COLLINS
COMPLETE GUIDE TO
BRITISH
BUTTERFLIES & MOTHS

Paul Sterry, Andrew Cleave
and Rob Read

WILLIAM
COLLINS

William Collins
An imprint of HarperCollinsPublishers
1 London Bridge Street
London SE1 9GF

WilliamCollinsBooks.com

HarperCollinsPublishers
Macken House, 39/40 Mayor Street Upper
Dublin 1, D01 C9W8, Ireland

First published in Great Britain
by William Collins in 2016

24 23
10 9 8 7 6

ISBN 978 0 00 810611 9

Dedication
This book is dedicated to the memory of the late Anthony Dobson, one of the last 'old school'
lepidopterists, and a gentleman naturalist.

Acknowledgements
The authors would like to express their sincere thanks to Barry Goater who has helped with the
preparation of this book in so many ways. In addition, the following people have helped with the
preparation of illustrations for the book: David Cooper, Penny Dobson, Brian Elliott, Mick Scott,
Christine Taylor of the Hampshire Cultural Trust, and Graham Vick. Over the years, Tim Norriss
and Mike Wall, pivotal members of the Hampshire lepidopterist community, have provided advice
on identification of various specimens. We would also like to thank Shane O'Dwyer for his design
skills, David Price-Goodfellow of D & N Publishing for his forbearance and patient management of
the project, and our publisher Myles Archibald without whom the project would not have become a
publishing reality.

Edited and designed by D & N Publishing, Baydon, Wiltshire

Colour reproduction by Nature Photographers Ltd
Printed and bound in Bosnia and Herzegovina by GPS Group

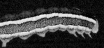

CONTENTS

HOW TO USE THIS BOOK

As its name suggests, *Complete British Butterflies and Moths* is aimed at naturalists with a general interest in entomology (the study of insects) and a specific enthusiasm for butterflies and moths, collectively known as Lepidoptera.

The main identification section has the text and main photographs for each species facing each other on the left and right pages, respectively. With a few exceptions, the right-hand pages show images that are larger than life, to allow enough detail to be seen for identification purposes; the sizes of species on any given page are roughly relative to one another. To allow direct size comparison with living specimens, life-size images are shown on the left-hand, text page, indicated by the abbreviation LS. In a few instances, where all the species on a given spread are large in life, images on the right-hand page are shown life size. The text has been written to complement the information conveyed by the photographs.

THE CHOICE OF SPECIES

The species description section begins with butterflies, and every species that occurs regularly in Britain and Ireland is included, along with a section dealing with the 'rarest of the rare' – extinct species or very rare immigrants. There follows the main section of the book, which covers our larger moths; every species that occurs regularly in Britain and Ireland is mentioned. After this, there is a section on 'rarest of the rare' larger moths – extinct species or very rare immigrants. And lastly, there is an introductory section to so-called 'micro-moths'. This covers the main families, other than those that appear in the main section of the book on the grounds of their larger size. For more detailed information about current understanding of butterfly and moth classification, please refer to p. 5.

SPECIES DESCRIPTIONS

At the start of each species description, the currently accepted English name is given. This is followed by the scientific name of the species in question, employing the nomenclature described on p. 5. The scientific name comprises the species' genus name first, followed by its specific name. Following the species' names are classification numbers that are unique to each species; see p. 5 for an explanation of how the numbering system works. Lastly, the wingspan of each species is given, represented in millimetres (mm).

In a few instances, reference is made, either in the species heading or the main body of the text, to a further subdivision – subspecies – where this is pertinent. In addition, geographical or colour variations, not assigned subspecies status, are referred to as forms (sometimes abbreviated as 'f.').

The text has been written in as concise a manner as possible. Each butterfly description begins with a summary of the species in question, which sometimes makes reference to habits and behaviour. A description of the ADULT butterfly or moth is given first. In the case of butterflies, and some moths, there follows information about the EGG, LARVA and PUPA; with most of the moths, however, only details about the LARVA are provided, including the foodplant, because information is generally sparse and other stages in the life cycle are seldom encountered by general naturalists. For all species, the description ends with information about their STATUS, providing an idea of their relative abundance or scarcity, geographical range and preferred habitats.

PHOTOGRAPHS

The illustrations used in the species identification section of the book have been created by digital manipulation of photographs. In most cases the source materials for the original photographs were either living individuals or specimens in the collection of the late Anthony Dobson.

In many moth species, resting individuals adopt a range of poses, for example sometimes settling with their wings spread and hindwings exposed, or alternatively with forewings close to the body and concealing the hindwings and abdomen. Depending on a range of factors, including level of activity, a resting moth's antennae may be concealed or evident. Wherever possible, we have tried to depict either a typical pose or a range of postures where appropriate.

BUTTERFLY AND MOTH STRUCTURE AND CLASSIFICATION

To understand how the natural world is ordered, and how animals and plants relate to one another, naturalists divide living things into groups, members of which have characters in common. In the animal kingdom, the most profound division is between vertebrates (animals with backbones) and invertebrates (animals without backbones). Invertebrates are classified into a number of subdivisions, each one of which is called a phylum. One of the most important invertebrate groups is the phylum Arthropoda, or arthropods – animals with an external skeleton, paired, jointed limbs, and internal muscles. Insects belong to a subdivision of the arthropods called class Insecta, and butterflies and moths, as a group, are further refined as the order Lepidoptera; a rough translation of this name is 'scale-wings'.

The body of a typical adult butterfly or moth is divided into three main regions: the head, which supports many sensory organs and the mouthparts; the abdomen, to which three pairs of legs and paired wings are attached (wings are absent in some species, or sexes); and the segmented abdomen, within which many of the main body organs are contained.

Insects are the only invertebrate group to have evolved wings and mastered the power of flight, and butterflies and moths are arguably the most showy and colourful representatives with this attribute. The wings are membranous and lent support by a network of rigid veins; the scales that cloak the wings are colourful in many species, serving a range of functions, from warning markings to camouflage patterns.

In strict scientific terms, there is no hard and fast distinction between butterflies and moths, or indeed between so-called 'macro-moths' and 'micro-moths'; in fact, it now turns out that, in classification terms, 'butterflies' are sandwiched in among families of micro-moths. Butterflies all fly in the daytime, but there again so do quite a number of moth species. So habits and behaviour do not provide a definitive answer to the conundrum: 'How do you tell a butterfly from a moth?'

Butterflies are treated as a stand-alone group at the start of the identification section; the running

Red Admiral.

order for the species follows conventions adopted by most British butterfly enthusiasts and organisations. The next section deals with larger moths, covering all the families of macro-moths, plus families of micro-moths whose representatives are a comparable size to most macro-moths; this anomaly highlights the problems surrounding the terms 'micro-moth' and 'macro-moth'. With the larger moth identification section, the current understanding of Lepidoptera classification has been respected and, by and large, the running order of species follows their evolutionary path from most primitive to most advanced. The order in which the species appear, in the main, follows the order adopted by the new *Checklist of the Lepidoptera of the British Isles* (Agassiz *et al.* 2013). At the end of the book, we have included an introduction to the remaining families of micro-moths.

All the moth species are identified by both their names and their unique 'new checklist' numbers. Take as an example the Silver Y: it is a member of the Noctuidae whose family number is 73, and its species number is 15; hence its unique Checklist number is 73.015. Prior to that, lepidopterists followed the order and numbering system of the 'Bradley checklist' (Bradley 2000). The incarnation of this publication was an update of Bradley and Fletcher's 1979 *A Recorder's Log Book or Label List of British Butterflies and Moths*. So most mature lepidopterists alive today grew up with the 'Bradley and Fletcher checklist' as their Lepidoptera bible. The Bradley and Fletcher number has been included as well (in brackets) for each moth species. Taking the Silver Y as an example again, its Bradley and Fletcher number is 2441 so its entry appears in the text as Silver Y *Autographa gamma* 73.015 (2441).

KEEPING RECORDS AND PHOTOGRAPHING BUTTERFLIES AND MOTHS

Step back in time 100 years, and any self-respecting lepidopterist would have had cabinets full of pinned and beautifully presented specimens of butterflies and moths, along with the tools of the trade needed to follow their passion: a panoply of nets, pots, killing jars, setting boards and pins. Some of the larger collections, generally created by men of independent means and with time on their hands, boasted dozens, sometimes hundreds, of specimens of the same species. It is tempting to speculate as to whether these Victorian and Edwardian lepidopterists had an impact on our butterfly and moth fauna. Of course, a century ago, there were far fewer lepidopterists and undoubtedly a far greater abundance of things to catch. But take a look at the numbers of Large Blues in any decent-sized collection and it is hard to imagine that collecting did not contribute to the native subspecies' decline; it eventually became extinct in 1979.

Today, there is still a case to be made for limited collecting; without reference collections of pinned specimens, the opportunity to study at first hand the characters needed for identification of tricky species would be lost. And not every species can be identified with certainty in the field; indeed, some can identified only by, for example, dissecting genitalia.

But thankfully the days of wholesale collecting for collecting's sake are gone. The emphasis today is on conservation rather than collecting, and observation and recording are rightly considered to be correct ways by which this goal is achieved. Serious lepidopterists have always taken meticulous notes, filling books with observations, with the relevant detailed data accompanying any pinned specimens. Nowadays, computers, tablets and even smartphones have a role to play in data collection. Whatever the method of collection and collation, however, there is always a need for detailed record-keeping.

The sheer beauty and variety of our butterflies and moths is what generates such an interest in the group. In the past, it was only by collecting what you saw that a permanent record could be maintained. Today, however, thanks to advances in digital technology, almost everyone has the ability to take photographs (with a camera or even on their phone). And so the beauty of butterflies and moths can be captured via a lens rather than with a net.

Capturing an image of a Cinnabar moth using a compact camera; the quality produced by such devices is quite astounding.

HABITATS THAT ARE SPECIAL
FOR BUTTERFLIES AND MOTHS

Adult butterflies and moths often wander – some species more than others – but their larval stages, and hence life cycles, are tied firmly to their foodplant. Although a few plant species are widespread and occur in a range of habitats, the vast majority are soil- and habitat-specific. So most of our butterflies and moths are inextricably linked to precise habitats. By being able to recognise these habitats, and understand the geological and geographical parameters that determine their occurrence, you will improve your chances of finding a given species by identifying its foodplant, and be more likely to identify a mystery specimen.

WOODLAND

Symbols of strength and endurance, trees are hugely important for British Lepidoptera. As individual species, they are important as larval foodplants for large numbers of moth species, and food for the caterpillars of a handful of butterflies. But the real significance of trees lies in the woodland habitat that, collectively, they form. Little wonder then that woods, and forested habitats generally, are dear to the hearts of all entomologists.

Very little British woodland is truly virgin and untouched, even though it may harbour native species and ancient trees. For millennia man has managed – some might say interfered – with the forested landscape, cutting down trees for fuel and building materials, and to clear areas for agriculture. However, this does not mean necessarily that its importance for moths and butterflies is diminished; on the contrary, it often enhances it. The fact that ecologists refer to most British and Irish woodland as 'semi-natural' is in no way derogatory.

ABOVE: **Silver-washed Fritillary, a classic butterfly of sunny woodland rides.**

LEFT: **Deciduous woodland in southern England, comprising a good range of tree and shrub species, plus open areas and dense cover.**

Native Pedunculate and Sessile oaks, and Silver and Downy birches, serve as larval foodplants for more species of moth than any others, the count running into the hundreds; this statistic is reflected in the dominance of these tree species themselves in the British landscape. Species of willow, notably Goat Willow, as well as Blackthorn and Hawthorn, are also really important, coming into their own in managed clearings, woodland edges and hedgerows; as with their larger cousins, they support hundreds of moth species.

A handful of butterfly species have trees and shrubs as their larval foodplants. Purple Hairstreaks, for example, favour mature oaks either in open rides or along neighbouring hedgerows. But for most woodland butterfly species, it is the habitats created by management that are important. Being sun-loving insects, the adults benefit from having open areas for flight. But of greater importance are the larval foodplants that are encouraged to grow on the woodland floor.

Each woodland butterfly species benefits in a subtly and uniquely different way from its cousins. Speckled Wood adults delight in frequenting sunny clearings and rides, and their larvae feed on grasses that typically flourish there. As adults, Silver-washed Fritillaries also favour sunny rides where the flowers of Bramble and thistles provide nectar. Their larvae feed on violets, which grow on the woodland floor in sufficient profusion only when coppicing creates enough light; this situation will last for a only few years, until the violets are crowded and shaded out by more vigorous vegetation.

But managing woodlands for butterflies is never straightforward. Like the fritillaries, White Admirals also like sunny clearings and rides as adults, but females will lay eggs only on Honeysuckle plants located in deep shade in neglected and slightly overgrown areas. And Purple Emperors require mature standard oaks as territorial lookout posts, and nearby large and mature Goat Willows on which to lay their eggs. So, manage a given area of woodland entirely for the benefit of the one species, and another is likely to suffer. An informed, small-scale and patchwork approach to woodland management is the key to success when it comes to encouraging butterflies, and moths too.

GRASSLAND AND MEADOWS

Full of wildflowers and native grass species, a good grassy meadow is a delight to anyone with an eye for colour and an interest in natural history. Prime sites are comparatively few and far between these days, either lost to the plough or degraded for native wildlife by modern intensive farming practices. When it comes to British meadows, the best ones are undisturbed (cut regularly, but not ploughed) and 'unimproved' (not sprayed or 'seeded' in any way). Find an area of sensitively managed grassland, and you will discover a wealth of insect life, including moths and butterflies.

As with other habitats, the species components (grasses themselves and other wildflowers) of unimproved meadows are influenced by factors such as geographical location and drainage. But more importantly, the biodiversity depends on soil chemistry. Grassland habitats on basic soils (chalk and limestone) tend to have greater botanical diversity than those on neutral or acid soils, and certainly harbour many species found nowhere else. Because the larvae of many butterfly and moth species feed on a very restricted range of plants – many feed only on one plant species – the precise nature of the grassland in question influences what Lepidoptera occur there.

A flower-rich meadow in summer will be full of grassland butterflies.

The Ringlet is a classic grassland butterfly.

Grassland and meadows, in all their forms, are arguably the most important British habitats when it comes to butterfly diversity: more species are found in meadows, in the loosest sense of the word, than any other habitat. Unmarked skipper species and the so-called 'browns' are the archetypal grassland butterflies, and their larvae feed on grasses. Some species are generalist feeders, while others have a much more restricted diet. Hence more generalist feeders such as Meadow Brown, Ringlet, Gatekeeper and Marbled White are widespread and locally common, while more specialist feeders such as Small Heath and Large Skipper occur only where their larval foodplants flourish.

Grasslands are much more than the sum of their component grass species, and many habitats support a rich array of wildflowers that bring colour to the scene in spring and summer. Where suitable larval foodplants occur, you will find Grizzled and Dingy skippers, Duke of Burgundy and Dark Green Fritillary, along with Common, Adonis and Chalk Hill blues, and Brown Argus. With these species, chalk and limestone grassland comes into its own, although of course you are most unlikely to find them all in the same location; certainly you will not find them at the same time of year.

Chalk Hill Blues are restricted to calcareous grassland where the larval foodplant – Horseshoe Vetch – flourishes. This pair began mating shortly after the female emerged from her pupa early one morning, and before her wings had had a chance to inflate and dry properly.

Among the moths, day-flying species such as the burnets can be easy to spot in suitable habitats, while their relatives the foresters are very local and restricted by precise habitat requirements. Moth species whose larvae feed on grass roots – the swifts, for example – can be locally common, but many people's attention is attracted by the presence of tiny micro-moths – so-called 'grass moths', members of the family Crambidae – that take to the wing in swarms when you walk through a grassy meadow at dusk.

HEDGEROWS AND SCRUB

Most hedgerows we see today owe their existence to man, having been planted – albeit centuries ago in many instances – as stock-proof barriers, to define land ownership and boundaries, and to serve as windbreaks. Although much neglected and abused, they are still a quintessential feature of the lowland British landscape. Over the years, hedgerows acquire the flora and fauna of the neighbouring countryside and take on the character of the margins of nearby woodlands. Their importance for wildlife – including butterflies and moths – cannot be overemphasised.

Scrub is a rather general term used to describe vegetation that encroaches on open land; it is the first stage of the natural vegetative succession that leads eventually to the formation of woodland. Scrub will usually have plant species in common with nearby hedgerows, ranging from low-growing herbaceous wildflowers to woody shrubs and climbers.

Hedgerows and areas of scrub are important habitats for wildlife, and the butterfly and moth species they support will depend on what potential larval foodplants are present. The moth and butterfly species found range from those whose larvae feed on trees and shrubs, to those that favour grasses. Moth species that feed on Hawthorn and Blackthorn are particularly well represented. By managing Blackthorn-dominated scrub and hedgerows sensitively, two very local butterfly species – Brown and Black hairstreaks – still survive in Britain. More widespread are the species of 'browns' that thrive where grassy margins flourish. And where Garlic Mustard and Hedge Mustard grow, Orange-tips and Green-veined Whites will benefit.

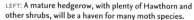

LEFT: A mature hedgerow, with plenty of Hawthorn and other shrubs, will be a haven for many moth species.

BELOW: The larvae of the December Moth feed on Hawthorn and other hedgerow shrubs.

RIGHT: Silver-studded Blue, the classic heathland butterfly in Britain.

BELOW: Lowland heath is at its most colourful in the summer months, just when butterflies such as Silver-studded Blue and Grayling are on the wing.

HEATHLAND

The heathlands of southern England are an entomologist's paradise, home to a fabulous array of specialist insects, including numerous moths and a few specialist butterflies. The habitat's name is clearly derived from the presence, and often dominance, of species of heathers – members of the heath family. These plants flourish on acid soils, and provide a stunning display from July to September, when the various species are in full bloom.

Heathland owes its existence to man and came about following forest clearance on acid, sandy soils. Regimes of grazing, cutting and periodic burning in the past helped maintain the habitat, and continued management is needed to ensure an appropriate balance is achieved between scrub encroachment and the maintenance of open habitats.

Two butterfly species in particular are strongly associated with heathland habitat: Grayling, whose larvae feed on grass species that thrive on free-draining acid soils; and Silver-studded Blue, whose larval foodplants are Bell Heather and related plants.

Specialist moths are also well represented, and many are active in the daytime, making observation easier. These include the magnificent Emperor Moth and Oak Eggar, along with smaller but equally striking species such as Common Heath, Beautiful Yellow Underwing, Clouded Buff and True Lover's Knot.

MOORLANDS AND MOUNTAINS

Apart from parts of the coast, moorlands and mountains are the only habitats in Britain and Ireland that still retain a feeling of 'wilderness'. Inhospitable terrain and often inclement weather mean they are challenging places for the naturalist to visit. But make the effort and you will discover some hardy Lepidoptera living there, including a handful of specialist butterflies and an array of upland moth species.

Upland vegetation is influenced by factors such as underlying soil type, rainfall and altitude. Vegetation on neutral soils is dominated by grasses and rushes, but where the underlying soil is acid, heather moors, reminiscent in appearance of lowland heaths, often develop; they are dominated

The Oak Eggar is a large and impressive day-flying moth of lowland heaths that is on the wing in July and August.

Upland butterflies and moths have to contend with a range of weather extremes. Clear, sunny days are comparatively rare, and cloud cover, wind and rain are to be expected; even snow in summer is not unknown.

by Heather and Bell Heather. And where limestone outcrops occur, the botanical diversity is reflected in the diversity of Lepidoptera too.

In Britain, the Mountain Ringlet is the classic upland butterfly species, restricted to areas where its larval foodplant, Mat-grass, flourishes. Despite its small size, it is found on the most windswept of slopes and is a truly hardy species. In more sheltered areas, with waterlogged soil and abundant Hare's-tail Cottongrass, look for the Large Heath. The range of the Scotch Argus arguably has a northern as well as upland bias, being found in open woodland on moors where Blue Moor-grass and Purple Moor-grass grow.

Upland moors support a surprising range of moths, the precise species found being influenced by soil type, altitude and geographical location. Species to look out for include Black Mountain Moth, Grey Mountain Carpet, Scotch Burnet, Broad-bordered White Underwing, Manchester Treble-bar and Netted Mountain Moth.

LEFT: As its name suggests, the Mountain Ringlet is restricted to upland areas. Given the often inclement weather of these habitats, the wings of this small, delicate butterfly soon become worn.

Reedbeds harbour a surprising range of moth species – generally specialists that are restricted to this habitat.

Larvae of the Drinker moth feed on a range of wetland grass species.

FRESHWATER WETLANDS

Reedbeds, comprising extensive stands of Common Reed, are home to a select band of moth species, many of which live as larvae within the stems. These include a mouthwatering array of wainscots, including Brown-veined, Silky, White-mantled and Fen. In addition, other species of interest include Drinker, Reed Leopard and Reed Dagger, the latter two having very restricted ranges.

Where bulrush species flourish, look for Bulrush, Rush and Webb's wainscots. Widespread reedbed plant species, such as Yellow Iris, support a large range of moth species, while the more unusual wetland Lepidoptera are often restricted to single larval foodplant species; this is reflected in their limited ranges. Hence, Swallowtails, whose larvae feed exclusively on Milk-parsley, are found only in the Norfolk Broads and nearby East Anglian wetlands.

COASTAL HABITATS

The coast is a source of inspiration for many people, naturalists included, and it is little wonder that most of us gravitate towards to the sea on a regular basis. Although the intertidal seashore does not provide any suitable habitats for Lepidoptera, coastal terrestrial habitats can be extremely productive.

Unsurprisingly, the coastal moth and butterfly fauna tends to be dominated by species associated elsewhere with open grassy habitats and many of these species are also widespread inland. However, various salt-tolerant coastal plants serve as larval foods for a small but select band of specialist moths.

Thrift, which grows in carpets in sea cliffs in western Britain, is a foodplant for Thrift Clearwing, Black-banded and Feathered Ranunculus, while Rock Sea-spurrey and Sea Campion are food for the larvae of Barrett's Marbled Coronet. Restricted to a scattering of saltmarsh locations, the larvae of the Striped Lychnis feed on Sea Aster, while Common Saltmarsh-grass supports Mathew's Wainscot. On sand dunes, Lyme-grass (the plant) supports the eponymous Lyme Grass moth, while Sea Sandwort is the foodplant for the Coast Dart, with Marram the mainstay of the Shore Wainscot.

Grassland butterfly species are often common on the coast in suitable habitats, but a couple of species are invariably found only within sight of the sea. The Glanville Fritillary has Sea Plantain as its larval foodplant, and is found only on the Isle of Wight and a neighbouring site on the mainland Hampshire coast, while the Lulworth Skipper, whose larval foodplant is Tor-grass, is pretty much restricted to the Dorset coast.

ABOVE: The tiny Thrift Clearwing is only found where Thrift grows in western Britain; its larvae feed exclusively on the roots of this maritime plant.

RIGHT: Thrift provides a stunning display of colour in June and July on Britain's west coasts, usually growing within sight of the sea.

A Glanville Fritillary sunning itself in coastal grassland on the Hampshire coast.

STUDY METHODS AND EQUIPMENT

If you have a keen eye, then strolls in the countryside and casual observations are bound to produce discoveries of an interesting range of Lepidoptera. But people who develop a more profound interest in the group soon realise that encounters with butterflies and moths are greatly improved by refining the way observations are made, and by using specialist equipment and techniques.

Many moths are highly seasonal in their appearance, a fact that is sometimes reflected in their names: the July Highflyer (*left*) is on the wing only in July and early August, while the December Moth (*right*) appears in the dead of winter.

The Buff-tip moth bears an uncanny resemblance to a snapped birch twig.

TIMING

As well as knowing *where* to look, knowing *when* to look is also extremely important for lepidopterists: some species may be long-lived but many are on the wing for only a brief few weeks. A knowledge of butterfly flight periods will improve your chances of observing a particular target species. And with moths, flight times provide clues to identification: for example, the Hebrew Character is on the wing mainly in March and April, while the superficially similar Setaceous Hebrew Character generally appears at least a month later, flying mainly in June and July. Of course, when it comes to flight times, no year is quite the same as the next. And the prevailing weather also has a profound influence on Lepidoptera activity: most butterflies fly only in sunshine, and with most moth species, nocturnal activity is influenced by air temperature and rainfall.

FINDING LEPIDOPTERA IN THE DAYTIME

If you are in the right habitat and looking at the right time of year, observing butterflies is relatively straightforward. On sunny days, they will be on the wing visiting flowers for nectar, or their activity will centre around areas where their larval foodplants

LEFT: A Peppered Moth's wings are a good match for lichen growing on tree bark.

BELOW: The shape, colour and markings of this Pale Prominent create the illusion of frayed wood.

flourish. On dull days, roosting butterflies can usually be found by careful inspection of the vegetation.

A small proportion of our moth species are day-flying and can be looked for in the same way, and in similar places to butterflies. Similarly, sunny days are usually more productive than dull ones, and nectar sources are important for many species. But most moths take to the wing only after dark and in the daytime remain hidden to avoid predation. Many have remarkably camouflaged wings when sited on substrates their markings and colours have evolved to mimic. Some resemble tree bark or lichens, while others are similar to leaves, either fallen or living. Unsurprisingly, they can be hard to spot at first, but once you have 'got your eye in', finding them becomes easier.

BELOW: Look at the leaves of shrubs and trees backlit with sunlight and you may see resting moths in silhouette. Insect-eating birds are also quick to spot a moth that has placed itself as inadvisably as this Mottled Umber.

NETTING

Nets are probably the piece of equipment with which lepidopterists are most associated. They are frowned upon in some circles, because of their association with 'killing and collecting'; you would not want to be seen wielding one, without permission, on a nature reserve for example. But no self-respecting serious lepidopterist would venture outdoors without one. Nets with fine mesh are ideal for capturing flying insects without damaging the scales on their wings. More robust versions, referred to as 'sweep nets', are used to sweep through vegetation; typically they will have a metal frame and nylon mesh.

Using a net to sample roosting grassland moths.

BEATING

A tried and tested method of sampling and finding Lepidoptera is called 'beating'. The clue is in the name: using a stout stick, overhanging branches are tapped vigorously over a purpose-bought beating tray or improvised upturned umbrella. Larvae and resting adult moths rain down and can be observed where they sit, or potted up for subsequent identification.

PHEROMONE LURES

Many female moths emit airborne sex-attractants known as pheromones, and males of the same species are attracted to them. Captive female moths will sometimes attract the attentions of several males if kept in a muslin container. But in the case of day-flying clearwing moths, the naturalist can employ a more direct approach: artificial pheromones can be purchased, and although their efficacy varies considerably, with some species the results are impressive.

Clearwing pheromones are supplied in impregnated rubber bungs – these male Six-belted Clearwings are being driven mad with desire by the scent given off.

DRAWN TO THE LIGHT

Few people need to be told that moths are attracted to light – leave an outdoor light on after dark in the summer months to demonstrate this for yourself. Taken a stage further, you can improve your catch by suspending a bulb over a white sheet outdoors. Alternatively, you can buy or make a light trap where the moths are collected in a box beneath the light. The best light source is a bulb that emits ultraviolet light, to which moths are particularly receptive. Captured moths are unharmed by the experience and can be released after they have been studied and identified.

BELOW: On warm, humid nights exceptional catches can be made using a trap that employs a mercury vapour lamp.

RIGHT: One theory has it that moths use the Moon for navigation. By maintaining a constant angle to this fixed reference point in the sky, they can fly a straight course: because the Moon is so far away, the angle hardly changes even if the moth flies a considerable distance. On overcast nights man-made light sources appear brighter than the moon to a moth's eyes and if they use it for orientation then they are in trouble: because the light source is so much closer to the moth than the Moon, the angle to the light changes dramatically over even a short flying distance. In an attempt to keep a constant angle, instead of flying in a straight line, the moth flies in a decreasing spiral, ever closer to the bulb.

A LIKING FOR SWEET THINGS

Another sure-fire method for attracting certain species of moth is to lure them with food. The classic mixture involves dissolving a bag of sugar and a tin of treacle in a pint or so of warmed red wine or brown ale. If the mixture is reduced slowly over heat, it becomes thick and, when cooled, can be painted onto tree trunks and posts. Some moths find the mixture irresistible. 'Sugaring', as the technique is called, is more of an art than a science, and catches are extremely variable; warm, muggy nights produce the best results.

Three Svennson's Copper Underwings and a Straw Underwing feasting on a sickly sweet 'sugaring' mixture.

BUTTERFLY AND MOTH LIFE CYCLES AND STAGES

Butterflies and moths have four stages in their life cycle: the egg, laid by a female of the previous generation; the larva, a growing stage that emerges from the egg; the pupa, an inactive stage inside which adult organs and tissues form; and the adult, which emerges from the pupa. In some species the life cycle is repeated two or three times each year, between spring and autumn. But in most, the life cycle is an annual event, adults emerging at the same time each year. If you find some moth eggs or larvae, you might like to try rearing them and following the life cycle all the way. But before you do so, be sure you know the identity of the species so you know what to feed it on. Daily supplies of fresh leaves, and the removal of old ones, is vital for the larvae. And at maturity, most need dry soil to burrow into before pupating, or dry leaves that they can form into a protective case.

Egg.

Newly emerged larva about to take its first meal.

Full-grown larva.

Pupa, suspended from a stem of the foodplant.

Newly emerged adult drying and hardening its wings.

THE LIFE CYCLE OF THE COMMA BUTTERFLY

In order to ensure successful fertilisation of the eggs, these mating Gatekeeper butterflies will remain joined together for nearly half an hour. Although mating butterflies such as these are able to fly short distances, they typically remain static, clinging onto a stem or leaf.

Egg.

Newly emerged larva eating its eggshell.

Larva, resting on its foodplant.

Pupa; prior to metamorphosing into a pupa, the larva digs into the soil and creates a silk-lined chamber.

Freshly emerged adult moth drying its wings, prior to taking its first flight as evening approaches.

THE LIFE CYCLE OF THE POPLAR HAWK-MOTH

BUTTERFLY AND MOTH LARVAE

Butterfly and moth larvae may lack the sophistication and elegance of their adult counterparts, but many species make up for this by being weird and wonderful to look at. Most have markings and colours that help them avoid being detected by predators, notably birds. But some species – those with some form of defence – go out of their way to be conspicuous. Here is a selection of some intriguing species.

Right up to the point where they disperse to pupate, Peacock butterfly larvae spend their lives in clustered groups on the leaves of their foodplant, Common Nettle.

Larvae have soft, juicy bodies and make succulent meals for insect-eating birds and other predators. The larvae of some species, such as this Pale Tussock, are armed with irritating hairs to discourage predation, these causing considerable discomfort if ingested. A bird or small mammal may try this once, but soon learns to avoid such hairy caterpillars.

ABOVE: The extraordinary plump-bodied larva of the Puss Moth has two whiplash tails that help ward off parasitic wasps. The head end can be swollen when alarmed, exaggerating the false eyespots, presumably to deter small birds.

RIGHT: The bold, stripy markings of the Cinnabar Moth larva warn potential predators that its body contains poisons accumulated from its foodplant, Ragwort.

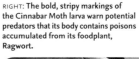

ABOVE: The Privet Hawk-moth larva is an impressive beast, being strikingly marked with an oblique stripe on each segment. It also has the hawk-moth trademark 'horn' at the tail end.

LEFT: The larvae of micro-moths are tiny and often inconspicuous. However, that of the *Stigmella aurella*, a leaf miner on Bramble, leaves a telltale sign of its presence: it lives and feeds inside Bramble leaves and its home shows up as a white streak.

RIGHT: Many moth larvae produce silk, either to help attach themselves to the leaf on which they are feeding, or in some cases to spin a cocoon in which to pupate. But some tiny larvae use it in a more active manner: in order to find new leaves on which to feed, or to reach the ground safely for pupation, they suspend themselves in silken strands and abseil in the breeze.

When full grown, a Lobster Moth larva bears a fanciful resemblance to its crustacean namesake.

ECOLOGY AND CONSERVATION

THE ECOLOGY OF BUTTERFLIES AND MOTHS

Butterflies and moths are vital elements in the ecology of our biologically rich environment. Many species are important pollinators of wildflowers and shrubs, and their larvae, which are herbivorous in the main, exert a controlling influence on plant growth and serve as food for predators; these range from other insects to birds and mammals. So, along with other creatures in the environment, butterflies and moths are integral to the general ecological well-being of natural habitats in Britain.

Butterflies and moths are relatively conspicuous insects, with many species being easy to observe. As well as being interesting in their own right, they serve as useful indicators of the state of health of the environment – an early warning system, if you like, of when things are going wrong, and when conservation land management is getting it right.

CONSERVATION

Over the last century, the biggest threat faced by British wildlife has been the loss and degradation of biologically rich natural habitats. Modern intensive farming practices and associated land uses are rightly singled out as the major culprits. But other contributors to the problem include industrial and housing 'creep' into rural areas, and human disturbance. Ineffective legal protection for both wildlife and natural habitats does little to curb the activities of those who see the land they own or manage as a resource to be exploited rather than a treasure to be cherished and protected.

A typical Blue Tit brood will contain around 10 chicks, each of which will need to be fed 100 or so caterpillars each day from hatching to fledging in order to survive. This means the parents may well need to find 20,000 caterpillars to raise a brood. So it is easy to imagine how significant moth populations are to the survival of bird species that feed their young on insects.

All is not doom and gloom, however. Fortunately for people who value native wildlife and natural habitats for their own sake, a commendable network of voluntary and charitable organisations exists to help. Their activities range from lobbying on behalf of wildlife, to the management and ownership of biologically rich land. Ownership of land, and hence its removal from the potential for degradation or destruction, is the future for conservation in Britain. So arguably the best thing any naturalist can do is to donate as much money as possible to conservation charities, and to include them when drafting their wills.

CONSERVATION CLOSER TO HOME: GARDENING FOR LEPIDOPTERA

Butterflies are a welcome addition to any garden and the sight of these delicate, colourful insects fluttering over the herbaceous border is guaranteed to lift the spirits. A knowledge of their habits, life cycles and ecological requirements can help boost their numbers and diversity, benefiting not only the insects themselves but also those who observe them. Of course the same principles apply to moths as well as butterflies.

Food for adult butterflies and moths, often in the form of nectar-rich flowers, is important. For this reason it is a good idea to plant your borders so that a succession of butterfly-friendly blooms appears from spring to autumn; many moth species will benefit too. But to provide the most effective help, butterflies and moths need more than just food for adults: the whole life cycle needs to be taken into consideration. The correct

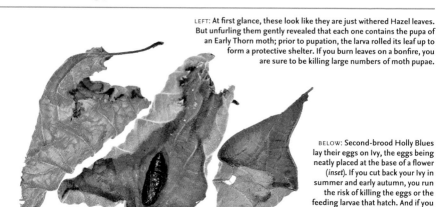

LEFT: At first glance, these look like they are just withered Hazel leaves. But unfurling them gently revealed that each one contains the pupa of an Early Thorn moth; prior to pupation, the larva rolled its leaf up to form a protective shelter. If you burn leaves on a bonfire, you are sure to be killing large numbers of moth pupae.

BELOW: Second-brood Holly Blues lay their eggs on Ivy, the eggs being neatly placed at the base of a flower (*inset*). If you cut back your Ivy in summer and early autumn, you run the risk of killing the eggs or the feeding larvae that hatch. And if you cut the Ivy back in winter, you will deprive Brimstone and Red Admiral of potential hibernation spots. Ivy presents conservation-minded gardeners with a real dilemma.

larval foodplants are vital, so use the text in this book's species accounts to familiarise yourself with what is required.

It is a good idea to consider the consequences of gardening methods, and their timing, for larval and pupal stages of butterflies and moths. Without realising it, you may inadvertently kill off a complete life cycle by, for example, strimming a nettle bed, pruning shrubs or tidying the herbaceous border at the wrong time, or burning dead leaves (containing unseen pupae) in autumn.

RIGHT: For some butterflies, the distinction between garden and home is blurred. A few days earlier, this Peacock butterfly would have been feeding on nectar in the herbaceous border, but now it has ventured indoors to find a place to hibernate.

BELOW: Ivy flowers are a rich source of nectar for butterflies such as this Red Admiral and, after dark, numerous moths too.

Within three years of allowing this area of garden lawn to become a meadow, seven species of grassland butterfly were breeding on the site: Meadow Brown, Ringlet, Gatekeeper, Marbled White, Common Blue, Large Skipper and Small Skipper. A large range of grassland moths were also present. Meadow management consisted of doing nothing more than cutting the grass for hay in early autumn.

Small Skipper *Thymelicus sylvestris* 25mm

antenna

Small butterfly with an active, buzzing flight. Basks on vegetation; forewings and hindwings are held in subtly different planes. **ADULT** has orange-brown upperwings and orange-buff underwings. Male has a dark sex brand (line of scent scales) on forewings. Brown underside to antennal tips allows separation from similar Essex Skipper. Feeds on grassland thistles and knapweeds. Flies Jul–Aug. **EGG** is laid in grass leaf sheaths. **LARVA** is green; feeds on various grasses. **PUPA** is formed within a 'tent' of leaves woven at base of grass stems. **STATUS** Common and widespread in Wales and England, as far as Lancashire in the W and Northumberland in the E.

LS

Essex Skipper *Thymelicus lineola* 25mm

antenna

Similar to Small Skipper but underside to antennal tips is black. Has a similar buzzing flight and basks on vegetation, with wings held at an angle; forewings and hindwings are held in subtly different planes. **ADULT** has orange-brown upperwings and orange-buff underwings. Male has a dark sex brand (line of scent scales) on forewings. Flies Jun–Jul. **EGG** is laid in grass leaf sheaths. **LARVA** is green; feeds on various grasses. **PUPA** is formed within a 'tent' of leaves woven at base of grass stems. **STATUS** Very locally common in SE England, E of a line from Lincolnshire to Dorset.

LS

adult basking

Lulworth Skipper

Thymelicus acteon 24–28mm

Active butterfly that makes short flights and basks on grass stems. Usually rests with its wings at an angle; forewings and hindwings are held in subtly different planes. **ADULT** has olive-brown to buffish-brown upperwings, darker in male than female. Female has a crescent of pale spots on forewings; forewings of male have a dark sex brand (line of scent scales). Flies Jun–Jul. **EGG** is laid in grass sheaths. **LARVA** is green and feeds on Tor-grass. Lives within a rolled grass leaf. **PUPA** is formed within a 'tent' of leaves woven at base of grass stems. **STATUS** Very locally common on Dorset coast between Weymouth and Swanage, usually within sight of sea.

LS

Chequered Skipper *Carterocephalus palaemon* 30mm

Well-marked little butterfly. Lives in a challenging climate and flies only on sunny days; in dull weather it hides deep in vegetation. **ADULT** has dark brown upperwings marked with pale spots, creating a chequered appearance. Underwings have similar colours and patterns to upperwings but are paler overall. Feeds on flowers of Bluebell and Bugle. Flies May–Jun. **EGG** is white and laid on underside of grass stem. **LARVA** feeds on Purple Moor-grass and lives inside a rolled leaf. **PUPA** is formed within a 'tent' of woven grasses. **STATUS** Widespread in NW Scotland in the general region of Fort William. Formerly occurred in England but extinct there since 1976.

LS

Small Skipper,
male underside

Small Skipper,
male

Small Skipper,
female

Essex Skipper,
male underside

Essex Skipper,
male

Essex Skipper,
female

Lulworth Skipper,
male underside

Lulworth Skipper,
male

Lulworth Skipper,
female

Chequered Skipper,
male underside

Chequered Skipper,
male

Chequered Skipper,
female

male basking

LS

Large Skipper
Ochlodes sylvanus 34mm
Active butterfly with a
buzzing flight. Noticeably
larger than Small Skipper
(p. 24), with which it often
occurs. Rests on vegetation
with wings held at an angle; forewings and hindwings
are held in subtly different planes. **ADULT** has dark
brown upperwings with pale markings. Males have
a dark sex brand (line of scent scales) on forewings.
Underwings are buffish orange with paler spots. Flies Jun–Jul. **EGG** is pale and
domed; laid on grass leaves. **LARVA** is green; feeds on grasses. **PUPA** is dark and
formed in a cocoon. **STATUS** Widespread and locally common in grassland.

Silver-spotted Skipper *Hesperia comma* 30–37mm
Similar to Large Skipper but has diagnostic white spots
on underside of hindwings; flight period is marginally
later. **ADULT** has rich brown upperwings adorned with
pale spots; male is smaller than female, with fewer
upperwing spots and a dark sex brand (line of scent scales)
on forewings. Underwings are yellowish buff, tinged greenish
on hindwings, which have silvery-white spots. Feeds on downland
flowers, notably Stemless Thistle. Flies Aug–Sep. **EGG** is white and laid on grass
stems. **LARVA** is buff with a dark head; feeds on Sheep's Fescue. **PUPA** is formed in
a cocoon near the ground. **STATUS** Local specialist of chalk downland in S England;
restricted to suitable areas in the Chilterns, South Downs and North Downs.

adult basking

LS

Dingy Skipper *Erynnis tages* 28–34mm
Rather sombre-looking butterfly. Often basks with wings
spread flat, when it looks superficially rather moth-like.
ADULT has grey-brown upperwings with rich brown
markings; these wear
off with time, creating a
more uniform coloration.
Underwings are buffish brown with pale spots.
Flies May–Jun. **EGG** is orange and ribbed; laid on
a plant leaf. **LARVA** is yellowish with a dark head;
feeds mainly on Common Bird's-foot Trefoil.
PUPA is formed in a cocoon at base of vegetation.
STATUS Widespread in rough grassland in
central and S England; local, scattered (often
coastal) colonies occur elsewhere in England,
and in Wales, Ireland and Scotland.

Grizzled Skipper *Pyrgus malvae* 24–28mm
Well-marked, active butterfly. Often basks with wings
spread flat. **ADULT** has blackish-brown upperwings adorned
with regular white spots, creating a chequered appearance.
Underwings are yellowish brown
with a similar pattern of pale spots
to upperwings. Often feeds on
flowers of Bugle. Flies May–Jun.
EGG is pale green and laid on a leaf.
LARVA feeds on herbaceous plants, including Wild
Strawberry and Creeping Cinquefoil. **PUPA** is formed
in a cocoon at base of vegetation. **STATUS** Widespread in
grassy areas in central and S England; very local in Wales.

Grizzled Skipper,
f. *taras*

LS

Large Skipper,
male underside

Large Skipper,
male

Large Skipper,
female

Silver-spotted Skipper,
male underside

Silver-spotted Skipper,
male

Silver-spotted Skipper,
female

Dingy Skipper,
male underside

Dingy Skipper,
male

Dingy Skipper,
female

Grizzled Skipper,
male underside

Grizzled Skipper,
male

Grizzled Skipper,
female

Swallowtail *Papilio machaon* 78–92mm

Iconic and unmistakable butterfly. Occurs in Britain as endemic ssp. *britannicus*, which is described here. **ADULT** has beautifully patterned upperwings. Forewings are stippled black with pale yellow spots. Hindwings have a tail streamer and blue-fringed red eyespot; otherwise they are pale yellow with a black submarginal band containing blue-stippled patches, and a marginal row of pale yellow crescents. Female is larger than male. Continental ssp. *gorganus* is similar to ssp. *britannicus* but overall paler with narrower, dark submarginal bands. Feeds on nectar of fenland flowers, notably Ragged Robin. Double-brooded: flies May–Jun, and Aug. **EGG** is yellow and laid on foodplant. **LARVA** is yellow-green with black and red markings; feeds on Milk-parsley. **PUPA** is attached to stem, supported by a thin silk harness. **STATUS** Local in fenland in Norfolk, especially the Norfolk Broads. Records elsewhere in Britain (a very rare event) are usually Continental ssp. *gorganus*; some may be immigrants but escapee captive-bred individuals are possible too.

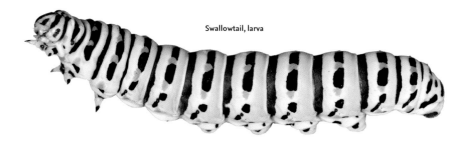

Swallowtail, larva

Wood White *Leptidea sinapis* 38–42mm

Slow-flying, delicate little butterfly. Usually rests with wings closed. **ADULT** is overall white with very rounded wings. Upperwings are chalky white with greyish-white marbling; forewings of male are marked with a sooty-grey patch at tip; this feature is much paler on female. Underwings of both sexes are chalky white, tinged with a faint yellow wash

LS

in some individuals, and showing faint grey marbling and venation. Second brood tends to be overall paler still than 1st brood. Double-brooded: flies May–Jun, and Jul. **EGG** is slender and laid on leaves of foodplant. **LARVA** is green with pale lengthways stripes. Feeds on Bitter-vetch and related plants. **PUPA** is attached to stems and supported by a thin silk harness. **STATUS** Very local in S and central England in open, flowery woodland rides. Also occurs in the Burren region of W Ireland, in more open, grassy habitats.

Cryptic Wood White *Leptidea juvernica* 38–42mm

Very similar to Wood White and not separable in the field (distinctions are based on differences in genitalia). Described as a new species in 2011. Usually rests with wings closed. **ADULT** is white with very rounded wings. Chalky-white upperwings have pale greyish marbling. Forewings of male have a sooty-grey patch at tip; this feature is much paler on

LS

female. Underwings of both sexes are white with faint grey markings and a subtle yellow wash in some individuals. Flies May. **EGG** is slender and laid on leaves of foodplant. **LARVA** is green and feeds on Common Bird's-foot Trefoil and related plants. **PUPA** is attached to stem and supported by a thin silk harness. **STATUS** Widespread in Ireland but absent from the Burren.

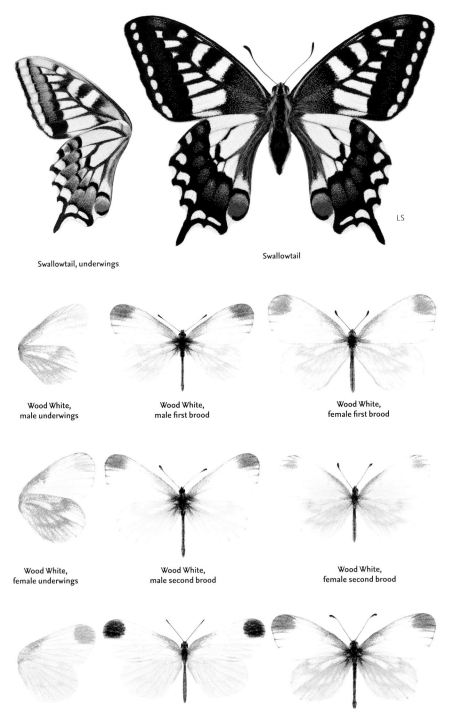

Swallowtail, underwings

Swallowtail

LS

Wood White,
male underwings

Wood White,
male first brood

Wood White,
female first brood

Wood White,
female underwings

Wood White,
male second brood

Wood White,
female second brood

Cryptic Wood White,
male underwings

Cryptic Wood White,
male

Cryptic Wood White,
female

Clouded Yellow *Colias croceus* 45–55mm

Fast-flying, active butterfly that seldom settles for long, and only occasionally reveals upperwings when at rest or feeding. **ADULT** has dark-bordered upperwings that are yellow in female, orange-yellow in male. Both sexes have yellow underwings with a few dark markings. In female form *helice*, upperwing ground colour is much paler (very pale lemon yellow); note that form *helice* is easily confused with Pale and Berger's clouded yellows (p. 68). **EGG** is pink and narrowly oval; laid on leaf of foodplant. **LARVA** is green and feeds on Lucerne and various clovers. **PUPA** is attached by a harness to stem. **STATUS** Summer migrant in varying numbers. Sometimes breeds but does not survive our winters. Commonest in coastal habitats in Jul–Sep.

Clouded Yellow, adult flying (*top*), and in typical pose (*above*).

Pale Clouded Yellow *Colias hyale* 52–60mm

Similar to Clouded Yellow (especially form *helice*). Settles with wings closed and seldom reveals upperwings except in flight. **ADULT** is overall much paler both above and below than Clouded Yellow. Has dark-bordered pale yellow upperwings, with a dark central spot on forewing. Both sexes have pale yellow underwings (intense lemon yellow in Clouded Yellow) with a few dark and red spots, and a red-ringed pale spot on hindwings. **EGG** is narrowly oval and laid on leaf of foodplant. **LARVA** is green and feeds on various clovers and Lucerne. **PUPA** is attached by a harness to stem. **STATUS** Rare immigrant from mainland Europe, seen mainly Jul–Aug along S coasts.

Brimstone *Gonepteryx rhamni* 55–65mm

Herald of spring and sometimes on the wing as early as March. **ADULT** has uniquely shaped wings. Male's brimstone-yellow colour is unmistakable; paler female can be mistaken for Large White (p. 34) in flight. Single-brooded – summer-flying adults (seen mainly Aug–Sep) hibernate and emerge the following spring (seen mainly Mar–Apr) on sunny days. **EGG** is flask-shaped and laid on stems and twigs of foodplant. **LARVA** is green and feeds on Buckthorn and Alder Buckthorn. **PUPA** is suspended by a harness from underside of leaf. **STATUS** Locally common in S half of England and Wales; local in Ireland.

TOP LEFT: **larva**
FAR LEFT: **eggs**
LEFT: **newly emerged adult**

Clouded Yellow,
male

Clouded Yellow,
female

Clouded Yellow,
f. *helice*

Pale Clouded Yellow

Pale Clouded Yellow,
underwings

Clouded Yellow,
underwings

Brimstone,
male underwings

Brimstone,
female underwings

Brimstone, male

Brimstone, female

Orange-tip *Anthocharis cardamines* 40–45mm

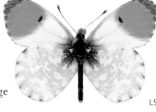

Attractive spring butterfly. **ADULT** has rounded wings. Forewings are dark-tipped but only male has an orange patch; hind underwings of both sexes are marbled green and white. Flies Apr–Jun. **EGG** is orange, flask-shaped and laid on flower stem of foodplant.

LARVA is green; feeds on seedpods of members of the cabbage family, notably Cuckoo-flower and Garlic Mustard. **PUPA** is attached by a harness to stem. **STATUS** Widespread in S Britain and Ireland.

LS

TOP: **egg**; ABOVE: **pupa**   larva   male

Green-veined White *Pieris napi* 45–50mm

Well-marked wayside butterfly. Similar to Small White (p. 34) but with distinctive dark veins. Represented here by 3 sspp. **ADULT** ssp. *sabellicae*, which occurs in England and Wales, has overall white upperwings with dark markings that are more intense in female than male: dark tip to forewings, dark veins on upperwings, and greyish-green veins on underwings, particularly hindwings. Ssp. *thomsoni*, from Scotland, is similar but has more intense dark markings and often a yellow suffusion on underwings. Ssp. *britannica*, from Ireland, is similar but overall smaller and with even more intense dark markings, and yellow on underside of hindwings. All ssp. are double-brooded except in uplands:

LS

flies Apr–May, and Jul–Aug. **EGG** is yellow, flask-shaped and laid singly on foodplant. **LARVA** feeds on Garlic Mustard and other wild cabbage family members. **PUPA** is attached by a harness to stem. **STATUS** Widespread and fairly common throughout, favouring verges, grassy areas and open scrub.

pupa   female

Orange-tip,
male underwings

Orange-tip,
male

Orange-tip,
female underwings

Orange-tip,
female

Green-veined White,
male underwings

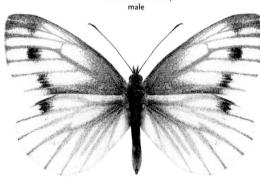

Green-veined White,
male

Green-veined White,
female underwings

Green-veined White,
female

Large White *Pieris brassicae* 58–62mm
The larger of our 2 common 'Cabbage White' butterflies. Often rests with wings spread. **ADULT** has white upperwings; male has a black tip to forewings while female has a black tip and 2 central black spots. Underside of hindwings is yellowish in both sexes. Underside of male's forewings is white with a yellow tip; female is similar but shows 2 black spots (as seen on upperwings). Male is smaller than female. Double-brooded: flies Apr–Jun, and Jul–Aug. **EGG** is yellow and laid in clusters

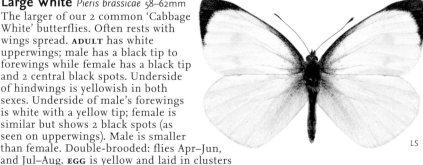

LS

on foodplant. **LARVA** is yellow at first with a black head; later instars are bristly and yellow with extensive black stippling. Feeds on a wide range of crucifers (including cultivated cabbage) and Nasturtium. **PUPA** is attached to vertical surface by a silken harness. **STATUS** Widespread and common throughout, although least numerous in N parts and absent from uplands. Favours a wide range of habitats, but particularly gardens.

LEFT: **eggs**; BELOW: **full grown larva**; BELOW RIGHT: **pupa**

Small White *Pieris rapae* 38–56mm
The smaller of our two common 'Cabbage White' butterflies. **ADULT** Upperwings are creamy white with a dark tip to forewings; female has 2 dark spots on each forewing. Underwings are yellowish. Male is smaller than female. Double-brooded: flies Apr–May, and Jul–Aug. **EGG** is slender, yellowish and laid singly on foodplant. **LARVA** is black and yellow; feeds on cabbages and other garden brassicas, as well as Nasturtium. **PUPA** is attached by a silk harness to a stem. **STATUS** Widespread and common throughout, although scarce or absent from N parts and uplands. Favours a wide range of habitats, but particularly gardens.

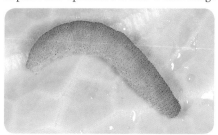

larva

LS

Large White,
male underwings

Large White,
male

Large White,
female underwings

Large White,
female

Small White,
male underwings

Small White,
male

Small White,
female underwings

Small White,
female

typical pose

Green Hairstreak
Callophrys rubi 27–34mm

underside　LS

Attractive little butterfly. Always rests with its wings closed, the green underwings providing excellent camouflage. Upperwings are seen mainly in flight, but the butterfly is extremely hard to follow when flying. **ADULT** has rather pointed wings, the hindwings showing a reduced tail streamer. Upperwings are shiny brown. Underwings are green, with small white spots on hindwings. Flies May–Jun. **EGG** is green, flattened and laid on leaf of foodplant. **LARVA** is green and flattened. Feeds on a range of plants, including Broom, Bilberry and Common Bird's-foot Trefoil. **PUPA** is brown and formed among debris on the ground. **STATUS** Widespread throughout, favouring areas of scrub; its precise occurrence is surprisingly patchy given the wide range of larval foodplants.

typical pose

Brown Hairstreak
Thecla betulae 36–45mm

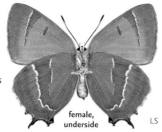

female, underside　LS

Well-marked butterfly that is sometimes rather lethargic and basks on vegetation. **ADULT** has pointed forewings and rather rounded hindwings with 2 tail streamers. Upperwings are brown with an orange-yellow patch on forewings that is much larger and more colourful in female than male; tail streamers are orange-tinged. Underwings are buffish brown with an orange wash towards tail-streamer region of hindwings; has 1 irregular white line on forewings, 2 irregular white lines on hindwings. Female is larger than male. Flies Aug–early Sep. **EGG** is white, flattened and laid on foodplant, in a fork of twigs. **LARVA** is green and rather flattened. Feeds on Blackthorn. **PUPA** is formed in leaf litter on the ground. **STATUS** Very local in S Britain, in areas of scrub; main range is centred on central S England, SW England, SW Wales and W Ireland.

typical pose

Purple Hairstreak
Favonius quercus 36–39mm

underside　LS

Attractive small butterfly whose life is linked to mature oaks; males in particular are seen flying around tree canopies. Individuals are sometimes found resting on low vegetation in dull weather. **ADULT** has pointed forewings and rather rounded hindwings with an angled bottom margin and tail streamer. Upperwings are brownish; in good light, male has a purple sheen across whole of upperwings, while in female sheen is restricted to forewing patch. Underwings of both sexes are grey with a black-bordered white 'hairstreak' line and orange-ringed eyespot. Flies Jul–Aug. **EGG** is a pale, flattened dome; laid at base of oak bud. **LARVA** is grey-brown and feeds on young oak leaves; it is a good match for oak bud scales. Feeds on Pedunculate and Sessile oaks. **PUPA** is brown and formed on the ground. **STATUS** Locally common only in S Britain, with colonies often restricted to specific mature trees.

pupa

Green Hairstreak,
male

Green Hairstreak,
female underside

Brown Hairstreak,
male

Brown Hairstreak,
male underside

Brown Hairstreak,
female

Purple Hairstreak,
female underside

Purple Hairstreak,
male

Purple Hairstreak,
female

White-letter Hairstreak

pupa

underside   LS

Satyrium w-album 26–34mm

Active little butterfly with diagnostic markings on underwings. Usually flies around tree tops and is hard to observe well, but sometimes feeds lower down on flowers of Wild Privet and Bramble. **ADULT** has pointed wings; hindwings have a tail streamer. Upperwings are grey-brown and seldom revealed, except in flight. Underwings are brown with a jagged white line; this forms a 'W' on hindwings. Hindwings also have a marginal row of semicircular orange spots framed by black. Flies Jul. **EGG** is circular and flattened, and laid on twigs of foodplant. **LARVA** is green and flattened, and well camouflaged on leaf buds and leaves. Feeds on Wych Elm and other elm species. **PUPA** is brown and fixed to underside of leaf by a silk harness. **STATUS** Widespread in England and lowland Wales, but local, favouring hedgerows and woodland margins; colonies are often faithful to just 1 tree, or group of trees.

Black Hairstreak *Satyrium pruni* 35–39mm

Unobtrusive and easily overlooked little butterfly. Superficially similar to White-letter Hairstreak, but separable with care by paying attention to underwing markings. Typically rather lethargic and often seen walking over leaves of larval foodplant or feeding on flowers of Privet. **ADULT** has pointed wings; hindwings have a tail streamer. Upperwings are grey-brown and seldom revealed, except in flight. Underwings

female   LS

are brown with a jagged white line that does not form a 'W' on hindwings. Hindwings also have a marginal orange band, inside which is a row of black spots; forewings have a subtle orange band. Flies Jun. **EGG** is brownish, domed and

ABOVE: **larva**; RIGHT: **pupa**;
FAR RIGHT: **typical pose**

laid on twig of larval foodplant. **LARVA** is green and flattened; feeds on Blackthorn. **PUPA** is brown with white markings (looks like a bird dropping) and attached to leaf by a silk harness. **STATUS** Rare and local, confined to a few areas of woody scrub in central England.

Small Copper *Lycaena phlaeas* 25–30mm

female, underside

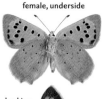

LS

basking

Active, fast-flying butterfly that can be hard to follow on the wing. However, often basks with wings spread, allowing its colours to be appreciated. Represented in our region by ssp. *eleus* (England, Wales and Scotland) and ssp. *hibernica* (Ireland). **ADULT** has colourful upperwings; forewings are largely orange with black dots and a brown margin, while hindwings are brown with a marginal orange band. Underwings have a similar pattern to upperwings but dark brown is replaced by grey-buff. Double-brooded (sometimes triple-brooded), with season extending May–Sep. **EGG** is pitted like a miniature golf ball; laid on foodplant. **LARVA** is green and feeds on Sheep's Sorrel. **PUPA** is formed among leaves on the ground. **STATUS** Locally common throughout in suitable grassy habitats.

White-letter Hairstreak,
male

White-letter Hairstreak,
female underside

Black Hairstreak,
male

Black Hairstreak,
underside

Small Copper,
male

Small Copper,
male underside

Small Copper,
female

Small Copper, female
f. *caeruleopunctata*

Small Blue *Cupido minimus* 19–26mm
Our smallest native butterfly. Hard
to follow in flight. **ADULT** has sooty-
brown upperwings; male is darker
than female, with a coating of blue
scales. Underwings of both sexes
are grey, with black dots and blue
scales towards base. Flies May–Jun.
EGG is laid in flowerhead of larval
foodplant. **LARVA** is brown and
grub-like; feeds on flowers of Kidney Vetch. **PUPA** is brown
and formed among debris on the ground. **STATUS** Local and
found in colonies; its main range is central and S England;
very local and mainly coastal in Wales, Scotland and Ireland.

male basking

ABOVE: Silver-studded Blue,
female

Silver-studded Blue *Plebejus argus* 27–31mm

Occurs here as 4 sspp. **ADULT** ssp. *argus* male has blue
upperwings with a black submarginal band and white
margin; female upperwings are brown with submarginal
black and orange spots on hindwings; underwings of both
sexes are grey, suffused blue towards base, with black dots
and submarginal row of orange and black spots. Compared to
ssp. *argus*, ssp. *cretaceus* and ssp. *masseyi* are larger, and males

are a brighter blue with a narrow dark margin; ssp. *caernensis*
is smaller, and males have a narrow dark border. Flies Jun–
Jul. **EGG** is laid on foodplant or the ground, and overwinters.
LARVA is often tended by ants. Foodplants include Bell
Heather and its relatives, Common Bird's-foot Trefoil and
Common Rock-rose. **PUPA** is often found in ants' nests.
STATUS Ssp. *argus* is locally common on heaths in S England;
ssp. *cretaceus* occurs on Portland, Dorset; ssp. *masseyi* is
found in Shropshire; ssp. *caernensis* occurs in N Wales.

male basking

Brown Argus *Aricia agestis* 25–30mm
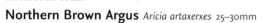
Atypical 'blue' butterfly. **ADULT** has brown upperwings with
submarginal orange spots and a white border and a central
dark crescent mark on forewings. Underwings are grey-buff
with white-ringed black spots and submarginal orange
spots. Double-brooded: flies May–Jun, and Aug–Sep. **EGG** is
white and laid on leaf of foodplant. **LARVA** is green and often
attended by ants; feeds on Common Rock-rose, Dove's-foot Crane's-bill and
Common Stork's-bill. **PUPA** is brown; often buried by ants. **STATUS** Widespread but
local in S and E England, and N and S Wales. Favours short grassland, mainly on
calcareous soils.

Northern Brown Argus *Aricia artaxerxes* 25–30mm
Occurs here as 2 sspp. **ADULT** is similar to Brown Argus but
has a central white spot on forewing, most obvious in ssp.
artaxerxes, less so (sometimes absent) in ssp. *salmacis*. Flies
Jun–Jul. **EGG** is
laid on leaf of
foodplant. **LARVA** feeds on Common
Rock-rose. **PUPA** is often buried by
ants. **STATUS** Very local on calcareous
grassland. Ssp. *artaxerxes* is found in
Scotland; ssp. *salmacis* is restricted
to N England.

Durham Argus, ssp. *salmacis*

Small Blue,
male underside

Small Blue,
male

Small Blue,
female

Silver-studded Blue,
male underside

Silver-studded Blue,
male

Silver-studded Blue,
female

Silver-studded Blue,
female underside

Silver-studded Blue,
male ssp. *caernensis*

Silver-studded Blue,
female ssp. *caernensis*

Brown Argus,
female underside

Brown Argus,
male

Brown Argus,
female

rn Brown Argus, female ssp.
salmacis underside

Northern Brown Argus,
male ssp. *artaxerxes*

Northern Brown Argus,
female ssp. *salmacis*

ABOVE: **male basking;**
BELOW: **egg**

female, variation

LS

Common Blue
Polyommatus icarus 30–35mm
Our most widespread blue
butterfly. Occurs here as 2
sspp. **ADULT** ssp. *icarus* male has
blue upperwings; female's are
usually brown, but sometimes
tinged blue in middle and with
a row of submarginal orange spots. Underwings of both
sexes are grey-brown with dark spots. Compared to ssp.
icarus, ssp. *mariscolore* is generally larger; female has more
blue on upperwings and more striking orange spots. Flies
Apr–Sep in successive broods. **EGG** is pale and button-
shaped; laid on foodplant. **LARVA** is green and feeds on
Common Bird's-foot Trefoil and related plants. **PUPA** is dull
green and formed on the ground. **STATUS** Locally common
in grassy places. Ssp. *icarus* is widespread in England, Wales
and Scotland; ssp. *mariscolore* occurs in Ireland.

male basking

female, variation

LS

Adonis Blue
Lysandra bellargus 30–40mm
The male is the most
intensely colourful British
'blue' butterfly. **ADULT** male
has bright blue upperwings,
bordered with a narrow black
edge and with a white margin
interrupted by dark lines. Female
has chocolate-brown upperwings with a white margin interrupted by dark lines.
Underside of male is grey-brown with white-ringed dark spots; female is similar but
ground colour is buffish brown. Double-brooded: flies May–Jun, and Aug–Sep. **EGG**
is pale green and flattened, and laid on leaf of foodplant. **LARVA** is grub-like, green
with yellow markings, and often attended by ants. Feeds on Horseshoe Vetch. **PUPA** is
brown and probably carried underground by ants. **STATUS** Very locally common on
suitable areas of chalk downland in S England where the larval foodplant flourishes.

Chalk Hill Blue *Lysandra coridon* 34–40mm
Distinctive butterfly of appropriately managed
calcareous grassland. **ADULT** male has pale blue
upperwings, edged with grey-brown and with a white
margin, clearly interrupted by dark lines. Female has
rich brown upperwings with a dusting of blue scales
near the body and a white margin interrupted by dark
lines. Underside of male is grey-brown with white-
ringed dark spots; female is similar but ground colour
is buffish brown. Flies Jul–Aug. **EGG** is white and flattened,
and laid on stem of foodplant. **LARVA** is grub-like, green with
yellow markings, and often attended by
ants. Feeds on Horseshoe Vetch. **PUPA** is
brown and probably carried underground
by ants. **STATUS** Very locally common on
chalk downland in S England.

female, underside

LS

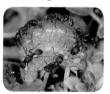

ABOVE: **larva, attended by ants**
RIGHT: **mating pair**
LEFT: **Chalk Hill Blue
aberrations**

Common Blue, female

Common Blue, male

Common Blue, female underside

Common Blue, male underside

Adonis Blue, female

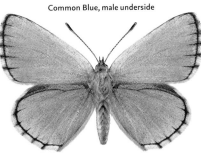

Adonis Blue, male

Adonis Blue, male underside

Chalk Hill Blue, male underside

Chalk Hill Blue, female

Chalk Hill Blue, male

Holly Blue
Celastrina argiolus 28–32mm

The most likely blue butterfly to be seen in gardens and woodlands. Looks silvery in flight. **ADULT** has violet-blue upperwings; male has a narrow blackish tip to forewings, female has a broad outer margin. Underwings are white with black dots. Double-brooded: flies Apr–May, and Aug–Sep. **EGG** is pale and button-shaped; laid at base of flower of foodplant.

egg

LARVA is green; feeds on flowers of Holly in spring, and flowers of Ivy in autumn. **PUPA** is brown and formed in a bark crevice. **STATUS** Widespread and fairly common in England and Wales; more local in Ireland, particularly in coastal regions.

Large Blue *Maculinea arion* ssp. *arion* 40–50mm

Our largest blue butterfly and a conservation icon. Inextricably linked to colonies of the red ant *Myrmica sabuleti*. **ADULT** has violet-blue upperwings with a dark grey border, and dark spots on forewings arranged in the shape of a semicircle or question mark. On average, males are paler than females. Underwings of both sexes are grey-buff, marked with black dots and flushed with blue scales towards base. Flies Jun–Jul. **EGG** is white and laid on flowerhead of Wild Thyme. **LARVA** is grub-like and feeds on Wild Thyme flowers for first 3 instars; thereafter becomes carnivorous and feeds on ant larvae inside colony. **PUPA** is formed in ant colony. **STATUS** Native ssp. *eutyphron* became extinct in 1979. Spp. *arion* has been successfully introduced from Sweden; easiest to see at Collard Hill, Somerset.

Duke of Burgundy *Hamearis lucina* 30–34mm

Beautifully patterned butterfly, reminiscent of a miniature fritillary. **ADULT** has brown upperwings, with a network of orange-yellow spots and patches, particularly striking on forewings. Underside of forewings has a similar pattern to upperwings but is overall paler; underside of hindwings is marked with silvery-white spots. Sexes are similar. Flies May–Jun. **EGG** is white and laid on leaf of larval foodplant. **LARVA** is grub-like and feeds on Cowslip and Primrose. **PUPA** is pale and marked with dark spots, and is formed in leaf litter. **STATUS** Extremely local and restricted mainly to calcareous grassland in S England; a few colonies occur in well-managed coppiced woodland.

mating pair

Holly Blue,
female

Holly Blue,
male

Holly Blue,
female underside

Holly Blue,
male underside

Large Blue,
male

Duke of Burgundy, male

Large Blue,
female

Duke of Burgundy,
female

Large Blue,
male underside

Duke of Burgundy,
male underside

White Admiral *Limenitis camilla* 60–65mm

A classic woodland butterfly with broad, rounded wings. Capable of rapid flight and also glides with ease. Fond of basking in the sun and often associated with patches of Bramble, the flowers of which are a source of nectar. **ADULT** has sooty-black upperwings with a broad band of white patches and spots, more complete on hindwings than forewings. Underwings are orange-brown with a similar pattern of white to that seen on upperwings. Sexes are similar but female has more rounded wings than male, and subtly browner

aberration *nigrina* underside

upperwings. In a rare aberration, upperwings are almost uniformly sooty black. Flies Jun–Jul. **EGG** is laid singly on leaves of Honeysuckle growing in deep shade. **LARVA** is green with a pale lateral band and numerous spikes. **PUPA** is wonderfully ornate, with a metallic sheen seen at certain angles. **STATUS** Very locally common in suitable well-managed woodland in S England; range extends to central England, where it is much more local.

FAR LEFT: **larva**
LEFT: **pupa**

Purple Emperor *Apatura iris* 70–90mm

A magnificent and iconic woodland butterfly. Rather enigmatic and spends much of its time in tree tops, making it hard to observe well. However, occasionally feeds on sap runs or on liquefying animal droppings on the ground. **ADULT** has broad but pointed forewings and rounded hindwings. Females are larger than males, but both sexes have overall dark upperwings with a band of contrasting white patches and spots. In female, ground colour of upperwings is brown; in male, ground colour appears blackish but at certain

angles an amazing purple sheen is revealed. In both sexes, underwings are orange-brown with white and grey bands and a striking eyespot on forewings. Flies Jun–Jul. **EGG** is laid on leaf of larval foodplant. **LARVA** is green and superficially slug-like, with 2 pale anterior projecting 'horns'. Feeds on Goat Willow. **PUPA** is green and remarkably leaf-like; suspended from the underside of a leaf. **STATUS** Extremely local and restricted to a few suitable woodlands in S England. Despite its size, easily overlooked because of its preference for tree tops.

larva   pupa

White Admiral, male

White Admiral, female

White Admiral, female aberration *nigrina*

White Admiral, male underside

Purple Emperor, male

Purple Emperor, larva

Purple Emperor, female underside

Purple Emperor, female

LIFE-SIZE PLATE

Red Admiral *Vanessa atalanta* 65–77mm

Sun-loving wayside butterfly and a frequent visitor to garden flowers. **ADULT** has rather angular forewings and rounded hindwings. Upperwings are sooty black with a red band (sometimes containing a small white dot) and white spots on forewings, and a red marginal band on hindwings. Underside of hindwings is marbled smoky grey; underside of forewings has patterns and colours reminiscent of upperwings, but with a marbled brown tip. Seen in many months but commonest May–Jun and Aug–Sep. **EGG** is green and barrel-shaped; laid singly on leaves of foodplant. **LARVA** is blackish with spiky bristles; feeds on Common Nettle and lives inside a 'tent' of leaves stitched together. **PUPA** is suspended within leaf tent. **STATUS** Most individuals seen in spring are migrants from mainland Europe; these breed and give rise to a new generation of adults in late summer. A few adults hibernate and survive our winters.

ABOVE: **newly emerged adult**

larva

Painted Lady *Vanessa cardui* 60–70mm

Subtly attractive butterfly that is active and fast-flying. **ADULT** has pinkish-buff upperwings marked with black spots; black tip to forewings is adorned with white spots. Underside of hindwings is marbled buffish grey with white spots; underside of forewings is marked with a similar pattern to upperwings but coloration is more pink. Seen from spring to autumn, but commonest May–Aug. **EGG** is green and ovoid; laid singly on leaves of foodplant. **LARVA** is blackish with spiky bristles; lives within a silk 'tent' constructed around leaves of thistles (the main foodplants). **PUPA** is suspended within a woven 'tent' of leaves. **STATUS** A migrant from mainland Europe in variable numbers; very occasionally abundant and always commonest near coasts. Migrants first appear Apr–May and sometimes breed; 2nd generation plus further migrants are seen in later months. Does not survive our winters.

Small Tortoiseshell *Aglais urticae* 45–60mm

Wayside species and a regular garden visitor. Sun-loving and fond of basking. **ADULT** has orange upperwings marbled with yellow and black, and with a row of blue spots inside a dark marginal band on both wings. Underwings are smoky brown with a dull yellow-buff patch on forewings. Double-brooded: emerges from hibernation Mar–Apr, producing a new generation of adults in Jul; a subsequent brood appears Aug–Sep and these adults hibernate. **EGG** is green and barrel-shaped; laid in clusters on leaves of foodplant. **LARVA** is yellow and black; gregarious and feeds on Common Nettle. **PUPA** is suspended at tail end from stem. **STATUS** Fairly common and widespread, but its fortunes have been mixed and it has declined in many areas. Commonest in S Britain.

larvae

pupa

Red Admiral, underside

Red Admiral

Red Admiral, larval 'tent' of Common Nettle leaves

Painted Lady, underside

Small Tortoiseshell, underside

Painted Lady

Small Tortoiseshell

larva

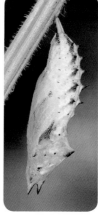

pupa

Peacock *Aglais io* 65–75mm
Distinctive and familiar visitor to garden flowers. Fond of basking in sunshine and often seen feeding on sap runs as well as flowers. **ADULT** has maroon upperwings with bold eye markings on each wing, and black markings on forewings. Underwings are marbled smoky grey-brown. Flies in many months, but commonest Jul–Sep and again in spring after emerging from hibernation. Sometimes hibernates indoors or in sheds and outbuildings. **EGG** is barrel-shaped; laid in clusters on leaves of foodplant. **LARVA** is blackish with spiky bristles; lives in clusters on Common Nettle foodplant. **PUPA** is suspended from stem or leaf by tail end. **STATUS** Common and widespread except in the far N of Britain, favouring a wide range of open habitats.

Comma *Polygonia c-album* 50–60mm
Attractive butterfly with distinctive ragged-edged wings, the shape unique to this species. Easy to observe when basking or feeding on nectar, but well camouflaged and hard to spot when resting with wings closed. **ADULT** has orange-brown upperwings with dark markings. Underwings are smoky brown with a white 'comma' mark. The form *hutchinsoni* (seen in summer) has paler underwings and more colourful upperwings. Variably single- or double-brooded depending on weather. Emerges from hibernation mainly Mar–Apr; 2nd brood appears Jun–Jul and typical individuals go into hibernation, whereas form *hutchinsoni* individuals produce another generation that appears Aug–Sep and then hibernates. Proportion of form *hutchinsoni* individuals is highest in warm seasons. **EGG** is green and barrel-shaped; laid singly on leaves of foodplant. **LARVA** is orange-brown with a white dorsal band; feeds on Common Nettle and Hop. **PUPA** is suspended from stem by tail end. **STATUS** Locally fairly common throughout S Britain, becoming rare towards the Scottish border. Favours open woodland, mature gardens and hedgerows.

ABOVE LEFT: **newly emerged adult**
LEFT: **larva**

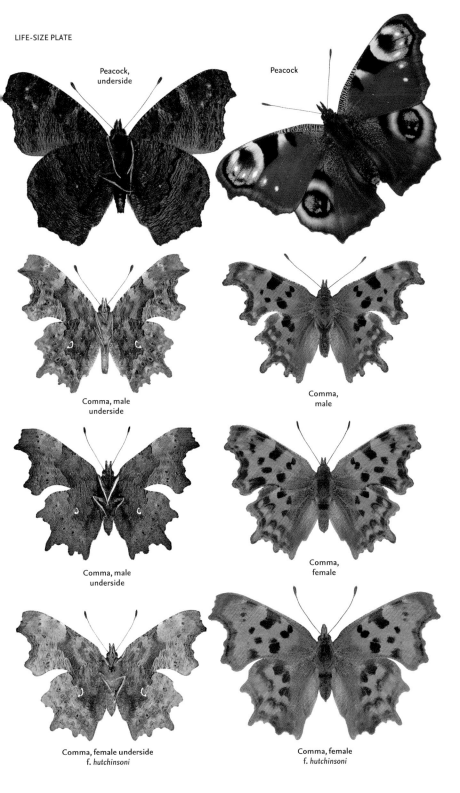

Peacock, underside

Peacock

Comma, male underside

Comma, male

Comma, male underside

Comma, female

Comma, female underside
f. *hutchinsoni*

Comma, female
f. *hutchinsoni*

Pearl-bordered Fritillary

Boloria euphrosyne 38–45mm

Sun-loving woodland butterfly that gets its
name from the silvery 'pearl' spots on underside
of hindwings. Very similar to Small Pearl-bordered
and best separated by studying markings on underside
of hindwings. Fond of basking and feeds on flowers of
plants such as Bugle. **ADULT** has rather rounded wings.
Upperwings are orange-brown, marked with a pattern of
black spots and squares; black submarginal crescent spots are separate from
dark wing margins (fused in similar Small Pearl-bordered). Underside of
forewings is orange-buff, with a pattern of dark markings similar to that on
upper surface. Underside of hindwings has a pattern of orange-brown and buff
cells, with 7 silver 'pearl' spots on margin and 2 in centre. Flies May–Jun; flight
time overlaps with that of Small Pearl-bordered, but typically Pearl-bordered
emerges a week or two before its cousin. **EGG** is yellowish and laid on underside
of leaf of foodplant. **LARVA** is blackish with spiky bristles; feeds mainly on
Common Dog-violet. **PUPA** is attached by tail end to stem. **STATUS** Has a very
patchy distribution: very locally common in S England (particularly SW); scattered
and very local in Wales; locally common in central Scotland; and extremely local
in W Ireland. Favours open deciduous woodland; these days, careful management
is often required to allow the larval foodplant to flourish.

LS

Small Pearl-bordered Fritillary, resting adult   Small Pearl-bordered Fritillary, basking

Small Pearl-bordered Fritillary

Boloria selene 36–42mm

Colourful and attractive butterfly that is similar
to Pearl-bordered. Fond of basking or feeding on
flowers of Bugle. **ADULT** has rather rounded wings.
Upperwings are orange-brown with a pattern of
black spots and squares; very similar to those of
Pearl-bordered, but unlike that species the black
submarginal crescent spots are fused to dark wing
margins. Underside of forewings is orange-buff with a pattern of dark markings
similar to that on upper surface. Underwings are marked with an intricate pattern
of white, orange-brown and buff. Markings on underside of hindwings are best
features for separation of this species from Pearl-bordered: shares that species'
7 silver marginal spots ('pearls'), but has several central silver 'pearl' spots (Pearl-
bordered has just 2 of these). Flies May–Jun. **EGG** is pale buff and laid on underside
of leaf of foodplant. **LARVA** is blackish with spiky bristles; feeds mainly on Common
Dog-violet. **PUPA** is attached by tail end to stem. **STATUS** Favours open woodland, as
well as suitable grassland, moorland and coastal cliff habitats where larval foodplants
are common. Widespread and locally common in Wales, Scotland and SW England,
but extremely local elsewhere and absent from most of central and E England.

LS

Pearl-bordered Fritillary,
male underside

Pearl-bordered Fritillary,
male

Pearl-bordered Fritillary,
female underside

Pearl-bordered Fritillary,
female

Small Pearl-bordered Fritillary,
male underside

Small Pearl-bordered Fritillary,
male

Small Pearl-bordered Fritillary,
female underside

Small Pearl-bordered Fritillary,
female

High Brown Fritillary *Argynnis adippe* 55–68mm

Fast-flying and well-marked butterfly. Can be confused with the very similar, and commoner, Dark Green Fritillary, and best separated by studying markings and colours on underside of hindwings. **ADULT** has broad and rather rounded wings. Upperwings are orange-brown with a pattern of black spots, squares and chevrons. Underside of forewings is orange-buff with black markings arranged in a similar pattern to that seen on upper surface. Underside of hindwings is overall buffish brown, adorned with silvery-white spots and chevrons; these align to form marginal and submarginal rows, between which there are brown spots. Flies Jun–Jul. **EGG** are laid in the vicinity of larval foodplants and remain dormant until the following spring. **LARVA** is brown with black and white dorsal markings, and spiny bristles. Feeds on a range of violet species, notably Common Dog-violet and Hairy Violet. **PUPA** is brown and formed within a 'tent' of woven withered leaves, attached by the tail end. **STATUS** Population and range have declined catastrophically over the last 40 years or so. Now restricted to SW England (particularly Exmoor and Dartmoor), Wales and NW England. Favours open (often coppiced) woodland and rough grassland where the larval foodplants flourish.

LS

Dark Green Fritillary *Argynnis aglaja* 60–65mm

Fast-flying butterfly that is fond of feeding on flowers of thistles and knapweeds. **ADULT** has broad, rather rounded wings. Upperwings are orange-brown with a pattern of black spots, squares and chevrons. Underside of forewings is orange-buff with black markings arranged in a similar pattern to that seen on upper surface. Underside of hindwings is tinged greenish overall (buffish brown in High Brown Fritillary) and adorned with silvery-white spots and chevrons; these align to form marginal and submarginal rows, but unlike High Brown Fritillary there are no brown spots between these rows. Flies Jul–Aug. **EGG** is laid on or near larval foodplants. **LARVA** hatches in summer and hibernates; the following spring it appears blackish with spiky bristles and a pale dorsal line. Feeds on Common Dog-violet and Hairy Violet. **PUPA** is brown and formed within a 'tent' of woven withered leaves, attached by the tail end. **STATUS** Widespread and locally common throughout much of Britain, although least numerous or absent from large parts of central and E England; mainly coastal in Ireland. Favours open grassland, typically on calcareous soils.

LS

basking adult

High Brown Fritillary,
female underside

High Brown Fritillary,
female

Dark Green Fritillary,
male underside

Dark Green Fritillary,
male

Dark Green Fritillary,
female underside

Dark Green Fritillary, female

Silver-washed Fritillary

Argynnis paphia 70–80mm

Large, colourful woodland butterfly that is easily observed in suitable habitats within its range. Fast-flying and active, but often feeds on flowers of thistles and Bramble. **ADULT** has broad wings; hindwings are rounded, forewings are rather pointed, more so in male than female. Upperwings are orange-brown with a network of black spots and squares. In male, upperwings are a more intense colour and forewings include 4 dark veins (known as sex brands) that contain special scales used in courtship. In both sexes, underside of forewings is orange-buff with black markings arranged in a similar pattern to that seen on upper surface. Underside of hindwings is greenish overall with streaks of shiny silver. Typical specimens are referred to as form *paphia*; in scarce form *valesina*, orange upperwing colour is replaced by olive-green. Flies Jun–Aug. **EGG** is yellow, ridged and laid on moss on shady side of tree trunk. **LARVA** is yellow at first, but becomes brown with a pale dorsal line and spiky bristles. Feeds mainly on Common Dog-violet. **PUPA** is attached by tail end to stem. **STATUS** Locally common in open woodland habitats in S England and S Wales; widespread but with a patchy distribution across Ireland.

LS

Silver-washed
Fritillary, female
f. *valesina*

LS

Marsh Fritillary *Euphydryas aurinia* 30–50mm

Colourful and intricately patterned butterfly that is particularly vivid when fresh; colours fade with age, leaving worn specimens looking rather shiny and waxen. Sun-loving and rather sluggish, often basking or resting for extended periods. **ADULT** has rather broad wings; hindwings are rounded while forewings are rather pointed. Upper surface of wings is overall reddish orange with a network of dark lines, some of which align and cross to form and frame yellow 'cells'. Underwings are overall orange-buff with pale spots and a suggestion of the upperwing patterns. Flies May–Jun. **EGG** is laid in a batch on underside of leaf of foodplant. **LARVA** is black with spiky bristles; lives within a colonial silk 'web' spun around leaves of foodplant, Devil's-bit Scabious. **PUPA** is attached by tail end to stem; it is white with beautiful black and yellow markings. **STATUS** Generally rather scarce and extremely local, occurring in small, discrete colonies. Range is mainly restricted to SW England, SW and NW Wales, SW Scotland and W Ireland.

LS

LS

Marsh Fritillary,
female ssp. *hibernica*

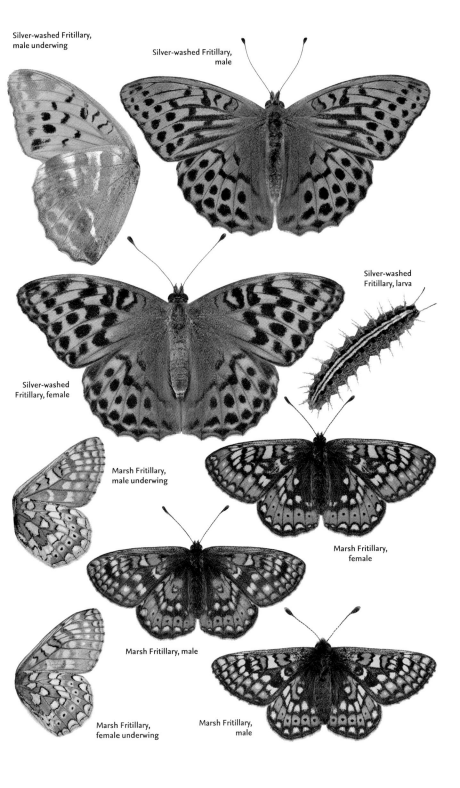

Silver-washed Fritillary, male underwing

Silver-washed Fritillary, male

Silver-washed Fritillary, larva

Silver-washed Fritillary, female

Marsh Fritillary, male underwing

Marsh Fritillary, female

Marsh Fritillary, male

Marsh Fritillary, female underwing

Marsh Fritillary, male

Glanville Fritillary *Melitaea cinxia* 40–50mm

Attractive and well-marked butterfly whose underwings are as beautifully patterned as its upperwings. Superficially similar to Heath Fritillary, but their geographical ranges do not overlap and subtle differences in markings also allow separation. A sun-loving species that disappears into cover in dull weather. **ADULT** has broad, rounded wings. Upperwings are orange-brown with a network of blackish veins and concentric cross-lines. Some of the resulting pale 'cells' on hindwings contain dark spots (absent in Heath Fritillary). Underside of forewings is orange-buff with a few dark spots, and a black-dotted white border. Underside of hindwings is white with dark markings and 2 concentric orange bands, the outer one containing black spots (absent in Heath Fritillary). Flies May–Jun. **EGG** is laid in a batch on underside of leaf of foodplant. **LARVA** is black with spiky bristles and a red head; lives colonially in a silk web spun over foodplant. Feeds on Ribwort Plantain. **PUPA** is suspended by tail end from stem. **STATUS** Restricted mainly to Isle of Wight, where it favours open coastal habitats, including cliffs and landslips. Occasional colonies also appear on S Hampshire coast; these are mainly ephemeral but colony at Hurst Castle appears stable for the present.

Heath Fritillary, basking adult

Glanville Fritillary, basking adult

Heath Fritillary *Melitaea athalia* 40–46mm

Sun-loving butterfly whose rounded wings are colourful and beautifully patterned on both upper and lower surfaces. Delights in basking, and fond of feeding on flowers of Bramble and Bugle. **ADULT** has broad, rounded wings. Upperwings are orange-brown with a network of blackish veins and concentric cross-lines; dark coloration is most intense towards wing bases. Unlike Glanville Fritillary, there are no dark spots inside pale cells on the hindwings. Underside of forewings is orange-brown with dark spots. Underside of hindwings is white with dark markings and 2 concentric orange bands; unlike Glanville Fritillary, there are no black spots on hindwings. Flies May–Jun. **EGG** is laid on underside of larval foodplant. **LARVA** is buffish grey with spiky black and orange bristles; colonial at first. Feeds mainly on Common Cow-wheat in SE England, but mainly on Ribwort Plantain in SW England. **PUPA** is suspended by tail end from stem. **STATUS** Extremely local and scarce. Colonies in SE England are restricted to appropriately managed coppiced woodland; colonies in SW England are found on grassy heathland.

Glanville Fritillary,
male underwing

Glanville Fritillary,
male

Glanville Fritillary,
female underwing

Glanville Fritillary,
female

Heath Fritillary,
male underwing

Heath Fritillary,
male

Heath Fritillary,
female underwing

Heath Fritillary,
female

LS

ssp. *insula*

resting
adult

Speckled Wood *Pararge aegeria* 46–55mm

Sun-loving butterfly that favours clearings and
sunny rides in woodlands. Rival males engage in
aerial battles. **ADULT** of widespread ssp. *tircis* has
dark brown upperwings with pale markings; row
of pale patches on hindwings contain eyespots
and forewings are marked with a single eyespot. Underwings are greyish buff
with subtle, pale marbling on hindwings, and suggestion of upperwing pattern
on forewings. Ssp. *insula* occurs on Isles of Scilly and is overall richer brown, with
the pale upperwing markings tinged orange. Ssp. *oblita*, from NW Scotland, lacks
colour and can look almost black and white. Ssp. *tircis* can be double- or triple-
brooded, flying Apr–Jun, Jul and Sep; ssp. *insula* is invariably triple-brooded, with
a similar flight period; ssp. *oblita* is double-brooded, flying May and Aug–Sep. **EGG**
is pale and ovoid; laid singly on foodplant. **LARVA** is green and feeds on various
grasses, notably Cock's-foot and Common Couch. Can overwinter either as larva
or pupa. **PUPA** is suspended by tail end low on a grass stem. **STATUS** Widespread
in England as far north as Lake District, Wales and Ireland; commonest in the S
and scarce or absent from upland areas and the N; very local in lowland Scotland.
Favours wooded habitats, including mature scrub, hedgerows and gardens.

Wall *Lasiommata megera* 45–52mm

Colourful, sun-loving, superficially fritillary-
like butterfly that is fond of basking on bare
ground, especially paths. **ADULT** has broad
wings, the upperwings brown with a striking
pattern of orange; orange band on hindwings
contains eyespots and there is a single eyespot
on forewings. Underside of hindwings is
marbled grey-buff and brown with subtle
eyespots; underside of forewings has a
suggestion of the pattern seen on upper
surface, and a striking eyespot. Double-
brooded: flies Jun, and Aug–Sep. **EGG** is pale and laid
singly on a grass stem or leaf. **LARVA** is green. Feeds on
a range of grasses, including species of bent (grass) and
Cock's-foot. **PUPA** is suspended by tail end low on a grass
stem. **STATUS** Formerly widespread but its range has
declined catastrophically in recent decades. Still occurs in
England, Wales, Ireland and S Scotland, but now restricted
primarily to coastal regions; absent from, or extremely
local, inland. Habitat degradation and loss are presumed
to be the cause of its decline. Favours dry grassland.

LS

eggs

Speckled Wood,
male underside

Speckled Wood,
male

Speckled Wood,
female underside

Speckled Wood,
female

Wall,
male underside

Wall,
male

Wall,
female underside

Wall,
female

Mountain Ringlet *Erebia epiphron* 32–40mm

LS

An upland moorland butterfly that is typically found at altitudes of 500–800m, invariably near sites where the larval foodplant flourishes. Sun-loving, it disappears into the cover of vegetation the moment the sun is obscured by cloud and consequently is almost impossible to find on dull days. ADULT ssp. *mnemon* has rich, dark brown upperwings with a row of orange patches on each wing, each patch containing an eyespot. Underside of hindwings is dark brown with small, subtle orange spots; underside of forewings is orange-brown with dark spots and a grey-brown border. Ssp. *scotica* is similar but larger overall, the orange markings and eyespots larger and more striking. Flies Jun–Jul. EGG is pale, barrel-shaped and laid on a grass stem. LARVA feeds on Mat-grass. PUPA is formed low in vegetation. STATUS Very local; ssp. *mnemon* is confined to the Lake District while ssp. *scotica* occurs in central W Scotland.

Scotch Argus *Erebia aethiops* 45–52mm

A broad-winged northern butterfly that is fond of basking. ADULT ssp. *aethiops* has rich brown upperwings, with an orange band on each wing containing dark eyespots. Underside of hindwings is brown with a grey band; underside of forewings is brown with an orange patch containing dark eyespots. Ssp. *caledonia* is similar but smaller, with more angular forewings and smaller, less colourful markings. EGG is spherical and laid on a grass stem. LARVA is buffish and feeds primarily on Blue Moor-grass. PUPA is formed in low vegetation. STATUS Widespread and locally common within its northern range: ssp. *aethiops* occurs in N England and SE Scotland; ssp. *caledonia* is found in W Scotland. Favours meadows and open grassy woodland.

male

LS

female underside

LS

Scotch Argus, basking adult   Ringlet, resting adult

Ringlet *Aphantopus hyperantus* 42–52mm

LS

Ringlet, male underside

Familiar dark-looking meadow butterfly. ADULT has smoky-brown velvety upperwings, darker in males than females, with variable numbers of small yellow-ringed eyespots that are more intense in female than male. Underwings are buffish brown with striking yellow-ringed eyespots. Flies Jun–Jul. EGG is yellowish and semi-ovoid; dropped in flight over grassland. LARVA is brown and feeds on various grasses, notably Cock's-foot and Common Couch. PUPA is formed in a cocoon at ground level. STATUS Widespread and fairly common across lowland Britain and Ireland, although absent from the far NW. Favours meadows, grassy woodland rides and hedgerows.

Mountain Ringlet,
Lake District

Mountain Ringlet,
Lake District

Mountain Ringlet,
Scotland

Mountain Ringlet,
Scotland

Scotch Argus,
female

Scotch Argus,
male

Ringlet,
male

Scotch Argus,
male underside

Ringlet,
female underside

Ringlet,
female

Marbled White
Melanargia galathea 54–58mm

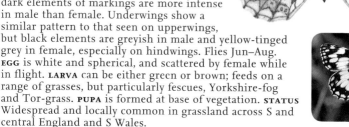

female underside

LS

Unmistakable butterfly with broad, rounded wings. Often feeds on knapweed flowers and is fond of basking in the mornings. Roosts on grass stems in late afternoon. **ADULT** has upperwings marked with a striking pattern of black and white; dark elements of markings are more intense in male than female. Underwings show a similar pattern to that seen on upperwings, but black elements are greyish in male and yellow-tinged grey in female, especially on hindwings. Flies Jun–Aug. **EGG** is white and spherical, and scattered by female while in flight. **LARVA** can be either green or brown; feeds on a range of grasses, but particularly fescues, Yorkshire-fog and Tor-grass. **PUPA** is formed at base of vegetation. **STATUS** Widespread and locally common in grassland across S and central England and S Wales.

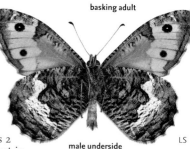

basking adult

Grayling *Hipparchia semele* 52–60mm
Sun-loving butterfly that rests with wings closed, aligned to the sun to create minimal shadow; underwings provide excellent camouflage against stony ground. **ADULT** has grey-buff upperwings with a band of yellow-buff on each wing containing eyespots; note, however, that upperwings are seldom revealed. Underside of hindwings is marbled buffish grey and white; underside of forewings is orange-buff with a grey-buff border; female has 2 striking dark eyespots, while in male one eyespot is bold, the other reduced in size. Several geographically isolated sspp. occur, each differing subtly in terms of average size and intensity of colour. Flies Jul–Aug. **EGG** is pale and spherical, and laid on a grass stem. **LARVA** is buffish with darker lengthways stripes; feeds on grasses, notably Bristle Bent, Red Fescue and Early Hair-grass. **PUPA** is formed at ground level, in a silk-lined cell. **STATUS** Widespread in Britain, but local and mostly coastal except in the S. Favours heaths and coastal cliffs.

male underside

LS

resting adult

Gatekeeper *Pyronia tithonus* 38–45mm
Wayside and hedgerow butterfly that often feeds on flowers of Bramble. **ADULT** has smoky-brown upperwings with an orange patch on each wing and a paired eyespot on forewing. Male is smaller than female, with overall darker upperwings and a brown band (sex brand) across the orange forewing

LS

patch. In both sexes, underside of hindwings is buff, marbled with greyish white and orange-brown; underside of forewings is orange with a darker border and a paired dark eyespot. Flies Jul–Aug. **EGG** is whitish, barrel-shaped and dropped among grasses. **LARVA** is pale brown and feeds on grasses, notably fescues and bents. **PUPA** is suspended among low grass stems. **STATUS** Locally common and widespread in S Britain and S Ireland in grassland.

basking adult

Marbled White,
male underside

Marbled White,
male

Grayling,
female underside

Marbled White,
female

Grayling,
female

Grayling,
male

Gatekeeper,
female

Gatekeeper,
male

Gatekeeper,
female underside

Gatekeeper,
male underside

Meadow Brown *Maniola jurtina*
40–60mm

Classic grassland and wayside
butterfly, and one of our commonest
species. **ADULT** male is smaller than
female. Both have brown upperwings:
male has small orange patch on forewings
containing an eyespot; orange patch and
eyespot are larger in female. Underside
of hindwings is stippled buffish brown
with a greyish border; underside of
forewings is orange-buff with a grey-brown
border and dark eyespot, this larger in female

LS

female

than male. Flies Jun–Aug. **EGG** is mottled brown and barrel-shaped, and laid or
dropped among grasses. **LARVA** is green and feeds on grasses, notably bents, False
Brome and Cock's-foot. **PUPA** is suspended from a grass stem. **STATUS** Common and
widespread throughout, and absent only from upland regions.

Small Heath *Coenonympha pamphilus* 33–36mm
Small grassland butterfly with rounded wings. Invariably rests with wings closed
so that upperwings are usually revealed only in flight.
ADULT male is smaller than female. Upperwings of
both species are buffish brown with a faint eyespot
on forewings and subtle marbling on hindwings.

Underside of forewings is
orange with an eyespot (colour
more intense in male than
female); underside of hindwings
is marbled grey, brown and buff.
Double-brooded: flies May–Jun, and

LS

female

Aug–Sep. **EGG** is beaker-shaped and laid on a grass stem.
LARVA is green and feeds on various grasses, notably fescues
and bents. **PUPA** is suspended by tail end low down on
a grass stem. **STATUS** Widespread but local throughout;
commonest in the S, absent from upland regions, and with
a very patchy distribution in Ireland. Favours heaths and
areas of open, dry grassland.

resting adult

Large Heath *Coenonympha tullia* 35–40mm
Northern and upland butterfly that always rests
with its wings closed; upperwings are revealed only in
flight. **ADULT** has rounded wings and sexes are similar.
Upperwings are buffish brown with subtle pale-ringed
dark eyespots. Underside of hindwings is grey-buff with
a jagged white band and white-ringed dark eyespots;
underside of forewings is orange-buff with a grey margin,
variable white band and white-ringed dark eyespots.
Eyespot intensity and size vary according to ssp.: ssp.
davus is darkest overall with bold eyespots; ssp. *scotica*
is palest with indistinct eyespots; ssp. *polydama* is
intermediate between the two. **EGG** is spherical and
laid on leaf of foodplant. **LARVA** is green and feeds
mainly on Hare's-tail Cottongrass. **PUPA** is attached by
tail end low down on a grass stem. **STATUS** Extremely
local, and associated with boggy moorland. Ssp. *davus*
is found in NW England; ssp. *polydama* is found in
N England, S Scotland and NW Wales; ssp. *scotica*
is found in N Scotland.

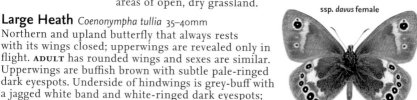

ssp. *davus* female

LS

male ssp. *scotica* resting adult

Meadow Brown,
male underside

Meadow Brown,
male

Meadow Brown,
female underside

Meadow Brown,
female

Small Heath,
female underside

Small Heath,
male underside

Small Heath,
male

Large Heath,
ssp. *davus* underside

Large Heath,
ssp. *davus*

Large Heath,
ssp. *polydama* underside

Large Heath,
ssp. *scotica* underside

Scarce Swallowtail *Iphiclides podalirius* 75–85mm

Unmistakable member of family Papilionidae. **ADULT** has broad triangular forewings and angular hindwings with a long tail streamer. Upperwings are creamy white; forewings have black cross-bands, hindwings have a dark margin with crescent-shaped blue spots and a red-framed blue eyespot. Underwings are similar to, but paler than, upperwings. **STATUS** Possible rare immigrant from mainland Europe.

Berger's Clouded Yellow
Colias alfacariensis 50–60mm

Member of family Pieridae. Upperwings are seldom revealed except in flight. **ADULT** has pale yellow upperwings; forewings have a dark tip and dark central spot, hindwings have an orange central spot. Underside of hindwings is yellow with an orange-ringed pale central spot; underside of forewings is pale yellow in male, whitish in female, with a yellow tip and dark central spot in both sexes. Compared to Clouded Yellow (even form *helice*; p. 30), underwings are much paler. Separation from Pale Clouded Yellow (p. 30) is tricky: orange spot on upper surface of hindwings is more intense in Berger's, and markings and colours on underwings show more contrast. **STATUS** Very rare immigrant, seen mainly Jul–Sep.

pupa

Bath White *Pontia daplidice* 50–52mm

Fast-flying small 'white' butterfly (family Pieridae) with angular forewings. **ADULT** has white upperwings with dark markings. Underside of hindwings is marbled yellowish and white; underside of forewings is white with a broad yellow margin and darkish patch on leading edge. **STATUS** Very rare immigrant from mainland Europe, seen mainly Jul–Sep.

Black-veined White *Aporia crataegi* 70–75mm

Member of family Pieridae, with broad rounded wings. **ADULT** has white wings, the wing margins and veins marked black above and below. **STATUS** Former British resident but extinct as a breeding species. Now a very rare immigrant from mainland Europe, seen mainly Jul–Sep along S coasts.

feeding adult

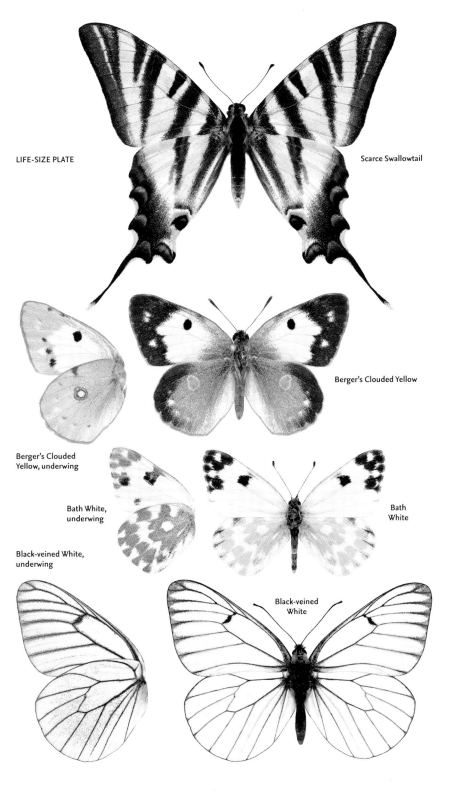

LIFE-SIZE PLATE

Scarce Swallowtail

Berger's Clouded Yellow

Berger's Clouded
Yellow, underwing

Bath White,
underwing

Bath
White

Black-veined White,
underwing

Black-veined
White

Large Copper *Lycaena dispar* 45–50mm
Stunning member of family Lycaenidae.
ADULT male has orange upperwings with a black
margin; female's upperwings are orange-yellow
with more extensive black markings. In both
sexes, underside of hindwings is grey with black
and orange spots; underside of forewings is orange
with black spots. STATUS Endemic ssp. *dispar*, a
former resident of East Anglian fens, has been extinct
since 1850s. Subsequent introductions have failed.

LS

Mazarine Blue *Cyaniris semiargus* 34–38mm
In both sexes, upperwings recall a Silver-studded
Blue (p. 40) but underwings are like those of Small
Blue (p. 40); larger than both species. Former
resident, now extinct.

LS

Geranium Bronze *Cacyreus marshalli* 20–25mm
Member of the Lycaenidae, with a 'tail' streamer on
hindwings. ADULT Upperwings are brown with a boldly
chequered black and white margin. Underwings are
beautifully marbled brown, buff and white; on hindwings,
has eyespot adjacent to 'tail' streamer. Larva feeds on cultivated geraniums and
pelargoniums. STATUS South African species introduced to Europe with garden
plants; first discovered in Britain in 1997 and established briefly. Turns up
from time to time in summer, but unlikely to survive our winters and become
established permanently.

LS

Long-tailed Blue *Lampides boeticus* 35–40mm
Member of family Lycaenidae, with paired 'tail'
streamers, similar to a hairstreak butterfly
(pp. 36–39). ADULT has blue upperwings with dark
margins; colour is brighter, and dark margins smaller,
in male than female. Underwings have bands of grey-
buff and white, with 2 eyespots on each hindwing.
STATUS Very rare immigrant from mainland Europe,
seen Jul–Sep on S coasts.

LS

Short-tailed Blue *Cupido argiades* 20–30mm
Member of family Lycaenidae and related to Small Blue
(p. 40), but with a tiny 'tail' streamer on hindwings.
ADULT male has blue upperwings; those of female are
brown. In both sexes, underwings are greyish white with
small black spots, and with orange eyespots on hindwings.
STATUS Very rare immigrant from mainland Europe, seen
mainly Jul–Sep along S coasts.

LS

Mazarine Blue

Mazarine Blue, underside

Large Copper, male

Large Copper, female

Geranium Bronze, underwing

Geranium Bronze

Short-tailed Blue, underwing

Short-tailed Blue

Long-tailed Blue, male

Long-tailed Blue, female

Long-tailed Blue, female underside

Queen of Spain Fritillary *Issoria lathonia* 35–55mm
Attractive fritillary (family Nymphalidae) with rather angular wings. **ADULT** has orange upperwings with black spots. Underwings are orange-buff; hindwings are marked with silvery patches, forewings with black spots. **STATUS** Very rare immigrant from mainland Europe, seen mainly Jul–Sep on S coasts.

Camberwell Beauty
Nymphalis antiopa 78–85mm
Unmistakable member of family Nymphalidae. **ADULT** has maroon upperwings with a fringe of blue spots and creamy-yellow border. Underwings are marbled smoky brown with a pale border. **STATUS** Very rare immigrant from mainland Europe, seen mainly Jul–Sep along S and E coasts.

LEFT: **larva**
BELOW LEFT: **pupa**
BELOW: **basking adult**

Large Tortoiseshell *Nymphalis polychloros* 70–75mm
Colourful member of family Nymphalidae. **ADULT** has orange-brown upperwings with black spots on forewings; dark margin contains blue spots on hindwings. Underwings are marbled grey-brown and buff. **STATUS** Very rare immigrant from mainland Europe, seen mainly Jul–Sep along S and E coasts.

Monarch *Danaus plexippus* 95–100mm
Impressive and unmistakable butterfly (family Nymphalidae). **ADULT** has orange upperwings with black veins and a white-spotted black border; underwings are paler than upperwings but show a similar pattern. **STATUS** Very rare vagrant from North America, seen mainly Sep–Oct in SW Britain.

Queen of
Spain Fritillary,
underwings

Camberwell Beauty

Queen of Spain Fritillary

LIFE-SIZE PLATE

Large
Tortoiseshell

Large Tortoiseshell,
underwings

Monarch

male

Orange Swift *Triodia sylvina*
3.001 (15) 30–38mm

LS

ADULT male has orange-brown forewings with dark-margined diagonal white lines; angle formed between lines is roughly 90 degrees. Female is larger and darker brown. Flies Jul–Sep. **LARVA** feeds on roots of various herbaceous plants. **STATUS** Widespread and locally common in England and Wales; scarce in Scotland. Favours waste ground and grassland.

Common Swift *Korscheltellus lupulina* 3.002 (17) 25–35mm

LS

ADULT male has buffish-brown forewings, typically with dark-margined white markings that form diagonal lines; angle formed between lines is greater than 90 degrees. Some individuals appear almost unmarked. Female is larger than male and has much fainter markings. Flies May–Jul. **LARVA** feeds on roots of various grasses and herbaceous plants. **STATUS** Widespread and locally common in England and Wales; scarce in Scotland. Favours waste ground and grassland.

Map-winged Swift *Korscheltellus fusconebulosa* 3.003 (18) 15–25mm

LS

ADULT male is smaller than female. Both have well-marked forewings with a variegated pattern of dark brown and buffish white of variable intensity; some individuals are uniform buff. Flies Jun–Jul. **LARVA** feeds on roots of Bracken. **STATUS** Widespread and locally common.

Gold Swift *Phymatopus hecta* 3.004 (16) 22–33mm

LS

ADULT male has orange-brown forewings with rows of white spots. Female is paler with much less intense markings. Flies Jun–Jul. **LARVA** feeds on Bracken. **STATUS** Widespread and locally common.

Ghost Moth *Hepialus humuli* 3.005 (14) 45–50mm

LS

ADULT has white wings, a fluffy yellow thorax and reddish legs. Female has yellow wings with a pattern of orange lines. In ssp. *thulensis* (Shetland Isles), male's wings are similar to those of female. Flies Jun–Aug. **LARVA** feeds on roots of various grasses and herbaceous plants. **STATUS** Widespread and locally common in England and Wales; much scarcer in Scotland and Ireland.

Ghost Moth male, ssp. *thulensis*

LS

FAR LEFT: Ghost Moth, male
MIDDLE LEFT: Ghost Moth, female
LEFT: Goat Moth, larva

Goat Moth *Cossus cossus* 50.001 (162) 70–95mm
ADULT has forewings whose colour and patterns resemble tree bark. Flies Jun–Jul. **LARVA** feeds inside trunks of deciduous trees; it smells of goats. **STATUS** Widespread but local; commonest in the S.

LS

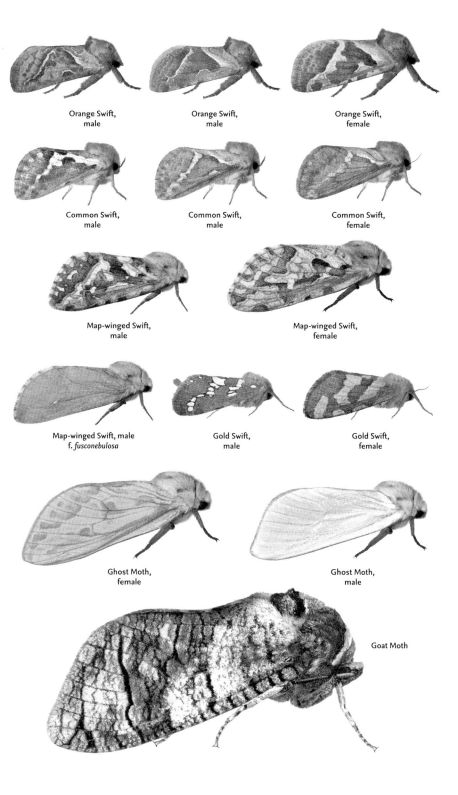

Orange Swift,
male

Orange Swift,
male

Orange Swift,
female

Common Swift,
male

Common Swift,
male

Common Swift,
female

Map-winged Swift,
male

Map-winged Swift,
female

Map-winged Swift, male
f. *fusconebulosa*

Gold Swift,
male

Gold Swift,
female

Ghost Moth,
female

Ghost Moth,
male

Goat Moth

Leopard Moth *Zeuzera pyrina* 50.002 (161) 35–60mm

ADULT has a furry white thorax marked with black spots, and white wings with black spots; these soon become worn and faded. Flies Jun–Aug. **LARVA** feeds on wood, inside deciduous trees. **STATUS** Widespread only in central and S England and E Wales.

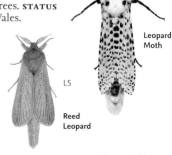

Leopard Moth

Reed Leopard

Phragmataecia castaneae 50.003 (160) 30–50mm
ADULT has a strikingly long abdomen that projects well beyond wings at rest; female is larger than male and has a proportionately longer abdomen. Forewings in both sexes are grey-buff with fine black spotting. Flies Jun–Jul. **LARVA** feeds inside stems of Common Reed. **STATUS** Rare and local, restricted to a few reedbeds in East Anglia; small population in Dorset.

Reed Leopard

Raspberry Clearwing *Pennisetia hylaeiformis* 52.001 (369a) 10–12mm

ADULT has 4 broad yellow bands on abdomen, and 3 narrower, indistinct ones; tail fan is yellowish with a dark centre. Margins to otherwise clear forewings are reddish orange. Flies Jun–Jul. **LARVA** feeds inside stems of Raspberry, forming a gall in its 2nd year. **STATUS** Introduced with Raspberry canes from mainland Europe; now established very locally in central England.

Hornet Moth

Sesia apiformis 52.002 (370) 35–45mm
ADULT is similar size and shape to true Hornet (*Vespa crabro*), with similar behaviour. Has striking black and yellow bands on abdomen, and a yellow head and 'shoulders'. Margins to otherwise clear wings are reddish. Flies Jun–Jul. **LARVA** feeds inside trunks of Black Poplar. **STATUS** Local and generally scarce, with most records from central England and East Anglia.

Hornet Moth, mating pair

pupal case

Lunar Hornet Moth, mating pair

Lunar Hornet Moth

Sesia bembeciformis 52.003 (371) 30–40mm
ADULT is similar to Hornet Moth, with similar Hornet- or wasp-like behaviour when disturbed. Separated from Hornet Moth by presence of yellow 'collar', and by black (not yellow) head and 'shoulders'. Flies Jun–Jul. **LARVA** feeds inside trunks of various willows (notably Grey Willow). **STATUS** Local and generally scarce throughout, but easily overlooked.

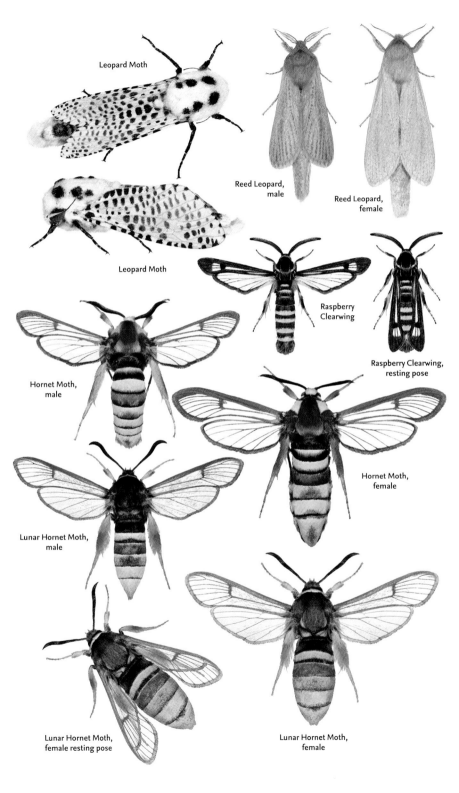

Leopard Moth

Reed Leopard, male

Reed Leopard, female

Leopard Moth

Raspberry Clearwing

Raspberry Clearwing, resting pose

Hornet Moth, male

Hornet Moth, female

Lunar Hornet Moth, male

Lunar Hornet Moth, female resting pose

Lunar Hornet Moth, female

Dusky Clearwing *Paranthrene tabaniformis* 52.004 (372) 28–32mm
ADULT has dusky-brown forewings and brown-margined smoky
hindwings. Abdomen is black with yellow bands (4 in male, 3 in
female). Flies Jun–Jul. **LARVA** feeds inside stems and trunks of
Aspen and other poplars, and Sea-buckthorn. **STATUS** Former
resident, probably extinct but possibly overlooked.

female

LS

Welsh Clearwing *Synanthedon scoliaeformis* 52.005 (376) 30–35mm
ADULT has a broad, dark central spot on forewing, yellow marginal
lines on thorax, 2 narrow yellow rings on abdomen, and an orange-red
tail fan. Flies Jun–Jul. **LARVA** feeds inside trunks of mature birches.
STATUS Extremely local, restricted to locations in N Wales, Cannock
Chase (Staffordshire) and Perthshire.

LS

White-barred Clearwing
Synanthedon spheciformis
52.006 (375) 26–30mm
ADULT looks rather dark
overall; has yellowish-white
marginal lines on thorax and
a yellowish-white ring on
abdomen. Flies Jun. **LARVA** feeds inside trunks
of birches and Alder. **STATUS** Extremely local
in S and central E England, and Wales.

LS

larva inside Osier stem   typical resting pose

Large Red-belted Clearwing *Synanthedon culiciformis* 52.007 (381) 24–26mm
ADULT has a broad red band on abdomen and red scales at base of
forewings. Flies May–Jun. **LARVA** feeds on wood of birches. **STATUS**
Widespread but patchy distribution in England; very local in Wales
and Scotland.

LS

Red-belted Clearwing *Synanthedon myopaeformis* 52.011 (379) 19–24mm
ADULT Marginally smaller and more slender than Large Red-belted
but best distinguished by absence of red scales at base of forewings.
Flies Jun–Aug. **LARVA** feeds under bark of mature fruit trees,
notably apples. **STATUS** Widespread only in S England.

LS

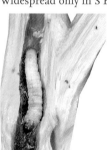

FAR LEFT: **Large Red-belted Clearwing,
resting pose**
MIDDLE LEFT: **Red-tipped
Clearwing, larva inside
Osier stem**
LEFT: **Red-tipped
Clearwing , resting pose**

Red-tipped Clearwing
Synanthedon formicaeformis 52.008 (380) 17–19mm
ADULT has red scaling on tip and leading edge of forewings, and red
band on abdomen. **LARVA** feeds inside stems of Osier and other willows.
Flies Jun–Aug. **STATUS** Widespread but local in England and Wales.

LS

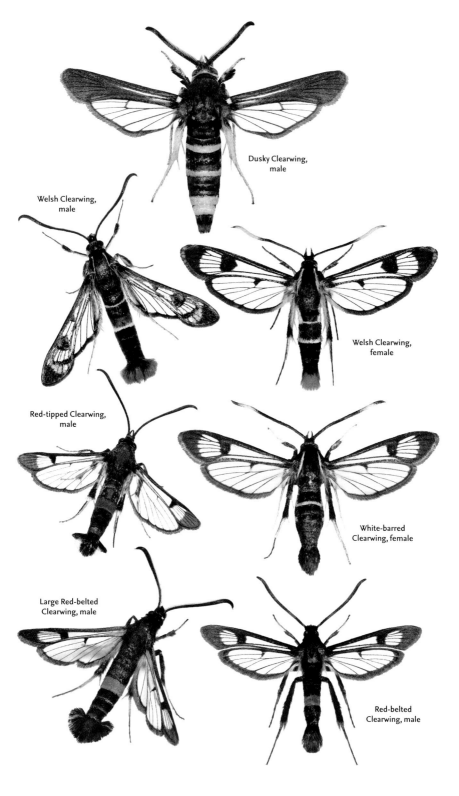

Dusky Clearwing, male

Welsh Clearwing, male

Welsh Clearwing, female

Red-tipped Clearwing, male

White-barred Clearwing, female

Large Red-belted Clearwing, male

Red-belted Clearwing, male

Sallow Clearwing *Synanthedon flaviventris* 52.009 (377) 18–20mm
ADULT has 3 yellow bands on abdomen and yellow outer-leg segments. Flies Jun–Jul. **LARVA** feeds inside stems of Grey Willow and relatives. **STATUS** Very local and restricted mainly to damp heaths in S central England.

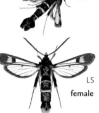

LS

Orange-tailed Clearwing
Synanthedon andrenaeformis 52.010 (378) 19–21mm
ADULT has narrow yellow bands on abdomen and a striking orange-yellow tail fan. Flies May–Jun. **LARVA** feeds inside stems of Wayfaring-tree and Guelder-rose. **STATUS** Widespread but local in central and S England.

LS
female

Yellow-legged Clearwing *Synanthedon vespiformis*
52.012 (374) 18–20mm
ADULT has mainly yellow legs, 4 yellow bands on abdomen and a yellow tail fan. Flies May–Jul. **LARVA** feeds on wood of oaks. **STATUS** Widespread but local in central and S England.

LS
female

LEFT: **Currant Clearwing, male;** MIDDLE LEFT: **Six-belted Clearwing, female;**
MIDDLE RIGHT: **Fiery Clearwing, male;** RIGHT: **Thrift Clearwing, male**

Currant Clearwing *Synanthedon tipuliformis* 52.013 (373) 18–20mm
ADULT has a yellow collar, yellow marginal lines on thorax, and narrow yellow bands on abdomen (3 in female, 4 in male). **LARVA** feeds inside stems of currants. Flies Jun–Jul. **STATUS** Very local in England and Wales.

LS
female

Six-belted Clearwing
Bembecia ichneumoniformis 52.014 (382) 15–20mm
ADULT has a dusting of orange-red scales on forewings, 6 yellow bands on abdomen and yellow margins to tail fan. Flies Jun–Aug. **LARVA** feeds on roots of Common Bird's-foot Trefoil and its relatives. **STATUS** Widespread and locally common in S and central England and S Wales.

LS

Fiery Clearwing *Pyropteron chrysidiformis* 52.015 (384) 16–22mm
ADULT has red forewings, red centre to tail fan, 2 pale bands on abdomen and orange-yellow legs. Flies Jun–Jul. **LARVA** feeds on roots of Common Sorrel and Sheep's Sorrel. **STATUS** Rare, protected and restricted to a few coastal sites in SE England.

LS
female

Thrift Clearwing *Pyropteron muscaeformis* 52.016 (383) 16–18mm
ADULT has 3 or 4 yellowish bands on abdomen, and pale marginal lines on thorax. Flies Jun–Jul. **LARVA** feeds on roots of Thrift. **STATUS** Widespread on suitable coasts of W Britain and NE Scotland.

LS

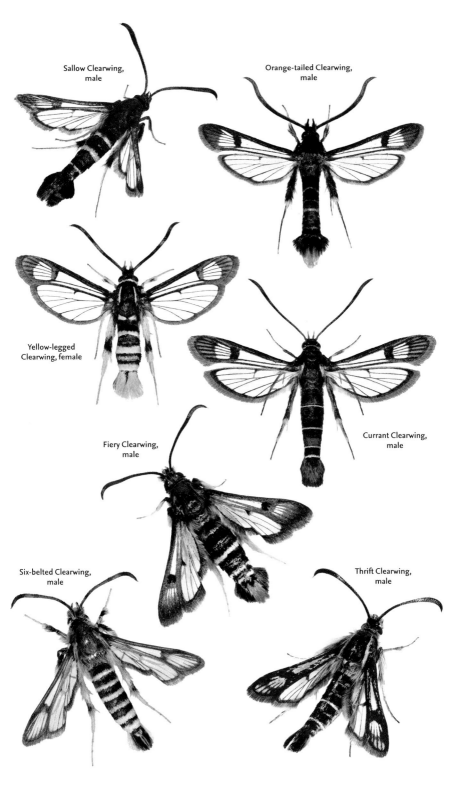

Sallow Clearwing,
male

Orange-tailed Clearwing,
male

Yellow-legged
Clearwing, female

Currant Clearwing,
male

Fiery Clearwing,
male

Six-belted Clearwing,
male

Thrift Clearwing,
male

Festoon *Apoda limacodes*
53.001 (173) 24–28mm
ADULT has forewings with 2 curved  LS
cross-lines that converge on leading
edge. Female is larger than male and
buffish rather than orange-brown.
Flies Jun–Jul. **LARVA** is green and flattened, and feeds on
oaks and Beech. **STATUS** Extremely local and restricted
to mature deciduous woodlands in S and central
England.

Triangle *Heterogenea asella*
53.002 (174) 19–21mm
ADULT has triangular forewings that
are held in a tent-like manner over body when at
rest; female is larger than male and has buff rather
than brown wings. Flies Jun–Jul. **LARVA** feeds on oaks,
Beech and Small-leaved Lime. **STATUS** Extremely local
and scarce, restricted to a few mature woodlands in
S England.

Festoon

Scarce Forester *Jordanita globulariae* 54.001 (165) 20–30mm
ADULT is day-flying and has bright, metallic green forewings
and greyish hindwings. Very similar to other foresters and best
distinguished by studying the antennae: in male, these taper to
a point and are feathery almost to the tip; in female, antennae
are slender and of uniform thickness along their length. Flies
Jun–Jul. **LARVA** feeds on Common Knapweed and Great Knapweed. **STATUS** Restricted
to a few chalk downland sites in S England, with its main range centred on Wiltshire.

Forester *Adscita statices*
54.002 (163) 25–28mm
ADULT is day-flying and has
bright, metallic green forewings
and greyish hindwings. Very
similar to other foresters and
best distinguished by studying the antennae: in male,
these are blunt-ended, the terminal 10 segments lacking
'feathery' projections; in female, antennae are slender
and narrow towards base. Flies May. **LARVA** feeds on
Common Sorrel. **STATUS** Widespread but very local;
favours undisturbed grassland but absent from many
seemingly suitable sites.

Cistus Forester
Adscita geryon
54.003 (164) 20–25mm
ADULT is day-flying and has
bright, metallic green forewings
Forester
and greyish hindwings. Very similar to other foresters
and best distinguished by studying the antennae: in male, these are blunt-ended, the
terminal 7 segments lacking 'feathery' projections; in female, antennae are slender and
narrow towards base. Flies Jun–Jul. **LARVA** feeds on Common Rock-rose. **STATUS** Very
local on calcareous grassland in England and N Wales.

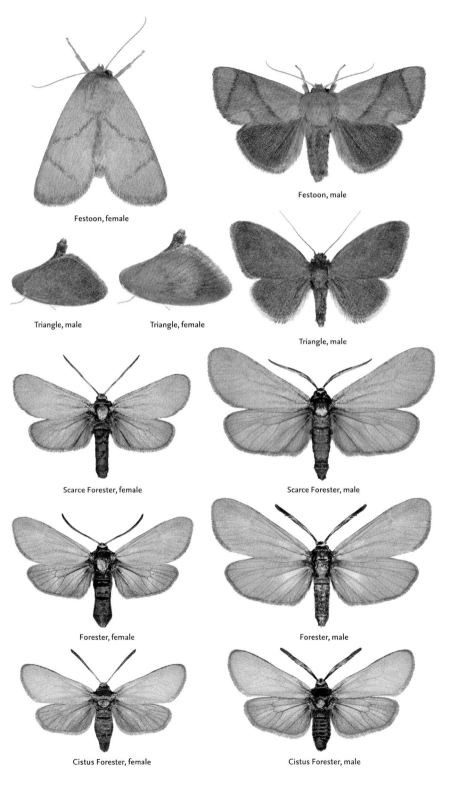

Festoon, female

Festoon, male

Triangle, male

Triangle, female

Triangle, male

Scarce Forester, female

Scarce Forester, male

Forester, female

Forester, male

Cistus Forester, female

Cistus Forester, male

Transparent Burnet

Zygaena purpuralis 54.004 (172) 30–34mm
ADULT has sparsely scaled wings. Forewings have 3 broad red streaks. Flies Jun–Jul. **LARVA** feeds on Wild Thyme. **STATUS** Very rare and local, favouring coastal grassland. Ssp. *sabulosa* occurs on the Burren, W Ireland; ssp. *caledonensis* occurs on some Hebridean islands and adjacent mainland sites.

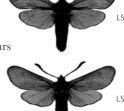

Slender Scotch Burnet *Zygaena loti* 54.005 (167) 25–35mm

ADULT has 5 red forewing spots; one near tip of forewings is a large patch (fused double spot). Red hindwings have a narrow black border. Flies Jun–Jul. **LARVA** feeds on Common Bird's-foot Trefoil. **STATUS** Very rare and restricted to coastal grassland on Inner Hebridean islands of Ulva and Mull.

Scotch Burnet *Zygaena exulans* 54.006 (166) 25–32mm

ADULT has 5 red forewing spots; one near tip of forewings is appreciably smaller than in Slender Scotch Burnet. Red hindwings have a broad dark margin. Flies Jul. **LARVA** feeds on Crowberry. **STATUS** Rare and very local, restricted to a few mountaintops in central Scotland.

New Forest Burnet *Zygaena viciae* 54.007 (168) 22–30mm

ADULT has 5 red forewing spots; compared to Five-spot Burnet, forewings are more rounded. Flies Jul. **LARVA** feeds on Common Bird's-foot Trefoil and Meadow Vetchling. **STATUS** New Forest ssp. *ytenensis* is now extinct in its namesake location; ssp. *argyllensis* is restricted to a single Scottish mountainside.

Six-spot Burnet

Zygaena filipendulae
54.008 (169) 30–36mm
ADULT has 6 red forewing spots. Flies Jun–Aug. **LARVA** feeds on Common Bird's-foot Trefoil. **STATUS** Widespread and common in lowland England and Wales; mainly coastal elsewhere.

Six-spot Burnet, mating pair

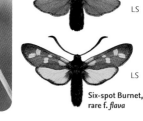

Six-spot Burnet, rare f. *flava*

Narrow-bordered Five-spot Burnet

Zygaena lonicerae 54.009 (171) 30–45mm
ADULT is hard to separate from Five-spot Burnet: both have 5 red forewing spots. On average, forewings are more pointed in Narrow-bordered and dark margin to red hindwings is narrower. Flies Jun–Jul. **LARVA** feeds on various members of the pea family. **STATUS** Widespread in lowland England and S Wales; absent or local elsewhere.

Five-Spot Burnet *Zygaena trifolii*

54.010 (170) 28–32mm
ADULT is similar to Narrow-bordered; see that species for description. Flies Jul–Aug. **LARVA** feeds on bird's-foot trefoil species. **STATUS** Locally common in SW Britain.

Five-spot Burnet, rare f. *lutescens*

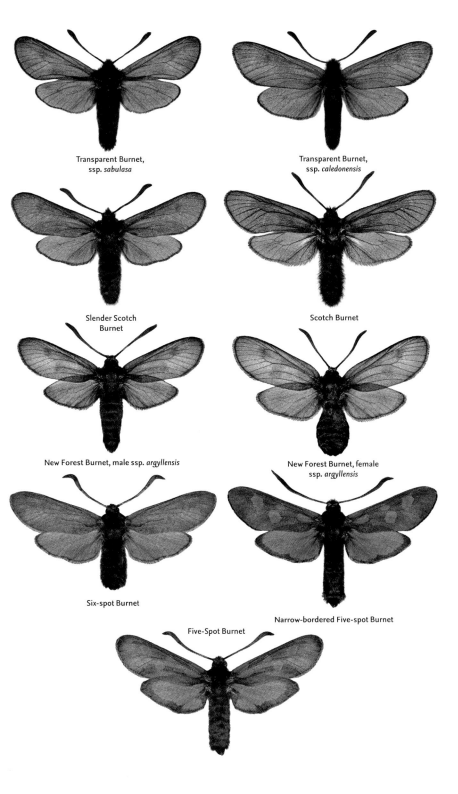

Transparent Burnet,
ssp. *sabulasa*

Transparent Burnet,
ssp. *caledonensis*

Slender Scotch
Burnet

Scotch Burnet

New Forest Burnet, male ssp. *argyllensis*

New Forest Burnet, female
ssp. *argyllensis*

Six-spot Burnet

Narrow-bordered Five-spot Burnet

Five-Spot Burnet

Scalloped Hook-tip *Falcaria lacertinaria* 65.001 (1645) 28–35mm

ADULT holds wings in a tent-like manner and resembles a dead leaf in shape and texture. Flies May–Jun. **LARVA** feeds on birches. **STATUS** Widespread in lowland Britain; commonest in the S.

larva

Oak Hook-tip *Watsonalla binaria* 65.002 (1646) 20–30mm

ADULT forewings are hook-tipped, hindwings are rounded. Wing colour is usually orange-brown in male, paler yellow-buff in larger female; both have 2 jagged pale lines on forewings that enclose 2 dark spots. Flies May–Jun. **LARVA** feeds on oaks. **STATUS** Locally common in S and central Britain.

Barred Hook-tip *Watsonalla cultraria* 65.003 (1647) 20–26mm

ADULT forewings are hook-tipped and buffish brown; dark brown central band contains a subtle dark spot. Double-brooded: flies May–Jun, and Jul–Aug. **LARVA** feeds on Beech. **STATUS** Locally common in S Britain.

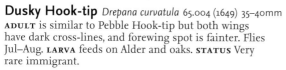

LS

Dusky Hook-tip *Drepana curvatula* 65.004 (1649) 35–40mm

ADULT is similar to Pebble Hook-tip but both wings have dark cross-lines, and forewing spot is fainter. Flies Jul–Aug. **LARVA** feeds on Alder and oaks. **STATUS** Very rare immigrant.

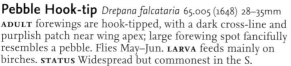

LS

Pebble Hook-tip *Drepana falcataria* 65.005 (1648) 28–35mm

ADULT forewings are hook-tipped, with a dark cross-line and purplish patch near wing apex; large forewing spot fancifully resembles a pebble. Flies May–Jun. **LARVA** feeds mainly on birches. **STATUS** Widespread but commonest in the S.

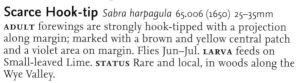

LS

Scarce Hook-tip *Sabra harpagula* 65.006 (1650) 25–35mm

ADULT forewings are strongly hook-tipped with a projection along margin; marked with a brown and yellow central patch and a violet area on margin. Flies Jun–Jul. **LARVA** feeds on Small-leaved Lime. **STATUS** Rare and local, in woods along the Wye Valley.

LS

Chinese Character *Cilix glaucata* 65.007 (1651) 19–22mm

ADULT rests with wings held in a tent-like manner and resembles a bird dropping. Double-brooded: flies May–Jun, and Aug. **LARVA** feeds on Hawthorn and Blackthorn. **STATUS** Widespread and common in S Britain.

LS

Peach Blossom *Thyatira batis* 65.008 (1652) 33–37mm

ADULT has brown forewings marked with pink spots. Flies Jun–Jul. **LARVA** feeds on Bramble. **STATUS** Widespread except in the N.

LS

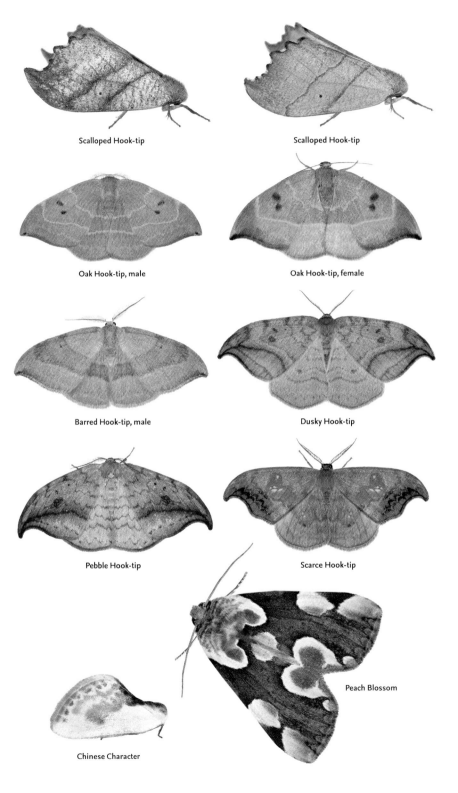

Scalloped Hook-tip

Scalloped Hook-tip

Oak Hook-tip, male

Oak Hook-tip, female

Barred Hook-tip, male

Dusky Hook-tip

Pebble Hook-tip

Scarce Hook-tip

Peach Blossom

Chinese Character

Buff Arches

Buff Arches
Habrosyne pyritoides
65.009 (1653) 35–40mm
ADULT has beautifully patterned
forewings that resemble a chipped fragment of
wood. Flies Jul–Aug. LARVA feeds on Bramble.
STATUS Widespread in S and central Britain.

 LS

Figure of Eighty
Tethea ocularis
65.010 (1654) 32–38mm
ADULT forewings have a central
band marked with an '80', of variable intensity. Flies May–
Jul. LARVA feeds on poplars. STATUS Widespread and
common in S and central Britain.

 LS

Poplar Lutestring *Tethea or* 65.011 (1655) 38–42mm
ADULT has grey-brown or buff forewings with wavy dark
cross-lines (the 'lutestrings'). Flies Jun–Jul. LARVA feeds on
Aspen and other poplars. STATUS Widespread but patchy
distribution, mainly S England and central Scotland.

 LS

Satin Lutestring *Tetheella fluctuosa* 65.012 (1656) 35–38mm
ADULT is similar to Common Lutestring but forewing central
band usually has a dark crescent mark. Flies Jun–Aug. LARVA
feeds mainly on birches. STATUS Local, mainly found in SE
England, Wales and central Scotland.

 LS

Common Lutestring *Ochropacha duplaris* 65.013 (1657) 28–32mm
ADULT has rather plain forewings, often with just 2 subtle
dark central spots, and a dark streak running in from tip.
Flies Jun–Aug. LARVA feeds on birches. STATUS Widespread and
fairly common throughout.

 LS

Oak Lutestring *Cymatophorima diluta* 65.014 (1658) 34–36mm
ADULT has 2 dark-bordered brown cross-bands on forewing.
Flies Aug–Sep. LARVA feeds on oaks. STATUS Local in S Britain.

 LS

Frosted Green *Polyploca ridens* 65.015 (1660) 30–34mm
ADULT has dark green forewings with dark markings, and
white-flecked tufts on thorax. Flies Apr–May. LARVA feeds on
oaks. STATUS Widespread and locally common in S Britain.

Yellow Horned
Achlya flavicornis 65.016 (1659) 36–39mm
ADULT has greyish forewings with
dark cross-lines and a pale spot
towards middle of leading edge.
Thorax is tufted. Antennae are orange-yellow. Flies
Mar–Apr. LARVA feeds on birches. STATUS Widespread
and fairly common throughout.

LS

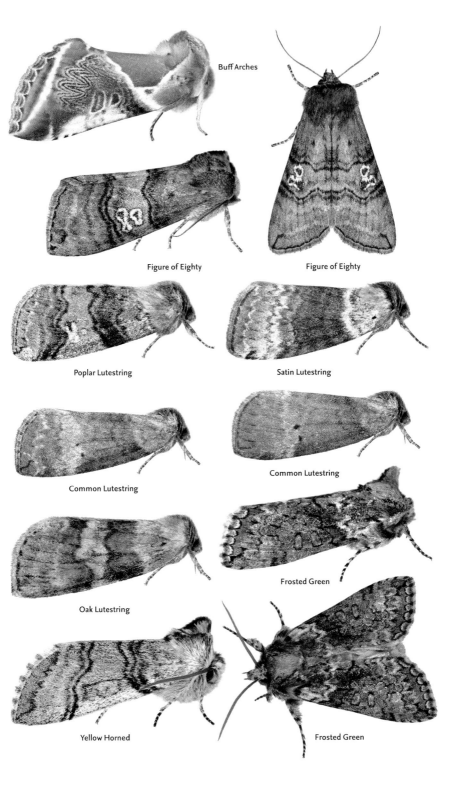

Buff Arches

Figure of Eighty

Figure of Eighty

Poplar Lutestring

Satin Lutestring

Common Lutestring

Common Lutestring

Oak Lutestring

Frosted Green

Yellow Horned

Frosted Green

December Moth, larvae

December Moth *Poecilocampa populi*
66.001 (1631) 30–45mm
ADULT male is smaller than female. Both have greyish-brown forewings with yellow markings and reddish-brown margins; thorax is 'fluffy' and pale at front. Flies Oct–Jan. **LARVA** is finely speckled grey and yellow; feeds on various deciduous trees. **STATUS** Widespread and fairly common, least so in the N.

LS

Pale Eggar *Trichiura crataegi*
66.002 (1632) 25–30mm
ADULT has overall pale greyish-white forewings with 2 dark cross-lines enclosing a subtly darker area. Flies Aug–Sep. **LARVA** feeds on a range of plants associated with heaths and margins: Heather, Blackthorn and Bilberry. **STATUS** Widespread and locally common throughout.

LS

Lackey
Malacosoma neustria 66.003 (1634) 25–35mm
ADULT forewing ground colour ranges from yellow-buff to brown, marked with 2 parallel cross-lines; in brown forms, area enclosed by lines is often darker than rest of wing. Flies Jul–Aug. **LARVA** is marked with longitudinal lines of red, white and blue; feeds colonially, inside web, on Hawthorn and Blackthorn. **STATUS** Widespread and locally common.

LS

Ground Lackey
Malacosoma castrensis
66.004 (1635) 25–35mm
ADULT is extremely variable. Male forewings can be pure yellow or marked with variable patterns of brown between the jagged cross-lines; female is larger, and

LS

female

usually buffish brown with a darker brown band between cross-lines. Flies Jul–Aug. **LARVA** is marked with broken lines of orange-red and blue; feeds on saltmarsh plants, including sea-lavenders and Sea Wormwood. **STATUS** Scarce and very local, confined to coastal saltmarsh in Kent, Essex and Suffolk.

Small Eggar *Eriogaster lanestris* 66.005 (1633) 30–40mm
ADULT has rich brown forewings with white spots and a dusting of whitish scales towards outer margin. Flies Feb–Mar. **LARVA** is brown with ginger hairs; feeds colonially, inside web, on Hawthorn and Blackthorn. **STATUS** Very local and generally scarce. Distribution is centred on central and SW England, and E Wales; extremely scarce elsewhere.

LS

December Moth, male

December Moth, female

Pale Eggar, female

Pale Eggar, male

Lackey, male

Lackey, female

Ground Lackey, female

Ground Lackey, male

Ground Lackey, male

Small Eggar, female

Small Eggar, male

Grass Eggar *Lasiocampa trifolii* 66.006 (1636) 40–55mm
ADULT has overall orange-brown wings; darker central band on
forewings contains a pale spot. So-called Pale Grass Eggar (form
flava) is similar but overall yellow-buff. Flies Aug–Sep. **LARVA**
is yellow-brown and hairy; feeds on a range of grasses and
herbaceous plants. **STATUS** Very local and restricted to a few
coastal grassland sites in S England, NW England and S
Wales; form *flava* is restricted to Dungeness, Kent.

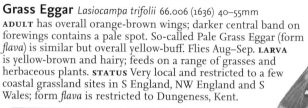

LS

FAR LEFT: Oak Eggar
LEFT: Oak Eggar,
larva

Oak Eggar,
egg

Oak Eggar,
f. *callunae*

LS

Oak Eggar
Lasiocampa quercus
66.007 (1637) 50–75mm
ADULT has broad wings,
the forewings pointed,
the hindwings rounded.
Male is rich brown with
a broad yellowish band on
forewings and a pale central spot;
hindwings have a narrow yellow band and
margin. Female is larger, and is yellow-buff with similar markings to male. So-called
Northern Oak Eggar (form *callunae*) is overall larger and darker. Flies Jul–Aug in the S,
Jun–Jul in the N. **LARVA** is hairy and brown with yellow markings;
feeds on a range of shrubs including heather, Bilberry and Bramble.
STATUS Widespread but local in many parts, favouring heaths and
moors; form *callunae* occurs on Scottish moors.

Fox Moth

Fox Moth
Macrothylacia rubi   larva
66.008 (1638) 45–65mm
ADULT male is overall brown
and smaller than grey-brown
female. Both have 2 pale
parallel cross-lines on each
forewing, the enclosed area
subtly darker than rest of
wing. Flies May–Jun. **LARVA**
is large and hairy, mainly

LS

orange-brown on dorsal surface with lateral black 'creases' appearing
between segments as body flexes; feeds on a range of plants, particularly
Heather and Bramble. **STATUS**. Widespread, particularly in W Britain,
and locally common on moors, heaths and open country.

Pine-tree
Lappet

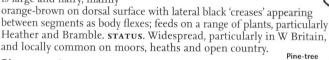

LS

Pine-tree Lappet *Dendrolimus pini* 66.009 (1639) 50–70mm
ADULT is superficially similar in shape to Fox Moth, but its
greyish forewings have a rich brown cross-band and a brown
patch near base. Flies Jul–Aug. **LARVA** feeds on a range of pine
trees. **STATUS** Very rare immigrant from mainland Europe;
established at 1 location in Scotland.

Grass Eggar, male

Grass Eggar, female

Oak Eggar, male

Pale Grass Eggar, female

Oak Eggar, female

Pale Grass Eggar, male

Fox Moth, female

Fox Moth, male

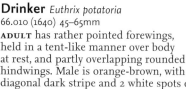

Drinker *Euthrix potatoria*
66.010 (1640) 45–65mm
ADULT has rather pointed forewings, held in a tent-like manner over body at rest, and partly overlapping rounded hindwings. Male is orange-brown, with a diagonal dark stripe and 2 white spots on forewings. Female is similar but larger and paler, usually yellow-buff. Flies Jul–Aug. **LARVA** is large and hairy, with lengthways bluish and orange lines and marginal tufts of white hairs; feeds on various grasses. **STATUS** Widespread and fairly common in S and central Britain; more local in Scotland and Ireland.

ABOVE: **Drinker larva**
BELOW: **Lappet larva**

Lappet *Gastropacha quercifolia*
66.012 (1642) 55–90mm
ADULT is impressive and unmistakable, with wing colours, markings and a shape that create the impression of dead Beech leaves; the projecting snout, which resembles a leaf stalk, completes the illusion. Forewing margin is scalloped and overall wing colour is reddish brown with a wash of lilac-grey. Flies Jun–Jul. **LARVA** is a contender for the largest British moth larva. Overall grey and brown, and hairy with fleshy marginal 'lappets'; it wraps itself lengthways around twigs and the lappets aid its camouflage. Feeds on Hawthorn and Blackthorn. **STATUS** Widespread and locally common in S and central England.

Small Lappet
Phyllodesma ilicifolia 66.011 (1641) 35–40mm
ADULT resembles a very small Lappet with wings that are orange-buff and grey, not deep red. Flies May. **LARVA** feeds on Bilberry. **STATUS** Former rare moorland resident but probably now extinct.

Kentish Glory, female

Small Lappet

Kentish Glory *Endromis versicolora* 67.001 (1644) 50–65mm
ADULT is well marked, the forewings with 2 irregular white-margined dark cross-lines, a blackish semicircular mark, and greyish-white markings towards margin; male is overall orange-brown while larger female is overall grey-buff. Flies Mar–May. **LARVA** feeds on birches and Alder. **STATUS** Restricted nowadays to woodland in the Scottish Highlands; extinct elsewhere in Britain.

Emperor Moth *Saturnia pavonia* 68.001 (1643) 40–60mm
ADULT is an unmistakable day-flying species with a large, bold eyespot on each of its broad, rounded wings. Male has overall brown forewings and orange hindwings, both finely marked and with a pale border. Female is larger than male and overall grey, but with similar markings. Flies Apr–May. **LARVA** is green with rings of yellow 'warts', from which tufts of bristles arise; feeds mainly on Heather, but also Bramble. **STATUS** Widespread and locally common, favouring heaths and moors.

Drinker,
female

Drinker, male

Small Lappet

Lappet

Kentish Glory,
male

Emperor Moth,
male

Emperor Moth,
female

Lime Hawk-moth *Mimas tiliae* 69.001 (1979) 55–70mm

ADULT is subtly attractive and well camouflaged when resting among dappled leaves. Wings have jagged outer edges and are held flat at rest. Wing colour is variable, but usually olive-green with pinkish marbling and darker markings. Flies May–Jun. **LARVA** is pale green with a pale diagonal stripe on each segment, numerous white dots, red spiracles, and a red-tinged 'horn' at tail end; head is rather angular-looking. Feeds mainly on limes. **STATUS** Common only in S Britain, becoming scarce further N; absent from Scotland and Ireland.

Eyed Hawk-moth *Smerinthus ocellata* 69.002 (1980) 70–80mm

ADULT is an intriguing moth with startling blue eye markings on its otherwise reddish hindwings; these are exposed by moth arching its body and spreading its forewings when disturbed. At rest, marbled grey-brown forewings obscure hindwings and afford the moth good camouflage when resting among leaves. Often double-brooded: flies May–Jun, and Jul–Aug. **LARVA** is bright green with a pale diagonal stripe on each segment and a 'horn' at tail end. Feeds on willows and apple. **STATUS** Common only in S and central Britain; scarce further N and in Ireland.

Eyed Hawk-moth, larva   Poplar Hawk-moth, larva

Poplar Hawk-moth *Laothoe populi* 69.003 (1981) 70–90mm

ADULT rests by day among leaves and is easy to overlook because of camouflage afforded by wing patterns and colours. Has grey-brown forewings with a darker central band containing a white crescent mark. At rest, hindwings project slightly in front of forewings but reddish mark on hindwings is obscured; this is exposed if moth becomes alarmed. Usually double-brooded: flies May–Jun, and Jul–Aug. **LARVA** is bright green with a pale diagonal stripe on each segment and a 'horn' at tail end. Feeds on poplars and willows. **STATUS** Common and widespread throughout most of the region, although scarce in N and upland regions.

Lime Hawk-moth

Eyed Hawk-moth,
resting pose

Lime Hawk-moth,
resting pose

Eyed Hawk-moth

Poplar Hawk-moth
resting pose

Eyed Hawk-moth,
wings spread in alarm

Poplar Hawk-moth

LIFE-SIZE PLATE

Convolvulus Hawk-moth

Agrius convolvuli 69.004 (1972) 85–120mm

pupa

ADULT is large and well marked, with narrow, pointed wings. At rest, forewings cover hindwings and most of abdomen, which has white, pink and black bands on each segment. Forewings are subtly marbled grey, black and white – a good match for tree bark; hindwings have grey and white bands. Often active at dusk, visiting fragrant long-tubed flowers such as tobacco-plants and ginger-lilies. Flies Jul–Oct. **LARVA** is green with a dorsal black band, a black and white diagonal stripe on each segment, and a red 'horn' at tail end; feeds on species of bindweed, but seldom encountered here, except very occasionally in the SW. **STATUS** Rare immigrant from mainland Europe, seen in good numbers in some years, mostly near the S coast.

Death's-head Hawk-moth

Acherontia atropos 69.005 (1973) 85–120mm

ADULT is iconic and unmistakable, with a bulky body and a diagnostic white marking on thorax that fancifully resembles a human skull. Body is massive and bulky, and insect is capable of

ABOVE: **larva**; RIGHT: **resting adult**

squeaking loudly if alarmed. Wings are relatively narrow and pointed. Forewings are overall blackish but with subtle blue, buffish-white and orange-brown marbling. Hindwings, which are concealed at rest, are yellow with black bands. Abdomen is yellow overall with a blue dorsal band. Flies Aug–Oct. **LARVA** is huge and yellowish, each segment marked with a triangular bluish patch on each side; has a wrinkly 'horn' at tail end. Feeds on Potato. **STATUS** Very rare immigrant from mainland Europe, with a few records each year; seen mainly on S coasts.

larva

pupa

Privet Hawk-moth

Sphinx ligustri 69.006 (1976) 95–120mm

ADULT is Britain's largest resident hawk-moth and an impressive insect. Wings are narrow and pointed. Forewings are streaked and marbled brown, pale buff and black; at rest, they are held in a tent-like manner covering hindwings and abdomen. Hindwings are marked with bands of pink and black. Abdomen has bands of pink and black on each segment, and a buff dorsal stripe. Thorax is blackish, stippled with greyish white. Flies Jun–Jul. **LARVA** is bright green with a diagonal violet and white stripe on each segment, and a black 'horn' at tail end; feeds on privets, lilac and Ash. **STATUS** Widespread and fairly common in S and central Britain.

Convolvulus Hawk-moth

Convolvulus Hawk-moth, resting pose

Death's-head Hawk-moth

Death's-head Hawk-moth

Privet Hawk-moth, resting pose

Privet Hawk-moth

Pine Hawk-moth
Sphinx pinastri 69.007 (1978) 65–80mm
ADULT has narrow, pointed wings. Forewings cover hindwings at rest and are grey with black streaks and brown patches; margin is chequered brown and white. Hindwings are grey with chequered margins, and thorax has black margins. Pristine specimens are seldom seen as moth loses wing scales easily. Flies May–Jun. **LARVA** is green with white markings and a black 'horn' at tail end; feeds on needles of Scots Pine. **STATUS** Widespread and locally common in conifer woodland in S and E England.

LS

Narrow-bordered Bee Hawk-moth
Hemaris tityus 69.008 (1982) 38–42mm
ADULT is day-flying and resembles a fast-flying bumblebee. Forewings are narrow and pointed; hindwings are rounded. Both are clear except for brown veins and margins; margins are appreciably narrower than in Broad-bordered Bee Hawk-moth, especially on the hindwings. Thorax is yellow and 'fluffy', and abdomen is adorned with areas of yellow, orange and black hairs. Flies May–Jun. **LARVA** is green and brown with a 'horn' at tail end; feeds on Devil's-bit Scabious and Field Scabious. **STATUS** Widespread but local and generally scarce. Found mainly in SW and NW Britain, favouring heaths and moors.

Narrow-bordered
Bee Hawk-moth

LS

larva

Broad-bordered Bee Hawk-moth
Hemaris fuciformis 69.009 (1983) 40–45mm
ADULT is day-flying and resembles a fast-flying bumblebee. Forewings are narrow and pointed; hindwings are rounded. Both are clear except for reddish-brown veins and margins; margins are appreciably broader than in Narrow-bordered Bee Hawk-moth, especially on hindwings. Thorax is yellow and 'fluffy', and abdomen is adorned with areas of yellow, orange and reddish-brown hairs. Flies May–Jun. **LARVA** is green with red spiracles, and a 'horn' at tail end; feeds on Honeysuckle. **STATUS** Widespread but local and generally scarce. Found mainly in S and E England, favouring woodland rides and clearings.

Broad-bordered
Bee Hawk-moth

LS

Hummingbird Hawk-moth
Macroglossum stellatarum 69.010 (1984) 40–50mm
ADULT is day-flying and extremely active, hovering at flowers while feeding on nectar. Wings are rather narrow and pointed, especially forewing. Forewings are brown with darker marbling, and hindwings are orange. Thorax is brown, and abdomen is hairy with patches of black and white. Flies Jun–Oct. **LARVA** is green with pale lengthways stripes and a 'horn' at tail end; feeds on various bedstraws. **STATUS** Regular immigrant from mainland Europe, sometimes in good numbers; mainly coastal but seen inland when large influxes occur.

feeding
adult

LS

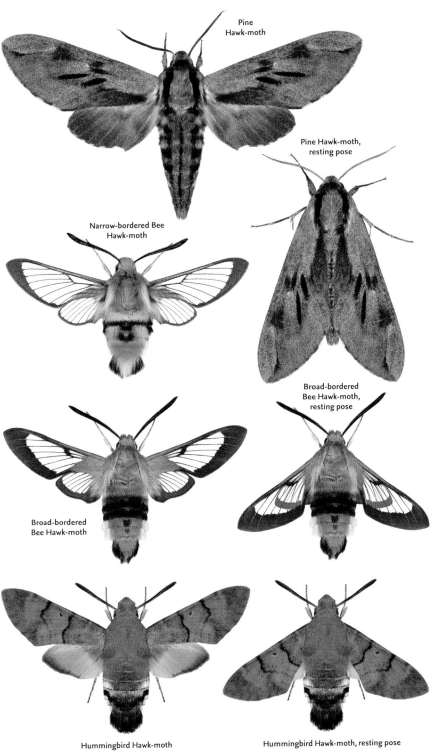

Pine Hawk-moth

Pine Hawk-moth, resting pose

Narrow-bordered Bee Hawk-moth

Broad-bordered Bee Hawk-moth, resting pose

Broad-bordered Bee Hawk-moth

Hummingbird Hawk-moth

Hummingbird Hawk-moth, resting pose

Oleander Hawk-moth *Daphnis nerii* 69.011 (1985) 90–125mm

ADULT is large and unmistakable, with narrow, pointed wings, the forewings with an incurved trailing edge. At rest, forewings cover most of hindwings; together with thorax, they are marbled with swirling patches of green, pink and lilac; dark-centred pale patches at base of forewings bear a passing resemblance to a pair of eyes. Flies Aug–Oct. **LARVA** is unlikely to be seen in this country but is green with a pale lengthways lateral band, a black-framed blue eyespot and a 'horn' at tail end; feeds on periwinkles and Oleander. **STATUS** Very rare immigrant from mainland Europe, seen mainly on S coasts.

larva eyespots

larva

Willowherb Hawk-moth *Proserpinus proserpina* 69.012 (1984a) 38–42mm

ADULT bears a passing resemblance to a miniature Lime Hawk-moth (p. 96). Forewings are pale green with a dark green central band and a jagged margin, and cover hindwings at rest; hindwings are orange-yellow with a dark margin. Flies May–Jul. **LARVA** is unlikely to be seen in this country; it is brown with a 'horn' at tail end, and feeds on willowherbs. **STATUS** Very rare immigrant from mainland Europe, seen mainly on S coasts.

Elephant Hawk-moth *Deilephila elpenor* 69.016 (1991) 45–60mm

ADULT is colourful and unmistakable, with narrow, pointed wings, especially forewings. Forewings are pink with olive-yellow bands, and hindwings are pink with a black basal patch. Thorax and abdomen are also marked with pink and olive-yellow. Flies May–Jul. **LARVA** is usually marbled brown, but sometimes green, and marked with black and white eyespots at head end; when larva is agitated, head end can be contracted and swollen, enhancing the 'eyes', presumably to deter predators. Feeds on willowherbs, particularly Rosebay Willowherb. **STATUS** Widespread across lowland areas and commonest in S and central Britain; favours a wide-range of open habitats.

pupa

larva , unusual green form

Small Elephant Hawk-moth *Deilephila porcellus* 69.017 (1992) 40–45mm

ADULT is a beautiful moth with narrow, pointed wings. Forewings cover hindwings at rest and are pink with yellow bands. Hindwings are pink and yellow, and abdomen and thorax are pink with a dusting of yellow hairs. Flies May–Jul. **LARVA** is marbled brown with eyespots similar to those seen on Elephant Hawk-moth; feeds on various bedstraws. **STATUS** Widespread but local, favouring open grassy habitats, especially on calcareous soils.

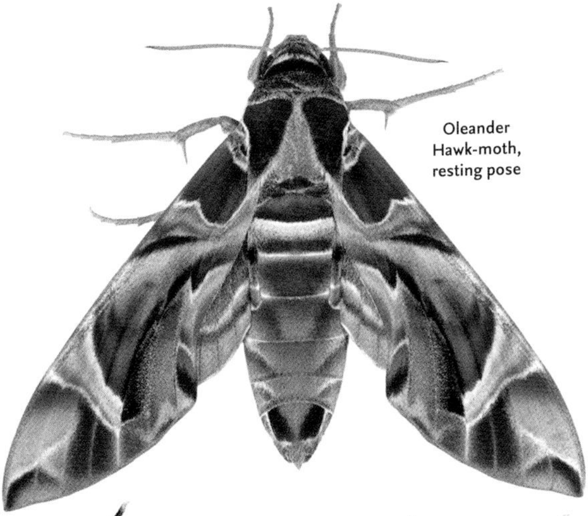

Oleander Hawk-moth, resting pose

Willowherb Hawk-moth, resting pose

Willowherb Hawk-moth

Elephant Hawk-moth

Elephant Hawk-moth

Small Elephant Hawk-moth

Small Elephant Hawk-moth, resting pose

Spurge Hawk-moth, larva

Spurge Hawk-moth *Hyles euphorbiae* 69.013 (1986) 55–75mm
ADULT has narrow, pointed wings. Forewings are olive-green with a broad pale stripe that tapers to a point and usually reaches wing's apex; pale elements of wing markings are sometimes tinged pink. Hindwings are marked with reddish pink, black and white. Flies Jul–Oct. **LARVA** has fantastically ornate markings: dark overall but stippled yellow, and with paired white spots on sides of each segment; red 'horn' at the tail end and red head add to the effect. Feeds on various spurges. **STATUS** Very rare immigrant from mainland Europe, seen mainly on S coasts; larvae have been found on occasions.

Bedstraw Hawk-moth *Hyles gallii* 69.014 (1987) 60–80mm
ADULT has pointed wings and is similar to Spurge Hawk-moth. Forewings are olive-green with a pale stripe that tapers to a point; it is narrower than stripe seen on Spurge Hawk-moth, and does not reach wing apex. Hindwings are marked with reddish pink, black and white. Flies May–Aug. **LARVA** is overall blackish with subtle yellow spotting on sides, and a red head and 'horn' at tail end; feeds on various bedstraws. **STATUS** Rare immigrant from mainland Europe, seen mainly on S coasts; larvae have been found on occasions.

Striped Hawk-moth *Hyles livornica* 69.015 (1990) 60–80mm
ADULT has pointed wings. Forewings cover hindwings at rest, and are olive-green with a narrow pale stripe that runs to wing apex and is crossed by whitish veins; hindwings are marked with reddish pink, black and white. Flies May–Oct. **LARVA** is blackish with extensive yellow spotting, and with a black head and red 'horn' at tail end; feeds on a range of herbaceous plants, including bedstraws. **STATUS** Rare immigrant from mainland Europe, seen mainly on S coasts; larvae have been found on occasions.

Silver-striped Hawk-moth *Hippotion celerio* 69.018 (1993) 70–80mm
ADULT has extremely narrow wings, the forewings with a deeply incurved trailing edge. Forewings are buffish brown with a curved, pale silvery stripe that tapers towards wing apex; additional pale and dark lines create a strongly patterned effect. Hindwings are flushed reddish pink with a dark submarginal band and dark veins. Flies Jun–Oct. **LARVA** is unlikely to be seen in this country; it is green with eyespots near head end, and feeds on bedstraws. **STATUS** Very rare immigrant from mainland Europe, seen mainly on S coasts.

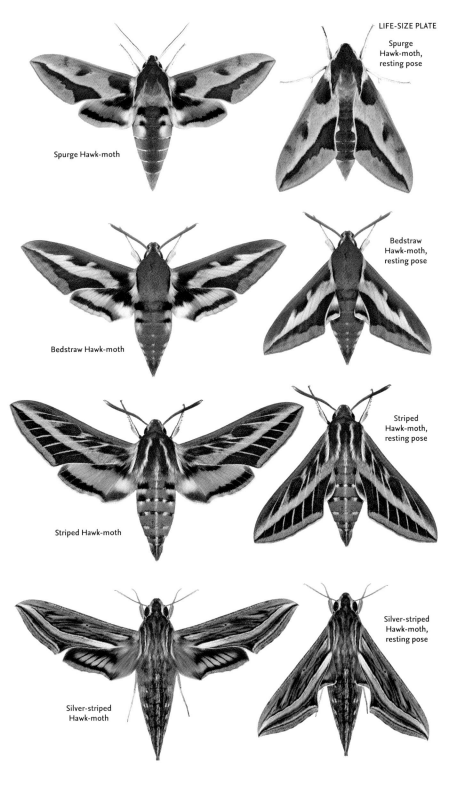

LIFE-SIZE PLATE

Spurge Hawk-moth, resting pose

Spurge Hawk-moth

Bedstraw Hawk-moth, resting pose

Bedstraw Hawk-moth

Striped Hawk-moth, resting pose

Striped Hawk-moth

Silver-striped Hawk-moth, resting pose

Silver-striped Hawk-moth

Ochraceous Wave *Idaea serpentata* 70.001 (1697) 20–22mm

ADULT is similar to Bright Wave but orange-brown ground colour of wings is more intense and cross-lines (usually 4 on forewings) are darker. Flies Jun–Jul. **LARVA** feeds on grasses. **STATUS** Resident on Jersey but very rare immigrant elsewhere.

Purple-bordered Gold *Idaea muricata* 70.002 (1698) 18–20mm

ADULT has beautifully patterned wings marked with pinkish purple and yellow; proportions of colours vary. Flies Jun–Jul. **LARVA** feeds on Marsh Cinquefoil. **STATUS** Local in S Britain, with hotspots in East Anglia, S Dorset and Hampshire; favours fens and marshes.

Bright Wave *Idaea ochrata* 70.003 (1696) 22–24mm

ADULT has yellowish wings overall; forewings have 3 dark reddish-brown cross-lines and marginal row of black dots. Flies Jul–Aug. **LARVA** feeds on flowers of various coastal plants. **STATUS** Local and rare resident of coastal dunes in S and SE England; also possibly a rare immigrant.

Least Carpet *Idaea rusticata* 70.004 (1699) 19–20mm

ADULT has whitish wings with a broad, dark brown band on forewings; base of forewings and thorax are also dark brown. Flies Jul–Aug. **LARVA** feeds on a range of plants, including Traveller's Joy and Ivy. **STATUS** Widespread and locally common in S and SE England; favours hedgerows, scrub and open ground.

Silky Wave *Idaea dilutaria* 70.005 (1704) 20–22mm

ADULT has creamy-buff wings with subtly darker wavy cross-lines; wing surfaces have a silky sheen. Flies Jul. **LARVA** feeds on Common Rock-rose. **STATUS** Rare and local, confined to calcareous grassland in S Britain; mostly coastal.

Dwarf Cream Wave *Idaea fuscovenosa* 70.006 (1705) 20–22mm

ADULT has creamy-buff wings with subtly darker wavy cross-lines and a single central dark dot on each wing. Flies Jun–Jul. **LARVA** feeds on a range of low-growing herbaceous plants. **STATUS** Widespread and locally common in S and SE England; local and mainly coastal in Wales and N England.

Isle of Wight Wave *Idaea humiliata* 70.007 (1706) 20–22mm

ADULT is similar to Dwarf Cream Wave but forewings are flushed reddish pink along leading edge. Flies Jul. **LARVA** feeds on coastal plants. **STATUS** Probably extinct as a resident on Isle of Wight, where it favoured coastal cliffs; possibly a very rare immigrant.

Ochraceous Wave

Purple-bordered Gold

Purple-bordered Gold

Bright Wave

Least Carpet

Silky Wave

Dwarf Cream Wave

Isle of Wight Wave

Small Dusty Wave *Idaea seriata* 70.008 (1707) 19–20mm
ADULT has buffish-grey to sooty-grey wings with fine dark speckles, each with a small central black spot and black dashes along margins. Double-brooded: flies Jun–Jul, and Aug–Sep. **LARVA** feeds on herbaceous plants. **STATUS** Widespread and locally common in England; local and patchy elsewhere.

 LS

Satin Wave *Idaea subsericeata* 70.009 (1709) 20–24mm
ADULT has whitish wings with subtle dark speckling and wavy cross-lines; wings have a silky sheen. Flies Jun–Jul. **LARVA** feeds on low-growing herbaceous plants. **STATUS** Widespread and fairly common in S Britain.

 LS

Dotted Border Wave *Idaea sylvestraria* 70.010 (1701) 20–22mm
ADULT has buffish-white to grey-buff wings with fine dark speckling, wavy cross-lines and a row of dark dots on margins. Flies Jul–Aug. **LARVA** feeds on low-growing plants. **STATUS** Restricted to heathland, mainly in S England.

 LS

Single-dotted Wave *Idaea dimidiata* 70.011 (1708) 15–18mm
ADULT has rounded forewings. Wings are buffish white with marginal black dots and a dark patch near trailing edge of forewings. Flies Jun–Aug. **LARVA** feeds on Cow-parsley and Burnet-saxifrage. **STATUS** Widespread and common except in the N.

 LS

Treble Brown Spot *Idaea trigeminata* 70.012 (1711) 23–25mm
ADULT has whitish wings; outer cross-line on forewings is expanded and forms 3 distinct dark blotches. Flies Jun–Jul. **LARVA** feeds on low-growing plants. **STATUS** Locally common in woods and hedgerows in S central and E Britain.

 LS

Small Fan-footed Wave *Idaea biselata* 70.013 (1702) 15–20mm
ADULT has a strongly curved tip to forewings. Wings are pale buff with wavy cross-lines, and each has a central black spot. Flies Jun–Aug. **LARVA** feeds on low-growing plants. **STATUS** Widespread and common except in uplands.

 LS

Weaver's Wave *Idaea contiguaria* 70.014 (1710) 19–20mm
ADULT has whitish wings marked with dark cross-lines that form dark patches on leading edge. Flies Jun–Jul. **LARVA** feeds mainly on Heather. **STATUS** Scarce moorland moth; N Wales only.

 LS

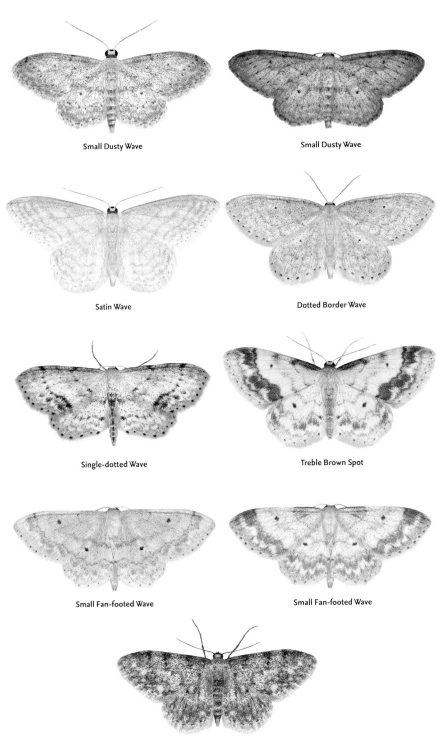

Small Dusty Wave

Small Dusty Wave

Satin Wave

Dotted Border Wave

Single-dotted Wave

Treble Brown Spot

Small Fan-footed Wave

Small Fan-footed Wave

Weaver's Wave

Small Scallop *Idaea emarginata* 70.015 (1712) 22–24mm
ADULT has buffish wings with scalloped margins, a dark central spot and wavy cross-lines. Flies Jun–Aug. **LARVA** feeds on low-growing plants. **STATUS** Common in woods in S and E England.

LS

LS

Riband Wave

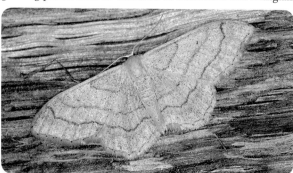

Riband Wave

Riband Wave *Idaea aversata* 70.016 (1713) 24–30mm
ADULT occurs in 2 forms. Typical form has a dark cross-band on each wing; form *remutata* has pale wings with 3 dark cross-lines, outer one with a kink. Flies Jun–Aug. **LARVA** feeds on low-growing plants. **STATUS** Widespread and common throughout, except in uplands and far N.

Portland Ribbon Wave
Idaea degeneraria 70.017 (1714) 27–30mm
ADULT is a similar shape to Riband Wave, but basal area of wings is dark reddish brown, as is leading edge to forewings. Flies Jun–Jul. **LARVA** feeds on low-growing plants. **STATUS** Rare resident, mainly around Portland, Dorset; rare immigrant elsewhere.

LS

Plain Wave *Idaea straminata* 70.018 (1715) 28–32mm
ADULT resembles *remutata* form of Riband Wave, but wings have a silky sheen and outer cross-line on forewings curves smoothly and is not kinked. Flies Jul. **LARVA** feeds on low-growing plants. **STATUS** Widespread throughout, but very local and distribution is patchy.

LS

Lewes Wave *Scopula immorata* 70.019 (1683) 20–25mm
ADULT has grey-buff wings with concentric, wavy cross-lines. Flies May–Aug. **LARVA** feeds on low-growing plants. **STATUS** Extinct as a resident; possibly a very rare immigrant.

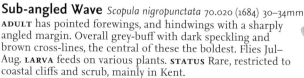
LS

Sub-angled Wave *Scopula nigropunctata* 70.020 (1684) 30–34mm
ADULT has pointed forewings, and hindwings with a sharply angled margin. Overall grey-buff with dark speckling and brown cross-lines, the central of these the boldest. Flies Jul–Aug. **LARVA** feeds on various plants. **STATUS** Rare, restricted to coastal cliffs and scrub, mainly in Kent.

LS

Lace Border *Scopula ornata* 70.021 (1687) 22–24mm
ADULT has white wings with a dark outer cross-line, beyond which is a beautiful pattern of grey and orange-buff. Flies May–Jun. **LARVA** feeds on thymes and Marjoram. **STATUS** Rare, restricted to downland habitat, mainly on the North Downs in SE England.

LS

Small Scallop, male

Small Scallop, female

Riband Wave

Riband Wave

Portland Ribbon Wave

Plain Wave

Lewes Wave

Sub-angled Wave

Lace Border

Tawny Wave *Scopula rubiginata* 70.022 (1688) 15–20mm
ADULT has rather rounded wings marked with bands of buff and reddish buff. Flies Jun–Jul. **LARVA** feeds on low-growing plants. **STATUS** Rare resident of Brecklands and dunes in East Anglia; very rare immigrant elsewhere.

LS

Mullein Wave *Scopula marginepunctata* 70.023 (1689) 26–28mm
ADULT is creamy white with fine dark speckling of varying intensity, and interrupted submarginal rows of black dots. Flies Jun–Aug. **LARVA** feeds on low-growing plants, including Yarrow. **STATUS** Local in S Britain; predominantly coastal.

LS

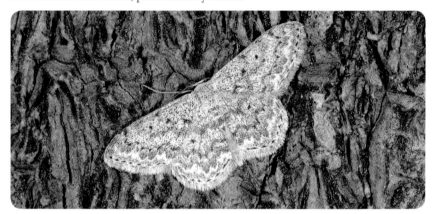

Small Blood-vein *Scopula imitaria* 70.024 (1690) 26–28mm
ADULT has pointed forewings and sharp-angled hindwings. Overall, similar to Blood-vein (p. 114) but smaller, with a less intense cross-line and lacking red wing margin. Flies Jul–Aug. **LARVA** Feeds on privets. **STATUS** Widespread but local in S Britain.

LS

Lesser Cream Wave *Scopula immutata* 70.025 (1692) 24–26mm
ADULT has whitish wings with faint concentric buff cross-lines and a dark central spot on each wing. Leading edge of forewings is straight. Flies Jul–Aug. **LARVA** feeds on Meadowsweet and Common Valerian. **STATUS** Local in S Britain, favouring damp meadows.

LS

Smoky Wave *Scopula ternata* 70.026 (1694) 20–28mm
ADULT has greyish-white wings, with fine dark speckling and faint brown concentric cross-lines; central black spots are absent. Flies Jun–Jul. **LARVA** feeds on Heather and Bilberry. **STATUS** Widespread but local on moorland in W and NW Britain.

LS

Cream Wave *Scopula floslactata* 70.027 (1693) 30–32mm
ADULT has creamy-white wings with pale buff cross-lines; usually has a faint dark spot only on hindwings. Leading edge of forewings is curved. Flies May–Jun. **LARVA** feeds on low-growing plants. **STATUS** Common in deciduous woods, mainly in the S.

LS

Rosy Wave *Scopula emutaria* 70.028 (1691) 24–26mm
ADULT has pointed forewings and sharp-angled hindwings. Wings are creamy white with a subtle pink tinge and central buffish-brown cross-line. Flies Jun–Jul. **LARVA** feeds on Sea Beet. **STATUS** Local and coastal, mainly in S and SE England.

LS

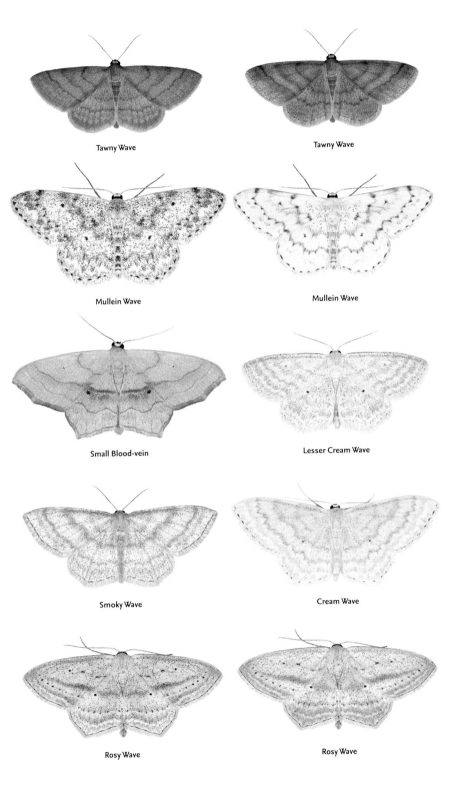

Tawny Wave

Tawny Wave

Mullein Wave

Mullein Wave

Small Blood-vein

Lesser Cream Wave

Smoky Wave

Cream Wave

Rosy Wave

Rosy Wave

Blood-vein

Blood-vein
Timandra comae
70.029 (1682) 24–28mm
ADULT has buffish wings
with red margins and a red
cross-line; at rest, lines on both
wings align and are continuous. Double-brooded: flies
May–Jul, and Aug–Sep. **LARVA** feeds on low-growing
plants. **STATUS** Widespread and common in central
and S Britain.

Dingy Mocha
Cyclophora pendularia
70.030 (1675) 26–28mm
ADULT has grey wings
marked with dark speckling
and a central reddish band. Flies Jul–Aug. **LARVA** feeds
on sallows. **STATUS** Very local; confined mainly to
Hampshire and Dorset heaths.

Mocha *Cyclophora annularia* 70.031 (1676) 22–26mm
ADULT has creamy-buff wings with a dark central cross-band
and dark-ringed spot on each wing. Double-brooded: flies
May–Jun, and Jul–Aug. **LARVA** feeds on Field Maple. **STATUS**
Scarce and local, restricted mainly to S England.

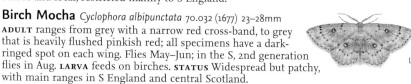

Birch Mocha *Cyclophora albipunctata* 70.032 (1677) 23–28mm
ADULT ranges from grey with a narrow red cross-band, to grey
that is heavily flushed pinkish red; all specimens have a dark-
ringed spot on each wing. Flies May–Jun; in the S, 2nd generation
flies in Aug. **LARVA** feeds on birches. **STATUS** Widespread but patchy,
with main ranges in S England and central Scotland.

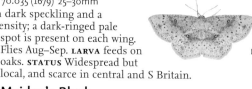
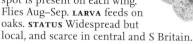

Blair's Mocha *Cyclophora puppillaria* 70.033 (1678) 28–34mm
ADULT has buffish-yellow wings with 2 rows of black spots and
a dark-ringed central spot on each wing. Flies Aug–Oct. **LARVA**
feeds on Evergreen Oak. **STATUS** Very rare immigrant.

False Mocha *Cyclophora porata* 70.035 (1679) 25–30mm
ADULT has yellow-buff wings with dark speckling and a
reddish cross-band of varying intensity; a dark-ringed pale
spot is present on each wing.
Flies Aug–Sep. **LARVA** feeds on
oaks. **STATUS** Widespread but
local, and scarce in central and S Britain.

Maiden's Blush
Cyclophora punctaria
70.036 (1680) 22–30mm
ADULT has buffish-yellow wings
with dark speckling; forewings
have a reddish cross-band and a
reddish flush of varying intensity. Double-brooded:
flies May–Jun, and Aug. **LARVA** feeds on oaks. **STATUS**
Widespread and locally common in S and central
England.

Maiden's Blush, spring form

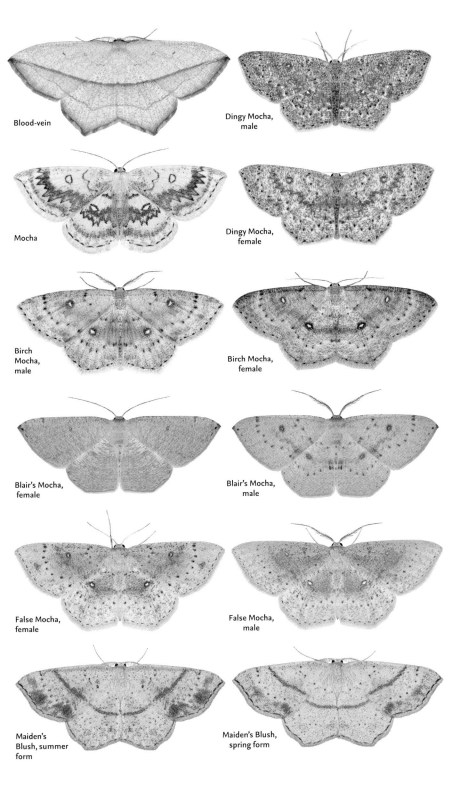

Blood-vein

Dingy Mocha, male

Mocha

Dingy Mocha, female

Birch Mocha, male

Birch Mocha, female

Blair's Mocha, female

Blair's Mocha, male

False Mocha, female

False Mocha, male

Maiden's Blush, summer form

Maiden's Blush, spring form

Clay Triple-lines *Cyclophora linearia* 70.037 (1681) 26–32mm
ADULT has yellow-buff wings with 3 brown cross-lines, the
central of these most intense. Flies May–Jul. LARVA feeds on
Beech. STATUS Widespread in central and S Britain.

Vestal
Rhodometra sacraria
70.038 (1716) 23–26mm
ADULT is usually yellow-

buff, the forewings with a diagonal reddish
stripe and reddish flush on leading edge;
some specimens are flushed pink. Holds
wings in a tent-like manner. Flies Jul–Oct.
LARVA feeds on low-growing plants. STATUS
Immigrant, mainly in the S.

Oblique Striped *Phibalapteryx virgata* 70.039 (1718) 22–24mm
ADULT has grey-buff wings; forewings have brown cross-
bands and a dark spot. Double-brooded: flies May–Jun, and
Aug. LARVA feeds on Lady's Bedstraw. STATUS Local in dry
grassland in the S.

Lead Belle *Scotopteryx mucronata* 70.040 (1733) 32–38mm
ADULT has greyish forewings with a broad, dark-margined
central band containing a teardrop-shaped dark spot, and a
zigzag outer cross-line. Flies May–Jun. LARVA feeds on gorse
and Broom. STATUS Widespread on heaths and moors,
mainly in the W and N.

July Belle *Scotopteryx luridata* 70.041 (1734) 32–38mm
ADULT is similar to Lead Belle but forewing spot is usually
smaller and round, not teardrop-shaped; outer zigzag cross-
line is indistinct. Flies Jun–Aug. LARVA feeds on gorse and
Petty Whin. STATUS Widespread on grassy heaths and
moors.

Spanish Carpet *Scotopteryx peribolata* 70.042 (1730) 28–33mm
ADULT has forewings marked with intricate concentric bands
of grey, brown and white, the outer bands wavy and kinked.
Flies Aug–Sep. LARVA feeds on Broom. STATUS Resident on
the Channel Islands; rare immigrant elsewhere.

Chalk Carpet *Scotopteryx bipunctaria* 70.043 (1731) 32–28mm
ADULT has pale forewings with subtle wavy central bands,
between which are paired black dots. Flies Jul–Aug. LARVA
feeds on bird's-foot trefoils and clovers. STATUS Local,
restricted to calcareous grassland, mainly in S Britain.

Clay Triple-lines

Vestal

Vestal

Oblique Striped, female

Oblique Striped, male

Lead Belle, male

July Belle

Lead Belle, female

Spanish Carpet

Chalk Carpet

Shaded Broad-bar *Scotopteryx chenopodiata* 70.045 (1732) 25–30mm
ADULT has buffish forewings with a central area comprising several cross-bands of varying intensity (outer and inner bands are usually dark brown, the central one often paler) and a single dark spot. Flies Jul–Aug. **LARVA** feeds on vetches and clovers. **STATUS** Widespread and locally common in open grassy habitats.

Oblique Carpet *Orthonama vittata* 70.046 (1719) 24–26mm
ADULT has rather pointed grey-buff forewings with an oblique darker stripe running from tip, and a dark central band containing a dark spot. Flies May–Jun. **LARVA** feeds on bedstraws. **STATUS** Widespread but local in wetland habitats.

Gem *Nycterosea obstipata* 70.047 (1720) 18–20mm
ADULT has rather pointed forewings. Male has buffish-brown forewings with a dark central band containing a dark spot; female is rich brown with a darker central band containing a white spot. Flies mainly Jul–Oct. **LARVA** feeds on low-growing plants. **STATUS** Scarce immigrant from mainland Europe, sometimes seen in reasonable numbers on S coasts.

Garden Carpet *Xanthorhoe fluctuata* 70.049 (1728) 20–24mm
ADULT has greyish forewings with dark bases (head and thorax are also dark), a dark leading half to central band and a dark patch near tip. Flies Apr–Sep in several broods. **LARVA** feeds on crucifers. **STATUS** Widespread and locally common throughout.

Balsam Carpet *Xanthorhoe biriviata* 70.050 (1721) 26–28mm
ADULT has forewings with a brown base, a dark central band with a pointed projection on outer margin, and a buffish-white outer region. Flies May–Jun. **LARVA** feeds on Orange Balsam. **STATUS** Confined to damp woods and river margins, mainly in the SE.

Red Twin-spot Carpet *Xanthorhoe spadicearia* 70.051 (1724) 24–26mm
ADULT has forewings with a central red band clearly defined by a black-edged white margin, and paired dark spots towards tip. Flies May–Jul, with 2nd generation in Aug in the S. **LARVA** feeds on low-growing plants. **STATUS** Widespread and locally common.

Dark-barred Twin-spot Carpet *Xanthorhoe ferrugata* 70.052 (1725) 19–21mm
ADULT usually has a darker central band than Red Twin-spot; inner edge has indented 'notch' near leading edge (not present in Red Twin-spot). Double-brooded: flies May–Jun, and Aug. **LARVA** feeds on low-growing plants. **STATUS** Common, except in the N.

Shaded Broad-bar

Shaded Broad-bar

Gem, female

Oblique Carpet

Gem, male

Garden Carpet

Balsam Carpet

Garden Carpet

Red Twin-spot
Carpet

Red Twin-spot
Carpet

Dark-barred
Twin-spot Carpet

Red Carpet *Xanthorhoe decoloraria* 70.048 (1723) 30–32mm
ADULT has pale grey-buff forewings with a dark-bordered
reddish cross-band (orange-buff in Shetland ssp. *hethlandica*).
Flies Jun–Aug. **LARVA** feeds on lady's-mantle. **STATUS** Confined
to rugged moors in upland and N Britain.

Flame Carpet *Xanthorhoe designata* 70.053 (1722) 26–28mm
ADULT forewings are grey with a dark-bordered red central band,
and red at base. Double-brooded: flies May–Jun, and Aug. **LARVA**
feeds on crucifers. **STATUS** Widespread and fairly common.

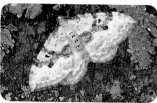

FAR LEFT: Flame Carpet
LEFT: Silver-ground
Carpet

Silver-ground Carpet *Xanthorhoe montanata* 70.054 (1727) 24–28mm
ADULT has whitish wings with a dark central band containing
a pale-framed black spot. Flies May–Jul. **LARVA** feeds on low-
growing woodland plants. **STATUS** Widespread and common.

Large Twin-spot Carpet
Xanthorhoe quadrifasiata 70.055 (1726) 30–32mm
ADULT has grey-buff forewings with a dark central band, the middle
of which is often bluish. Flies Jun–Jul. **LARVA** feeds on low-growing
plants. **STATUS** Local; woods in E and central England.

Large
Twin-spot
Carpet

Royal Mantle *Catarhoe cuculata* 70.056 (1736) 22–26mm
ADULT has a broad white central area on forewings. At rest,
dark innerwing aligns with dark head and thorax; forewings
also show dark patches near tip. Flies Jun–Jul. **LARVA** feeds on
bedstraws. **STATUS** Widespread on calcareous grassland in S
England; local outpost in central Scotland.

Royal
Mantle

Ruddy Carpet *Catarhoe rubidata* 70.057 (1735) 26–30mm
ADULT has orange-red forewings with a wavy-edged dark
central band and dark base. Flies Jun–Jul. **LARVA** feeds on
bedstraws. **STATUS** Widespread in grassland and open scrub
in the S.

Ruddy
Carpet

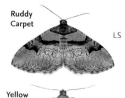

Yellow Shell
Camptogramma bilineata
70.059 (1742) 20–24mm
ADULT is variable.
Forewings are typically
yellow with wavy,
concentric brown, black
and white cross-lines of
varying intensity. N and Irish
individuals are darker. Flies
Jun–Aug. **LARVA** feeds on
low-growing plants. **STATUS**
Widespread and locally common.

Yellow
Shell

Yellow Shell,
ssp. *hibernica*

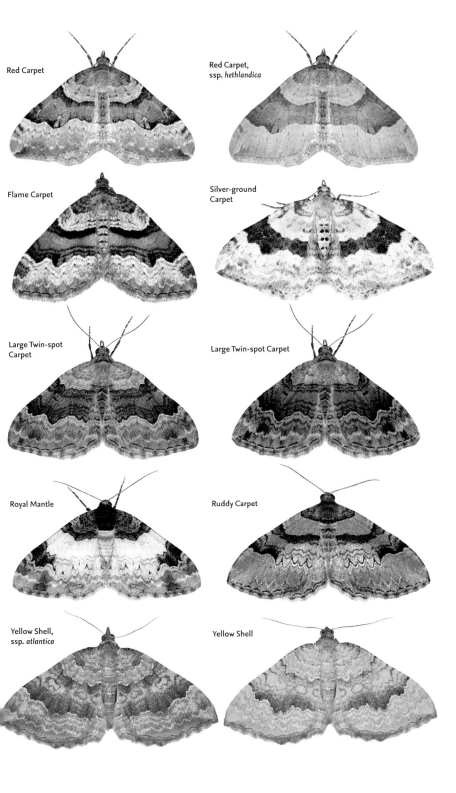

Red Carpet

Red Carpet,
ssp. *hethlandica*

Flame Carpet

Silver-ground
Carpet

Large Twin-spot
Carpet

Large Twin-spot Carpet

Royal Mantle

Ruddy Carpet

Yellow Shell,
ssp. *atlantica*

Yellow Shell

Small Argent and Sable *Epirrhoe tristata* 70.060 (1737) 24–26mm
ADULT has wings marked with bands of white and marbled black
and brown; margins are chequered. Flies May–Jul. LARVA feeds
on Heath Bedstraw. STATUS Widespread on moors in the W
and N.

Common Carpet *Epirrhoe alternata* 70.061 (1738) 20–24mm
ADULT forewings have bands of blackish brown and white; broad
central band is complete. Double-brooded: flies May–Jun, and
Aug–Sep. LARVA feeds on bedstraws. STATUS Occurs throughout.

Wood Carpet *Epirrhoe rivata* 70.062 (1739) 29–33mm
ADULT is similar to Common Carpet but larger, and broad white
outer band lacks central grey line seen in that species. Flies
Jun–Aug. LARVA feeds on bedstraws. STATUS Local in central
and S Britain, favouring scrub, open woodland and sea cliffs.

Galium Carpet *Epirrhoe galiata* 70.063 (1740) 28–32mm
ADULT is similar to Wood Carpet but forewing outer margin is
straight, not curved, and dark central band is broader, with much
more jagged margins. Flies Jun–Aug. LARVA feeds on bedstraws.
STATUS Local on dry (often calcareous) grassland; commonest
near coasts.

Cloaked Carpet *Euphyia biangulata* 70.064 (1793) 26–30mm
ADULT has dark inner forewings with a broad, jagged-edged white
outer band and a greyish margin. Flies Jun–Jul. LARVA feeds on low-
growing plants. STATUS Local in woods in SW Britain.

Sharp-angled Carpet
Euphyia unangulata 70.065 (1794) 25–28mm
ADULT forewings have banded brown inner half, with a white outer
band and a marbled grey margin; outer edge of central brown cross-
band extends as a sharp point into white cross-band. Flies Jun–Jul.
LARVA feeds on low-growing plants. STATUS Widespread in
S Britain and Ireland, favouring hedgerows and woods.

Shoulder-stripe *Earophila badiata* 70.066 (1746) 25–30mm
ADULT has deep brown forewings with a pale cross-band that varies
from orange-buff to whitish. Flies Mar–Apr. LARVA feeds on roses.
STATUS Widespread in lowland Britain, favouring hedgerows
and scrub.

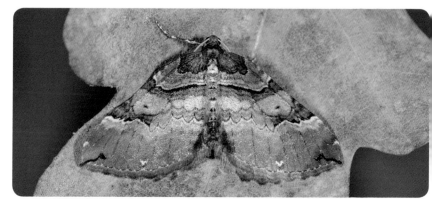

Small Argent and Sable

Common Carpet

Wood Carpet

Galium Carpet

Cloaked Carpet

Sharp-angled Carpet

Shoulder-stripe

Sharp-angled Carpet

Shoulder-stripe

Streamer *Anticlea derivata*
70.067 (1747) 25–30mm
ADULT has brown or pinkish-
brown forewings with a tapering,
wavy dark streak running
diagonally from leading edge;

pale central cross-band has a dark inner edge. Flies Apr–
May. **LARVA** feeds on Dog-rose. **STATUS** Widespread and
locally common in lowland Britain, favouring hedgerows
and scrub.

Beautiful Carpet *Mesoleuca albicillata* 70.068 (1748) 34–38mm
ADULT has creamy-white forewings, marked with purple and
brown at base and towards tip of leading edge. Flies Jun–Jul.
LARVA feeds on Bramble and related plants. **STATUS** Widespread
but local throughout lowland Britain, favouring open
woodland.

Dark Spinach *Pelurga comitata* 70.069 (1749) 25–30mm
ADULT has forewings marked with cross-bands of yellow-buff
and orange-brown; central cross-band contains a small black
dot, and outer margin has a striking projection. Flies Jul–Aug.
LARVA feeds on goosefoots and oraches. **STATUS** Widespread
but local throughout; commonest in E half of Britain.

Mallow *Larentia clavaria* 70.070 (1745) 38–40mm
ADULT has rather pointed forewings that are brown with a
white-edged, darker brown central cross-band. Flies Sep–Oct.
LARVA feeds on Common Mallow. **STATUS** Widespread and
locally common in S Britain, favouring waste ground
and verges.

Yellow-ringed Carpet *Entephria flavicinctata* 70.071 (1743) 35–40mm
ADULT has forewings that are overall grey, but beautifully patterned
with yellow and black cross-lines. Flies Jul–Aug. **LARVA** feeds on
saxifrages and stonecrops. **STATUS** Local in the N; main range is
central and NW Scotland, but it also occurs sparingly as far S
as N Yorkshire.

Grey Mountain Carpet
Entephria caesiata 70.072 (1744) 32–40mm
ADULT has grey forewings, boldly marked with a central brown
cross-band and brown cross-lines; cross-band lacks yellow scaling
seen in Yellow-ringed Carpet. Flies Jul–Aug. **LARVA** feeds on
Heather and Bilberry. **STATUS** Widespread and locally common
on moorland from N Wales to N Scotland.

White-banded Carpet *Spargania luctuata* 70.073 (1786) 30–34mm
ADULT has brown forewings, boldly marked with a fairly narrow
and well-defined white cross-band; projection into white area by
dark central cross-band is double-lobed. Double-brooded: flies
May–Jun, and Aug. **LARVA** feeds on Rosebay Willowherb. **STATUS**
Local, restricted to woods in Kent and East Anglia.

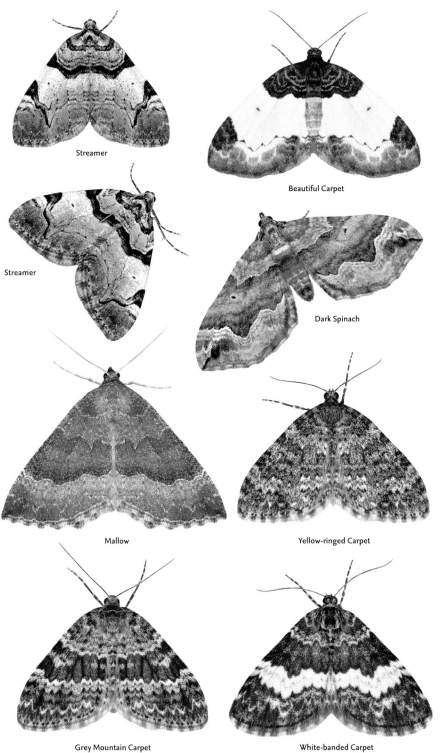

Streamer

Beautiful Carpet

Streamer

Dark Spinach

Mallow

Yellow-ringed Carpet

Grey Mountain Carpet

White-banded Carpet

July Highflyer *Hydriomena furcata*
70.074 (1777) 24–30mm

ADULT forewings are variable but usually green with dark cross-lines; yellow and buff forms also occur. Forewing base is 'shouldered' (like May and Ruddy highflyers). Single apical forewing streak allows separation from congeners. Flies Jul–Aug. **LARVA** feeds on shrubs: southern form mainly sallows, northern form mainly Bilberry. **STATUS** Widespread and locally common.

May Highflyer *Hydriomena impluviata* 70.075 (1778) 30–34mm

ADULT is variable but usually has grey-brown forewings with a broad central greyish cross-band. Has 2 or 3 parallel dark streaks near apex of outer margin of forewings. Flies May–Jun. **LARVA** feeds on Alder. **STATUS** Widespread and locally common in lowland Britain, favouring woodland and hedgerows.

Ruddy Highflyer *Hydriomena ruberata* 70.076 (1779) 32–36mm

ADULT is variable, but forewings are usually reddish brown with a pale central cross-band; usually shows a dark apical streak and additional dark streak running parallel to leading edge. Flies May–Jun. **LARVA** feeds on Eared Willow and other willows. **STATUS** Widespread but local, mainly in W Britain.

Pine Carpet *Pennithera firmata* 70.077 (1767) 30–34mm

ADULT has orange-brown forewings of variable intensity, with a subtly darker central cross-band, the inner margin of which is deeply and sharply indented. Flies Aug–Nov. **LARVA** feeds on Scots Pine. **STATUS** Widespread and locally common throughout.

Chestnut-coloured Carpet *Thera cognata* 70.078 (1770) 26–28mm

ADULT has brown forewings; darker central cross-band is jagged but not sharply indented, with a dark band alongside trailing margin. Flies Jul–Aug. **LARVA** feeds on Juniper. **STATUS** Local in central Scotland; occasional elsewhere.

Spruce Carpet *Thera britannica* 70.079 (1769) 18–24mm

ADULT has grey-brown forewings with a darker cross-band, within which darker veins create 'cells' of subtly brighter colour near trailing edge. Double-brooded: flies May–Jul, and Sep–Oct. **LARVA** feeds on spruces and Douglas-fir. **STATUS** Widespread.

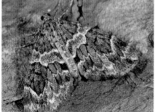

Grey Pine Carpet
Thera obeliscata 70.081 (1768) 28–36mm

ADULT has variably brown forewings with a darker central cross-band; unlike Pine Carpet, inner margin is not deeply indented. Double-brooded: flies May–Jul, and Sep–Oct. **LARVA** feeds on pines and spruces. **STATUS** Widespread and locally common.

Spruce Carpet

July
Highflyer

July
Highflyer

July
Highflyer

May
Highflyer

May
Highflyer

May
Highflyer

Ruddy
Highflyer

Ruddy
Highflyer

Pine
Carpet

Chestnut-
coloured Carpet

Spruce
Carpet

Spruce
Carpet

Grey Pine
Carpet

Grey Pine
Carpet

Grey Pine
Carpet

Juniper Carpet *Thera juniperata* 70.082 (1771) 26–28mm
ADULT has grey-buff forewings with a dark-bordered brown central band; within this, dark veins often create oval 'cells' of colour towards trailing margin. Flies Oct–Nov. **LARVA** feeds on junipers. **STATUS** Widespread but local.

Cypress Carpet *Thera cupressata* 70.083 (1771a) 28–32mm
ADULT has pointed forewings that are grey with an incomplete brown central band, and a dark diagonal stripe running from forewing apex. Double-brooded: flies May–Jun, and Aug–Sep. **LARVA** feeds on Leyland Cypress and Monterey Cypress. **STATUS** Relative newcomer to Britain, now established in S England.

Cypress Carpet

Blue-bordered Carpet
Plemyria rubiginata 70.084 (1766) 22–26mm
ADULT ssp. *rubiginata* has rounded wings, forewings white with brown at base and on leading edge and with a marbled bluish margin. In N, ssp. *plumbata* is duller, with a more complete central band. Brown form *semifumosa* is seen in both ssp. Flies Jun–Aug. **LARVA** feeds on shrubs, notably Blackthorn. **STATUS** Widespread.

Barred Yellow
Cidaria fulvata 70.085 (1765) 20–24mm
ADULT has yellow-buff forewings with a darker brown central cross-band and a pale triangle at wing apex. Flies Jun–Jul. **LARVA** feeds on Dog-rose. **STATUS** Widespread but local.

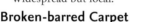
Barred Yellow

Broken-barred Carpet
Electrophaes corylata 70.086 (1773) 20–28mm
ADULT has grey-buff wings, dark at base and with a jagged dark cross-band interrupted or pinched in towards trailing margin. Form *albocrenata* (found in Scotland) lacks central band. Flies May–Jun. **LARVA** feeds on various shrubs and trees. **STATUS** Widespread in scrub and woodland throughout lowland Britain.

Purple Bar *Cosmorhoe ocellata* 70.087 (1752) 20–24mm
ADULT has white forewings with a marbled purplish base and cross-band, both of which have a narrow orange margin. Flies May–Aug. **LARVA** feeds on bedstraws. **STATUS** Widespread and locally common.

Purple Bar

Netted Carpet *Eustroma reticulata* 70.088 (1772) 20–24mm
ADULT has brown forewings strongly 'netted' with white veins and cross-lines. Flies Jul–Aug. **LARVA** feeds on Touch-me-not Balsam. **STATUS** Rare, restricted to a few Lake District sites.

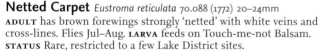

Phoenix *Eulithis prunata* 70.089 (1754) 30–34mm
ADULT has brown forewings, with a broad darker cross-band; has dark triangular marks near apex. Flies Jul–Aug. **LARVA** feeds on various currants. **STATUS** Widespread in lowland Britain.

Cypress Carpet

Juniper
Carpet

Juniper
Carpet

Barred Yellow

Blue-bordered Carpet,
f. *semifumosa*

Blue-bordered
Carpet

Broken-barred Carpet
f. *alboerenata*

Broken-barred
Carpet

Broken-barred
Carpet

Purple Bar

Purple Bar

Phoenix

Netted Carpet

Chevron *Eulithis testata* 70.090 (1755) 26–34mm

ADULT is variable, wings ranging from yellow-buff to brown. Darker forewing cross-band is sharply angled and chevron-like; has a diagonal white line at wing apex. Flies Jul–Aug. **LARVA** feeds on shrubs and trees. **STATUS** Widespread; locally common.

LS

Northern Spinach
Eulithis populata 70.091 (1756) 26–30mm

Northern Spinach, dark northern form

ADULT is variable, with wing colour ranging from yellow-buff to brown. Forewings have broad, darker central cross-band with a double-lobed projection on outer margin. Flies Jul–Aug. **LARVA** feeds on Bilberry. **STATUS** Widespread in the W and N.

Northern Spinach, dark northern form

LS

Spinach *Eulithis mellinata* 70.092 (1757) 28–30mm

ADULT usually rests with wings widely spread, trailing edge of hindwings slightly furled, and abdomen curled upwards. Forewings are yellow-buff with a broad, dark-margined cross-band showing a single projection on outer edge; wing margin is chequered. Flies Jun–Aug. **LARVA** feeds on currants. **STATUS** Widespread; locally common only in central and S Britain.

Spinach
LS

Barred Straw

Barred Straw *Gandaritis pyraliata* 70.093 (1758) 28–32mm

ADULT rests with wings spread wide; forewings cover hindwings and trailing edges of both are slightly furled, with abdomen curled upwards. Forewings are yellow-buff, with a narrow, dark-margined central cross-band. Flies Jun–Aug. **LARVA** feeds on bedstraws. **STATUS** Widespread and common in grassy habitats.

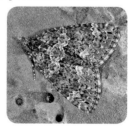

LS

Small Phoenix *Ecliptopera silaceata* 70.094 (1759) 24–26mm

ADULT rests with abdomen curled upwards. Forewings are boldly marked with a white-margined dark cross-band dissected by white veins, and several white-framed dark tooth-like marks near margin. Double-brooded: flies May–Jul, and Aug–Sep. **LARVA** feeds on willowherbs. **STATUS** Widespread; locally common in the S.

LS

Red-green Carpet *Chloroclysta siterata* 70.095 (1760) 30–35mm

ADULT has narrow forewings variably marked with bright green and reddish brown, and with a dark bar along trailing margin of cross-band. Flies Sep–Oct, and Mar–Apr after hibernation. **LARVA** feeds on deciduous trees. **STATUS** Widespread and locally common.

LS

Autumn Green Carpet *Chloroclysta miata* 70.096 (1761) 34–38mm

ADULT has greenish forewings; these are broader than in Red-green Carpet and lack that species' dark bar on trailing edge of cross-band. Flies Sep–Oct, and Mar–Apr after hibernation. **LARVA** feeds on sallows and Rowan. **STATUS** Widespread but local.

LS

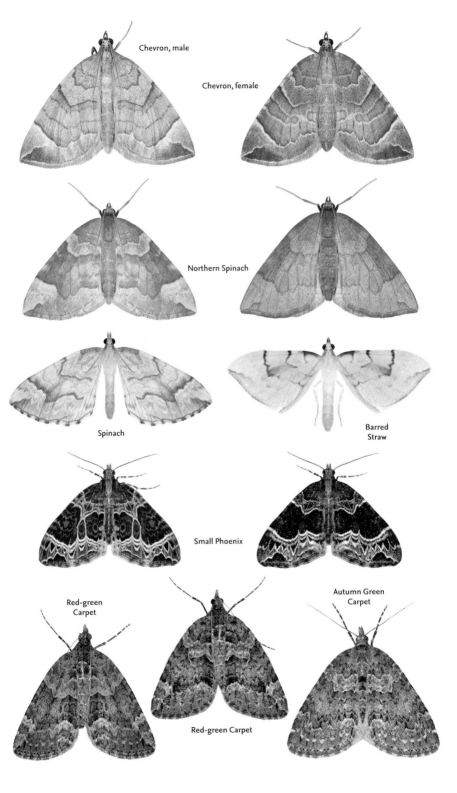

Chevron, male

Chevron, female

Northern Spinach

Spinach

Barred
Straw

Small Phoenix

Red-green
Carpet

Autumn Green
Carpet

Red-green Carpet

Common Marbled Carpet
Dysstroma truncata truncata 70.097 (1764) 24–30mm
ADULT is variably marbled grey-buff and brown; forewing band has a lobed projection on outer margin, less distinct than in Dark Marbled Carpet. Distinct form has an orange-buff central band. Double-brooded: flies May–Jun, and Aug–Oct. **LARVA** feeds on low-growing plants. **STATUS** Widespread and common.

Arran Carpet *Dysstroma truncata concinna* 70.097a (1763) 24–30mm
ADULT is variable and similar to Common Marbled; formerly considered to be a separate sp., now treated as a ssp. of its widespread cousin. Outer edge of cross-band has a subtly more pointed projection. Flies Jul–Aug. **LARVA** feeds on Heather. **STATUS** Restricted mainly to Arran and some Hebridean islands.

Dark Marbled Carpet
Dysstroma citrata 70.098 (1762) 24–30mm
ADULT is variable; similar to Common Marbled but projection on outer margin of forewing cross-band is more angular and pointed. Differences also exist in shape of cross-line on underside of hindwings. Flies Jul–Aug. **LARVA** feeds on shrubs, including Bilberry. **STATUS** Widespread and locally common.

forewing

Beech-green Carpet *Colostygia olivata* 70.099 (1774) 22–26mm
ADULT is green, fading to yellowish green. Darker central band on forewings has a black margin with a white border beyond. Flies Jul–Aug. **LARVA** feeds on bedstraws. **STATUS** Widespread; fairly common in the N, local in the S, mainly on dry calcareous grassland.

Green Carpet

Green Carpet *Colostygia pectinataria* 70.100 (1776) 22–26mm
ADULT has fresh green forewings, although colour fades eventually to yellow-buff; forewing cross-band is dark-margined with a white border beyond. Flies May–Jul. **LARVA** feeds on bedstraws. **STATUS** Widespread in open grassy habitats.

Mottled Grey *Colostygia multistrigaria* 70.101 (1775) 26–30mm
ADULT has grey-buff forewings with subtly darker cross-lines and a central cross-band. Flies Mar–Apr. **LARVA** feeds on bedstraws. **STATUS** Widespread but local in open woods and heaths.

Striped Twin-spot Carpet *Coenotephria salicata* 70.102 (1753) 28–30mm
ADULT has grey-buff forewings with subtle white and dark grey cross-lines, some defining a central cross-band containing a dark central spot. Flies May–Jul. **LARVA** feeds on bedstraws. **STATUS** Widespread on moors in the N and W.

Arran Carpet

Arran Carpet, underwings

Common Marbled Carpet

Common Marbled Carpet

Common Marbled Carpet, underwings

Common Marbled Carpet

Dark Marbled Carpet

Dark Marbled Carpet, underwings

Dark Marbled Carpet

Dark Marbled Carpet

Beech-green Carpet

Green Carpet

Mottled Grey, male

Striped Twin-spot Carpet

Striped Twin-spot Carpet

Mottled Grey, female

Northern Winter Moth *Operophtera fagata*
70.105 (1800) 32–40mm (male)
ADULT female has vestigial wings. Male has rounded wings;
forewings are grey-buff with a subtly darker cross-band. Similar
to Winter Moth but marginally larger and usually paler. Flies
Oct–Dec. **LARVA** feeds on birches and other trees. **STATUS**
Widespread but rather local; commonest in the N.

LS

LS

Winter
Moth

FAR LEFT: **Winter
Moth, mating pair;**
LEFT: **November
Moth**

Winter Moth *Operophtera brumata* 70.106 (1799) 24–28mm (male)
ADULT female has vestigial wings. Male has rounded wings;
forewings are grey-buff with a subtly darker cross-band.
Usually smaller and darker than Northern Winter Moth.
Flies Nov–Feb. **LARVA** feeds on trees and shrubs. **STATUS**
Widespread and common, least so in the N.

November Moth *Epirrita dilutata* 70.107 (1795) 39–43mm
ADULT has rounded wings. Forewings are variable, but usually grey-buff
with wavy dark cross-lines; if present, black dot in central band is
usually close to outer margin. Flies Sep–Nov. **LARVA** feeds on trees
and shrubs. **STATUS** Widespread but commonest in the S.

LS

Pale November Moth *Epirrita christyi* 70.108 (1796) 38–40mm
ADULT is very similar to November, Autumnal and Small Autumnal
moths, and some individuals (of all four species) are impossible to
separate without dissection of genitalia. Rounded forewings are variable,
but usually grey-buff with wavy dark cross-lines; if present, black dot
in central band is usually located away from outer margin. Flies
Sep–Nov. **LARVA** feeds almost exclusively on Beech. **STATUS**
Widespread but local, commonest in the S.

LS

Autumnal Moth *Epirrita autumnata* 70.109 (1797) 38–42mm
ADULT has rounded wings that are variable, but usually grey-buff
with wavy dark cross-lines; if present, black dot in central band
is usually located away from outer margin. Flies Sep–Oct.
LARVA feeds on birches and Alder. **STATUS** Widespread and
locally common.

LS

Small Autumnal Moth *Epirrita filigrammaria* 70.110 (1798) 30–36mm
ADULT is similar to Autumnal Moth but most individuals are
appreciably smaller, fly earlier and have more precise habitat
preferences. Has rounded wings that are variable, but usually
grey-buff with wavy dark cross-lines. Flies Aug–Sep. **LARVA** feeds
on Heather and Bilberry. **STATUS** Widespread on moors, only in
the N and W.

LS

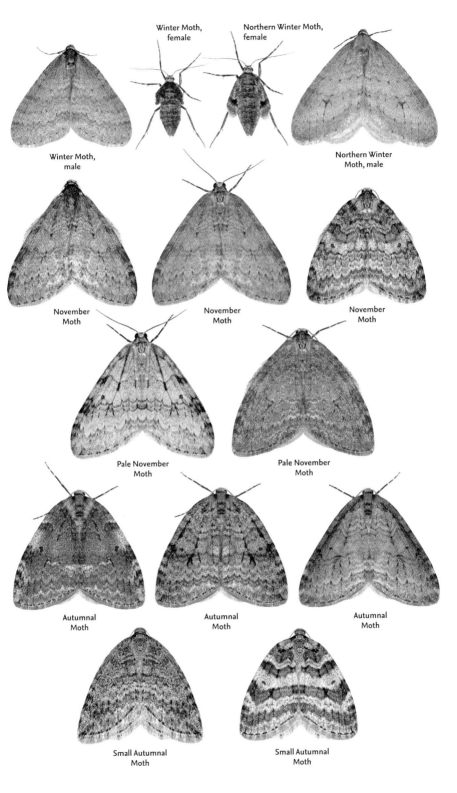

Winter Moth, female

Northern Winter Moth, female

Winter Moth, male

Northern Winter Moth, male

November Moth

November Moth

November Moth

Pale November Moth

Pale November Moth

Autumnal Moth

Autumnal Moth

Autumnal Moth

Small Autumnal Moth

Small Autumnal Moth

Water Carpet *Lampropteryx suffumata* 70.103 (1750) 26–32mm
ADULT forewings have curved leading edge and are marked
with variably intense brown, and with white and buff cross-lines;
broad, central dark band is usually obvious, with a double-lobed
projection on outer margin. Form *porrittii*, from Yorkshire,
has striking black and white banding. Flies Apr–May. **LARVA** feeds on
bedstraws. **STATUS** Widespread and locally common.

Devon Carpet *Lampropteryx otregiata* 70.104 (1751) 28–30mm
ADULT has marbled brown and grey-buff forewings; white-edged
dark central band has a double-lobed projection on outer margin.
Double-brooded: flies May–Jun, and Aug–Sep. **LARVA** feeds on
Common Marsh-bedstraw. **STATUS** Locally common in SW
England and W Wales.

Small White Wave *Asthena albulata* 70.111 (1875) 14–18mm
ADULT has subtly shiny white wings with concentric, wavy
buffish-brown cross-lines. Flies May–Jul. **LARVA** feeds on birches,
Hazel, and other shrubs and trees. **STATUS** Locally common only in
S and central Britain.

Dingy Shell *Euchoeca nebulata* 70.112 (1874) 23–25mm
ADULT has rounded wings and usually rests with these folded
above its body in the manner of a resting butterfly. Upper and
lower wing surfaces are yellow-buff with darker speckling and
concentric brown cross-lines. Flies Jun–Jul. **LARVA** feeds on Alder.
STATUS Locally common in S and central Britain.

Waved Carpet *Hydrelia sylvata* 70.113 (1877) 28–30mm
ADULT has pale grey-buff wings with concentric, wavy brown cross-
lines. Flies Jun–Jul. **LARVA** feeds on deciduous trees and shrubs.
STATUS Local, favouring damp woods and scrub in SW Britain and
SW England.

Small Yellow Wave *Hydrelia flammeolaria* 70.114 (1876) 15–20mm
ADULT has pale yellow-buff wings with rich orange-buff cross-lines;
forewings have a dark central spot. Flies Jun–Jul. **LARVA** feeds on
Field Maple and Alder. **STATUS** Locally common in S and central
Britain, becoming much scarcer further N.

Welsh Wave *Venusia cambrica* 70.115 (1873) 28–30mm
ADULT has pale grey-buff wings, the forewings with subtle buffish-
brown cross-lines, and dark cross-lines defining a central band, the
outer margin of which has paired spiky projections. Flies Jul–Aug.
LARVA feeds on Rowan. **STATUS** Widespread but local in upland
habitats in W and N Britain.

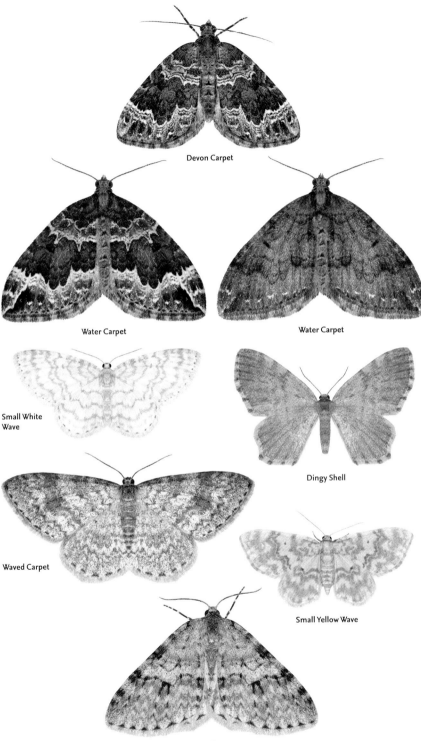

Devon Carpet

Water Carpet

Water Carpet

Small White Wave

Dingy Shell

Waved Carpet

Small Yellow Wave

Welsh Wave

Blomer's Rivulet *Venusia blomeri* 70.116 (1872) 24–28mm
ADULT has dark-speckled greyish forewings flushed orange-red at base and with a broad reddish terminal patch. Flies Jun–Jul. **LARVA** feeds on Wych Elm. **STATUS** Scarce and local, mainly in SW and NE England, and W Wales.

Drab Looper
Minoa murinata
70.117 (1878) 14–18mm
ADULT is a day-flying species that has subtly shiny, uniformly sooty-brown wings. Double-brooded: flies May–Jun, and Aug. **LARVA** feeds on Wood Spurge. **STATUS** Local and generally scarce, restricted to mature woodland in S England and the Welsh borders.

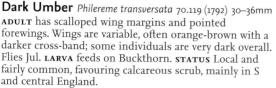

Brown Scallop *Philereme vetulata* 70.118 (1791) 24–30mm
ADULT has variable brown wings with subtle, pale cross-lines usually defining a dark cross-band. Forewings are pointed; wings have scalloped margins, most noticeable on hindwings. Flies Jul. **LARVA** feeds on Buckthorn. **STATUS** Local, favouring calcareous scrub, mainly in S and central England.

Dark Umber *Philereme transversata* 70.119 (1792) 30–36mm
ADULT has scalloped wing margins and pointed forewings. Wings are variable, often orange-brown with a darker cross-band; some individuals are very dark overall. Flies Jul. **LARVA** feeds on Buckthorn. **STATUS** Local and fairly common, favouring calcareous scrub, mainly in S and central England.

Argent and Sable *Rheumaptera hastata* 70.120 (1787) 34–38mm
ADULT is day-flying and has distinctive black and white markings on wings. Flies Jun–Jul. **LARVA** feeds mainly on birches in the S, and mostly on Bog-myrtle in the N. **STATUS** Widespread but very local in S and central Britain; more widespread in W Scotland.

Scallop Shell *Hydria undulata* 70.121 (1789) 26–30mm
ADULT has wings that grade from yellow-buff to brown, beautifully patterned with wavy, concentric dark cross-lines. Flies Jun–Jul. **LARVA** feeds on Bilberry and sallows. **STATUS** Widespread but local in S and central Britain.

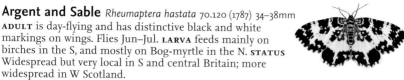

Barberry Carpet *Pareulype berberata* 70.124 (1785) 28–32mm
ADULT has intricately patterned forewings with cross-lines and bands of black, brown and grey-buff; projections on outer margin of cross-band are emphasised in black, and has a black streak at wingtip. Double-brooded: flies May–Jun, and Aug. **LARVA** feeds on Barberry. **STATUS** Rare and local in S England.

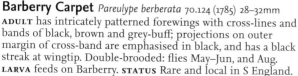

Brown Scallop

Blomer's Rivulet

Brown Scallop

Drab Looper

Dark Umber

Argent and Sable

Dark Umber

Argent and Sable

Barberry Carpet

Scallop Shell

Scarce Tissue *Hydria cervinalis* 70.122 (1788) 40–46mm
ADULT is similar to Tissue, but forewings are
narrower and have a straighter leading edge.
Wings are brown, marked with marbled darker
brown bands and pale cross-lines; scalloped hindwing
margin has shallower indentations than in Tissue. Flies
May–Jun. **LARVA** Feeds on Barberry. **STATUS** Scarce in S and
central Britain, particularly East Anglia.

LS

Tissue *Triphosa dubitata* 70.123 (1790) 38–46mm
ADULT has broader wings than Scarce Tissue,
with a straighter leading edge; hindwing margin
is deeply scalloped. Flies Aug–Sep, and Apr after
hibernation. **LARVA** feeds on Alder Buckthorn and
Buckthorn. **STATUS** Local in central and S Britain.

LS

Slender-striped Rufous
Coenocalpe lapidata 70.125 (1780) 30–33mm
ADULT has buffish-brown wings with well-defined, wavy
dark cross-lines. At rest, wings are spread wide, with the
narrow, pointed forewings mostly covering hindwings,
which are held away from abdomen. Flies Sep. **LARVA** feeds on Meadow
Buttercup. **STATUS** Rare, confined to moorland in central and N Scotland.

LS

Small Waved Umber
Horisme vitalba 70.126 (1781) 30–34mm
ADULT has narrow, pointed forewings that are buffish
brown with subtle dark cross-lines and a dark central
band. Double-brooded: flies May–Jun, and Aug. **LARVA**
feeds on Traveller's Joy. **STATUS** Local in S Britain, favouring
hedgerows and scrub, mainly on calcareous soils.

LS

Fern *Horisme tersata* 70.127 (1782) 32–36mm
ADULT has narrow, pointed forewings that are
brown and very subtly marked with cross-lines; dark
line across abdomen aligns with short dark line on
trailing edge of forewings. Flies Jun–Jul. **LARVA** feeds
on Traveller's Joy. **STATUS** Local in S Britain, favouring
hedgerows and scrub, mainly on calcareous soils.

LS

Pretty Chalk Carpet
Melanthia procellata 70.128 (1784) 28–32mm
ADULT has white forewings with dark brown patches
at base, on leading edge and on margin. Flies Jul–Aug.
LARVA feeds on Traveller's Joy. **STATUS** Local in S
Britain, favouring hedgerows and scrub, mainly
on calcareous soils.

LS

Dentated Pug *Anticollix sparsata* 70.129 (1863) 20–25mm
ADULT is grey-brown with dark speckling and subtle
cross-lines. Hindwings have a scalloped margin with
a large indentation near leading edge. Flies Jun–Jul.
LARVA feeds on Yellow Loosestrife. **STATUS** Very local;
found in wetlands, mainly in S and E England.

LS

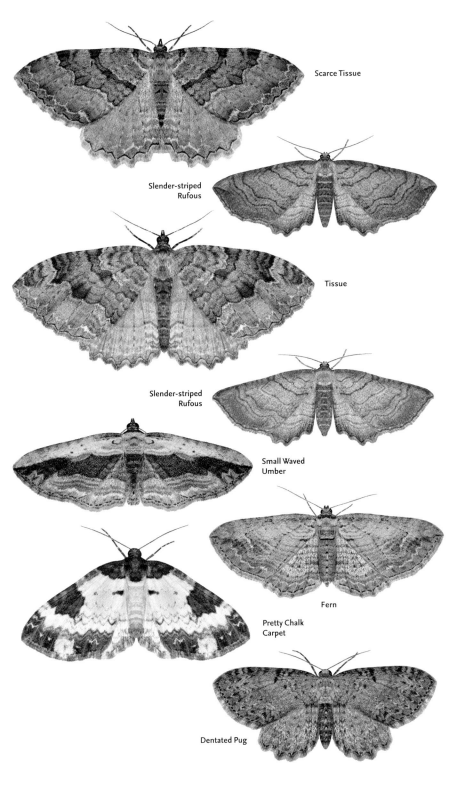

Scarce Tissue

Slender-striped
Rufous

Tissue

Slender-striped
Rufous

Small Waved
Umber

Fern

Pretty Chalk
Carpet

Dentated Pug

Chimney Sweeper *Odezia atrata* 70.130 (1870) 24–26mm
ADULT flies in daytime and has uniformly sooty-black wings with a narrow white margin around forewing tip. Flies Jun–Jul. LARVA feeds on Pignut. STATUS Widespread but local in grassland and open woods.

Twin-spot Carpet *Mesotype didymata* 70.131 (1809) 24–28mm
ADULT is variable, ground colour ranging from greenish yellow to grey-buff; N populations are usually reddish brown. All specimens have paired tooth-like black spots towards forewing tip. Flies Jun–Aug. LARVA feeds on Heather, Bilberry and sallows. STATUS Widespread on heaths and moors.

ABOVE: **Twin-spot Carpet**

Rivulet *Perizoma affinitata* 70.132 (1802) 26–30mm
ADULT has rounded wings that are dark brown with a white cross-band; this has a single indentation on inner margin. Flies May–Jul. LARVA feeds inside seed capsules of Red Campion. STATUS Widespread and fairly common in England and Wales; more local elsewhere.

Small Rivulet *Perizoma alchemillata* 70.133 (1803) 14–18mm
ADULT Similar to Rivulet, but appreciably smaller and with paired indentations on inner margin of white cross-band on forewings. Flies Jun–Jul. LARVA feeds inside the seed capsules of Common Hemp-nettle and related plants. STATUS Widespread and locally common except in the N, favouring open woodland.

Barred Rivulet *Perizoma bifaciata* 70.134 (1804) 20–25mm
ADULT has grey-brown forewings with a central white-edged dark cross-band and dark patches near wingtip. Flies Jul–Aug. LARVA feeds on the seeds of Red Bartsia. STATUS Widespread but local in S Britain.

Heath Rivulet *Perizoma minorata* 70.135 (1805) 18–20mm
ADULT is day-flying and has grey-buff forewings with a dark central cross-band and white cross-lines. Flies Jul–Aug. LARVA feeds on seeds of eyebrights. STATUS Local in grassland, mainly in Scotland.

Pretty Pinion *Perizoma blandiata* 70.136 (1806) 20–22mm
ADULT has white forewings with grey marbling, a wavy white marginal cross-line and a dark patch on leading edge. Flies Aug–Sep. LARVA feeds on eyebrights. STATUS Local in grassland, mainly in Scotland and W Wales.

Chimney Sweeper

Twin-spot Carpet

Twin-spot Carpet

Rivulet

Small Rivulet

Barred Rivulet

Heath Rivulet

Pretty Pinion

Grass Rivulet *Perizoma albulata* 70.137 (1807) 20–25mm

ADULT has greyish-white forewings with dark cross-lines and a
marbled dark cross-band; some individuals are very faintly marked.
Flies May–Jul. **LARVA** feeds on the seeds of Yellow-rattle. **STATUS**
Widespread but local in dry grassland on calcareous soils.

Sandy Carpet *Perizoma flavofasciata* 70.138 (1808) 26–32mm

ADULT has yellow-buff forewings with a white cross-band and
cross-lines. Flies Jun–Jul. **LARVA** feeds on the seeds of campions.
STATUS Widespread but commonest in the S.

Barred Carpet *Martania taeniata* 70.139 (1801) 26–28mm

ADULT has buffish-brown forewings with dark brown at base and a
dark brown cross-band. Flies Jul–Sep. **LARVA** feeds on low-growing
plants. **STATUS** Widespread but extremely local and scarce, favouring
damp woodland.

Marsh Carpet *Gagitodes sagittata* 70.140 (1810) 28–34mm

ADULT has orange-buff forewings with a dark band at base and
a jagged dark central cross-band. Flies Jun–Jul. **LARVA** feeds on
Common Meadow-rue. **STATUS** Rare and local, confined to fens
in East Anglia.

Double-striped Pug *Gymnoscelis rufifasciata* 70.141 (1862) 16–18mm

ADULT has tapering, pointed forewings with a straight leading edge,
typically reddish brown with numerous cross-lines and dark markings
on outer margin of otherwise paler cross-band. Double-brooded: flies
Apr–May, and Aug. **LARVA** feeds on shrubs and climbers, including
Ivy. **STATUS** Widespread and locally common in lowland Britain.

V-Pug *Chloroclystis v-ata* 70.142 (1858) 14–18mm

ADULT has green wings when fresh (colour soon fades); forewings
have a diagnostic black 'V' mark. Flies May–Jun, with partial 2nd
generation flying Aug. **LARVA** feeds on shrubs, including brambles
and Elder. **STATUS** Widespread but commonest in S and central Britain.

Bilberry Pug *Pasiphila debiliata* 70.145 (1861) 18–20mm

ADULT has rounded, pale, faintly green wings; margins of cross-band
(particularly outer margin) are marked with a line of black dots. Flies
Jun–Jul. **LARVA** feeds on Bilberry. **STATUS** Local and generally scarce
on heaths and moors in central and S Britain and Ireland.

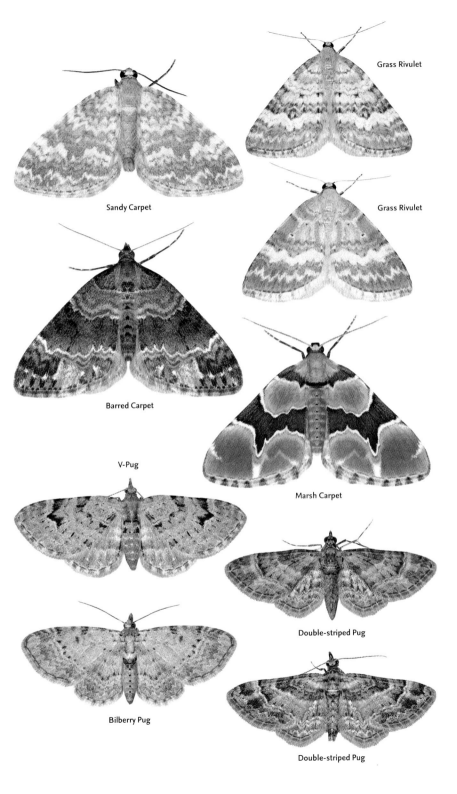

Grass Rivulet

Grass Rivulet

Sandy Carpet

Barred Carpet

V-Pug

Marsh Carpet

Double-striped Pug

Bilberry Pug

Double-striped Pug

Sloe Pug *Pasiphila chloerata* 70.143 (1859) 18–20mm
ADULT is similar to a dull Green Pug, but margin of cross-band is not edged with black and anterior segments of abdomen are pink. Flies May–Jun. **LARVA** feeds on Blackthorn. **STATUS** Widespread but generally local in S and central Britain.

 LS

Green Pug *Pasiphila rectangulata* 70.144 (1860) 17–20mm
ADULT is variable but often green, forewings with a dark-edged cross-band; abdomen has a dark segment near base. Some forms are very dark. Flies Jun–Jul. **LARVA** feeds on the flowers of apples and other fruit trees. **STATUS** Widespread and locally common.

 LS

Haworth's Pug *Eupithecia haworthiata* 70.146 (1813) 12–14mm
ADULT has rounded wings that are rather uniformly grey and with only faint, pale cross-lines; anterior abdominal segments are a distinctive orange-pink. Flies Jun–Jul. **LARVA** feeds on Traveller's Joy. **STATUS** Widespread on calcareous soils in the S.

 LS

Slender Pug *Eupithecia tenuiata* 70.147 (1811) 14–16mm
ADULT has rather plain grey-buff wings, with only subtle cross-lines but a distinctive central black spot on forewings. Flies Jun–Jul. **LARVA** feeds on sallow catkins. **STATUS** Widespread and fairly common, especially in the S.

 LS

Maple Pug *Eupithecia inturbata* 70.148 (1812) 13–15mm
ADULT is similar to Slender Pug but with narrower, more pointed forewings that have a reddish-brown hue and only a faint black spot. Flies Jul–Aug. **LARVA** feeds on flowers of Field Maple. **STATUS** Widespread but local, in woods mainly in the S.

 LS

Cloaked Pug *Eupithecia abietaria* 70.149 (1815) 20–22mm
ADULT has grey-brown wings, the forewings with numerous cross-lines and a dark-edged cross-band containing a bold black spot. Flies Jun–Jul. **LARVA** feeds inside cones of spruces and firs. **STATUS** Scarce and scattered resident, and occasional immigrant.

 LS

Toadflax Pug *Eupithecia linariata* 70.150 (1816) 18–20mm
ADULT has orange-brown forewings with a broad dark cross-band. Flies Jul–Aug. **LARVA** feeds on flowers and seeds of Common Toadflax. **STATUS** Widespread in central and S Britain.

 LS

Foxglove Pug *Eupithecia pulchellata* 70.151 (1817) 20–22mm
ADULT is similar to Toadflax Pug, but larger, and forewings have a more jagged-edged dark cross-band and are dark at base. Flies May–Jun. **LARVA** feeds on Foxglove flowers. **STATUS** Widespread and common.

 LS

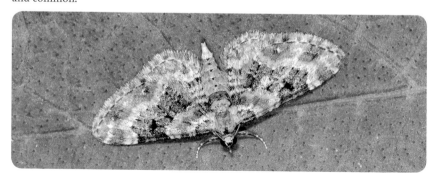

Green Pug

Green Pug,
melanic form

Sloe Pug

Haworth's Pug

Slender Pug

Maple Pug

Cloaked Pug

Toadflax Pug

Foxglove Pug

Channel Islands Pug *Eupithecia ultimaria* 70.152 (1855a) 14–17mm
ADULT has grey-buff wings, the forewings with subtle cross-lines and a striking black central streak. Flies Jun–Jul. LARVA feeds on Tamarisk. STATUS Recent colonist; rare on the S coast.

LS

Lead-coloured Pug *Eupithecia plumbeolata* 70.153 (1814) 14–15mm
ADULT has grey-brown wings with subtle cross-lines; similar to Haworth's Pug (p. 146) but lacks that species' pink coloration on abdomen. Flies May–Jun. LARVA feeds on flowers of Common Cow-wheat. STATUS Widespread but very local.

LS

Marsh Pug *Eupithecia pygmaeata* 70.154 (1822) 15–18mm
ADULT is dark brown, forewings with subtle buffish and white cross-lines, and a white spot on trailing edge. Flies May–Jun. LARVA feeds on flowers and seeds of Field Mouse-ear. STATUS Local.

LS

Netted Pug *Eupithecia venosata* 70.155 (1823) 18–22mm
ADULT has buff wings with black lines. Northern Scottish island races (e.g. ssp. *ochracae* from Orkney) have richer colours and less intense dark lines. Irish ssp. *plumbea* is duller overall. Flies May–Jun. LARVA feeds on seeds of Bladder Campion and Sea Campion. STATUS Very local.

LS

Brindled Pug *Eupithecia abbreviata* 70.156 (1852) 20–22mm
ADULT is buffish brown, forewings with a marbled reddish-brown cross-band, cross-lines and patches, and a dark central streak; melanistic form *hischkei* is uniformly dark. Flies Apr–May. LARVA feeds on oaks and Hawthorn. STATUS Widespread and common.

LS

Oak-tree Pug *Eupithecia dodoneata* 70.157 (1853) 20–22mm
ADULT is similar to Brindled Pug, with reddish-brown, buff and grey marbling on wings; forewings have a rounded dark central spot, not a streak. Flies May–Jun. LARVA feeds on oaks and Hawthorn. STATUS Widespread in central and S Britain.

LS

Juniper Pug *Eupithecia pusillata* 70.158 (1854) 18–20mm
ADULT is variable but usually dark grey-brown; edges of forewing cross-band are marked with black wedge-shaped marks; dark central streak is bordered by pale outer patch. Flies Jul–Sep. LARVA feeds on junipers. STATUS Widespread.

LS

Cypress Pug *Eupithecia phoeniceata* 70.159 (1855) 18–22mm
ADULT has grey-buff wings with black streaks and oblique cross-lines. Flies Aug–Sep. LARVA feeds on Monterey Cypress. STATUS Recent arrival, now established in the S.

LS

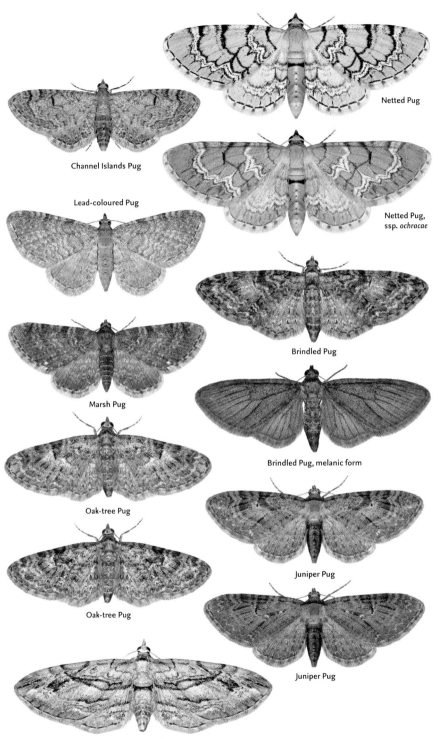

Channel Islands Pug

Netted Pug

Lead-coloured Pug

Netted Pug,
ssp. *ochracae*

Brindled Pug

Marsh Pug

Brindled Pug, melanic form

Oak-tree Pug

Juniper Pug

Oak-tree Pug

Juniper Pug

Cypress Pug

White-spotted Pug *Eupithecia tripunctaria* 70.160 (1835) 18–20mm
ADULT is grey-brown with a bold white spot near trailing corner
of both wings, and a row of smaller white spots on forewings.
Double-brooded: flies May–Jun, and Jul–Aug. LARVA feeds on
flowers and seeds of Wild Angelica and Hogweed. STATUS Local,
mainly in central and S Britain and Ireland.

Golden-rod Pug *Eupithecia virgaureata* 70.161 (1851) 18–22mm
ADULT has grey-brown wings with an oval, bold black spot on
forewings; some individuals have a chequered appearance to
veins. Easily confused with commoner Grey Pug (p. 156).
Double-brooded: flies May–Jun, and Jul–Aug. LARVA feeds
on flowers of Asteraceae (daisy family); this includes Goldenrod
for 2nd generation. STATUS Widespread, mainly in the N and W.

Dwarf Pug *Eupithecia tantillaria* 70.162 (1857) 17–19mm
ADULT is grey-brown with dark cross-lines and a large black central
spot on forewings. Flies Jun–Jul. LARVA feeds on spruces and firs.
STATUS Widespread but local.

Larch Pug *Eupithecia lariciata* 70.163 (1856) 20–22mm
ADULT has grey-brown wings, the forewings with wavy, angled
cross-lines and a dark central spot. Pale spot at base of abdomen
is characteristic. Flies May–Jun. LARVA feeds on larches.
STATUS Widespread and locally common.

Pauper Pug *Eupithecia egenaria* 70.164 (1824) 22–24mm
Also called Fletcher's Pug. ADULT has grey-buff wings, the forewings
with subtle dark cross-lines and a dark streak-like central spot. Flies
May–Jun. LARVA feeds on Small-leaved and Large-leaved limes.
STATUS Rare and local in S and central England.

Pimpinel Pug *Eupithecia pimpinellata* 70.165 (1845) 20–24mm
ADULT has grey-buff wings overall, but forewings have a rufous
patch on trailing half and a bold black central streak. Flies Jun–Jul.
LARVA feeds on seeds of Burnet-saxifrage. STATUS Restricted to
calcareous soils, mainly in S and E England.

Plain Pug *Eupithecia simpliciata* 70.166 (1842) 21–23mm
ADULT has grey-buff wings, the forewings with a dark central spot,
reddish-brown cross-band and cross-lines, and distinct white outer
cross-line. Flies Jun–Aug. LARVA feeds on seeds of oraches and
goosefoots. STATUS Widespread but rather local in central and
S Britain.

White-spotted Pug

Golden-rod Pug

Dwarf Pug

Larch Pug

Larch Pug,
melanic form

Pauper Pug

Pimpinel Pug

Plain Pug

Narrow-winged Pug *Eupithecia nanata* 70.168 (1846) 14–17mm
ADULT has narrow brown forewings with concentric pale, dark brown
and black cross-lines. Flies Apr–Jun. LARVA feeds on Heather. STATUS
Locally common on heaths and moors.

 LS

Angle-barred Pug *Eupithecia innotata* 70.169 (1848, 1849, 1850) 18–22mm
Complex taxon comprising 'forms' formerly treated as species.
Form *innotata* (Angle-barred Pug) is grey-brown, the forewings
with a dark central spot and sharp-angled cross-lines; larva feeds
on Sea-buckthorn; coastal E England only. Form *fraxinata* (Ash
Pug) is similar; larva feeds on Ash; widespread in lowlands. Form *tamarisciata*
(Tamarisk Pug) is similar; larva feeds on Tamarisk; rare in the S. Unmarked melanistic
forms of *E. innotata* also occur. All are double-brooded, flying May–Jun and Aug.

 LS

Marbled Pug *Eupithecia irriguata* 70.170 (1818) 18–20mm
ADULT has narrow greyish-white wings, the forewings with brown
and black marbling on leading edge and outer margin, and a streak-
like black central spot. Flies Apr–May. LARVA feeds on oaks. STATUS
Local, mainly in SW England.

 LS

Ochreous Pug *Eupithecia indigata* 70.171 (1844) 16–18mm
ADULT is grey-buff; forewings have a streak-like black central spot
and subtle row of dark marks on leading edge. Flies Apr–May. LARVA
feeds on larches and Scots Pine. STATUS Widespread and common.

 LS

Thyme Pug *Eupithecia distinctaria* 70.172 (1843) 16–18mm
ADULT is grey-buff; forewings have a streak-like black central spot,
black marks on leading edge and 2 discrete dark cross-lines. Flies
Jun–Jul. LARVA feeds on thymes. STATUS Widespread but scarce and
very local.

Lime-speck Pug

Lime-speck Pug *Eupithecia centaureata* 70.173 (1825) 18–20mm
ADULT has white forewings marked with a large dark patch on
leading edge and brown marginal marbling; head and thorax are
white, and abdomen is black with a white tip. Flies Apr–Sep. LARVA
feeds on low-growing plants. STATUS Widespread and common.

 LS

Pinion-spotted Pug *Eupithecia insigniata* 70.174 (1820) 19–21mm
ADULT has lilac-grey wings marked with a network of dark cross-
lines and veins, and brown patches on leading edge of forewings.
Flies Apr–May. LARVA feeds on Hawthorn and apple species.
STATUS Local and scarce in S and E England.

 LS

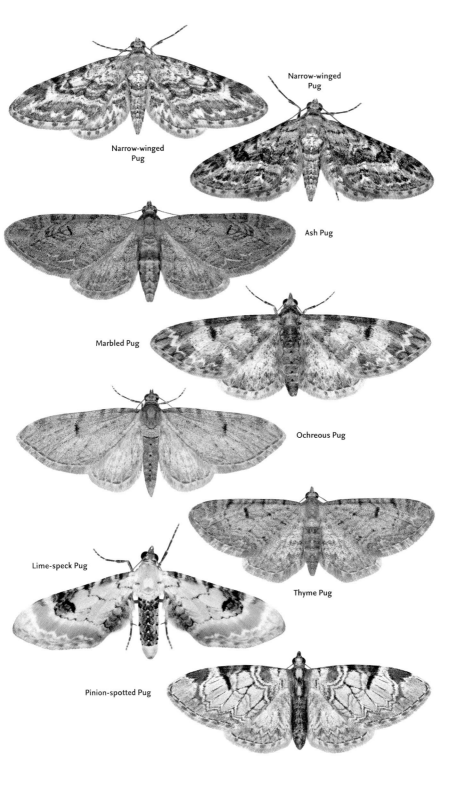

Narrow-winged
Pug

Narrow-winged
Pug

Ash Pug

Marbled Pug

Ochreous Pug

Lime-speck Pug

Thyme Pug

Pinion-spotted Pug

Triple-spotted Pug *Eupithecia trisignaria* 70.175 (1826) 18–21mm

ADULT is plain grey-brown; forewings have 3 black spots arranged in a triangle, 2 on leading edge, 1 central. Flies Jun–Jul. LARVA feeds on Hogweed and Wild Angelica flowers. STATUS Local, mainly in central and S Britain.

Eupithecia intricata 70.176 (1827) 22–24mm

Our region is home to 3 ssp. that fly May–Jun; larval foods include junipers and cypresses. **Freyer's Pug** (ssp. *arceuthata*) is common and is grey-buff, the forewings with dark cross-lines angled near leading edge and a dark central spot. **Edinburgh Pug** (ssp. *millieraria*), from N Britain, has subtler dark markings on forewings. **Mere's Pug** (ssp. *hibernica*), from the Burren, W Ireland, has more intense cross-lines.

Satyr Pug *Eupithecia satyrata* 70.177 (1828) 20–22mm

ADULT is grey-buff; forewings have a dark central spot, chequered veins and white spots, the largest near trailing corner. Flies May–June. LARVA feeds on various plants. STATUS Ssp. *satyrata* occurs in S England, ssp. *callunaria* on moors on N Britain and Ireland, and ssp. *curzoni* in the Northern Isles.

LEFT: **larva**

Satyr Pug, ssp. *callunaria*

Scarce Pug *Eupithecia extensaria* 70.178 (1847) 22mm

ADULT has pale wings, the forewings with neatly aligned, oblique brown cross-bands. Easily confused with Narrow-winged Pug (p. 152). Flies Jun–Jul. LARVA feeds on Sea Wormwood. STATUS Restricted mainly to coastal NE Norfolk.

Wormwood Pug *Eupithecia absinthiata* 70.179 (1830) 20–22mm

ADULT is buff-brown; forewings have a dark central spot, dark marks on leading edge and a white spot near trailing corner; abdomen has a black and white band. Flies Jun–Jul. LARVA feeds on low-growing plants. STATUS Widespread and common. Form *goossensiata* (known as Ling Pug) is usually smaller and greyer, and lives on heaths; its larva feeds on Heather.

Ling Pug

Bleached Pug *Eupithecia expallidata* 70.180 (1833) 22–24mm

ADULT is pale grey-buff; forewings have subtle dark marks on leading edge, a striking streak-like dark central spot and a dotted cross-line. Flies Jul–Aug. LARVA feeds on Goldenrod. STATUS Local, mainly in central and S Britain.

Valerian Pug *Eupithecia valerianata* 70.181 (1821) 17–19mm

ADULT is buff with a white spot near trailing corner of both wings; forewings have a zigzag white cross-line near margin. Flies Jun–Jul. LARVA feeds on Common Valerian. STATUS Very local.

Currant Pug *Eupithecia assimilata* 70.182 (1832) 19–22mm

ADULT is brown with a white spot near trailing corner on both wings; forewings have a dark central streak and bold, dark markings on leading edge. Flies May–Jun, sometimes Aug. LARVA feeds on currants and Hop. STATUS Widespread, commonest in the S.

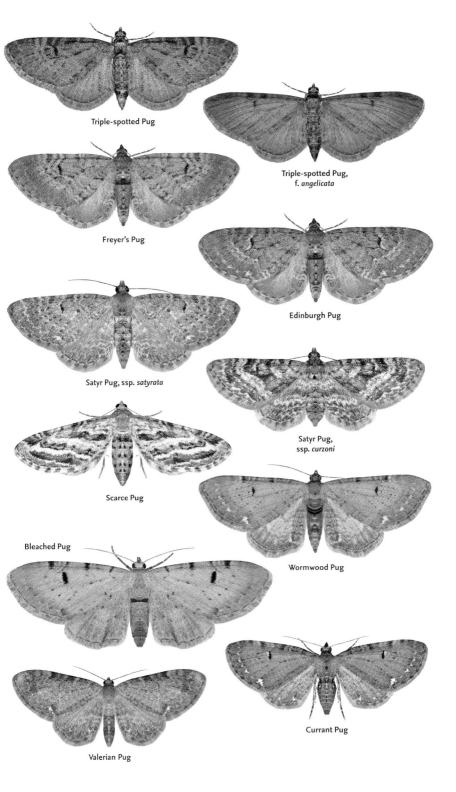

Triple-spotted Pug

Triple-spotted Pug,
f. *angelicata*

Freyer's Pug

Edinburgh Pug

Satyr Pug, ssp. *satyrata*

Satyr Pug,
ssp. *curzoni*

Scarce Pug

Bleached Pug

Wormwood Pug

Valerian Pug

Currant Pug

Common Pug *Eupithecia vulgata* 70.183 (1834) 16–18mm
ADULT ssp. *vulgata* is brown; forewings have a curved leading edge, dark cross-lines, an indistinct central spot and a small white spot near trailing corner. Flies May–Aug. **LARVA** feeds on shrubs. **STATUS** Ssp. *vulgata* is widespread; ssp. *scotica* occurs in Scotland and Ireland; ssp. *clarensis* (paler and greyer) occurs in the Burren, W Ireland.

ssp. *scotica*

Mottled Pug *Eupithecia exiguata* 70.184 (1819) 20–22mm
ADULT is grey-buff; forewings have dark cross-bands interrupted by buff-brown. Flies May–Jun. **LARVA** feeds on trees and shrubs. **STATUS** Widespread; generally common but scarce in the N.

Campanula Pug *Eupithecia denotata* 70.185 (1836) 18–20mm
ADULT is brown; forewings have a dark central spot and wavy white outer cross-line. Flies Jul. **STATUS** Ssp. *denotata* is local in S England; larva feeds on Nettle-leaved Bellflower. Smaller ssp. *jasioneata* (Jasione Pug) is greyer and found in SW Britain; its larva feeds on Sheep's-bit.

Yarrow Pug *Eupithecia millefoliata* 70.186 (1841) 20mm
ADULT is grey-brown; forewings have numerous cross-lines, these angled near leading edge, which is straight. Flies Jun–Jul. **LARVA** feeds on Yarrow. **STATUS** Local in S and SE England.

Tawny Speckled Pug *Eupithecia icterata* 70.187 (1838) 20–22mm
ADULT form *subfulvata* has a distinctive orange patch on otherwise marbled brown forewing; in other forms, orange area is greatly reduced. Flies Jul–Aug. **LARVA** feeds on Yarrow and Sneezewort. **STATUS** Widespread and common in lowland areas.

Bordered Pug *Eupithecia succenturiata* 70.188 (1839) 20–22mm
ADULT has a white tip to abdomen and white 'shoulders'; forewings have a white central area and marbled grey and brown border. Flies Jul–Aug. **LARVA** feeds on Mugwort. **STATUS** Widespread and locally common in S and central Britain.

Shaded Pug *Eupithecia subumbrata* 70.189 (1840) 18–20mm
ADULT is grey-buff; forewings have a very indistinct central spot and subtle cross-lines, angled near leading edge, which is straight. Flies Jun–Jul. **LARVA** feeds on low-growing plants. **STATUS** Local, mainly in damp grassland in SE England.

Grey Pug *Eupithecia subfuscata* 70.190 (1837) 18–20mm
ADULT is grey-buff (sometimes much darker) with wavy cross-lines and a dark central spot on forewings. Can be confused with Valerian Pug (p. 154). Flies May–Jun. **LARVA** feeds on low-growing plants. **STATUS** Widespread and locally common.

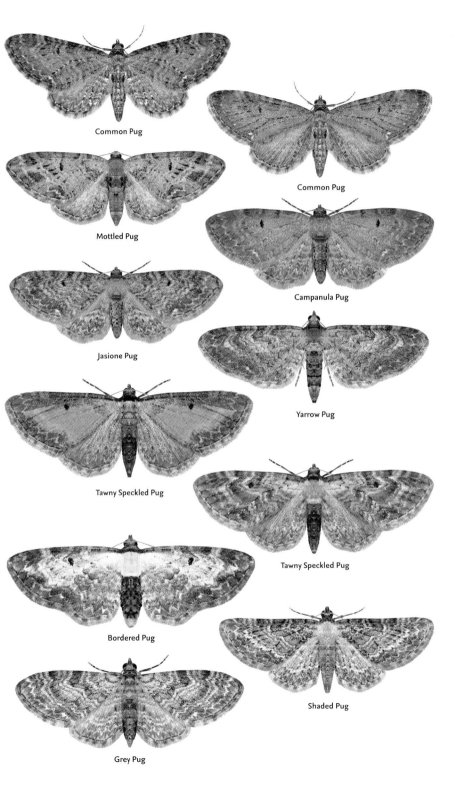

Common Pug

Common Pug

Mottled Pug

Campanula Pug

Jasione Pug

Yarrow Pug

Tawny Speckled Pug

Tawny Speckled Pug

Bordered Pug

Shaded Pug

Grey Pug

Manchester Treble-bar *Carsia sororiata* 70.191 (1866) 22–30mm
ADULT at rest holds wings flattish, creating a triangular outline.
Forewings are lilac-grey with bold reddish-brown cross-bands.
Sometimes active in daytime. Flies Jul–Aug. LARVA feeds on
Bilberry. STATUS Restricted to damp moorland, mainly in N
England and Scotland.

Treble-bar *Aplocera plagiata*
70.192 (1867) 38–42mm
ADULT at rest holds wings flattish,
creating a triangular outline.
Forewings are lilac-grey with
several dark cross-bands; these
contain dark cross-lines and
are darkest towards leading
edge. Compared to Lesser Treble-bar, inner cross-band
shows a rounded curve towards leading edge (sharply
angled in Lesser). Sometimes active in daytime. Flies
Jul–Aug. LARVA feeds on various St John's-worts. STATUS
Widespread throughout but commonest in the S.

Lesser Treble-bar
Aplocera efformata 70.193 (1868) 36–40mm
ADULT is very similar to Treble-bar.
Forewings are lilac-grey with several
dark cross-bands; these contain dark
cross-lines and are darkest towards
leading edge. Inner cross-band is
sharply angled towards leading edge (rounded
in Treble-bar). Sometimes active in daytime.
Double-brooded: flies May–Jun, and Aug–Sep.
LARVA feeds on various St John's-worts.
STATUS Widespread only in central and S Britain.

Purple Treble-bar *Aplocera praeformata* 70.194 (1869) 34–38mm
ADULT is similar to Treble-bar but larger, with reddish flush beyond outer cross-band
and reddish band inside inner cross-band of forewings. Flies Jul–Aug. LARVA feeds
on St John's-worts. STATUS Very rare immigrant from Europe; only 2 records here (not
illustrated).

Streak *Chesias legatella*
70.195 (1864) 30–35mm
ADULT has narrow, pointed forewings
that cover hindwings at rest. These
are marked with a pale lengthways
streak and an elliptical black and
white mark, and are otherwise finely
patterned like tree bark. Flies Sep–
Oct. LARVA feeds on Broom. STATUS
Widespread and locally common.

Broom-tip *Chesias rufata* 70.196 (1865) 28–32mm
ADULT is similar in shape to Streak and also rests with forewings
covering hindwings. Ssp. *rufata* has grey wings with marbled orange
bands, particularly dark and intense on leading half of central cross-band.
Ssp. *scotica* is similar but wings are blue-grey; darker markings are intense
and usually maroon. Flies Apr–Jul. LARVA feeds on Broom. STATUS
Widespread but local; ssp. *rufata* occurs in the S, ssp. *scotica* occurs
in N England and Scotland.

Manchester Treble-bar

Broom-tip

Treble-bar

Streak

Lesser Treble-bar

Grey Carpet *Lithostege griseata* 70.197 (1871) 28–30mm
ADULT has pointed, pale grey forewings, with a very subtle buffish
outer cross-band often discernible. Flies May–Jul. LARVA feeds on
seeds of Flixweed and Treacle Mustard. STATUS Scarce and local,
restricted to the Brecklands of East Anglia.

Seraphim *Lobophora halterata* 70.198 (1879) 20–24mm
ADULT has rounded forewings that are held flat at rest, covering
hindwings. Forewings are grey but with variable pale and dark cross-
bands and lines, but invariably a dark cross-band near base of wings.
Flies May–Jun. LARVA feeds on Aspen and other poplars. STATUS
Widespread, common only in central and S Britain.

Small Seraphim *Pterapherapteryx sexalata* 70.199 (1882) 23–25mm
ADULT has forewings with grey and brown cross-bands; central cross-
band is typically grey in trailing half but darker in leading half, with
an obvious dark spot near inner margin. Double-brooded: flies May–
Jun, and Jul–Aug. LARVA feeds on sallows. STATUS Widespread but
local, mainly in S England and Wales.

Yellow-barred Brindle
Acasis viretata 70.200 (1883) 26–28mm
ADULT has green forewings when fresh,
fading rapidly to yellow; broad, dark
central band is a good distinguishing
feature in all individuals. Flies May–Jun, with occasional
2nd brood in autumn in the S. LARVA feeds on shrubs,
including Holly and Ivy. STATUS Widespread but
commonest in the S.

Barred Tooth-striped *Trichopteryx polycommata* 70.201 (1880) 34–36mm
ADULT has grey forewings with a dark reddish-brown cross-band that
divides towards leading edge of wing. Flies Mar–Apr. LARVA feeds
on Wild Privet and Ash. STATUS Scarce and local, with scattered populations
in S England, NW England and W Scotland.

Early Tooth-striped
Trichopteryx carpinata 70.202 (1881) 30–34mm
ADULT is variable, forewings ranging from
pale grey-buff to darker greenish brown;
wings are marked with several narrow
dark cross-bands that range in intensity
with the wings' ground colour (i.e. more
intense in darker specimens). Flies Apr–May. LARVA feeds
on a range of shrubs. STATUS Widespread and locally
common.

Grey Carpet

Seraphim

Small Seraphim

Seraphim

Small Seraphim

Yellow-barred Brindle

Barred Tooth-striped

Yellow-barred Brindle

Early Tooth-striped

Early Tooth-striped

Orange Underwing
Archiearis parthenias 70.203 (1661) 30–40mm

ADULT is day-flying. Forewings are marbled brown with pale stippling and a pale central band that is well defined only towards leading edge. Hindwings have a broad orange-yellow band; on their underside, orange band has an obvious central projection. Flies Mar–Apr. **LARVA** feeds on birches and moth is seldom seen far from foodplant trees. **STATUS** Widespread, but its precise range is strongly tied to the presence of birches; commonest in central and S England and Wales, and central Scotland.

Light Orange Underwing
Boudinotiana notha 70.204 (1662) 34–36mm

ADULT is day-flying. Forewings are marbled brown with pale stippling; pale central band is much less obvious than in Orange Underwing. Hindwings have a broad orange-yellow band; on their underside, orange band lacks an obvious central projection. Flies Mar–Apr, usually 2 weeks earlier than Orange Underwing. **LARVA** feeds on Aspen and moth is seldom seen far from foodplant trees. **STATUS** Locally common only in S England.

Magpie
Abraxas grossulariata 70.205 (1884) 35–40mm

ADULT is broad-winged and very distinctive. Wings have a white ground colour, forewings with blotchy black spots, these aligning along outer margin to form a

cross-band containing orange-yellow coloration that is also seen at base of wings. A wide range of odd forms have been produced by captive breeding; these are unknown in the wild. All stages in the life cycle have elements of adult's warning colours. Flies Jul–Aug. **LARVA** feeds on currants. **STATUS** Widespread. Formerly very common but now much less so; decline is most marked in suburban areas.

Clouded Magpie
Calospilos sylvata 70.206 (1885) 36–42mm

ADULT has broad rounded wings that are whitish with subtle grey blotches, especially on forewings; also note the dark-centred orange-buff patches on trailing margins of all wings, and at base of forewings. Flies Jun–Jul. **LARVA** feeds on Wych and English elms. **STATUS** Widespread but local in central and S Britain.

Clouded Border
Lomaspilis marginata 70.207 (1887) 24–26mm

ADULT has white wings marked with a variable broad black border that is particularly striking on forewings. Flies May–Jul. **LARVA** feeds on sallows, Aspen and other poplars. **STATUS** Widespread and fairly common.

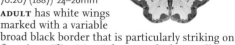

Light Orange Underwing

Orange Underwing

Orange Underwing

Light Orange Underwing

Magpie, larva

Magpie, typical form

Magpie, pupa

Magpie, aberrant form

Magpie, aberrant form

Clouded Magpie

Clouded Border

Scorched Carpet *Ligdia adustata* 70.208 (1888) 20–25mm
ADULT has broad whitish wings, the forewings with a dark outer cross-band and dark basal patch that runs across abdomen. Double-brooded: flies May–Jun, and Aug. **LARVA** feeds on Spindle. **STATUS** Widespread and fairly common, mainly in central and S Britain.

BELOW: **Scorched Carpet**

Ringed Border *Stegania cararia* 70.209 (1888b) 20–22mm
ADULT has broad, pale wings that are strongly stippled with reddish brown, the same colour creating broad, semicircular marginal 'rings'. Flies Jul–Aug. **LARVA** feeds on poplars. **STATUS** Very rare immigrant (not illustrated).

Dorset Cream Wave
Stegania trimaculata 70.210 (1888a) 26–28mm
ADULT has broad creamy-white wings. Forewings are pointed. Wavy dark cross-line on hindwings aligns with the posterior of the 2 cross-lines on forewings. Double-brooded: flies Apr–May, and Aug. **LARVA** feeds on poplars. **STATUS** Very rare immigrant.

Peacock Moth *Macaria notata* 70.211 (1889) 28–30mm
ADULT has angular wing margins, with a central projection on both wings. Wings are creamy white, marbled with grey-buff; forewings have orange-brown marks along leading edge and a dark central 'pawprint'. Note the well-defined dark marginal line around hindwings. Flies May–Jun. **LARVA** feeds on birches. **STATUS** Locally common in S Britain and central Scotland only.

Sharp-angled Peacock
Macaria alternata
70.212 (1890) 22–26mm
ADULT is similar to Peacock but dark central 'pawprint' is much reduced. Hindwing margin is marked with a series of dark dashes, not a continuous line. Flies May–Jun. **LARVA** feeds on sallows and Blackthorn. **STATUS** Locally common only in the S.

Dusky Peacock *Macaria signaria* 70.213 (1891) 28–30mm
ADULT has angular wing margins, with a central projection on both wings. Wings are marbled grey-buff with interrupted darker cross-bands, most heavily marked towards leading edge of forewings. Flies May–Jul. **LARVA** feeds on various shrubs. **STATUS** Very rare immigrant, now very locally established in the S.

Tawny-barred Angle
Macaria liturata
70.214 (1893) 20–26mm
ADULT has pointed forewings; hindwings have a marginal projection. Colour is variable. Typical form has dark-stippled grey wings with narrow dark cross-bands, the outer one flushed orange towards leading edge. Dark form (*nigrofulvata*) is dark brown with orange bands on both wings. Flies Jun–Jul. **LARVA** feeds mainly on Scots Pine. **STATUS** Widespread and common.

Scorched Carpet

Dorset Cream Wave

Dorset Cream Wave

Peacock Moth

Sharp-angled Peacock

Dusky Peacock

Tawny-barred Angle

Tawny-barred Angle

Tawny-barred Angle

V-Moth *Macaria wauaria* 70.215 (1897) 25–30mm

LS

ADULT has grey-buff wings with dark stippling and a reddish-buff flush towards margin of forewings; black marks on leading edge include a striking black 'V'. Flies Jul–Aug. **LARVA** feeds on Gooseberry and currants. **STATUS** Widespread but local.

Netted Mountain Moth *Macaria carbonaria* 70.216 (1895) 22–24mm

LS

ADULT is day-flying. Wings are dark grey-brown with concentric, wavy black and white cross-lines. Flies Apr–Jun. **LARVA** feeds on Bearberry. **STATUS** Rare, on upland moors and mountains in central Scotland.

Rannoch Looper *Macaria brunneata* 70.217 (1896) 25–30mm

LS

ADULT is day-flying. Has yellow-buff wings with dark speckling and 4 dark cross-lines; these are more intense in female than male. Flies Jun–Jul. **LARVA** feeds on Bilberry. **STATUS** Rare, in open woodland in central Scotland; also an immigrant to S England.

Latticed Heath *Chiasmia clathrata* 70.218 (1894) 20–25mm

LS

ADULT is superficially rather butterfly-like and sometimes flies by day. Wings are creamy white, with a lattice network of black cross-lines and veins. Double-brooded: flies May–Jun, and Aug–Sep. **LARVA** feeds on clovers and Lucerne. **STATUS** Widespread and common except in the far N.

Tamarisk Peacock *Chiasmia aestimaria* 70.219 (1894a) 22–24mm

ADULT has pointed forewings and hindwings with a sharp-angled margin. Overall grey-buff, with dark speckling and an oblique black-edged white forewing stripe from tip to trailing edge. Double-brooded: flies Apr–May, and Sep–Oct. **LARVA** feeds on Tamarisk. **STATUS** Very rare immigrant (not illustrated).

Frosted Yellow *Isturgia limbaria* 70.220 (1899) 26–28mm

LS

ADULT has dark-bordered orange-yellow forewings and speckled yellow hindwings. Double-brooded: flies May–Jun, and Jul–Aug. **LARVA** feeds on Broom. **STATUS** Extinct resident; possible very rare immigrant.

Little Thorn *Cepphis advenaria* 70.221 (1901) 24–26mm

LS

ADULT is day-flying. Has grey-buff upperwings with subtly darker cross-lines; rests with wings partly folded, showing speckled orange-buff underwings with a white-edged dark cross-line. Flies May–Jun. **LARVA** feeds on Bramble and Bilberry. **STATUS** Local in S England and Wales.

Netted Mountain
Moth

Rannoch Looper,
male

Rannoch Looper,
female

Frosted Yellow

V-Moth

Latticed Heath

Latticed Heath

Little Thorn

Brown Silver-line *Petrophora chlorosata* 70.222 (1902) 32–36mm

ADULT has pointed grey-buff forewings with 2 dark brown cross-lines, between which is a dark spot. Flies Jul–Sep. LARVA feeds on Bracken. STATUS Widespread and locally common.

LS

Barred Umber *Plagodis pulveraria*

70.223 (1903) 28–32mm
ADULT is reddish buff, the forewings with dark speckling and a broad, rich brown cross-band. Flies May–Jun. LARVA feeds on various deciduous trees. STATUS Widespread but local; mainly in the W.

male

LS

Scorched Wing

Plagodis dolabraria
70.224 (1904) 28–32mm
ADULT has wavy-margined wings whose subtle dark cross-lines and dark purplish-brown patches give it a passing resemblance to a scorched piece of paper. Flies May–Jun. LARVA feeds on oaks, birches and other deciduous trees. STATUS Widespread and fairly common, especially in the S.

ABOVE: **Barred Umber, larva**
BELOW: **Scorched Wing**

LS

LS

Horse Chestnut

Horse Chestnut *Pachycnemia hippocastanaria* 70.225 (1905) 28–32mm

ADULT has narrow forewings that are grey-buff with variable dark streaks and cross-bands; at rest, forewings overlap one another. Head and thorax are typically paler than wings. Double-brooded: flies May–Jun, and Aug. LARVA feeds on Heather. STATUS Very local, on heaths in S England.

Brimstone Moth *Opisthograptis*

luteolata 70.226 (1906) 32–36mm
ADULT has angular wings that are bright yellow; forewings have chestnut markings along leading edge, the one nearest the tip being the largest. Flies Apr–Oct in several generations. LARVA feeds on Hawthorn, Blackthorn and other shrubs. STATUS Widespread and locally common.

Brimstone Moth

LS

Brimstone
Moth

Bordered Beauty *Epione repandaria* 70.227 (1907) 26–28mm

ADULT has wings with wavy margins; they are yellow-orange with subtle darker cross-lines and a broad, wavy-edged dark outer border that tapers to a point at tip. Flies Jul–Sep. LARVA feeds on sallows. STATUS Widespread but commonest in central and S Britain, favouring damp woodland and scrub.

Bordered Beauty

LS

Dark Bordered Beauty

Epione vespertaria 70.228 (1908) 26–28mm
ADULT is similar to Bordered Beauty. Male is orange-yellow with a reddish-brown border of fairly uniform width. Female is yellow with a dark border that tapers but does not reach a point at tip. Flies Jul–Aug. LARVA feeds on Creeping Willow. STATUS Extremely local; restricted to a few sites, mainly in NE England.

LS

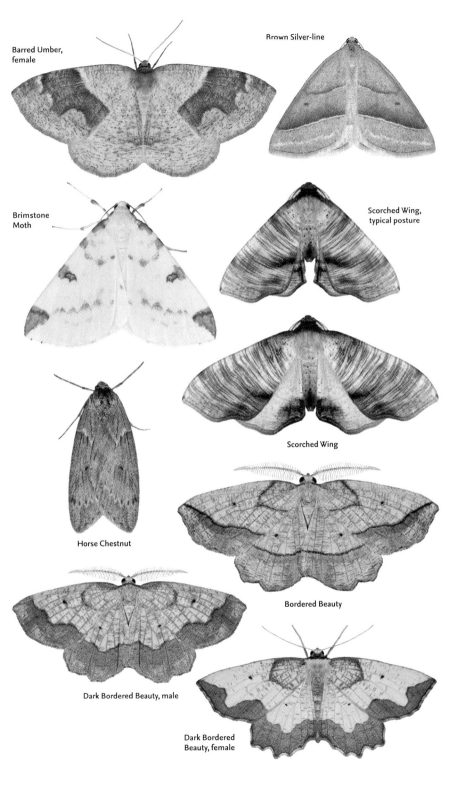

Barred Umber, female

Brown Silver-line

Brimstone Moth

Scorched Wing, typical posture

Horse Chestnut

Scorched Wing

Bordered Beauty

Dark Bordered Beauty, male

Dark Bordered Beauty, female

Speckled Yellow

Pseudopanthera macularia
70.229 (1909) 24–28mm
ADULT is day-flying and
distinctive. Wings are rich
yellow with brown blotches.
Flies May–Jun. **LARVA** feeds on Wood-sage.
STATUS Widespread only in S England and
W Britain, reflecting range of larval foodplant.

LS

Orange Moth *Angerona prunaria* 70.230 (1924) 35–45mm

female f. *corylaria*

ADULT is brightly coloured and variable. Male is
typically orange with dark crosswise flecking of
varying intensity; female is typically similar overall
but yellow. Form *corylaria* has brown wings with a
broad cross-band that is orange in male, yellow in
female. Antennae are feathered only in males. Flies Jun–
Jul. **LARVA** feeds on deciduous shrubs and trees. **STATUS**
Local in woods and on heaths, mainly in S and SE England.

LS

Lilac Beauty *Apeira syringaria*

70.231 (1910) 38–42mm
ADULT has wings with
jagged, scalloped margins.
They are yellowish buff,
marked with pinkish lilac
and a dark red oblique cross-line
on forewings. At rest, leading half of forewings is folded
lengthways and the overall effect produced is that of a
crumpled leaf. Flies Jun–Jul. **LARVA** feeds on privets and
Honeysuckle. **STATUS** Locally common in central and
S Britain.

LS

Large Thorn *Ennomos autumnaria* 70.232 (1911) 40–50mm

ADULT has wings with a jagged, scalloped margin. They are
yellow-buff with dark speckling; cross-line is indistinct
at best. Flies Sep–Oct. **LARVA** feeds on deciduous trees
and shrubs. **STATUS** Scarce and local, mainly in S
England and East Anglia.

LS

Canary-shouldered Thorn

Ennomos alniaria
70.234 (1913) 38–40mm
ADULT has wings with
jagged, scalloped margins.
They are orange-buff to
yellow-buff, with dark
speckling and 2 distinct dark
cross-lines; outer cross-line on forewings curves smoothly
towards leading edge. Thorax is 'furry' and bright yellow.
Flies Jul–Oct. **LARVA** feeds on deciduous trees and shrubs.
STATUS Widespread and locally common.

LS

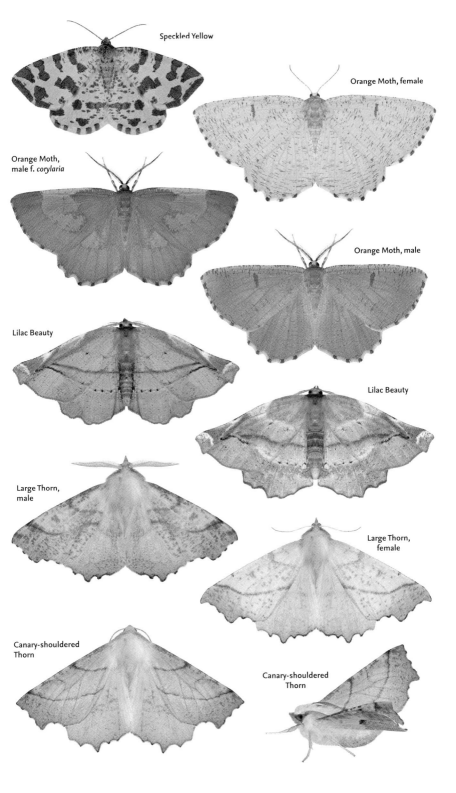

Speckled Yellow

Orange Moth, female

Orange Moth, male f. *corylaria*

Orange Moth, male

Lilac Beauty

Lilac Beauty

Large Thorn, male

Large Thorn, female

Canary-shouldered Thorn

Canary-shouldered Thorn

August Thorn *Ennomos quercinaria* 70.233 (1912) 42–50mm
ADULT has yellow to orange-buff wings with jagged, scalloped margins; they are held at an angle at rest. Forewings have 2 dark cross-lines, the outer one kinked where it meets the leading edge, the inner one acutely angled at leading edge. Flies Aug–Sep. **LARVA** feeds on deciduous trees. **STATUS** Widespread and locally common in central and S Britain.

LS

Dusky Thorn *Ennomos fuscantaria* 70.235 (1914) 35–45mm
ADULT has overall buffish-brown wings with jagged, scalloped margins; they are held at an angle at rest. Forewings have 2 dark cross-lines; region beyond outer cross-line is flushed purplish brown. Flies Aug–Oct. **LARVA** feeds on Ash. **STATUS** Widespread and locally common in central and S Britain.

LS

September Thorn *Ennomos erosaria* 70.236 (1915) 38–40mm
ADULT has yellow-buff wings with jagged, scalloped margins; they are held at an angle at rest. Forewings have 2 dark cross-lines; compared to August Thorn, both cross-lines meet leading edge at less of an angle. Flies Jul–Sep. **LARVA** feeds on oaks and birches. **STATUS** Widespread, but commonest in central and S Britain.

LS

Early Thorn *Selenia dentaria* 70.237 (1917) 35–45mm
ADULT has wings with jagged, scalloped margins, held folded flat over back at rest (unlike other 'thorns'); they are variably marbled with orange, lilac-grey and brown. Underwings (seen at rest) have 2 cross-lines, with white crescent on hindwings. Second-generation moths are paler and smaller than 1st generation; unusual form *harrisoni* is overall brown. Double-brooded: flies Apr–May, and Aug–Sep. **LARVA** feeds on deciduous trees. **STATUS** Widespread and common.

f. harrisoni

LS

LS

Lunar Thorn *Selenia lunularia* 70.238 (1918) 38–42mm
ADULT has wings with jagged, scalloped margins; they are held at an angle at rest. Both wings are typically yellow-buff with a darker orange central band containing white 'crescent moon' marks; hindwings have a particularly deep scalloped central indentation. Flies May–Jun. **LARVA** feeds on deciduous trees. **STATUS** Widespread but local.

LS

Purple Thorn *Selenia tetralunaria* 70.239 (1919) 32–38mm
ADULT has wings with jagged, scalloped margins; they are held at an angle at rest. Inner half of underside to both wings is reddish brown and darker than outer half, which is marbled brown and grey; has a white 'crescent moon' mark on both wings. Second-generation moths are paler and

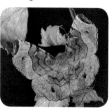

2nd generation

1st generation

LS

smaller than 1st generation. Double-brooded: flies Apr–May, and Jul–Aug. **LARVA** feeds on deciduous trees. **STATUS** Widespread, commonest in central and S Britain.

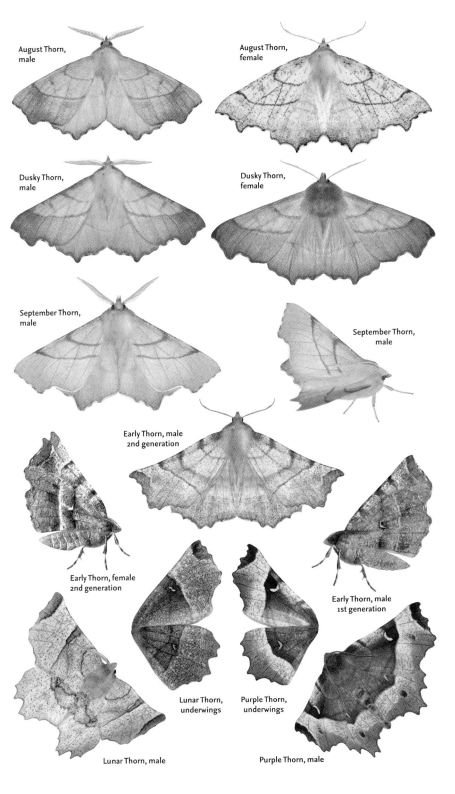

August Thorn, male

August Thorn, female

Dusky Thorn, male

Dusky Thorn, female

September Thorn, male

September Thorn, male

Early Thorn, male 2nd generation

Early Thorn, female 2nd generation

Early Thorn, male 1st generation

Lunar Thorn, underwings

Purple Thorn, underwings

Lunar Thorn, male

Purple Thorn, male

Scalloped Hazel *Odontopera bidentata* 70.240 (1920) 32–38mm

ADULT has wings with jagged, scalloped margins; they are held flat at rest. Colour varies from yellow-buff to grey-buff, with furry abdomen the same colour as wings; forewings have dark-framed, subtly darker cross-bands containing a black-ringed spot. Dark form *nigra* has dark brown wings that contrast with paler thorax. Flies May–Jun. **LARVA** feeds on various shrubs and trees. **STATUS** Widespread and locally common.

Scalloped Oak   LS

FAR LEFT: **Scalloped Hazel**
LEFT: **Scalloped Oak**

Scalloped Oak *Crocallis elinguaria* 70.241 (1921) 32–40mm

ADULT has wings with gently scalloped margins; they are typically yellow to yellow-buff with a darker central cross-band containing a dark spot. Flies Jul–Aug. **LARVA** feeds on a range of trees and shrubs. **STATUS** Widespread and fairly common.

Dusky Scalloped Oak *Crocallis dardoinaria* 70.242 (1921a) 48–50mm

ADULT recalls a Scalloped Oak but is much duller overall and black spot comprises 4 black spots. Flies Jul–Sep. **LARVA** feeds on Broom. **STATUS** Rare immigrant, possibly established on Guernsey (not illustrated).

Swallow-tailed Moth

Ourapteryx sambucaria 70.243 (1922) 40–50mm
ADULT has broad, pale yellow wings. Forewings have 2 cross-lines; hindwings have 1 cross-line and an extended tail streamer flanked at base by dark brown spots. Flies Jul. **LARVA** feeds on a range of plants, including Ivy. **STATUS** Widespread and fairly common; absent from N Scotland.

Swallow-tailed Moth   LS

Feathered Thorn   LS

FAR LEFT:
Swallow-tailed Moth
LEFT:
Feathered Thorn

Feathered Thorn *Colotois pennaria* 70.244 (1923) 35–45mm

ADULT male has feathery antennae. Wings of both sexes are brown with darker speckling; forewings have 2 cross-lines containing a dark spot, and a white spot near wingtip. Flies Sep–Nov. **LARVA** feeds on a range of trees and shrubs. **STATUS** Widespread and fairly common, least so in the N.

LS

March Moth

March Moth *Alsophila aescularia* 70.245 (1663) 25–35mm (male)

ADULT female is virtually wingless. Male has narrow wings that overlap one another at rest. Forewings are overall grey-brown with a subtly darker central band, the outer margin of which is jagged. Flies Mar–Apr. **LARVA** feeds on deciduous trees and shrubs. **STATUS** Widespread and fairly common, except in the N.

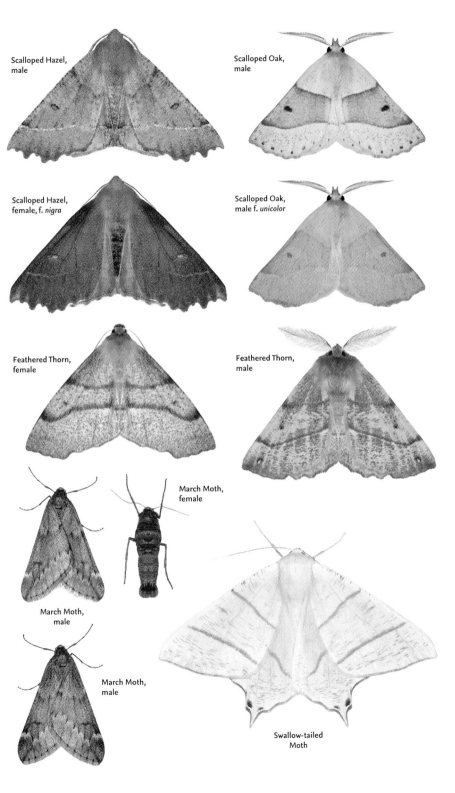

Scalloped Hazel, male

Scalloped Oak, male

Scalloped Hazel, female, f. *nigra*

Scalloped Oak, male f. *unicolor*

Feathered Thorn, female

Feathered Thorn, male

March Moth, female

March Moth, male

March Moth, male

Swallow-tailed Moth

Small Brindled Beauty *Apocheima hispidaria* 70.246 (1925)

30–34mm (male)

ADULT female is wingless. Male has yellow-buff forewings with variably intense dark speckling and cross-lines; outerwing margin is typically palest. Much smaller than similar Brindled Beauty and flies earlier, in Feb–Mar. **LARVA** feeds mainly on oaks. **STATUS** Fairly common only in S Britain.

LS

Pale Brindled Beauty *Phigalia pilosaria* 70.247 (1926)

36–40mm (male)

ADULT female is wingless. Male is typically pale yellow-buff with a grey wash, dark speckling and dark markings (interrupted cross-lines); confusingly, also occurs as uniformly dark form *monacharia*. Flies Jan–Mar. **LARVA** feeds on deciduous trees. **STATUS** Widespread and fairly common, least so in the N.

LS

Brindled Beauty

Brindled Beauty

Lycia hirtaria 70.248 (1927) 35–45mm

ADULTS of both sexes are winged; only male has feathery antennae. Wing colour is variable but typically yellow-buff with dark speckling and dark cross-lines. Flies Mar–Apr. **LARVA** feeds on deciduous trees. **STATUS** Has a disjunct distribution: locally common in central and S England and Wales; also occurs in central Scotland.

LS

Rannoch Brindled Beauty *Lycia lapponaria*

70.249 (1929) 32–34mm (male)

ADULT female is wingless. Both sexes have a line of dull pink spots running from thorax down centre of abdominal segments. Male has semi-transparent grey-buff wings with dark veins and cross-lines. Flies Apr. **LARVA** feeds on Heather and Bog-myrtle. **STATUS** Rare, restricted to damp moorland in central Scotland.

LS

Belted Beauty *Lycia zonaria* 70.250 (1928) 28–30mm (male)

ADULT female is wingless. Male's forewings have a pale buffish-white ground colour with broad brown cross-bands and dark veins. Flies Mar–Apr. **LARVA** feeds on Burnet-rose and Creeping Willow. **STATUS** Rare, restricted to stable dunes on coasts of Cheshire and NE Wales, and machair grassland in Outer Hebrides.

LS

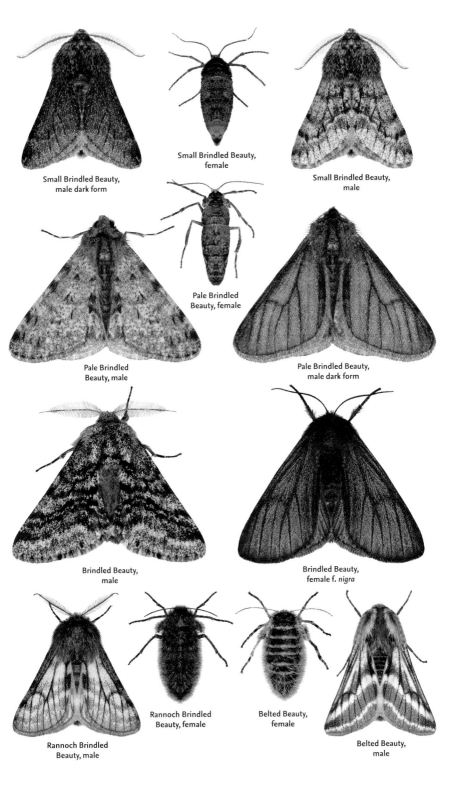

Small Brindled Beauty,
male dark form

Small Brindled Beauty,
female

Small Brindled Beauty,
male

Pale Brindled
Beauty, female

Pale Brindled
Beauty, male

Pale Brindled Beauty,
male dark form

Brindled Beauty,
male

Brindled Beauty,
female f. *nigra*

Rannoch Brindled
Beauty, male

Rannoch Brindled
Beauty, female

Belted Beauty,
female

Belted Beauty,
male

Oak Beauty *Biston strataria* 70.251 (1930) 40–50mm

ADULT has dark-speckled white wings with 2 broad, black-edged reddish-brown cross-bands. Only male has feathered antennae; pectination runs to tip, cf. male Peppered Moth. Flies Mar–Apr. **LARVA** feeds on deciduous trees. **STATUS** Widespread, mainly in S and central Britain.

LS

Peppered Moth, natural resting pose

Peppered Moth

Biston betularia 70.252 (1931) 35–55mm

ADULT occurs in a range of forms. Typical form has white wings with dark speckling. At the other extreme, form *carbonaria* is uniformly sooty black. A range of additional forms, including form *insularia*, are intermediate in appearance. Flies May–Aug. **LARVA** feeds on a range of trees and shrubs. **STATUS** Widespread and locally common.

LS

Peppered Moth, intermediate colour

Spring Usher *Agriopis leucophaearia* 70.253 (1932) 25–30mm (male)

ADULT female's wings are reduced to tiny stumps. Male has narrow wings with variable markings, but typical form has reddish-brown forewings with a broad white central band that is curved on inner margin, wavy on outer. Almost uniformly pale buff and dark brown forms also occur. Flies Feb–Mar. **LARVA** feeds on oaks. **STATUS** Widespread, commonest in S and central Britain.

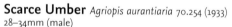

LS

Scarce Umber *Agriopis aurantiaria* 70.254 (1933) 28–34mm (male)

ADULT female is flightless with only short wing stumps. Male has orange-yellow forewings with brown cross-lines and speckling. Flies Oct–Nov. **LARVA** feeds on deciduous trees and shrubs. **STATUS** Widespread and locally common.

LS

Dotted Border *Agriopis marginaria* 70.255 (1934) 28–32mm (male)

ADULT female is flightless with short fan-shaped wings. Male is variable, but typical form has dull orange-buff forewings with dark speckling, a row of black marginal dots, and 2 dark cross-lines, the inner one straight and the outer one straight along trailing half but kinked towards leading edge. Uniformly dark brown form *fuscata* also occurs. Flies Feb–Apr. **LARVA** feeds on deciduous trees and shrubs. **STATUS** Widespread, commonest in S and central Britain.

LS

Mottled Umber *Erannis defoliaria* 70.256 (1935) 30–40mm (male)

ADULT female is wingless. Male is very variable. Typical form has reddish-brown cross-bands on forewings enclosing a broad paler central band containing a dark spot. Confusingly, orange-buff and speckled brown forms also occur and some lack the dark black forewing spot. Flies Oct–Dec. **LARVA** feeds on deciduous trees and shrubs. **STATUS** Widespread, commonest in the S.

LS

Oak Beauty,
male

Peppered Moth,
female typical form

Peppered Moth,
male melanic form

Spring Usher,
male

Spring Usher,
female

Spring Usher,
male

Scarce Umber,
female

Dotted Border,
male

Dotted Border,
female

Scarce Umber,
male

Dotted Border,
female

Dotted Border,
melanic form

Mottled Umber,
male

Mottled Umber,
female

Mottled Umber,
male

Waved Umber *Menophra abruptaria*
70.257 (1936) 38–40mm
ADULT has buff wings, the forewings with a dark
oblique stripe from tip to midway, the hindwings
with a broad dark band. Flies Apr–Jun. **LARVA** feeds
on privets and Lilac. **STATUS** Commonest in the S.

LS

Willow Beauty *Peribatodes rhomboidaria* 70.258 (1937) 32–38mm
ADULT ranges from grey-buff to brown, all variations
with dark speckling and 2 dark cross-lines on
forewings; outer central cross-line is straight
along much of its length; note the dark squarish
spot where the 2 cross-lines converge at trailing
edge. Flies Jul–Aug, sometimes also Sep. **LARVA** feeds
on deciduous trees and shrubs. **STATUS** Widespread,
commonest in S and central Britain.

LS

Feathered Beauty *Peribatodes secundaria*
70.260 (1937a) 40–42mm
ADULT is similar to Willow Beauty but with
bolder markings and darker stippling. Outer
cross-line on forewings is jagged (not straight), with
a noticeable deep curve towards trailing margin. Flies
Jul–Aug. **LARVA** feeds on Norway Spruce and other conifers.
STATUS Scarce immigrant, established locally in the SE.

female
LS

Bordered Grey *Selidosema brunnearia*
70.262 (1938) 38–42mm
ADULT has dark-stippled grey-buff wings with 3
incomplete dark cross-lines on forewings, and brown
outer margin on both wings. Flies Jul–Aug. **LARVA** feeds
on Common Bird's-foot Trefoil, Heather and other
low-growing plants. **STATUS** Scarce and local; New Forest
heaths and coastal dunes in the S are strongholds.

female

LS

Ringed Carpet *Cleora cinctaria* 70.263 (1939) 30–34mm
ADULT has a straight leading edge to forewings. Has
2 central dark cross-lines: outer one partly embraces a
pale inner patch; inner one provides a margin to dark
cross-band near wing base. Ssp. *cinctaria* (S Britain) is
brown overall; ssp. *bowesi* (Scotland) is greyer. Flies
Apr–May. **LARVA** feeds on Bog-myrtle and birches.
STATUS Scarce and local; disjunct distribution.

LS

Satin Beauty *Deileptenia ribeata*
70.264 (1940) 30–40mm
ADULT has broad wings that vary from buff to
grey-brown. Forewings have 3 dark cross-lines.
Flies Jun–Aug. **LARVA** feeds on Yew and other
conifers. **STATUS** Fairly common only in the S.

male

LS

Mottled Beauty *Alcis repandata* 70.265 (1941) 30–40mm
ADULT has a scalloped margin to hindwings. Wing
ground colour varies from grey-buff to rich
brown. Forewings have 2 dark central cross-
lines; unlike similar Willow Beauty, these do
not converge at trailing edge. Flies Jun–Jul.
LARVA feeds on trees and shrubs. **STATUS**
Widespread and locally common.

LS

Willow Beauty,
male typical form

Waved Umber

Willow Beauty,
male f. *perfumaria*

Willow Beauty,
male f. *rebeli*

Feathered
Beauty,
male

Bordered Grey,
male

Ringed Carpet,
male

Satin Beauty,
male f. *nigra*

Satin Beauty,
female typical form

Mottled Beauty,
typical form

Mottled Beauty,
f. *conversaria*

Dotted Carpet *Alcis jubata* 70.266 (1942) 28–32mm
ADULT has white wings with dark speckling, a black
central spot and blackish cross-lines that are darkest
near leading edge. Flies Jul–Sep. **LARVA** feeds on
tree lichens, including beard lichens. **STATUS** Local
in SW England, W Wales and Scotland.

LS

Great Oak Beauty *Hypomecis roboraria*
70.267 (1943) 40–50mm
ADULT has grey wings, heavily marked
with dark speckling. Central cross-lines
on forewings converge at trailing edge
and thicken to form a squarish black
patch; hindwings have a dark central
spot. Form *infuscata* is similar but overall
much darker. Flies Jun–Jul. **LARVA** feeds on oaks.
STATUS Local, confined mainly to S and SE England.

LS

Pale Oak Beauty *Hypomecis punctinalis*
70.268 (1944) 48–52mm
ADULT has grey wings with dense, fine
speckling. Unlike Great Oak Beauty, central
cross-lines on forewings do not converge at
trailing edge to form a black patch; hindwings
have a dark-ringed central spot. Has a pale spot
near tip of underside of forewing. Flies May–Jul.
LARVA feeds on oaks and birches. **STATUS** Local,
mainly in S and SE England.

LS

Engrailed *Ectropis (crepuscularia) bistortata*
70.270 (1947) 30–40mm
ADULT has whitish wings heavily stippled with grey,
brown and buff. Forewings have dark cross-lines,
the outer central one being the most complete and
intense, with projecting dark dashes; beyond this,
towards tip, a white-framed black 'W' is usually
visible. In some forms, wings are almost uniformly
dark brown. Double-brooded: flies Mar–Apr, and
Jul–Aug. **LARVA** feeds on deciduous trees and shrubs.
STATUS Widespread and locally common.

LS

Engrailed

Small Engrailed
Ectropis (crepuscularia) crepuscularia
70.271 (1948) 35–40mm
ADULT is very similar to Engrailed; considered
conspecific by some but treated here as separate
species. Typically, overall paler then Engrailed and
with more striking dark cross-lines, the outer ones
sometimes framing orange-buff coloration. Some forms
have uniformly dark wings. Flies May–Jun. **LARVA** feeds on birches and
sallows. **STATUS** Widespread, commonest in central and S Britain.

LS

Square Spot *Paradarisa consonaria* 70.272 (1949) 40–45mm
ADULT has rounded wings that vary from grey-buff to
brown with dark speckling; forewings have dark
cross-lines and a dark square patch just inside
pale outer cross-line. Flies Apr–Jun. **LARVA** feeds
on various trees. **STATUS** Local, mainly in S and
SW Britain.

LS

Great Oak Beauty

Dotted Carpet

Pale Oak Beauty

Great Oak Beauty

Engrailed, typical
2nd generation

Engrailed, typical
1st generation

Small Engrailed,
typical form

Engrailed,
dark form

Small Engrailed,
dark form

Square Spot,
typical form

Square Spot,
dark form

Brindled White-spot *Parectropis similaria* 70.273 (1950)
34–38mm
ADULT has buff wings marked with dark concentric, crosswise flecks. Forewings have bold black cross-lines, the outermost framing a square, striking white patch. Flies May–Jun. **LARVA** feeds on oaks and birches. **STATUS** Local, mainly in S and SE England.

Grey Birch *Aethalura punctulata* 70.274 (1951) 30–34mm
ADULT has grey wings with fine, dark stippling; forewings have variably incomplete dark cross-lines, most intense towards leading edge. Flies May–Jun. **LARVA** feeds mainly on birches. **STATUS** Widespread, commonest in central and S Britain.

Common Heath
Ematurga atomaria
70.275 (1952) 24–28mm
ADULT is day-flying. Wing ground colour varies from grey to yellow. All forms show dark speckling and dark cross-lines that are black in grey forms, brown in yellow forms. Uniformly dark-winged forms also occur. Flies May–Jun. **LARVA** feeds mainly on Heather and clovers. **STATUS** Widespread and locally common, favouring heaths and moors in particular.

Bordered White *Bupalus piniaria* 70.276 (1954) 26–32mm
ADULT male is active in daytime and after dark. Both sexes rest with wings folded above body, revealing a white streak on hindwings. Sexually dimorphic: male upperwings are speckled white or pale yellow with a broad blackish border; on female, upperwing pattern is more subtle, and yellow and brown colours are typical. Male has feathery antennae. Flies May–Jun. **LARVA** feeds on pines. **STATUS** Widespread and locally common.

male, southern form

Common White Wave *Cabera pusaria* 70.277 (1955)
28–34mm
ADULT has broad white wings with subtle dark speckling on outer margins and forewing leading edge; has 3 straightish grey-brown cross-lines on forewings, 2 on hindwings. Flies May–Aug with overlapping broods. **LARVA** feeds on birches and other trees. **STATUS** Widespread and locally common.

Common Wave *Cabera exanthemata* 70.278 (1956) 32–34mm
ADULT is similar to Common White Wave but wings usually show more extensive brown speckling; brown cross-lines (3 on forewings, 2 on hindwings) are curved (not straight). Flies May–Aug with overlapping broods. **LARVA** feeds on sallows and poplars. **STATUS** Widespread and locally common.

White-pinion Spotted *Lomographa bimaculata* 70.279 (1957)
23–25mm
ADULT has white wings; forewings have 2 dark spots on leading edge and a row of dark spots. Flies May–Jun. **LARVA** feeds on Hawthorn and Blackthorn. **STATUS** Common in central and S Britain.

Brindled White-spot, f. *variegata*

Brindled White-spot, typical form

Grey Birch

Common Heath, female

Common Heath, male

Common Heath, male

Bordered White, male northern form

Bordered White, female

Common White Wave

Bordered White, male typical resting posture

Common Wave

White-pinion Spotted

Clouded Silver *Lomographa temerata* 70.280 (1958) 23–25mm
ADULT has broad white wings. Forewings have a variable extent
of blackish-brown scaling towards outer margin, including
incomplete outer cross-band. Flies May–Jun. **LARVA** feeds on
deciduous shrubs, including Hawthorn. **STATUS** Widespread
and fairly common except in the N.

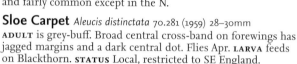

Sloe Carpet *Aleucis distinctata* 70.281 (1959) 28–30mm
ADULT is grey-buff. Broad central cross-band on forewings has
jagged margins and a dark central dot. Flies Apr. **LARVA** feeds
on Blackthorn. **STATUS** Local, restricted to SE England.

Early Moth *Theria primaria*
70.282 (1960) 33–36mm (male)
ADULT female is flightless, its wings
reduced to stumps. Male has rather
narrow wings that typically overlap
one another at rest. Forewings are
buffish brown with a darker central cross-band that has
rather smooth margins. Flies Jan–Feb. **LARVA** feeds on
Hawthorn and Blackthorn. **STATUS** Locally common,
except in the N.

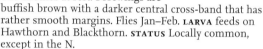

Light Emerald *Campaea margaritaria* 70.283 (1961) 30–40mm
ADULT is light green when fresh, but soon fades to almost
white. Hindwings have a straight white cross-line;
forewings have 2 cross-lines and a small red wedge
near tip. Flies Jun–Aug. **LARVA** feeds on deciduous trees
and shrubs. **STATUS** Widespread and locally common.

Barred Red

Brussels Lace

Barred Red *Hylaea fasciaria* 70.284 (1962) 30–40mm
ADULT is orange-buff, with a broad, subtly darker, pale-edged
cross-band on forewings. Rare form *prasinaria* is green. Flies
Jun–Aug. **LARVA** feeds on Scots Pine and Norway Spruce.
STATUS Widespread and locally common.

Brussels Lace *Cleorodes lichenaria* 70.288 (1945) 32–36mm
ADULT ground colour varies from whitish to buff, tinged
green. All forms show dark speckling and 2 dark cross-lines
on forewings, the outer one very jagged. Flies Jun–Aug. **LARVA**
feeds on epiphytic tree lichens. **STATUS** Locally common only
in W Britain and Ireland.

Clouded Silver

Clouded Silver

Sloe Carpet

Early Moth,
female

Early Moth,
male

Light Emerald

Barred Red,
male

Barred Red,
female

Brussels Lace,
male

Brussels Lace,
female

Scotch Annulet *Gnophos obfuscata* 70.285 (1963) 42–45mm
ADULT has rather triangular forewings and rounded
hindwings. Wings are grey-buff with dense, dark
speckling; forewings have scalloped cross-lines and a
dark central spot. Flies Jul–Aug. **LARVA** feeds on Heather
and other moorland plants. **STATUS** Local, on upland moors
in Scotland and W Ireland.

Irish Annulet *Odontognophos dumetata* 70.286 (1962a) 24–26mm
ADULT has rather triangular forewings and scalloped margins
to both wings. Forewings are grey with dark speckling
and part-broken dark cross-lines, the inner central one
sharply angled towards leading edge. Flies Aug. **LARVA**
feeds on Buckthorn. **STATUS** Restricted to the Burren
in W Ireland.

Annulet *Charissa obscurata* 70.287 (1964) 28–30mm
ADULT has rather broad forewings and scalloped margins
to both wings. Colour varies from pale grey to almost
black. In most forms, wings are grey with dark speckling
and curved, jagged cross-lines (2 on forewings, 1 on
hindwings); both wings have a dark-ringed central spot.
Flies Jul–Aug. **LARVA** feeds on Heather and related plants.
STATUS Widespread but local, with a bias towards heathland
and coastal habitats.

Black Mountain Moth *Glacies coracina* 70.289 (1965) 40–45mm
ADULT has broad, rounded wings that are grey-buff with dark
speckling; forewings have 2 jagged central cross-lines containing
a dark spot. Flies Jun–Jul. **LARVA** feeds on Crowberry. **STATUS**
Scarce and local, restricted to mountains in central Scotland at
altitudes above 500m.

Black-veined Moth *Siona lineata* 70.291 (1966) 35–40mm
ADULT is day-flying. Upperwings are creamy white
with dark veins; underwings are similar but also
have a dark cross-line. Flies May–Jul. **LARVA** feeds on
herbaceous plants. **STATUS** Rare and protected, restricted
to a few downland sites in Kent.

Grey Scalloped Bar *Dyscia fagaria* 70.292 (1969) 32–38mm
ADULT has rather narrow forewings and rounded hindwings, pale
grey to buffish grey in colour, with black and orange-buff
speckling. Forewings have 2 dark cross-lines (outer one
scalloped) and a dark central spot; hindwings have 1
cross-line. Flies Jun–Jul. **LARVA** feeds on Heather and
related plants. **STATUS** Local, confined to heaths and moors.
Most widespread in the N but with outposts as far S as New
Forest heaths.

Scotch Annulet

Scotch Annulet

Irish Annulet

Annulet

Annulet

Black Mountain Moth, female

Black-veined Moth

Black Mountain Moth, male

Grey Scalloped Bar, male

Grey Scalloped Bar, female

Straw Belle *Aspitates gilvaria* 70.293 (1967) 25–30mm
ADULT has triangular forewings with an oblique reddish-brown stripe running from tip to trailing edge. Male has feathered antennae; female has denser brown speckling than male. Flies Jul–Aug. LARVA feeds on downland plants, including Wild Thyme. STATUS Rare, restricted to calcareous grassland; ssp. *gilvara* occurs on the North Downs in Kent and Surrey; ssp. *burrenensis* is restricted to the Burren in W Ireland.

LS

Yellow Belle *Aspitates ochrearia* 70.294 (1968) 30–32mm
ADULT has triangular buffish-yellow forewings with brown speckling and 2 brown cross-lines. Male has feathery antennae. Double-brooded: flies May–Jun, and Aug–Sep. LARVA feeds on Sea Carrot and Buck's-horn Plantain. STATUS Local; favours dry coastal grassland in S Britain.

LS

Grass Wave *Perconia strigillaria* 70.295 (1970) 38–40mm
ADULT has dark-speckled grey-buff wings with brown cross-lines. Male has feathery antennae. Flies Jun–Jul. LARVA feeds on Heather, Broom and related plants. STATUS Has scattered populations throughout, favouring heaths and moors.

LS

male

Rest Harrow *Aplasta ononaria* 70.296 (1664) 28–30mm
ADULT has triangular, warm buff wings with subtle reddish speckling and cross-bands. Flies Jun–Jul. LARVA feeds on Restharrow. STATUS Rare, restricted to coastal grassland in S and SE England; seen elsewhere as a very rare immigrant.

LS

Grass Emerald *Pseudoterpna pruinata* 70.297 (1665) 32–34mm
ADULT is bright green when fresh but fades to greyish white. Forewings have 2 jagged, dark central cross-lines, plus a pale marginal one. Flies Jun–Jul. LARVA feeds on Broom, Petty Whin and related plants. STATUS Locally common on heaths and moors, mainly in central and S Britain and Ireland. SIMILAR SPECIES **Jersey Emerald** *Pseudoterpna coronillaria*, 70.298 (1665a), 36–38mm, has a similar shape and markings but is grey-buff in colour; it is restricted to Jersey (not illustrated).

LS

Large Emerald
Geometra papilionaria 70.299 (1666) 40–50mm
ADULT rests with its bright green wings spread in the manner of a basking butterfly. Both wings have an obvious jagged white central cross-line, plus an inner, more subtle one and an outer row of white dots. Flies Jun–Jul. LARVA feeds on birches. STATUS Widespread and locally common.

Large Emerald

LS

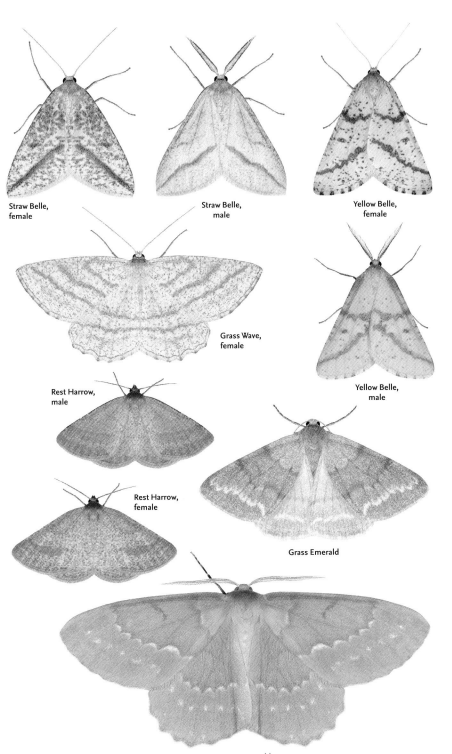

Straw Belle,
female

Straw Belle,
male

Yellow Belle,
female

Grass Wave,
female

Rest Harrow,
male

Yellow Belle,
male

Rest Harrow,
female

Grass Emerald

Large Emerald

Blotched Emerald *Comibaena bajularia* 70.300 (1667) 24–26mm

L

ADULT has bright green wings with brown and white blotches near trailing corners of both forewings and hindwings. Wing margins are rounded and chequered. Flies Jun–Jul. **LARVA** feeds on oaks. **STATUS** Locally common in S and central England; scarcer in Wales.

Small Emerald *Hemistola chrysoprasaria* 70.302 (1673) 28–30mm

ADULT has broad, bright green wings; hindwings have an angled margin. Forewings have 2 white cross-lines and hindwings have 1. Flies Jul–Aug. **LARVA** feeds on Traveller's Joy. **STATUS** Locally common in S Britain, mainly on calcareous soils.

LS

Small Emerald

Small Emerald

Little Emerald *Jodis lactearia* 70.303 (1674) 24–26mm

ADULT is a subtle blue-green when fresh but fades much paler. Hindwings have an angled margin. Forewings have 2 white cross-lines and hindwings have 1. Flies May–Jun. **LARVA** feeds on trees and shrubs, including birches. **STATUS** Widespread and locally common in S and central Britain and Ireland.

Sussex Emerald *Thalera fimbrialis* 70.304 (1672) 25–30mm

ADULT is bright green with triangular forewings and 2 angular projections on hindwings. Wing margins are chequered with red; forewings have 2 white cross-lines, hindwings have 1. Flies Jul–Aug. **LARVA** feeds on Sea Carrot. **STATUS** Rare and protected, restricted to stable shingle at Dungeness in Kent.

LS

Common Emerald *Hemithea aestivaria* 70.305 (1669) 26–30mm

ADULT is deep green; forewings are pointed and hindwings have a single projection (2 in Sussex Emerald). Wing margins are chequered with red; forewings have 2 wavy, angular white cross-lines, hindwings have 1. **LARVA** feeds on Hawthorn, Blackthorn and other shrubs. **STATUS** Widespread and locally common in S and central Britain and Ireland.

LS

Small Grass Emerald *Chlorissa viridata* 70.306 (1670) 24–26mm

ADULT has deep green wings that do not fade. Forewings are triangular and pointed, with 2 white cross-lines; hindwings have an angular margin and 1 white cross-line. Flies Jun–Jul. **LARVA** feeds on birches and Heather. **STATUS** Scarce and very local on heaths in S England; New Forest and Exmoor are hotspots.

LS

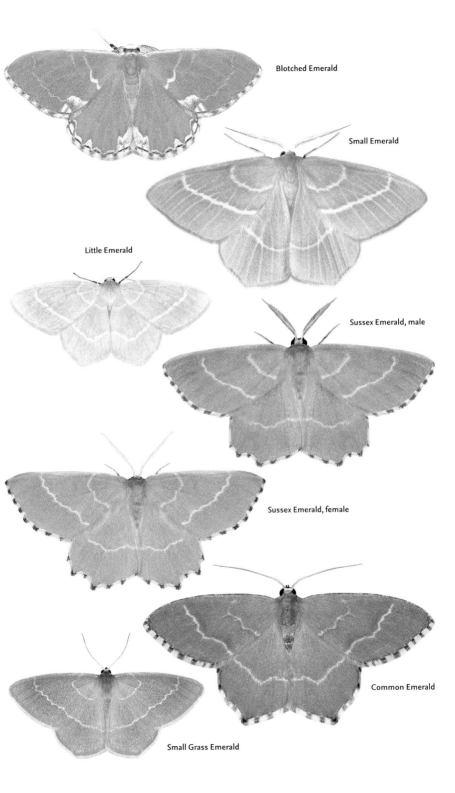

Blotched Emerald

Small Emerald

Little Emerald

Sussex Emerald, male

Sussex Emerald, female

Common Emerald

Small Grass Emerald

Pine Processionary *Thaumetopoea pityocampa* 71.002 (2021) 25–35mm

ADULT holds wings in a tent-like manner over body at rest. Forewings are grey with dark speckling and 2 dark jagged cross-lines containing a dark crescent. Flies May–Jul. **LARVA** feeds on pines and is covered in irritating hairs; forms nose-to-tail lines when on the move. **STATUS** Possible rare immigrant. **SIMILAR SPECIES Oak Processionary** *Thaumetopoea processionea*, 71.001 (2022), 25–35mm is browner overall with a pale patch at wing base; larvae feed on oaks. Recently established in the Greater London area.

LS

LS

Puss Moth *Cerura vinula* 71.003 (1995) 50–70mm

ADULT has broad white wings, the forewings with concentric, deeply indented black lines, dark cross-lines and orange veins. Thorax and legs are white and very furry. Flies May–Jul. **LARVA** is green, plump and angular, with false eye marks and 2 whip-like 'tails' that are waved around when larva is agitated. Feeds on Aspen and willows. **STATUS** Widespread and locally common, especially in central and S Britain.

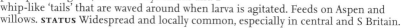
LS

FAR LEFT:
Puss Moth, larva
LEFT:
Sallow Kitten, larva

Sallow Kitten *Furcula furcula* 71.005 (1997) 28–34mm

ADULT is white with a grey thorax and grey central band on forewings; outer margin of this is rather jagged and usually defined in black only on leading half (cf. similar Poplar Kitten). Double-brooded in the S: flies May–Jun, and Aug. **LARVA** resembles a miniature Puss Moth larva, with a dark brown 'saddle'; feeds on sallows and Aspen. **STATUS** Widespread; locally common only in central and S Britain.

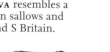
LS

Alder Kitten *Furcula bicuspis* 71.006 (1996) 30–34mm

ADULT is white with a blackish dorsal patch on thorax, and a blackish cross-band and wedge near tip of leading edge on forewings. Flies May–Jul. **LARVA** feeds on Alder and birches. **STATUS** Patchy distribution, with centres in SE and SW England, East Anglia and Wales.

LS

Poplar Kitten *Furcula bifida* 71.007 (1998) 38–42mm

ADULT is similar to Sallow Kitten but larger; central grey cross-band on forewings has a more smoothly curved outer margin that is defined by a black line along its entire length. Flies May–Jul. **LARVA** resembles a miniature Puss Moth larva, with a reddish 'saddle'; feeds on poplars, including Aspen. **STATUS** Widespread in central and S Britain.

LS

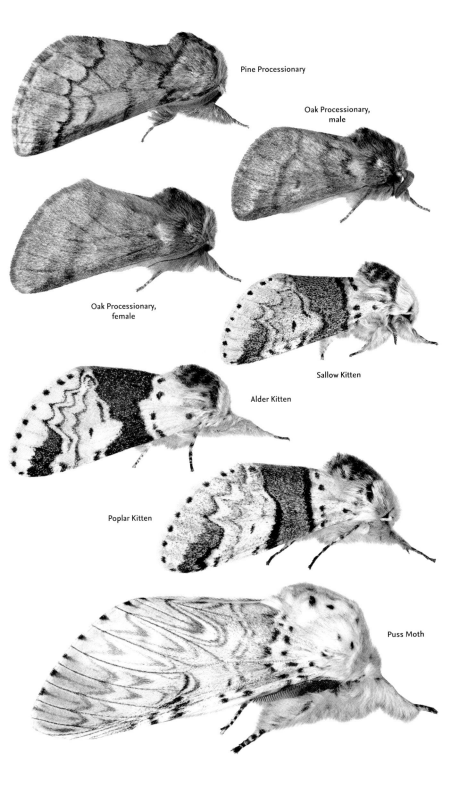

Pine Processionary

Oak Processionary,
male

Oak Processionary,
female

Sallow Kitten

Alder Kitten

Poplar Kitten

Puss Moth

larva

Lobster Moth *Stauropus fagi*
71.009 (1999) 50–60mm
ADULT rests with wings held flattish, hindwings partly protruding beyond forewings. Forewings are grey-brown, with yellow speckling and an orange-red flush along trailing edge. Thorax and legs are furry. Flies May–Jul. **LARVA** is ant-like in 1st instar but fancifully crustacean-like when fully grown. Feeds on Beech and oaks. **STATUS** Locally common in S Britain.

L

female dark form

Marbled Brown *Drymonia dodonaea* 71.010 (2014) 35–38mm
ADULT has grey forewings with a dark central cross-band and outerwing separated by a whitish band. Flies May–Jun. **LARVA** feeds on oaks. **STATUS** Widespread; commonest in S Britain.

LS

Lunar Marbled Brown *Drymonia ruficornis* 71.011 (2015) 36–40mm
ADULT is variable but typically overall grey with a broad central whitish cross-band containing a dark crescent mark. Flies Apr–May. **LARVA** feeds on oaks. **STATUS** Widespread, but common only in S Britain.

LS

Iron Prominent *Notodonta dromedarius* 71.012 (2000) 36–40mm
ADULT rests with wings held in a tent-like manner; dorsal tuft of hairs is seen in profile. Forewings are sooty grey with orange-brown markings and jagged cross-lines; N forms are often darker than S individuals. Double-brooded: flies May–Jun, and Aug. **LARVA** is green with orange-tipped dorsal 'humps'; feeds on birches. **STATUS** Widespread and locally common.

LS

Pebble Prominent *Notodonta ziczac* 71.013 (2003) 40–45mm

Pebble Prominent, larva

ADULT has buff forewings with an oval blotch marked with black, white and brown; note dorsal tuft of hairs when resting moth is viewed in profile. Flies May–Aug. **LARVA** is grey-brown with a pale lateral line and dorsal 'humps'; feeds on sallows and poplars. **STATUS** Widespread and locally common.

LS

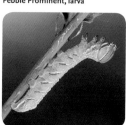

Great Prominent, larva

Great Prominent *Peridea anceps*
71.016 (2005) 55–65mm
ADULT is grey-brown, the forewings with dense yellow speckling, and beautifully patterned with orange-brown and black markings and cross-lines. Flies Apr–Jun. **LARVA** is green with diagonal stripes on each segment, like a hawk-moth larva; feeds on oaks. **STATUS** Locally common only in S Britain.

LS

Plumed Prominent *Ptilophora plumigera*
71.024 (2013) 36–42mm
ADULT has orange-brown forewings with dark veins and pale cross-lines. Male has feathery antennae. Flies Nov–Dec. **LARVA** feeds on Field Maple. **STATUS** Scarce and very local on calcareous soils in S England.

LS

Lobster Moth, male

Lobster Moth, female dark form

Marbled Brown

Lunar Marbled Brown

Marbled Brown

Lunar Marbled Brown

Iron Prominent

Pebble Prominent

Great Prominent

Plumed Prominent, male

Swallow Prominent *Pheosia tremula* 71.017 (2007) 45–55mm
ADULT forewings are white and buffish orange with a black band running along trailing edge and up outer corner; into this, white streaks run from the margin. Flies May–Jul. **LARVA** feeds on poplars and sallows. **STATUS** Widespread and fairly common.

Lesser Swallow Prominent *Pheosia gnoma* 71.018 (2006) 45–50mm
ADULT is similar to Swallow Prominent but black band has a wedge-shaped, bold white mark running into it (much larger than other white lines). Double-brooded: flies May–Jun, and Aug. **LARVA** feeds on birches. **STATUS** Widespread and locally common.

White Prominent *Leucodonta bicoloria* 71.019 (2012) 40–42mm
ADULT is pure white, the forewings with black-bordered orange markings; thorax and legs are furry. Flies Jun–Jul. **LARVA** feeds on birches. **STATUS** Very rare, restricted to County Kerry in SW Ireland; former resident in England but now extinct there.

Pale Prominent *Pterostoma palpina* 71.020 (2011) 35–50mm
ADULT rests with long palps extended and hair tufts protruding at rear end. Forewings are buff with darker lines and bands; shape, colour and markings make moth look like a fragment of wood. Double-brooded in S: flies May–Jun, and Aug. **LARVA** feeds on poplars and sallows. **STATUS** Widespread, but commonest in the S.

Coxcomb Prominent *Ptilodon capucina* 71.021 (2008) 38–40mm
ADULT forewings vary from orange-buff to dark brown; broad profile and scalloped margin give resting moth a leaf-like appearance. Has a forward-pointing tuft of pale hairs on dorsal surface of thorax. Double-brooded: flies May–Jun, and Aug. **LARVA** feeds on birches. **STATUS** Widespread and fairly common.

BELOW: Maple Prominent, larva

Maple Prominent *Ptilodon cucullina* 71.022 (2009) 35–40mm
ADULT forewings are marbled brown and buff, with a greyish-white band along margin; in profile, has a tuft of hairs on abdomen and a forward-pointing tuft on thorax. Flies May–Jul. **LARVA** feeds on Field Maple. **STATUS** Locally common in SE England.

Scarce Prominent *Odontosia carmelita* 71.023 (2010) 40–44mm
ADULT forewings grade from reddish brown to greyish white; margin is scalloped and shows a white 'wedge' on leading edge. Flies Apr–May. **LARVA** feeds on birches. **STATUS** Local in mature woodland, mainly in S and NE England, and central Scotland.

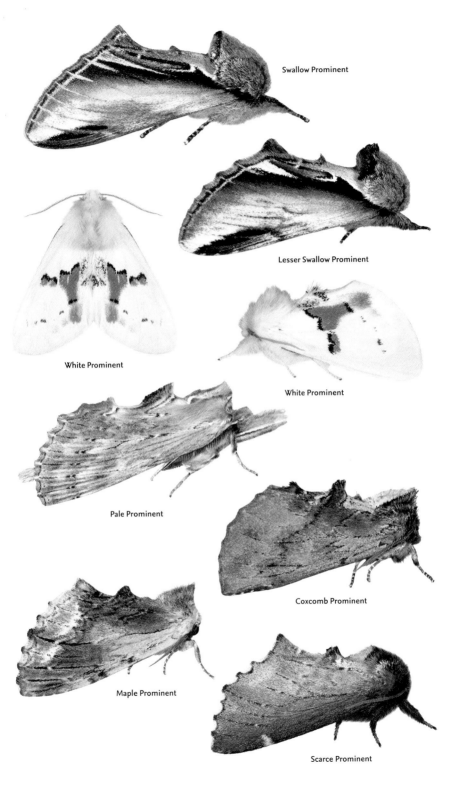

Swallow Prominent

Lesser Swallow Prominent

White Prominent

White Prominent

Pale Prominent

Coxcomb Prominent

Maple Prominent

Scarce Prominent

Buff-tip *Phalera bucephala*
71.025 (1994) 45–50mm
ADULT resembles a snapped-off piece of birch twig. Forewings are grey with dark speckling, black and reddish cross-lines, and a dark-framed yellow patch at tip. Flies Jun–Jul. **LARVA** is yellow and black, and hairy; gregarious, feeding on birches and other trees. **STATUS** Widespread and locally common.

Chocolate-tip *Clostera curtula*
71.027 (2019) 28–34mm
ADULT has grey-buff forewings with white cross-lines; reddish-

Buff-tip, camouflaged adult

Buff-tip, larva

brown patch at tip is defined by the white outer cross-line. At rest, moth often raises its abdomen tip. Double-brooded: flies Apr–May, and Aug–Sep. **LARVA** feeds on Aspen and other poplars, and sallows. **STATUS** Locally common in S England and E Wales, with an isolated outpost in central Scotland.

Chocolate-tip

Small Chocolate-tip *Clostera pigra* 71.028 (2017) 24–26mm
ADULT forewings are grey with dark speckling and dark-edged white cross-lines; orange-red coloration is reduced to a small patch on leading edge. Double-brooded: flies Apr–May, and Aug. **LARVA** feeds on Eared Willow and Creeping Willow. **STATUS** Widespread but generally scarce and very local, favouring boggy heaths and moors.

Scarce Chocolate-tip
Clostera anachoreta 71.029 (2018) 34–36mm
ADULT forewings are grey-brown with white cross-lines; dark reddish-brown patch near tip is rather wedge-shaped and extends beyond pale outer cross-line. Double-brooded: flies Apr, and Aug. **LARVA** feeds on sallows and poplars. **STATUS** Very rare, restricted to stabilised shingle at Dungeness, Kent.

Herald *Scoliopteryx libatrix*
72.001 (2469) 40–45mm
ADULT forewings are broad with an indented, ragged margin and hooked tip; overall grey-brown, marked with white cross-lines and veins, and intense orange-red patches towards base of wings and on thorax. Flies Sep–Nov, and again after hibernation in Apr–May. **LARVA** feeds on willows and poplars. **STATUS** Widespread and fairly common.

Herald

Straw Dot *Rivula sericealis*
72.002 (2474) 20–22mm
ADULT has a triangular outline when resting. Forewings are yellow-buff with a darker reddish-brown margin and central kidney-shaped spot. Double-brooded: flies Jun–Jul, and Aug. **LARVA** feeds on various grasses. **STATUS** Widespread, but commonest in central and S Britain and Ireland.

Straw Dot

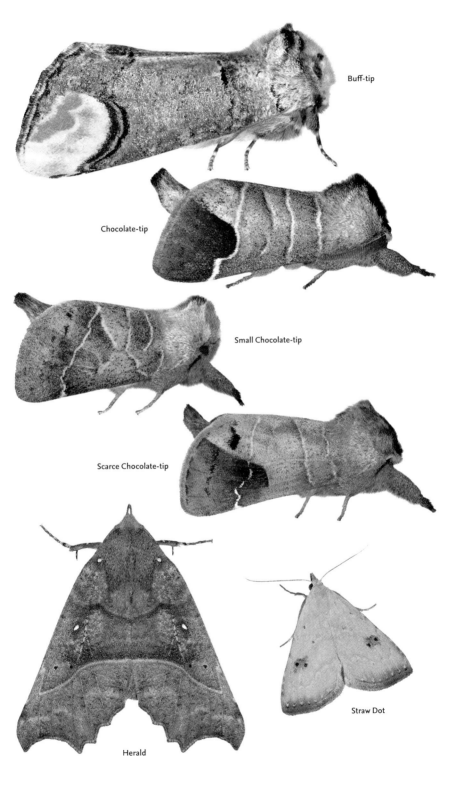

Buff-tip

Chocolate-tip

Small Chocolate-tip

Scarce Chocolate-tip

Herald

Straw Dot

Snout *Hypena proboscidalis*
72.003 (2477) 30–35mm

larva

ADULT rests with wings flat, creating a broadly triangular outline, and with palps projecting. Forewings have distinct cross-lines. Double-brooded: spring generation (Jun–Jul) is larger and browner than darker grey 2nd generation (Aug–Oct). **LARVA** feeds on Common Nettle. **STATUS** Widespread and common.

LS

Buttoned Snout

Buttoned Snout *Hypena rostralis* 72.004 (2480) 28–30mm
ADULT rests with wings flat, creating a narrow triangular outline, and with palps projecting. Forewings are brown with a diagonal dark streak at tip and a central black mark, which in some individuals fancifully resembles a buttonhole. Flies Aug–Oct, and again in Apr–May after hibernation. **LARVA** feeds on Hop. **STATUS** Locally common only in SE England and SE Wales.

LS

Bloxworth Snout *Hypena obsitalis*
72.006 (2478) 30–34mm

LS

ADULT rests with wings flat, creating a broadly triangular outline, and with palps projecting. Forewings are brown with a dark streak at tip, and a dark central patch on leading edge defined by a wavy white cross-line. Double-brooded: flies Jul–Aug, and Sep–Oct; 2nd generation hibernates. **LARVA** feeds on Pellitory-of-the-wall. **STATUS** Rare immigrant but also a recently established local resident of coastal SW England. **SIMILAR SPECIES** Paignton Snout *Hypena obesalis*, 72.005 (2479), 38–40mm, is larger; more pointed forewings have only incomplete pale cross-lines. Very rare immigrant (not illustrated).

Beautiful Snout

Beautiful Snout
Hypena crassalis 72.007 (2476) 30–33mm

LS

ADULT rests with wings flat, creating a broadly triangular outline, and with palps projecting. Forewings are grey with a broad reddish-brown central patch and brown streak at tip. Flies Jun–Jul. **LARVA** feeds on Bilberry. **STATUS** Local in S England and W Britain, favouring heaths, moors and acid woodland.

Black V Moth

LS

Black V Moth
Arctornis l-nigrum 72.008 (2032) 38–40mm

ADULT has white wings with a silky sheen. Forewings are broadly triangular with a central black 'V' mark. Flies Jun–Jul. **LARVA** feeds on Beech and birches. **STATUS** Very rare immigrant.

TOP: Bloxworth Snout, resting; ABOVE: Bloxworth Snout

White Satin Moth *Leucoma salicis* 72.009 (2031) 40–50mm
ADULT has broad, rather rounded white wings with a satin-like sheen. Thorax is very furry. Flies Jul–Aug. **LARVA** feeds on sallows and poplars. **STATUS** Widespread but rather local, commonest in S and E England.

LS

Snout, 1st generation

Snout, 2nd generation

Bloxworth Snout

Beautiful Snout

Buttoned Snout

White Satin Moth

Black V Moth

Black Arches *Lymantria monacha*
72.010 (2033) 35–50mm

LS

ADULT male is smaller than female and has feathery antennae; otherwise sexes are similar, with broad white forewings marked with jagged, concentric black cross-lines; abdomen has pink banding on segments. Flies Jul–Aug. **LARVA** feeds mainly on oaks. **STATUS** Widespread and locally common in S Britain.

Gypsy Moth *Lymantria dispar* 72.011 (2034) 35–55mm

LS

ADULT male has brown forewings with jagged, concentric dark cross-lines; female is larger, with creamy-white forewings marked with dark cross-lines that are darkest towards leading edge. Flies Jul–Aug. **LARVA** feeds on a range of deciduous trees. **STATUS** Very rare immigrant, extinct as a resident species.

Brown-tail *Euproctis chrysorrhoea*
72.012 (2029) 38–40mm

LS

ADULT has white wings, and a furry white thorax and legs; if disturbed, abdomen is often raised, revealing a tuft of brown hairs at tip. **LARVA** is covered in irritating hairs; feeds on Hawthorn and Blackthorn. Flies Jul–Aug. **STATUS** Local, mainly in S and SE England, and commonest near coasts.

larvae in colonial web

Yellow-tail *Euproctis similis* 72.013 (2030) 30–35mm

LS

ADULT has white wings, and a furry white thorax and legs; if disturbed, abdomen is often raised, revealing a tuft of yellow hairs at tip. Flies Jul–Aug. **LARVA** is covered in irritating hairs; feeds on deciduous trees and shrubs. **STATUS** Widespread and locally common in central and S Britain.

Pale Tussock
Calliteara pudibunda
72.015 (2028) 45–55mm

Pale Tussock

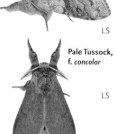

LS

ADULT male is pale grey (rarely darker), with cross-lines defining a darker central cross-band; thorax and legs are very furry. Female is larger; area between central cross-lines is usually same colour as rest of wing. Flies May–Jun. **LARVA** is yellow,

Pale Tussock, f. *concolor*

LS

larva

with lateral bristles, a red tuft of hairs at tail end, and tufts of rich yellow hairs on 4 segments at head end; feeds on Hop and deciduous shrubs. **STATUS** Widespread and locally common in central and S Britain.

Dark Tussock *Dicallomera fascelina* 72.016 (2027) 35–45mm
ADULT is similar to Pale Tussock, but typically darker grey and with dark cross-lines edged with orange-red; thorax and legs are very furry. Flies Jul–Aug. **LARVA** is grey-brown, with lateral bristles, tuft of hairs at tail end, and tufts of black-tipped white hairs on 5 segments at head end; feeds on Heather, Broom and related plants. **STATUS** Widespread but local, on heaths in S England and moors in N Britain.

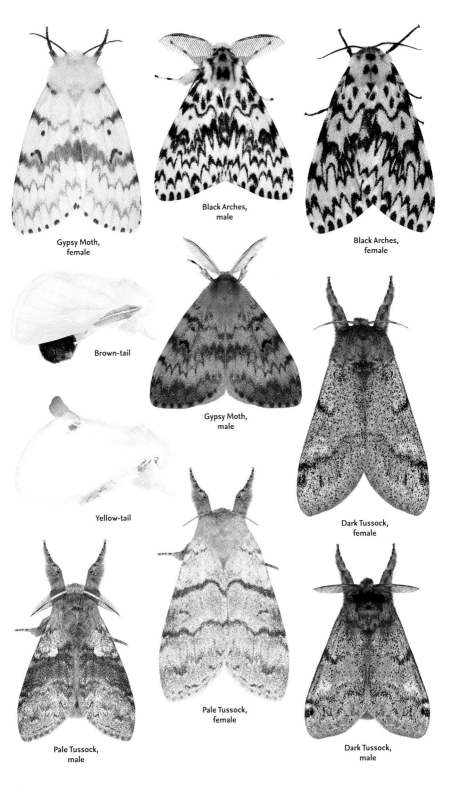

Gypsy Moth,
female

Black Arches,
male

Black Arches,
female

Brown-tail

Gypsy Moth,
male

Dark Tussock,
female

Yellow-tail

Pale Tussock,
male

Pale Tussock,
female

Dark Tussock,
male

Vapourer
Orgyia antiqua 72.017
(2026) 25–30mm (male)
ADULT male flies by
day, as well as night.
Forewings are broadly
triangular and rich
brown, with darker cross-

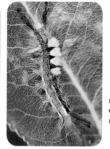

FAR LEFT: **female with egg cluster;** LEFT: **larva**

lines and a black-framed white spot near trailing
corner. Flies Jul–Sep. Female is grey, furry and
flightless, with tiny wing stumps. **LARVA** is
colourful and hairy, with tufts of yellow and red
hairs; feeds on deciduous trees. **STATUS**
Widespread, commonest in the S.

Scarce Vapourer *Orgyia recens*
72.018 (2025) 35–40mm (male)
ADULT male flies by day. Forewings are broadly
triangular, similar overall to Vapourer but with
additional orange and white spots near tip, and
white-framed dark patches on leading edge and
at base. Flies Jun–Jul. Female is brown, furry and
flightless, with only tiny wing stumps. **LARVA** is

LEFT: **Scarce Vapourer, female**

hairy and colourful, with 4 prominent dorsal tufts of orange hairs;
feeds on Hawthorn and other shrubs. **STATUS** Rare and local, restricted
to a few locations in E England.

Buff Ermine *Spilosoma luteum* 72.019 (2061) 30–40mm
ADULT is variable, but typically forewings are buffish yellow with rows
of black dots; thorax is very furry. In some forms wings are very pale; in
others (very rare in the wild) black markings are more extensive, forming
streaks or consolidating around wing borders. Flies May–Jul. **LARVA** has
a pale lateral line and long orange-brown hairs; feeds on a wide range
of herbaceous plants and shrubs. **STATUS** Widespread and common,
especially in central and S Britain.

White Ermine
Spilosoma lubricipeda 72.020 (2060) 35–45mm
ADULT is typically white, the forewings with
a variable scattering of black dots; thorax is
furry, hindwings have a central black spot,
and abdomen is yellow and black above.
In Scotland and Ireland, pale buff forms are
encountered. Flies May–Jul. **LARVA** is dark and

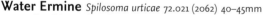

hairy with a reddish dorsal line; feeds on herbaceous plants. **STATUS**
Widespread and locally common.

Water Ermine *Spilosoma urticae* 72.021 (2062) 40–45mm
ADULT is white with a few small black spots on forewings; thorax is very
furry, and hindwings lack central black spot (seen in White Ermine). Flies
Jun–Jul. **LARVA** is hairy and grey-buff, with dorsal lines of black spots;
feeds on wetland plants, including Water Mint and Water Dock. **STATUS**
Scarce and local, mainly in coastal S and SE England.

Muslin Moth *Diaphora mendica* 72.022 (2063) 30–35mm
ADULT male is grey-brown with dark spots. Female is white, with black
spots on its diaphanous forewings; thorax is white. Flies Apr–Jun. **LARVA**
is grey with reddish-brown hairs; feeds on low-growing plants. **STATUS**
Widespread in central and S Britain.

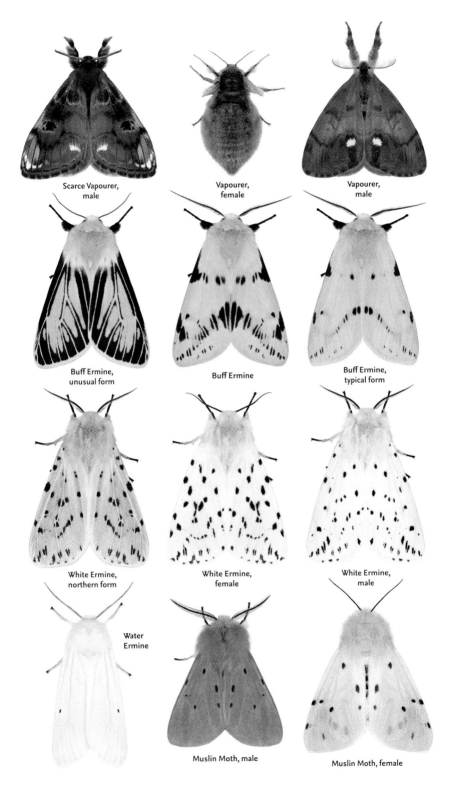

Scarce Vapourer, male

Vapourer, female

Vapourer, male

Buff Ermine, unusual form

Buff Ermine

Buff Ermine, typical form

White Ermine, northern form

White Ermine, female

White Ermine, male

Water Ermine

Muslin Moth, male

Muslin Moth, female

Clouded Buff *Diacrisia sannio* 72.023 (2059) 35–50mm

ADULT male is active in sunshine as well as after dark; forewings are rich orange-yellow with a pinkish-red margin and red central spot. Female is nocturnal, smaller than male, and dull orange with darker red veins. Flies Jun–Jul. **LARVA** is hairy and dark brown with a yellow dorsal stripe; feeds on Heather and related plants. **STATUS** Widespread but local, restricted to heaths and moors throughout.

LS

Ruby Tiger *Phragmatobia fuliginosa* 72.024 (2064) 30–35mm

LS

ADULT typically has deep pinkish-brown forewings and a furry thorax; abdomen is red with a dark dorsal line, and hindwings are pink with a dark submarginal band. Northern ssp. *borealis* is darker overall with mainly blue-grey hindwings. Double-brooded in the S: flies Apr–Jun, and Aug–Sep. **LARVA** is dark brown and very hairy; feeds on herbaceous plants. **STATUS** Widespread and locally common.

Wood Tiger *Parasemia plantaginis* 72.025 (2056) 34–38mm

ADULT male is often active in sunshine as well as at night. Both sexes have black forewings with an extensive and variable white pattern. Hindwings are typically yellow with variable black markings that are more extensive in female than male; in N, male sometimes has white hindwing ground colour (form *hospita*). Flies May–Jul. **LARVA** is dark with black and brown hairs; feeds on low-growing plants. **STATUS** Widespread but local; commonest in W and N Britain.

LS

Garden Tiger, larva

LS

Garden Tiger, dark form

Garden Tiger *Arctia caja* 72.026 (2057) 45–65mm

ADULT has very variably patterned white and chocolate-brown forewings; hindwings are orange with very variable blue spots. Thorax is furry and brown with a red band, and abdomen is mainly orange. Flies Jul–Aug. **LARVA** is reddish and black, with very long hairs; feeds on a wide range of low-growing plants. **STATUS** Widespread; still locally common but has declined greatly in gardens and suburbia generally.

Cream-spot Tiger *Arctia villica* 72.027 (2058) 45–60mm

ADULT has black forewings with variable white markings; hindwings are yellow with variable black spots. Thorax is black with white lateral bands, and abdomen is yellow, flushed red towards tip. Flies May–Jun. **LARVA** is hairy and black, with red 'feet'; feeds on a range of low-growing plants. **STATUS** Local and restricted to open grassy habitats in S England and SE Wales; commonest in coastal areas.

Clouded Buff, female

Clouded Buff, male

Ruby Tiger, ssp. *borealis*

Garden Tiger

Ruby Tiger

Wood Tiger, female

Wood Tiger, male

Garden Tiger

Wood Tiger

Cream-spot Tiger

Cream-spot Tiger

Scarlet Tiger

Callimorpha dominula 72.029 (2068) 45–55mm
ADULT flies by day as well as at dusk. Forewings are black with a metallic green sheen and variable white spots; hindwings are typically red with variable black spots; in very rare form *rossica*, hindwing ground colour is yellow. Flies May–Jun. **LARVA** is black and yellow, and bristly; feeds on comfreys. **STATUS** Locally common in S and SW England and W Wales, favouring marshes and water meadows.

f. bimaculata

LS

Jersey Tiger

Euplagia quadripunctaria 72.030 (2067) 45–50mm
ADULT flies by day as well as at night. Forewings are black with broad creamy-white bands. Hindwings are pinkish red with variable black spots; in form *lutescens*, hindwing ground colour is yellow. Flies Jul–Sep. **LARVA** is brown and bristly, with a lateral row of white spots; feeds on herbaceous plants. **STATUS** Locally common in SW England; range has expanded E recently, and it is now found along the S coast and in London.

f. lutescens

LS

Cinnabar

Tyria jacobaeae 72.031 (2069) 35–40mm
ADULT is sometimes active in daytime. Forewings are sooty grey with red spots on margin and red stripe along leading edge. Hindwings are red. In rare form *flavescens*, red coloration is replaced by yellow. Flies May–Jul. **LARVA** is bristly with orange and black stripes; feeds on Ragwort. **STATUS** Widespread and locally common, although absent from much of N Scotland.

larva

LS

Speckled Footman

Coscinia cribraria 72.032 (2053) 30–35mm
ADULT rests in the manner of some micromoths, with wings wrapped around body. Forewings of ssp. *bivittata* are white with variable brown spotting and dark streaks. Flies Jul–Aug. **LARVA** feeds on low-growing plants. **STATUS** Very rare resident of Dorset heaths; immigrant elsewhere (much paler ssp. *arenaria*).

Speckled Footman

LS

LS

Feathered Footman

Coscinia striata 72.033 (2052) 30–35mm
ADULT is day-flying and rests with wings wrapped around body. Forewings are yellow with variable black streaks (many aligning with veins) and a black margin. Male has feathery antennae. Flies May–Aug. **LARVA** feeds on low-growing plants. **STATUS** Very rare immigrant from mainland Europe.

Feathered Footman

Crimson Speckled

LS

Crimson Speckled

Utetheisa pulchella 72.034 (2054) 30–40mm
ADULT is day-flying. Forewings are white with numerous black and red spots. Flies Jul–Oct. **LARVA** feeds on low-growing plants. **STATUS** Very rare immigrant from mainland Europe.

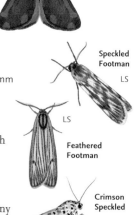

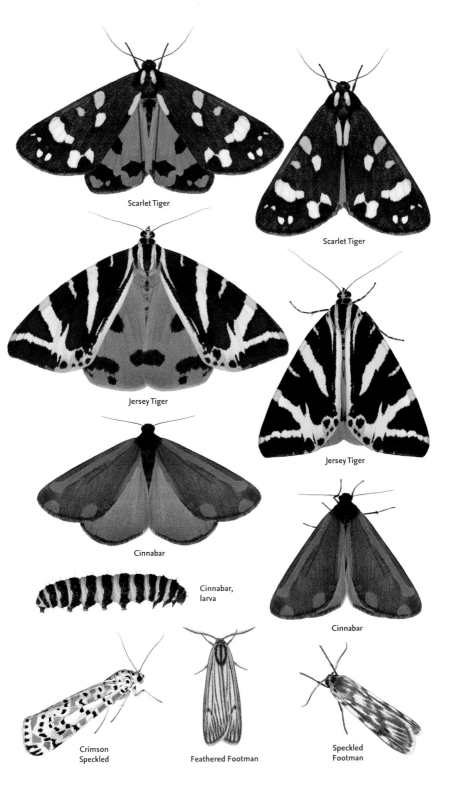

Scarlet Tiger

Scarlet Tiger

Jersey Tiger

Jersey Tiger

Cinnabar

Cinnabar, larva

Cinnabar

Crimson Speckled

Feathered Footman

Speckled Footman

Rosy Footman
Miltochrista miniata
72.035 (2037) 25–27mm
ADULT forewings are broad with a curved leading edge; typically pinkish orange (rarely yellow) with a wavy black cross-line and black dots. Flies Jul–Aug. **LARVA** is brown and hairy; feeds on lichens growing on trees. **STATUS** Locally common in S Britain.

Muslin Footman *Nudaria mundana* 72.036 (2038) 20–22mm
ADULT forewings are broad and rounded; diaphanous grey-buff, with darker central cross-lines and a central spot. Flies Jun–Aug. **LARVA** is bristly and dark with a dorsal row of yellow spots; feeds on lichens growing on stone walls, weathered fences and the like. **STATUS** Widespread; commonest in the W.

Round-winged Muslin *Thumatha senex* 72.037 (2035) 15–20mm
ADULT forewings are broad and rounded; diaphanous buff, with 2 rows of black dots and a central black spot. Flies Jul–Aug. **LARVA** feeds on lichens. **STATUS** Widespread but local, mainly in central and S Britain.

Four-dotted Footman *Cybosia mesomella* 72.038 (2040) 25–30mm
ADULT forewings are usually greyish white, with a yellow margin and a black dot on both leading and trailing edges (because forewings overlap at rest, only 3 dots are visible in life); in form *flava*, forewings are uniformly orange-yellow. Flies Jun–Aug. **LARVA** feeds on epiphytic algae and lichens. **STATUS** Widespread but local on heaths and dry habitats.

Dotted Footman *Pelosia muscerda* 72.039 (2041) 26–28mm
ADULT forewings are grey-buff with an indistinct row and a central pair of dark dots. Flies Jul–Aug. **LARVA** feeds on epiphytic tree algae. **STATUS** Scarce and local, restricted mostly to the Norfolk Broads.

Small Dotted Footman *Pelosia obtusa* 72.040 (2042) 23–25mm
ADULT forewings are broad and rounded; grey-buff with a sharply angled row of black spots. Flies Jun–Jul. **LARVA** feeds on algae growing on fallen wood. **STATUS** Rare; Norfolk Broads only.

Four-spotted Footman
Lithosia quadra
72.041 (2051) 40–55mm
ADULT male has mostly grey forewings; wing base, thorax and head are yellow. Female is yellow, the forewings with a bold black spot on both leading and trailing edges (because wings overlap at rest, only 3 spots are visible in life). Flies Jul–Sep. **LARVA** is bristly, and black with red spots; feeds on epiphytic tree lichens. **STATUS** Locally common only in S and SW Britain.

LS

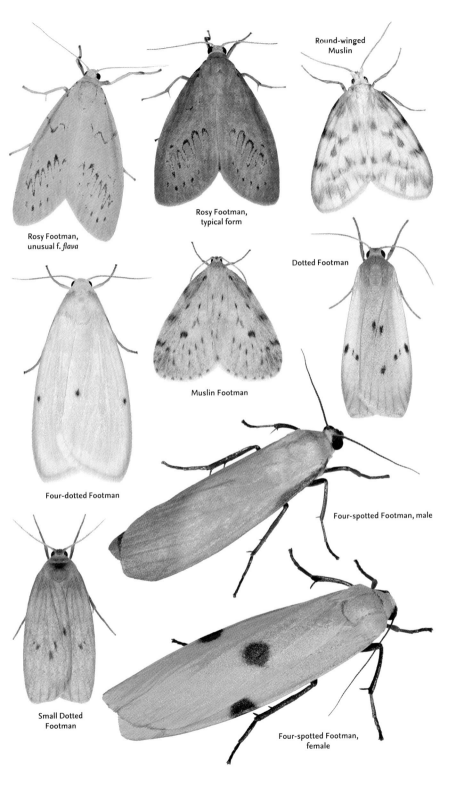

Rosy Footman,
unusual f. *flava*

Rosy Footman,
typical form

Round-winged
Muslin

Dotted Footman

Muslin Footman

Four-dotted Footman

Four-spotted Footman, male

Small Dotted
Footman

Four-spotted Footman,
female

Red-necked Footman *Atolmis rubricollis* 72.042 (2039) 25–35mm

ADULT is sometimes active in daytime but also flies after dark. Forewings and thorax are dark, sooty grey except for the bold orange-red 'collar' behind head; underside of abdomen is marked with yellow. Flies Jun–Jul. **LARVA** feeds on lichens and algae that are epiphytic on trees. **STATUS** Widespread but local; commonest in woodland in W Britain.

Buff Footman *Eilema depressa* 72.043 (2049) 30–34mm

ADULT male has grey-buff forewings with a yellowish margin; hindwings are pale buff with a dark margin. Female's forewings are buffish grey with an orange border on leading edge; hindwings are grey-buff. In unusual form *unicolor*, forewings are uniformly buffish yellow. Flies Jul–Aug. **LARVA** feeds on algae and lichens that are epiphytic on trees. **STATUS** Locally common in central and S Britain.

Dingy Footman *Eilema griseola* 72.044 (2044) 34–38mm

ADULT is similar to Buff Footman but forewings are broader and rounded, their appearance enhanced by curved leading edge; hindwings are grey-brown. Forewings are typically grey with an orange-yellow leading edge; in unusual form *stramineola*, forewings are uniform yellow-buff. Flies Jul–Aug. **LARVA** feeds on lichens. **STATUS** Locally common in central and S Britain.

Common Footman, larva

Common Footman
Eilema lurideola
72.045 (2050) 30–34mm

ADULT rests with wings flattish or at most only slightly rolled around body. Forewings are grey except for tapering yellow stripe on leading edge; hindwings are yellow-buff. Flies Jul–Aug. **LARVA** feeds on lichens. **STATUS** Widespread and locally common, although very local in Scotland.

Scarce Footman *Eilema complana* 72.046 (2047) 30–34mm

ADULT rests with wings tightly rolled around body. Forewings are grey with a yellow stripe of even width on leading edge, extending down outer margin; hindwings are yellow-buff. Flies Jul–Aug. **LARVA** feeds on lichens. **STATUS** Locally common only in S Britain. **SIMILAR SPECIES Northern Footman** *E. complana* f. *sericea*, 72.046 (2048), 30–34mm, is very similar to Scarce Footman (treated here as a form of that species), but differs in having a grey leading edge to hindwings. Confined to N Britain.

Scarce Footman, wings

Northern Footman, wings

Dew Moth *Setina irrorella*
72.050 (2036) 28–32mm

ADULT flies by day as well as at night. Forewings are rich yellow with 3 rows of black dots. Flies Jun–Jul. **LARVA** feeds on lichens growing on rocks and stabilised shingle. **STATUS** Very local; with a few exceptions, most populations are coastal, scattered from S England to W Wales and W Scotland.

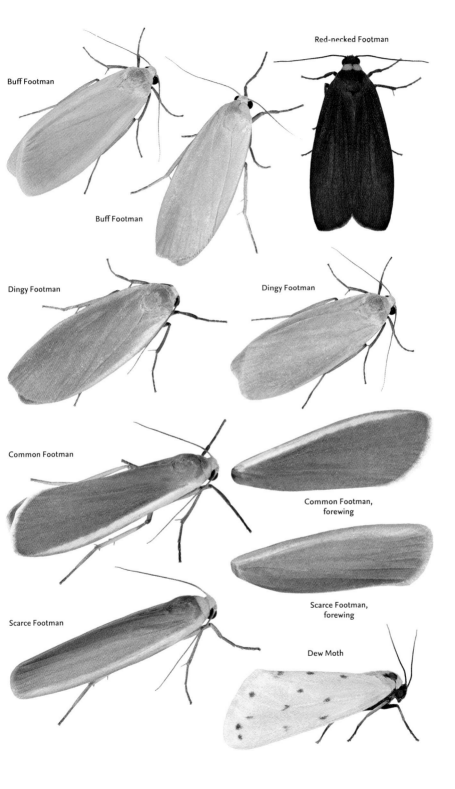

Buff Footman

Red-necked Footman

Buff Footman

Dingy Footman

Dingy Footman

Common Footman

Common Footman, forewing

Scarce Footman, forewing

Scarce Footman

Dew Moth

Hoary Footman *Eilema caniola* 72.047 (2045) 30–34mm
ADULT rests with wings rolled tightly around body. Forewings are narrow and pale grey with a pale yellow stripe along leading edge (stripe is white in unusual form *lacteola*). Flies Jul–Sep. **LARVA** feeds on lichens growing on rocks and stones. **STATUS** Confined to S Britain; most populations are coastal.

Pigmy Footman *Eilema pygmaeola* 72.048 (2046) 26–28mm
ADULT rests with wings rolled tightly around body. Forewings are pale grey in ssp. *pygmaeola*, yellow in ssp. *pallifrons*; hindwings are pale yellow with a dark leading edge in both sspp. Flies Jul–Aug. **LARVA** feeds on lichens. **STATUS** Rare, confined to coastal shingle and dunes, mainly in Kent and East Anglia; ssp. *pallifrons* is found at Dungeness, Kent.

Orange Footman *Eilema sororcula* 72.049 (2043) 28–30mm
ADULT forewings are orange-yellow, their rounded appearance enhanced by curved outer half to leading edge. Flies May–Jun. **LARVA** feeds on lichens that are epiphytic on oaks and Beech. **STATUS** Locally common in S Britain, particularly in woodland in SE England.

Orange Footman

Blackneck

Blackneck *Lygephila pastinum* 72.063 (2466) 38–40mm
ADULT has marbled grey-buff forewings with fine patterning and a narrow black kidney-shaped mark; top of head and 'collar' at front of thorax are black. Flies Jun–Jul. **LARVA** feeds on Tufted Vetch. **STATUS** Local in central and S Britain.

Scarce Blackneck *Lygephila craccae* 72.064 (2467) 40–44mm
ADULT is similar to Blackneck, but forewings have pale veins and 4 dark marks on leading edge, and kidney-shaped mark reduced to dark spots. Flies Jul–Aug. **LARVA** feeds on Wood Vetch and related plants. **STATUS** Scarce and local, confined mainly to N Devon coast.

Pinion-streaked Snout *Schrankia costaestrigalis* 72.061 (2484) 18–20mm
ADULT could be confused with a micromoth species. Forewings are narrow and grey-buff or brown with a dark-edged pale oblique outer central cross-line, and a dark central streak. Flies Jul–Sep. **LARVA** feeds on wetland plants. **STATUS** Widespread but scarce and local, probably overlooked; favours damp meadows.

White-line Snout *Schrankia taenialis* 72.062 (2482) 20–22mm
ADULT could be confused with a micromoth species. Forewings are broader than those of Pinion-streaked, and grey-brown with a dark-edged white cross-line. Flies Jul–Aug. **LARVA** feeds on wetland plants. **STATUS** Scarce and local; wetland habitats in S Britain.

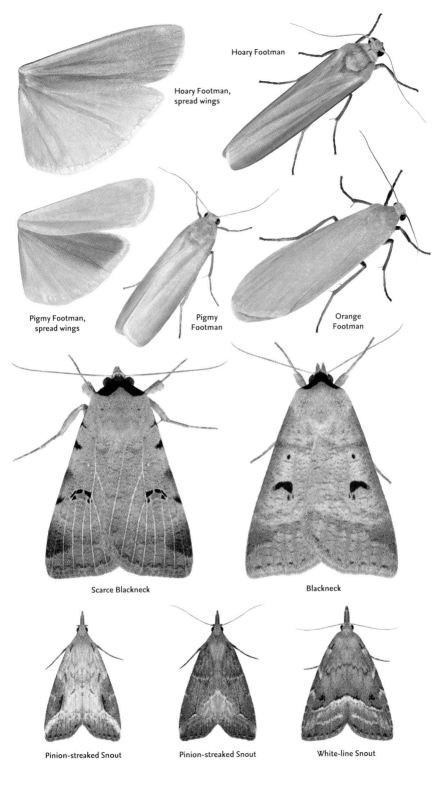

Hoary Footman

Hoary Footman, spread wings

Pigmy Footman, spread wings

Pigmy Footman

Orange Footman

Scarce Blackneck

Blackneck

Pinion-streaked Snout

Pinion-streaked Snout

White-line Snout

Marsh Oblique-barred *Hypenodes humidalis* 72.060 (2485) 15mm
ADULT is tiny and easily confused with a micromoth species. Forewings
are grey-buff with oblique dark cross-lines, the outermost reaching
wingtip. Flies Jun–Aug. LARVA feeds on sedges and rushes. STATUS
Widespread but very local on heaths and moors.

Clay Fan-foot *Paracolax tristalis* 72.051 (2494) 30–34mm
ADULT has triangular buffish-brown forewings with 2 dark central
cross-lines, the outer one curving strongly towards leading edge.
Flies Jul–Aug. LARVA feeds on oaks. STATUS Scarce and local, mainly
in SE England; rare immigrant elsewhere.

Dotted Fan-foot *Macrochilo cribrumalis* 72.052 (2493) 28–30mm
ADULT has triangular, pale grey-buff forewings with 2 cross-rows of dark
dots and a central black spot. Flies Jun–Aug. LARVA feeds on grasses and
sedges. STATUS Scarce and local; East Anglia is its stronghold.

Fan-foot *Herminia tarsipennalis* 72.053 (2489) 32–34mm
ADULT has triangular brown forewings with 3 dark cross-lines, the inner
one curving gently, the middle one resembling a question mark and the
outer one straight. Outer margin has a series of dark dashes. Flies Jun–
Jul. LARVA feeds on trees and shrubs. STATUS Widespread
and locally common in central and S Britain.

Shaded Fan-foot *Herminia tarsicrinalis* 72.054 (2491) 30–32mm
ADULT has triangular buffish-brown forewings with 3 dark cross-lines,
the inner one curving strongly towards leading edge, the middle one
resembling a jagged question mark and the outer one straight. Outer
margin has a dark line (not dashes). Flies Jun–Jul. LARVA feeds on
withered leaves of Bramble. STATUS Rare, restricted to Bramble
patches on open ground in East Anglia.

Small Fan-foot

Small
Fan-foot

Small Fan-foot *Herminia grisealis* 72.055 (2492) 24–26mm
ADULT has grey-brown forewings with 3 dark cross-lines, the inner one straight, the
middle one sharply angled and the outer one curved, reaching wingtip. Flies Jun–Aug.
LARVA feeds on withered tree leaves. STATUS Widespread and locally common.

Common Fan-foot *Pechipogo strigilata* 72.056 (2488) 30–35mm
ADULT has grey-buff forewings with 3 cross-lines (often indistinct), the
inner one sharply angled towards leading edge, the middle one jagged
and the outer one straightish. Flies May–Jun. LARVA feeds on withered
tree leaves. STATUS Scarce; S England only.

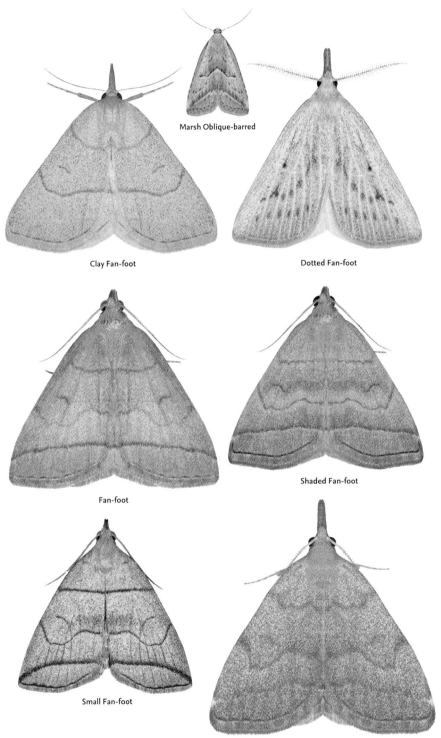

Marsh Oblique-barred

Clay Fan-foot

Dotted Fan-foot

Fan-foot

Shaded Fan-foot

Small Fan-foot

Common Fan-foot

Waved Black

Waved Black
Parascotia fuliginaria
72.066 (2475) 20–25mm

L

ADULT rests with wings spread flat; they are sooty black, stippled and marbled with buff, and with wavy buff cross-lines and a pale patch near trailing corners. Flies Jun–Aug. **LARVA** feeds on bracket fungi. **STATUS** Local, mainly in SE England and Welsh/English border counties.

Small Purple-barred
Phytometra viridaria
72.067 (2470) 18–20mm

L

ADULT flies by day as well as after dark. Forewings are yellow-buff with pinkish-purple outer cross-bands and leading edge; hindwings have a dull purple outer margin. Flies May–Jul. **LARVA** feeds on milkworts. **STATUS** Widespread and locally common, on heaths and chalk downs; commonest in the S.

Beautiful Hook-tip
Laspeyria flexula
72.069 (2473) 24–26mm
ADULT has hook-tipped forewings, grey with dark speckling, 2 dark-edged pale cross-lines and a reddish patch near wingtip. Flies Jun–Aug. **LARVA** feeds on lichens that are epiphytic on trees. **STATUS** Locally common only in S Britain.

Beautiful Hook-tip

Olive Crescent

L

Olive Crescent
Trisateles emortualis
72.070 (2495) 30–34mm

L

ADULT has buff wings; hindwings have 1 pale cross-line, while forewings have 2 pale cross-lines and a pale central crescent. Flies Jun–Jul. **LARVA** feeds on withered and fallen leaves of oaks and Beech. **STATUS** Rare, resident in a few woodland sites in SE England; very rare immigrant elsewhere.

Purple Marbled *Eublemma ostrina* 72.072 (2407) 20–24mm
ADULT has pointed buff forewings, with a broad, marbled purple and brown outer half, and a dark-edged pale jagged cross-line near margin. Flies May–Oct. **LARVA** feeds on flowers and seeds of Carline Thistle. **STATUS** Rare immigrant from mainland Europe.

LS

Small Marbled *Eublemma parva* 72.073 (2408) 15–17mm
ADULT is tiny; forewings are buff with 2 jagged central cross-lines, the inner one defining darker reddish-brown inner half to wing. Flies Jun–Jul. **LARVA** feeds on Common Fleabane and Ploughman's-spikenard. **STATUS** Rare immigrant from mainland Europe.

LS

Beautiful Marbled *Eublemma purpurina* 72.074 (2409a) 22–24mm
ADULT has yellow-buff inner half to forewings, and a pink outer half with a purple oblique cross-line running from tip. Flies Jun–Aug. **LARVA** feeds on thistles. **STATUS** Very rare immigrant.

LS

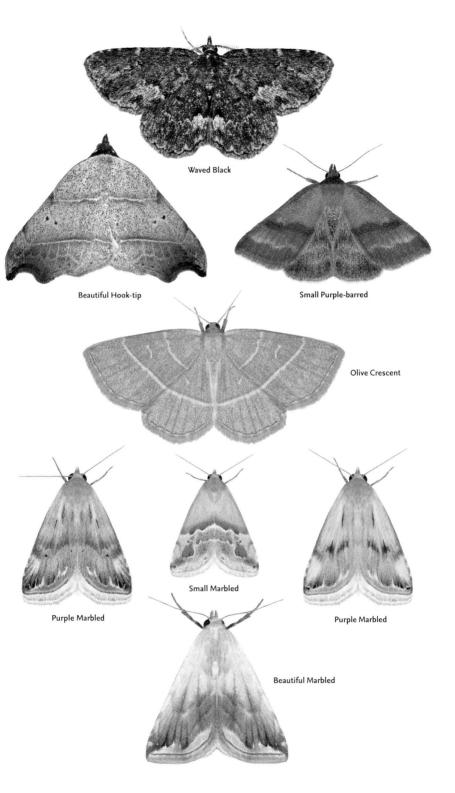

Waved Black

Beautiful Hook-tip

Small Purple-barred

Olive Crescent

Purple Marbled

Small Marbled

Purple Marbled

Beautiful Marbled

Oak Yellow Underwing
Catocala nymphagoga 72.075 (2455a) 38–42mm
ADULT has grey-brown forewings with dark speckling and cross-lines; hindwings are usually concealed, but when moth is agitated it reveals yellow coloration with a broad dark margin and cross-band. Flies Jul–Aug. **LARVA** feeds on oaks. **STATUS** Very rare immigrant from mainland Europe.

Red Underwing
Catocala nupta 72.078 (2452) 65–75mm
ADULT has grey wings with dark speckling, and jagged, dark-edged pale cross-lines. Hindwings (usually concealed except when moth is agitated) are pinkish red with a dark margin and dark cross-band that is strongly curved and tapering, almost reaching trailing edge. Flies Aug–Sep. **LARVA** feeds on willows and poplars. **STATUS** The commonest of the 'red' underwings. Widespread and locally common in central and S Britain, although absent from the W.

Red Underwing

Rosy Underwing
Catocala electa 72.079 (2453) 65–75mm
ADULT has grey forewings with only limited dark speckling; dark cross-lines are bold, the outer one with a paired projection. Hindwings (usually concealed except when moth is agitated) are rosy pink with a dark margin and a kinked, abruptly truncated cross-band. Flies Jul–Sep. **LARVA** feeds on sallows and poplars. **STATUS** Very rare immigrant from mainland Europe.

Dark Crimson Underwing
Catocala sponsa 72.081 (2455) 60–70mm
ADULT has dark grey-brown forewings with dark speckling and subtle dark-edged pale cross-lines. Hindwings (usually concealed except when moth is agitated) are pinkish red with a dark margin and relatively narrow, tapering dark cross-band that is kinked like the letter 'W'. Flies Aug–Sep. **LARVA** feeds on oaks. **STATUS** Rare and local in S England; New Forest, Hampshire, is the species' stronghold.

Light Crimson Underwing
Catocala promissa 72.082 (2454) 60–65mm
ADULT is similar to Dark Crimson Underwing but forewings are paler, with bands of grey and jagged, bold, dark-edged white cross-lines. Hindwings are pinkish red with a dark margin and relatively narrow, tapering dark cross-band that is wavy rather than sharply kinked. Flies Jul–Aug. **LARVA** feeds on oaks. **STATUS** Rare and local in S England; New Forest, Hampshire, is the species' stronghold.

Red Underwing

Red Underwing

Rosy Underwing

Rosy Underwing

Dark Crimson Underwing

Dark Crimson Underwing

Light Crimson Underwing

Light Crimson Underwing

Clifden Nonpareil

Catocala fraxini 72.076 (2451) 80–90mm

ADULT is large and impressive, the grey forewings with dark speckling and jagged, dark-edged white cross-lines. Hindwings (usually concealed except when moth is agitated) are black with a white margin and pale lilac-blue cross-band. Flies Aug–Oct. **LARVA** feeds on Aspen. **STATUS** Rare immigrant from mainland Europe.

LS

Burnet Companion

Euclidia glyphica 72.083 (2463) 25–30mm

ADULT is day-flying. Forewings are grey-brown with dark cross-bands and a squarish dark patch on leading edge, near tip. Hindwing inner half is brown; outer half is orange-yellow with a dark band and veins. Flies May–Jul. **LARVA** feeds on clovers and trefoils. **STATUS** Widespread in central and S Britain, but common only in the S.

LS

Mother Shipton *Callistege mi* 72.084 (2462)

25–30mm

ADULT is day-flying. Forewings are grey-brown, with a white-edged dark marking that bears a fanciful resemblance to the head of the eponymous witch, complete with eye. Hindwings are brown with pale bands. Flies May–Jun. **LARVA** feeds on clovers and grasses. **STATUS** Widespread but locally common only in central and S Britain.

LS

Lunar Double-stripe *Minucia lunaris*

72.086 (2456) 55–60mm

ADULT forewings are grey-buff with 2 pale yellow cross-lines containing a dark compressed kidney-shaped mark. Hindwings have a burnished sheen and dark central band. Flies May–Jun. **LARVA** feeds on oaks. **STATUS** Scarce immigrant from mainland Europe.

LS

Passenger *Dysgonia algira* 72.087 (2460)

40–45mm

ADULT has broad triangular forewings that are reddish brown and boldly marked with a pinkish-white cross-band and outer margin; the latter contains a dark wedge at tip. Hindwings are brown with a pale cross-band. Flies Jun–Aug. **LARVA** feeds on sallows and Bramble. **STATUS** Very rare immigrant from S Europe. **SIMILAR SPECIES Geometrician** *Grammodes stolida*, 72.088 (2461), 40–45mm, has narrower wings and 2 whitish cross-lines, the inner one straight and the outer one scalloped. Very rare immigrant from S Europe.

LS

Burnet Companion

Clifden Nonpareil

Burnet Companion

Mother Shipton

Passenger

Lunar Double-stripe

Spectacle *Abrostola tripartita* 73.001 (2450) 28–30mm

LS

ADULT seen head on, has 2 circles of pale hairs that fancifully resemble a pair of spectacles. Forewings are grey with a dark central cross-band. Double-brooded in the S: flies Jun–Jul, and Sep. **LARVA** feeds on Common Nettle. **STATUS** Widespread and locally common.

Dark Spectacle

Dark Spectacle

LS

Dark Spectacle *Abrostola triplasia* 73.002 (2449) 28–30mm
ADULT is similar to Spectacle but base of wing and thorax are reddish buff and dark central band is defined by reddish-brown cross-lines. Flies Jun–Jul. **LARVA** feeds on Common Nettle. **STATUS** Widespread and locally common in central and S Britain.

Ni Moth *Trichoplusia ni* 73.003 (2432) 34–38mm

LS

ADULT is similar to both Silver Y and Scarce Silver Y (p. 230); compared to former, has 2 white markings (not a single Y); compared to latter, forewings are paler and more intricately patterned. Flies Jul–Sep. **LARVA** feeds on Sea Rocket and other herbaceous plants. **STATUS** Scarce immigrant from S Europe.

Slender Burnished Brass *Thysanoplusia orichalcea* 73.004 (2433) 38–42mm

LS

ADULT forewings are brown with a narrow curved, metallic golden patch; head and front of thorax are reddish orange. Flies Aug–Oct. **LARVA** feeds on low-growing plants. **STATUS** Rare immigrant from S Europe.

Scar Bank Gem *Ctenoplusia limberina* 73.005 (2430) 40–45mm

LS

ADULT is similar to Silver Y (p. 228), but ornate forewings usually have a purple sheen and white marking is a subtly different shape; compressed kidney-shaped pink mark near middle of outer margin is a good identification feature. Flies Jun–Sep. **LARVA** feeds on low-growing plants. **STATUS** Rare immigrant from S Europe.

Golden Twin-spot *Chrysodeixis chalcites* 73.008 (2428) 35–40mm

LS

ADULT forewings are marbled grey-brown and reddish buff, with 2 pale cross-lines and 2 pale, metallic gold spots. Flies Sep–Oct. **LARVA** feeds on Viper's-bugloss. **STATUS** Rare immigrant from S Europe.

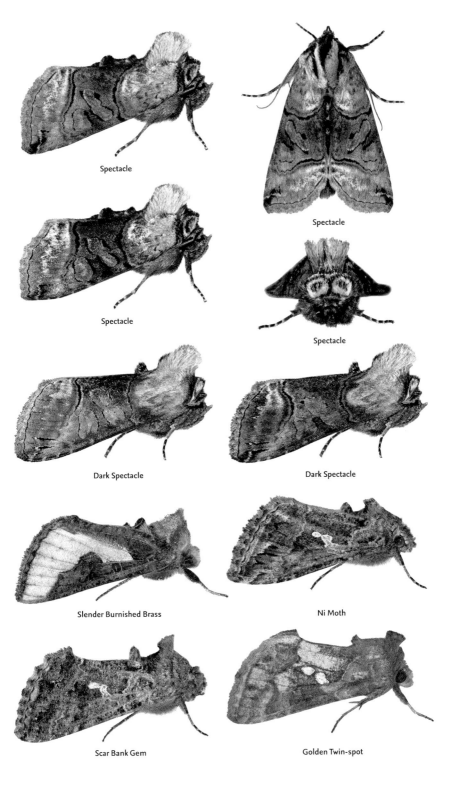

Spectacle

Spectacle

Spectacle

Spectacle

Dark Spectacle

Dark Spectacle

Slender Burnished Brass

Ni Moth

Scar Bank Gem

Golden Twin-spot

Dewick's Plusia *Macdunnoughia confusa* 73.010 (2436) 34–38mm
ADULT is pinkish buff to grey-buff, the trailing half of central
band on forewings reddish orange, defined on inner edge and
leading margin by a bold white line. Flies Jul–Oct. **LARVA** feeds
on Common Nettle. **STATUS** Rare immigrant from S Europe.

L

Scarce Burnished Brass *Diachrysia chryson* 73.011 (2435)
46–52mm
ADULT forewings are rich reddish brown with a squarish,
metallic yellow patch near tip (much less extensive than in
Burnished Brass). Flies Jul–Aug. **LARVA** feeds on Hemp-agrimony.
STATUS Scarce and very local, mainly in S Hampshire and SW Wales.

L

Burnished Brass *Diachrysia chrysitis* 73.012 (2434) 30–34mm
ADULT forewings are grey-buff with a variable area of metallic
yellow, much more extensive in typical form *juncta* than in form
aurea. Double-brooded: flies Jun–Jul, and Sep. **LARVA** feeds on
Common Nettle. **STATUS** Widespread and locally common.

L

FAR LEFT:
Burnished Brass
LEFT: Silver Y

Silver Y *Autographa gamma* 73.015 (2441) 35–40mm
ADULT forewings have a bold 'Y' marking in all individuals;
forewing colour is variable but typically marbled grey and
brown, with pale cross-lines; in rare form *nigricans*, forewings are
uniformly dark. Flies May–Sep. **LARVA** feeds on low-growing
plants. **STATUS** Immigrant from S Europe; very common in some years.

LS

Beautiful Golden Y

Beautiful Golden Y
Autographa pulchrina
73.016 (2442) 35–40mm
ADULT forewings are marbled
reddish brown and pinkish buff,
the central cross-band usually darker and defined by pale
cross-lines; central white markings comprise a 'V' and a
spot. Kidney mark is obvious and partly outlined in pale
yellow. Flies Jun–Jul. **LARVA** feeds on low-growing plants.
STATUS Widespread and locally common.

LS

Plain Golden Y
Autographa jota
73.017 (2443) 40–44mm
ADULT forewings are pinkish
buff; the trailing half of the
central cross-band is a rich reddish brown and contains white markings that comprise
a 'V' and a spot. Compared to Beautiful Golden Y, forewing pattern is more uniform and
less ornate, and kidney mark is not obvious. Flies Jun–Aug. **LARVA** feeds on Common
Nettle and other herbaceous plants. **STATUS** Widespread and locally common.

LS

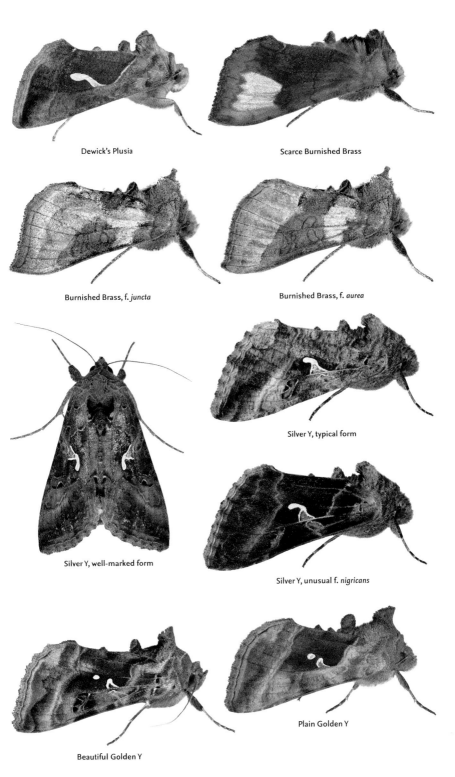

Dewick's Plusia

Scarce Burnished Brass

Burnished Brass, f. *juncta*

Burnished Brass, f. *aurea*

Silver Y, well-marked form

Silver Y, typical form

Silver Y, unusual f. *nigricans*

Beautiful Golden Y

Plain Golden Y

Golden Plusia *Polychrysia moneta* 73.014 (2437) 34–36mm

ADULT in profile has fan-like tufts of hair on thorax and projecting, recurved palps. Broad forewings are yellow-buff with grey outer and inner margins, and a bold white kidney mark (abutting, paired white circles). Flies Jun–Aug. **LARVA** feeds on delphiniums (native and cultivated). **STATUS** Widespread but local, mainly in the S.

 LS

Gold Spangle *Autographa bractea* 73.018 (2444) 38–40mm

ADULT forewings are grey-brown with a broad, rich reddish-brown central band on trailing half; this contains a large, pale metallic spot. Flies Jul–Aug. **LARVA** feeds on low-growing plants. **STATUS** Widespread and locally common in central and N Britain.

 LS

Stephens' Gem *Megalographa biloba* 73.019 (2445) 40–42mm.

ADULT recalls Gold Spangle but greyer overall, with contrasting orange-brown hue to trailing half of central cross-band; central white marking is double-lobed. **LARVA** feeds on low-growing plants. **STATUS** Very rare vagrant from N America.

 LS

Scarce Silver Y *Syngrapha interrogationis* 73.021 (2447) 36–38mm

ADULT recalls Silver Y (p. 228), but white marking is a different shape (more of a white squiggle than a Y, like a question mark and a spot), and wings are darker, marbled grey-brown and blackish. Flies Jun–Aug. **LARVA** feeds on Heather and Bilberry. **STATUS** Widespread but local on moors, mainly in N and W Britain.

 LS

Gold Spot *Plusia festucae* 73.022 (2439) 38–42mm

ADULT is orange and yellow-buff, the forewings with paired, pale metallic central spots and a tapering silvery streak near wingtip. Flies Jun–Sep. **LARVA** feeds on wetland plants. **STATUS** Widespread and locally common in marshes and river margins.

 LS

Lempke's Gold Spot *Plusia putnami* 73.023 (2440) 34–40mm

ADULT is similar to Gold Spot, the orange and yellow-buff forewings with paired, pale metallic central spots, but silvery streak near wingtip is rectangular, not tapering. Flies Jul–Aug. **LARVA** feeds on species of small-reed grasses. **STATUS** Widespread and locally common only in the N.

 LS

Marbled White Spot *Deltote pygarga* 73.024 (2410) 20–22mm

ADULT is grey-brown, the forewings with a broad dark central band and striking white patch near trailing corner. Flies May–Jul. **LARVA** feeds on Tufted Hair-grass, False Brome and Purple Moor-grass. **STATUS** Locally common in central and S Britain, favouring heaths and open woodland on acid soils.

 LS

Pretty Marbled *Deltote deceptoria* 73.025 (2411) 22–24mm

ADULT forewings are banded purple-brown and white. Flies May–Jun. **LARVA** feeds on grasses. **STATUS** Rare immigrant.

LS

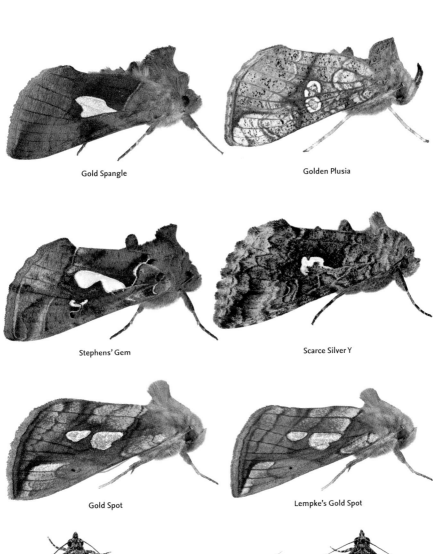

Gold Spangle

Golden Plusia

Stephens' Gem

Scarce Silver Y

Gold Spot

Lempke's Gold Spot

Marbled White Spot

Pretty Marbled

Marbled White Spot

Silver Hook *Deltote uncula* 73.026 (2412) 20–22mm
ADULT has grey-buff forewings with a broad, white-edged reddish-brown central band on trailing two-thirds of wing, indented with a grey-buff projection. Flies May–Jul. **LARVA** feeds on wetland sedges. **STATUS** Widespread but very local, restricted to bogs and fens.

LS

Silver Barred *Deltote bankiana* 73.027 (2413) 24–26mm
ADULT forewings are reddish brown with 2 broad diagonal white cross-lines and a pale margin. Flies Jun–Jul. **LARVA** feeds on Smooth Meadow-grass and Purple Moor-grass. **STATUS** Rare and very local, restricted to fens, bogs and marshes mainly in East Anglia.

LS

Pale Shoulder *Acontia lucida* 73.028 (2415) 28–30mm
ADULT forewings are marbled reddish purple and brown, with a creamy-white base (and thorax) and creamy-white patches on leading edge and trailing corner. Flies May–Aug. **LARVA** feeds on mallows and Field Bindweed. **STATUS** Rare immigrant from S Europe.

LS

Four-spotted *Tyta luctuosa* 73.031 (2465) 23–25mm
ADULT has marbled grey and brown forewings with a white patch on middle of leading edge; hindwings are black with a pale margin and white central cross-band. Flies May–Aug. **LARVA** feeds on Field Bindweed. **STATUS** Very scarce and local, restricted mainly to disturbed ground and open habitats with free-draining soils in E England.

LS

ABOVE: **Nut-tree Tussock**
BELOW: **Figure of Eight**

Nut-tree Tussock
Colocasia coryli
73.032 (2425) 28–32mm
ADULT is variable, its ground colour ranging from grey to brown. All forms typically have a broad, darker central cross-band containing a dark-framed, dark-centred pale spot; with wings seen together, these resemble a pair of eyes. Double-brooded in the S: flies Apr–Jun, and Aug–Sep. **LARVA** feeds on deciduous shrubs, notably Hazel and birches. **STATUS** Widespread; locally common in S Britain, absent from much of central Britain, and local and patchy in Scotland.

LS

Figure of Eight
Diloba caeruleocephala
73.033 (2020) 32–38mm
ADULT forewings are grey-buff, with a darker central cross-band that is defined by wavy black and white cross-lines and contains a dark-centred white marking resembling the number '8'. Flies Oct–Nov. **LARVA** is grey with bold black and yellow markings; feeds on Blackthorn and Hawthorn. **STATUS** Widespread and locally common in central and S Britain and Ireland.

Silver Barred

Silver Hook

Pale Shoulder

Four-spotted

Four-spotted

Pale Shoulder

Nut-tree Tussock

Nut-tree Tussock

Figure of Eight

Nut-tree Tussock

Scarce Merveille du Jour

Moma alpium 73.034 (2277) 30–35mm

ADULT is marbled bluish green, black and white – a good match for tree lichens. Flies Jun–Jul. **LARVA** is grey with orange hairs and orange and white spots; feeds on oaks. **STATUS** Very local in mature woodland; mainly the New Forest and SE England.

LS

Reed Dagger *Simyra albovenosa* 73.035 (2290) 34–38mm

ADULT is pale buff and recalls a wainscot (*Mythimna* spp.; pp. 294–6). Forewings have subtle dark speckling and dark lengthways streaks. Double-brooded: flies May–Jun, and Aug. **LARVA** feeds on Common Reed. **STATUS** Local, in reedbeds; mainly in East Anglia and SE England.

LS

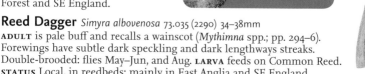

Alder Moth *Acronicta alni* 73.036 (2281) 34 36mm

ADULT is typically grey, the forewings with a dark trailing border and central cross-band; the latter often frames a central dark-centred spot. Much darker forms also occur. Flies May–Jun. **LARVA** is black and yellow when mature, with club-tipped hairs; feeds on Alder and birches. **STATUS** Locally common in central and S Britain.

LS

Dark Dagger *Acronicta tridens* 73.037 (2283) 36–44mm

ADULT is variably grey with dagger-like dark streaks and a wavy outer cross-line. Not reliably separable from Grey Dagger without examination of genitalia. Flies Jun–Jul. **LARVA** is black and hairy, with an orange and white dorsal line and red spots along flanks; feeds on Hawthorn and Blackthorn. **STATUS** Locally common in central and S Britain.

LS

Grey Dagger *Acronicta psi*

73.038 (2284) 34–40mm

Grey Dagger, larva

ADULT is variably grey with dagger-like dark streaks and a wavy outer cross-line. Not reliably separable from Dark Dagger without examining genitalia. Flies Jun–Jul. **LARVA** is very different from Dark Dagger: black and hairy with lateral red spots, a yellow dorsal line and a projection behind head. Feeds on deciduous shrubs. **STATUS** Widespread and locally common.

LS

Sycamore *Acronicta aceris*

73.039 (2279) 36–44mm

Sycamore, larva

Sycamore

ADULT is variably grey with fine dark and orange speckling, and a pale outer cross-line shaped like a question mark. Flies Jun–Jul. **LARVA** is covered in yellow hairs, with orange tufts and black-ringed white dorsal spots; feeds on Field Maple and Sycamore. **STATUS** Locally common only in S and SE England.

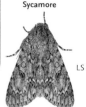

LS

Miller *Acronicta leporina* 73.040 (2280) 36–44mm

ADULT is usually whitish, the forewings finely speckled with grey and with a few dark markings; darker forms sometimes occur. Flies Jun–Aug. **LARVA** is pale green with long pale hairs and black dorsal tufts; feeds on birches. **STATUS** Widespread and locally common.

LS

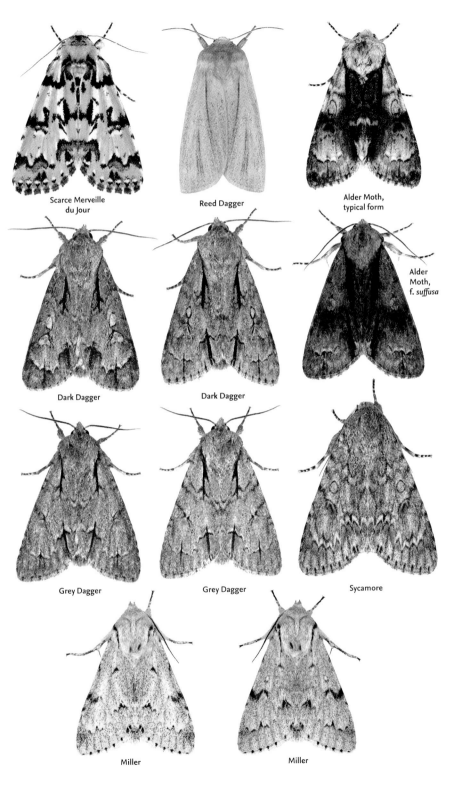

Scarce Merveille
du Jour

Reed Dagger

Alder Moth,
typical form

Dark Dagger

Dark Dagger

Alder
Moth,
f. *suffusa*

Grey Dagger

Grey Dagger

Sycamore

Miller

Miller

Light Knot Grass *Acronicta menyanthidis* 73.042 (2286) 34–40mm
ADULT ssp. *menyanthidis* is variably grey with irregular black cross-lines,
between which is a small black-ringed oval that lacks a central spot,
and a dark-framed kidney-shaped mark. Ssp. *scotica* is larger, with
bolder markings and dark hind wing. Flies May–Jul. **LARVA** is hairy
and black, with red lateral spots; feeds on Bog-myrtle and Bilberry.
STATUS Widespread on moorland. Ssp. *menyanthidis* is found in Wales
and N England; ssp. *scotica* occurs in Scotland.

LS

Sweet Gale Moth *Acronicta cinerea* 73.044 (2288) 34–38mm
ADULT is grey, the forewings with fine, dense dark and yellow speckling,
wavy dark cross-lines and a dark-ringed oval that contains a dark spot.
Flies May–Jun. **LARVA** is hairy and black, with red lateral spots and
yellow dorsal spots; feeds on Heather and other moorland plants.
STATUS Local on moorland in central and NE Scotland.

LS

ABOVE: **Knot Grass, larva**

Knot Grass *Acronicta rumicis* 73.045 (2289) 32–34mm
ADULT is variably grey with rather narrow forewings that are coated
with dense, dark speckling and have a dark-ringed oval containing
a dark spot; middle of trailing edge has a white mark, these aligning
in resting moths. Double-brooded in the S: flies May–Jun, and Aug.
LARVA is hairy and brown, with bold white dorsal spots, and a lateral
white line adorned with red spots; feeds on herbaceous plants. **STATUS**
Widespread and locally common, least so in the N.

LS

Poplar Grey *Subacronicta megacephala* 73.046 (2278) 42–44mm
ADULT is variably grey, the forewings with dense, dark speckling and
indistinct cross-lines; oval is dark-ringed with a dark centre, and wing
shows a pale patch towards margin. Flies May–Aug. **LARVA** is grey-brown
with yellow and black speckling; feeds on poplars. **STATUS** Widespread;
locally common only in the S.

LS

Coronet *Craniophora ligustri* 73.047 (2291) 32–34mm
ADULT forewings are rather broad and rounded; ground colour varies
from grey-brown to rich brown, with yellow-green and black marbling,
and with wavy black cross-lines and a pale patch beyond the kidney mark.
Flies Jun–Jul. **LARVA** feeds on Ash and privets. **STATUS** Widespread, but
locally common only in the S.

LS

Small Yellow Underwing *Panemeria tenebrata* 73.048 (2397) 20–22mm
ADULT is day-flying. Forewings are reddish brown with darker brown
cross-bands; hindwings are black with a broad yellow band. **LARVA** feeds
on seeds of Common Mouse-ear and related plants. **STATUS** Widespread
and locally common in central and S Britain.

LS

Light Knot
Grass

Light Knot
Grass

Sweet Gale
Moth

Knot
Grass

Knot
Grass

Poplar
Grey

Coronet

Coronet

Poplar
Grey

Coronet

Coronet

Small Yellow Underwing

Wormwood *Cucullia absinthii* 73.050 (2211) 34–38mm

ADULT at rest has a forward-projecting tuft of hairs on thorax. Forewings are grey-buff with blackish central blotches and 2 rows of black dots. Flies Jul. **LARVA** is patterned buff, green and brown, and closely resembles its foodplant flowers and seedheads; feeds on Wormwood and Mugwort. **STATUS** Very local, restricted to central and S Britain.

Shark *Cucullia umbratica* 73.052 (2216) 44–50mm

ADULT at rest has a forward-projecting tuft of hairs on thorax. Forewings are grey-buff with dark veins, and a dark streak running through oval and kidney marks; fine streaks on margin do not extend into fringe. Hindwing fringe is subtly 2-banded: buff at base, fading paler towards tips. Flies Jun–Jul. **LARVA** feeds on sow-thistles. **STATUS** Widespread, favouring areas of disturbed ground; commonest in the S.

Shark

Chamomile Shark *Cucullia chamomillae* 73.053 (2214) 40–42mm

ADULT at rest has a forward-projecting tuft of hairs on thorax. Very similar to Shark. Forewings are grey-buff with dark veins; fine streaks on margin extend into fringe. Hindwing fringe is distinctly 3-banded: buff–brown–white. Flies Apr–Jun. **LARVA** is pale green with wavy, dark green lengthways stripes; feeds on Chamomile and related plants. **STATUS** Widespread and locally common.

Star-wort *Cucullia asteris* 73.055 (2217) 44–48mm

ADULT at rest has a forward-projecting tuft of hairs on thorax. Forewings are grey-brown with orange-brown leading and trailing edges. Flies Jun–Aug. **LARVA** is green with black and yellow lengthways stripes; feeds on Sea Aster and Goldenrod. **STATUS** Local; mainly coastal in S and SE England and W Wales.

Striped Lychnis *Cucullia lychnitis* 73.057 (2219) 44–46mm

ADULT at rest has a forward-projecting tuft of hairs on thorax. Forewings are grey-buff with dark blackish-brown leading and trailing edges. Underside of hindwings lacks a dark discal spot. Flies Jun–Jul. **LARVA** is pale yellowish green with black and yellow bands and spots on each segment; feeds on Dark Mullein. **STATUS** Very local on calcareous soils in S England.

larvae

underwings

Mullein *Cucullia verbasci* 73.058 (2221) 45–55mm

ADULT at rest has a forward-projecting tuft of hairs on thorax. Forewings are buffish brown with blackish-brown leading and trailing edges. Underside of hindwings has a dark discal spot. Flies Apr–May. **LARVA** is whitish with numerous bold black spots and yellow patches; feeds on mulleins, particularly Great Mullein. **STATUS** Widespread in central and S Britain.

underwings

larva

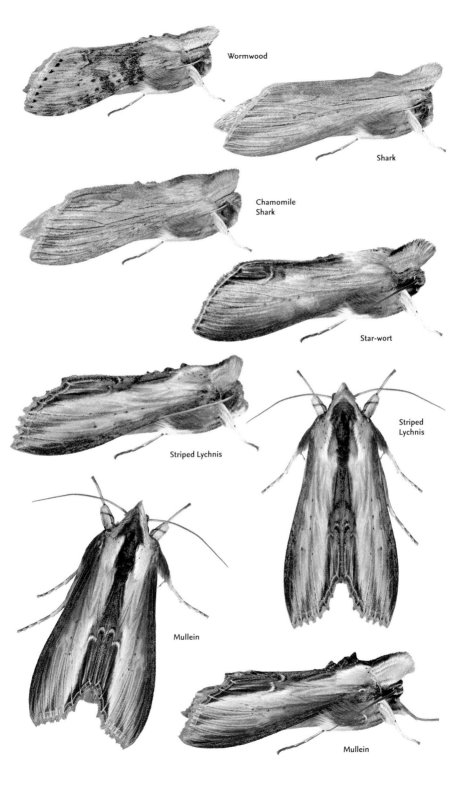

Wormwood

Shark

Chamomile Shark

Star-wort

Striped Lychnis

Striped Lychnis

Mullein

Mullein

Toadflax Brocade *Calophasia lunula*
73.059 (2223) 28–30mm
ADULT forewings are marbled grey-buff with a dark central cross-band containing a white spot and streak, and defined by white cross-lines. Flies Jul–Aug. **LARVA** is green, heavily marked with black and yellow; feeds on toadflaxes. **STATUS** Scarce and local, mainly on coastal shingle in S and SE England.

Toadflax Brocade, larva

Anomalous *Stilbia anomala* 73.061 (2394) 30–35mm
ADULT forewings are variably grey, with a darker patch between the oval and kidney marks; seen from above, thorax has a white-ringed dark central spot. Flies Aug–Sep. **LARVA** feeds on Wavy Hair-grass and other grasses. **STATUS** Associated with moorland, and hence widespread and locally common only in W Britain.

Copper Underwing
Amphipyra pyramidea 73.062 (2297) 40–50mm

Copper Underwing, underwing

ADULT forewings are brown with wavy pale cross-lines and a dark central band containing a dark-centred white spot. Hindwing upper side is orange; underside is orange only on outer third, defined by a black band. Seen head on, palps are uniformly pale brown. Flies Aug–Oct. **LARVA** feeds mainly on oaks. **STATUS** Widespread and locally common in central and S Britain.

Svensson's Copper Underwing
Amphipyra berbera 73.063 (2298) 40–50mm
ADULT forewings are similar to those of Copper Underwing. Hindwing upper side is orange; on underside, orange extends along trailing edge. Seen head on, palps are dark with white tips. Flies Jul–Sep. **LARVA** feeds mainly on oaks. **STATUS** Widespread and locally common in central and S Britain.

Svensson's Copper Underwing, underwing

Mouse Moth *Amphipyra tragopoginis* 73.064 (2299) 34–38mm
Mouse Moth

ADULT forewings are variably grey-brown, with a silky sheen and 3 black spots. Scuttles away like a mouse when disturbed. Flies Jul–Sep. **LARVA** feeds on a range of plants. **STATUS** Widespread and locally common.

Sprawler *Asteroscopus sphinx* 73.065 (2227) 40–48mm
ADULT forewings are grey-buff, with black streaks and a jagged marginal line. Thorax and legs are hairy. Flies Nov–Dec. **LARVA** is green with yellow lengthways stripes; feeds on deciduous trees. **STATUS** Locally common only in central and S Britain.

Rannoch Sprawler *Brachionycha nubeculosa*
73.066 (2228) 50–60mm
ADULT is grey-brown with black streaks and a large pale kidney mark, framed black on trailing edge. Flies Mar–Apr. **LARVA** feeds on birches. **STATUS** Local in ancient birch woods in Scottish Highlands.

Sprawler

LS

Toadflax Brocade

Anomalous,
male

Anomalous,
female

Copper
Underwing

Copper
Underwing

Sprawler

Rannoch
Sprawler

Rannoch
Sprawler

Svensson's Copper
Underwing

Mouse
Moth

ABOVE: **Green-brindled Crescent**
BELOW: **Early Grey**

Green-brindled Crescent
Allophyes oxyacanthae
73.068 (2245) 35–45mm
ADULT has marbled green and brown forewings with a pale outer margin and pale oval and kidney marks; thorax is pale. Flies Sep–Nov. **LARVA** feeds on shrubs. **STATUS** Widespread and common.

Early Grey *Xylocampa areola*
73.069 (2243) 34–38mm
ADULT is grey, the forewings with black speckling and lines, framing pale oval and kidney marks; sometimes subtly flushed pink. Flies Mar–May. **LARVA** feeds on Honeysuckle. **STATUS** Widespread, but commonest in the S.

Bordered Sallow *Pyrrhia umbra*
73.070 (2399) 28–34mm
ADULT forewings are orange-yellow with red cross-lines on inner two-thirds, and reddish brown on outer third. Flies Jun–Jul. **LARVA** feeds on flowers of restharrows. **STATUS** Widespread but local; restricted to coastal habitats and calcareous grassland in the S.

Marbled Clover

Marbled Clover *Heliothis viriplaca*
73.072 (2401) 32–34mm
ADULT flies by day and at night. Forewings are pale buff with a darker brown cross-band and brown margin; hindwings have black and buffish-white bands. Flies Jun–Jul. **LARVA** feeds on low-growing plants. **STATUS** East Anglian Breckland resident; also a regular migrant.

Shoulder-striped Clover

Shoulder-striped Clover *Heliothis maritima* 73.073 (2402) 32–34mm
ADULT flies by day and at night. Forewings have a dark cross-band, dark basal streak and dark patch on trailing edge; hindwings have black and whitish bands. Flies Jun–Jul. **LARVA** feeds on Heather and Cross-leaved Heath. **STATUS** Rare; S heaths only.

Bordered Straw *Heliothis peltigera* 73.074 (2403) 36–40mm
ADULT forewings are yellow-buff to orange-brown with a dark kidney mark and adjacent brown patch on leading edge, and a brown patch near leading corner. Flies Jun–Aug. **LARVA** feeds mainly on Sticky Groundsel and cultivated marigolds. **STATUS** Immigrant from S Europe in varying numbers.

Bordered Straw

Scarce Bordered Straw *Helicoverpa armigera* 73.076 (2400) 32–38mm
ADULT forewings range from buff with darker markings, to brown with paler orange-buff markings. Flies Aug–Oct. **LARVA** feeds on low-growing plants. **STATUS** Scarce immigrant from Europe; larvae imported with tomatoes.

Reddish Buff *Acosmetia caliginosa* 73.078 (2393) 26–30mm
ADULT forewings are reddish buff; very wavy cross-lines define darker central band. Male is larger than female. Flies May–Jun. **LARVA** feeds on Saw-wort. **STATUS** Rare, Isle of Wight only; formerly mainland Hampshire.

Green-brindled Crescent

Green-brindled Crescent

Early Grey

Early Grey

Bordered
Sallow

Marbled Clover

Marbled Clover

Bordered
Straw

Shoulder-striped Clover

Shoulder-striped Clover

Reddish Buff, female

Scarce Bordered Straw

Reddish Buff, male

Latin *Callopistria juventina* 73.080 (2308) 35–38mm
ADULT has hairy legs. Forewings are marbled pink and green, with pale veins, kidney mark and patch near leading tip. Flies Jun–Jul. **LARVA** feeds on Bracken. **STATUS** Rare immigrant from Europe.

LS

Tree-lichen Beauty *Cryphia algae* 73.082 (2292) 26–28mm
ADULT is camouflaged against tree lichens. Forewings usually have a blue-green base of variable intensity, and a marbled black and blue-green outer area. Flies Aug. **LARVA** feeds on epiphytic lichens on trees. **STATUS** Scarce immigrant and recent colonist.

Marbled Beauty

LS

Tree-lichen Beauty

Marbled Grey
Bryophila raptricula
73.083 (2294) 30–34mm
ADULT forewings are grey with a darker central band defined by a wavy inner cross-line and an outer cross-line curved like a question mark. Flies Jul–Aug. **LARVA** feeds on lichens. **STATUS** Rare immigrant.

LS

Marbled Grey

Marbled Beauty
Bryophila domestica
73.084 (2293) 20–24mm
ADULT forewings are marbled, the colour varying from greyish white to buff; dark central cross-band is defined by a jagged, complete inner central cross-line. Flies Jul–Aug. **LARVA** feeds on lichens. **STATUS** Widespread and fairly common, except in the N.

LS

Marbled Beauty

Marbled Green *Nyctobrya muralis* 73.085 (2295) 28–32mm
ADULT varies from blue-green to orange-buff; forewing inner central cross-line does not reach trailing margin and hence dark central cross-band is incomplete. **LARVA** feeds on lichens. **STATUS** Local and mainly coastal in S Britain.

LS

Marbled Green

Small Mottled Willow *Spodoptera exigua* 73.087 (2385) 28–30mm
ADULT rests with wings rolled around body. Forewings are grey-brown with orange oval and kidney marks. Flies mainly Jul–Oct. **LARVA** feeds on low-growing plants. **STATUS** Immigrant from Europe.

LS

Dark Mottled Willow *Spodoptera cilium* 73.088 (2386c) 30–32mm
ADULT forewings are grey with jagged central cross-lines and white-framed oval and kidney marks. **LARVA** feeds on low-growing plants. **STATUS** Rare immigrant from S Europe.

LS

Mediterranean Brocade *Spodoptera littoralis* 73.089 (2386) 34–36mm
ADULT forewings are marbled brown and bluish violet, with black and white central cross-lines, white veins and a diagonal band. Flies Jul–Oct. **LARVA** feeds on numerous plants. **STATUS** Possibly a very rare immigrant; also imported with cultivated plants.

LS

Tree-lichen Beauty

Tree-lichen Beauty

Tree-lichen Beauty

Latin

Marbled Grey

Marbled Green

Marbled Beauty

Marbled Beauty

Marbled Green

Small Mottled Willow

Marbled Green

Dark Mottled Willow

Dark Mottled Willow

Mediterranean Brocade

Rosy Marbled *Elaphria venustula* 73.091 (2396) 20–22mm
ADULT is tiny. Forewings are pinkish white with a dark central patch on trailing margin, and a lengthways pink central stripe. Flies May–Jun. **LARVA** feeds on low-growing plants. **STATUS** Local, in open woodland, in SE England only.

Mottled Rustic *Caradrina morpheus* 73.092 (2387) 34–36mm
ADULT forewings are brown with a diffuse dark oval mark and relatively large (compared to similar species) dark kidney mark. Flies Jun–Aug. **LARVA** feeds on low-growing plants of disturbed ground. **STATUS** Widespread and locally common except in the N.

Pale Mottled Willow

Pale Mottled Willow *Caradrina clavipalpis* 73.095 (2389) 28–34mm
ADULT forewings are grey-buff with an orange hue to kidney mark (partly framed with white dots) and to submarginal line; leading edge has 4 dark dots. Flies Jul–Sep. **LARVA** feeds on cereal grains. **STATUS** Widespread and fairly common, except in the N.

Uncertain *Hoplodrina octogenaria* 73.096 (2381) 30–32mm
ADULT forewings are buff to reddish brown, with white-framed dark oval and kidney marks, and dark central and submarginal bands. Flies Jun–Aug. **LARVA** feeds on low-growing plants. **STATUS** Widespread and common in central and S Britain.

Rustic *Hoplodrina blanda* 73.097 (2382) 32–34mm
ADULT is similar to Uncertain; some individuals are not separable in the field. Forewings are grey-brown, with dark speckling and pale-framed dark kidney and oval marks; central cross-band is less distinct than in Uncertain. Double-brooded in the S: flies Jun–Aug, and Oct. **LARVA** feeds on low-growing plants. **STATUS** Widespread and common, except in the N.

Vine's Rustic *Hoplodrina ambigua* 73.099 (2384) 32–34mm
ADULT forewings are pale grey-brown, with subtle darker oval and kidney marks framed with pale buff; surface appears faintly speckled and has cross-rows of dark dots. Hindwings are paler than in similar species. Double-brooded: flies May–Jun, and Sep–Oct. **LARVA** feeds on low-growing plants. **STATUS** Locally common in the S.

Silky Wainscot *Chilodes maritima* 73.100 (2391) 30–35mm
ADULT forewings have a curved leading edge. Ground colour is buff, but markings are extremely variable; some have black dots, others a black central streak. Flies Jun–Aug. **LARVA** lives inside stems of Common Reed and is partly carnivorous on other moth pupae. **STATUS** Very local, in reedbeds, mainly in S and SE England.

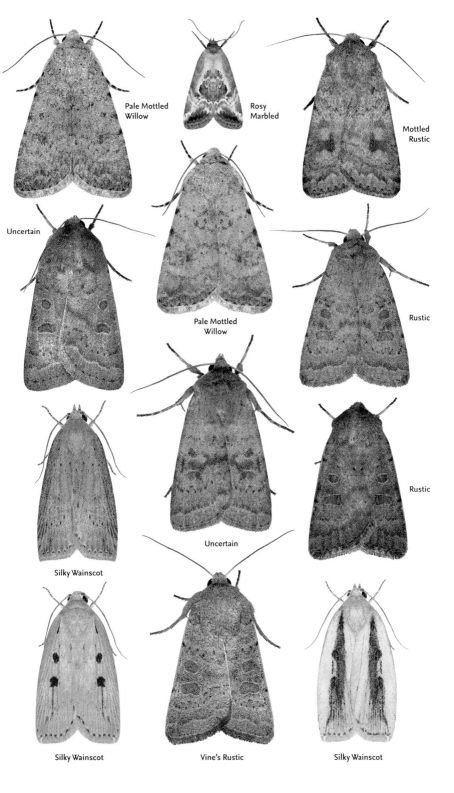

Pale Mottled
Willow

Rosy
Marbled

Mottled
Rustic

Uncertain

Pale Mottled
Willow

Rustic

Silky Wainscot

Rustic

Uncertain

Silky Wainscot

Vine's Rustic

Silky Wainscot

Treble Lines

Brown Rustic

LS

Marsh
Moth

LS

Bird's
Wing

LS

Orache
Moth

LS

Treble Lines *Charanyca trigrammica*
73.101 (2380) 35–40mm
ADULT ranges from pale buff to brown. Forewing has 3 bold, dark cross-lines. Flies May–Jul. **LARVA** feeds on low-growing plants. **STATUS** Widespread and locally common in central and S Britain.

Brown Rustic *Rusina ferruginea*
73.102 (2302) 34–38mm
ADULT forewings are broad and dark brown, with 5–6 white spots on leading edge and a broad, darker central band. Male has feathery antennae and broader wings than female. Flies Jun–Jul. **LARVA** feeds on low-growing plants. **STATUS** Widespread and locally common.

Marsh Moth *Athetis pallustris*
73.103 (2392) 20–34mm
ADULT male is much larger than female. Both sexes are buffish brown with 2 curved central cross-lines containing a dark, dart-like oval mark and a dark kidney mark. Flies May–Jun. **LARVA** feeds on low-growing plants. **STATUS** Rare and local, confined to the Lincolnshire coast.

Bird's Wing *Dypterygia scabriuscula* 73.105 (2301) 34–36mm
ADULT has rich brown forewings with a pale buff band along trailing edge; in aligned wings this is continuous with pale buff thorax. Flies Jun–Jul. **LARVA** feeds on docks and knotgrasses. **STATUS** Local and fairly common only in S and SE England.

Orache Moth *Trachea atriplicis* 73.106 (2304) 40–42mm
ADULT forewings are brown, marbled with green, including the oval and kidney marks, and with an oblique, bold white central streak. Flies Jun–Jul. **LARVA** feeds on oraches and goosefoots. **STATUS** Former resident; now a scarce immigrant from Europe.

feeding on 'sugaring' mixture

L

Old Lady *Mormo maura*
73.107 (2300) 58–64mm
ADULT is easily disturbed daytime, and often attracted indoors by lights after dark. Forewings are broad and grey-brown, with a broad, dark brown central patch. Flies Jul–Aug. **LARVA** feeds on Blackthorn and other shrubs. **STATUS** Widespread, but commonest in central and S Britain.

Straw Underwing *Thalpophila matura* 73.109 (2303)
40–44mm
ADULT forewings are grey-brown, with white cross-lines defining a dark central band that contains a pale-ringed oval and kidney. Hindwings are yellow-buff with a brown margin. Flies Jul–Aug. **LARVA** feeds on grasses. **STATUS** Widespread in central and S Britain; commonest in the S and E.

L

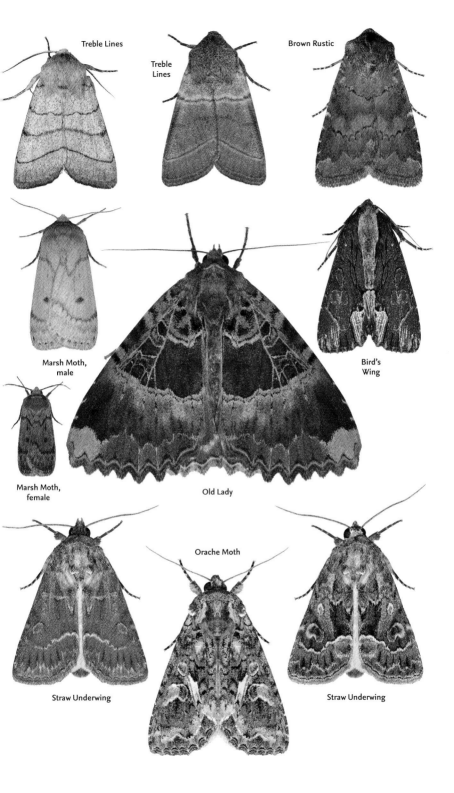

Treble Lines

Treble Lines

Brown Rustic

Marsh Moth, male

Bird's Wing

Marsh Moth, female

Old Lady

Straw Underwing

Orache Moth

Straw Underwing

Saxon *Hyppa rectilinea* 73.110 (2320) 40–42mm

ADULT is grey-buff, the forewings with a broad rufous-brown central band defined by cross-lines, the inner of which is very jagged. Has a black bar parallel to trailing edge, a bold black streak at base of wing adjacent to thorax, and black streaks on outer margin. Flies Jun–Jul. **LARVA** feeds on Bearberry and Bramble. **STATUS** Local on moorland in Scotland and SW Ireland.

Purple Cloud *Actinotia polyodon* 73.111 (2097) 32–34mm

ADULT forewings are yellow-buff, marbled and streaked with pinkish purple and white; pale kidney mark is dark-framed and margin has jagged black streaks. Flies May–Jun. **LARVA** feeds on St John's-worts. **STATUS** Rare immigrant to Britain.

Pale-shouldered Cloud *Chloantha hyperici* 73.112 (2097a) 32–38mm

ADULT forewings are grey-buff, with a dark basal bar aligned with trailing edge, and pale kidney and oval marks framed with black and reddish brown. Flies Jun–Aug. **LARVA** feeds on St John's-worts. **STATUS** Rare immigrant from mainland Europe.

Angle Shades *Phlogophora meticulosa* 73.113 (2306) 45–50mm

ADULT has jagged wing margins and rests with wings folded lengthways, the effect like a crumpled, dry leaf. Forewings are grey-buff with a green and pink central triangle, greenish inner trailing edge and greenish margin. Multiple-brooded: flies Apr–Oct. **LARVA** feeds on a range of herbaceous plants. **STATUS** Widespread and common, especially in the S.

ABOVE: **Angle Shades**
BELOW: **Small Angle Shades**

Small Angle Shades *Euplexia lucipara* 73.114 (2305) 28–30mm

ADULT rests with wings slightly creased, like Angle Shades. Broad forewings are pinkish buff with a dark brown central cross-band, whitish kidney mark and dark margin. Flies Jun–Jul. **LARVA** feeds on a range of plants, including Bracken. **STATUS** Widespread and fairly common, especially in the S.

Burren Green *Calamia tridens* 73.116 (2366) 38–40mm

ADULT is bright green, the forewings with a white margin and white oval and kidney marks. Flies Jul–Aug. **LARVA** feeds on Blue Moor-grass. **STATUS** Restricted to the Burren, W Ireland.

Haworth's Minor *Celaena haworthii* 73.118 (2367) 26–30mm

ADULT male is active on sunny days, as well as after dark. Forewings are brown with white veins, cross-lines and oval mark, and usually a pale outer cross-band. Flies Aug–Sep. **LARVA** feeds on cotton-grasses. **STATUS** Widespread on moorland, mainly in W and NW Britain and Ireland.

Saxon

Angle
Shades

Purple
Cloud

Pale-shouldered Cloud

Small Angle Shades

Haworth's Minor

Burren
Green

Small Angle Shades

Crescent *Helotropha leucostigma* 73.119 (2368) 38–42mm
ADULT ranges from grey-buff to rich brown, the forewings with pale veins, a pale trailing edge and submarginal band, and white-ringed oval and kidney marks. Flies Aug–Sep. LARVA feeds on wetland plants, including Yellow Iris. STATUS Widespread but local, in marshes and on damp moorland.

Dusky Sallow *Eremobia ochroleuca* 73.120 (2352) 35–37mm
ADULT is sometimes active by day, as well as after dark. Forewings are buff, marbled with white, including irregular cross-bands that define a broken, dark central band and a pale submarginal band. Flies Jul–Sep. LARVA feeds on various grasses. STATUS Locally common in dry grassland in SE England, including dunes and chalk downland.

Frosted Orange *Gortyna flavago* 73.121 (2364) 36–40mm
ADULT is brown, the forewings with a broad orange-yellow cross-band marked with rich orange cross-lines and pale oval and kidney marks. Flies Aug–Oct. LARVA feeds inside stems of thistles and related plants. STATUS Widespread and locally common in lowland Britain and Ireland.

Fisher's Estuarine Moth *Gortyna borelii* 73.122 (2365) 45–55mm
ADULT recalls an outsized Frosted Orange. Forewings are yellow-buff with a dark border to inner leading edge, framing white oval mark and abutting white kidney mark. Flies Sep–Oct. LARVA feeds inside stems and roots of Hog's-fennel. STATUS Rare and very local, found at a few sites on coasts of N Kent and Essex.

Rosy Rustic *Hydraecia micacea* 73.123 (2361) 30–42mm
ADULT forewings have a velvety texture, and are pinkish buff with a darker brown cross-band, the outer edge of which is straight and oblique. Flies Aug–Oct. LARVA feeds on roots of low-growing plants. STATUS Widespread and locally common.

Butterbur *Hydraecia petasitis* 73.124 (2362) 46–48mm
ADULT is similar to Rosy Rustic but larger and greyer buff in colour. Forewings have rather pointed tips and a subtly darker central cross-band framing paler oval and kidney marks. Flies Aug–Sep. LARVA feeds inside roots of Butterbur. STATUS Widespread but very local, reflecting range of larval foodplant.

Marsh Mallow Moth *Hydraecia osseola* 73.125 (2363) 42–48mm
ADULT is similar to Butterbur but overall much paler. Forewings are buff with subtle dark cross-lines, submarginal band and kidney mark. Flies Sep. LARVA feeds inside roots of Marsh-mallow. STATUS Rare and local in coastal marshes, in Sussex and Kent.

Crescent

Crescent

Dusky Sallow

Fisher's Estuarine
Moth

Frosted Orange

Rosy Rustic

Butterbur

Marsh Mallow Moth

Saltern Ear *Amphipoea fucosa* 73.126 (2358) 30–34mm

ADULT cannot be separated reliably from other 'ear' moth species without examining genitalia. However, it is usually the palest of the set: grey-buff to pale brown. Forewings are slightly hook-tipped and have dark cross-lines and an orange or white kidney mark. Flies Aug–Sep. **LARVA** feeds on grasses. **STATUS** Mainly coastal, in England and Wales.

Large Ear *Amphipoea lucens* 73.127 (2357) 32–36mm

ADULT is very similar to Saltern Ear but tends to be darker. However, cannot be separated reliably from that or other 'ear' moth species without examining genitalia. Flies Aug–Sep. **LARVA** feeds on Purple Moor-grass and other species associated with acid soils. **STATUS** Widespread in W Britain and Ireland.

Ear Moth *Amphipoea oculea* 73.128 (2360) 30–33mm

ADULT cannot be separated reliably from other 'ear' moth species without examining genitalia. Like its relatives, forewings range from buff to brown, with darker cross-lines, an orange or buff oval mark and orange or white kidney mark. Flies Jul–Sep. **LARVA** feeds on grasses. **STATUS** Widespread; locally common in central and S Britain.

Crinan Ear *Amphipoea crinanensis* 73.129 (2359) 31–33mm

ADULT cannot be separated reliably from other 'ear' moth species without examining genitalia. Forewing description is the same as for its relatives. Flies Aug–Sep. **LARVA** feeds on wetland plants. **STATUS** Local, on moors and in marshes in the N.

Ear Moth

Flounced Rustic *Luperina testacea* 73.131 (2353) 32–34mm

ADULT ranges from grey-buff to brown, with a dark central bar running parallel to trailing edge between central cross-lines. Flies Aug–Sep. **LARVA** feeds on grass stems and roots. **STATUS** Widespread; locally common in central and S Britain and Ireland.

Sandhill Rustic *Luperina nickerlii* 73.132 (2354) 34–40mm

ADULT ranges from grey-buff to brown. Forewings have a subtle central bar and central cross-lines, and a small round oval and pale-framed kidney marks. **LARVA** feeds on coastal grasses, including Common Saltmarsh-grass and Sand Couch. **STATUS** Rare, local and coastal: ssp. *demuthi*, N Kent to Suffolk; ssp. *leechi*, Cornwall; ssp. *gueneei*, N Wales; and ssp. *knilli*, SW Ireland.

Large Wainscot *Rhizedra lutosa* 73.134 (2375) 44–50mm

ADULT ranges from pale buff to orange-brown. Forewings have a row of black dots. Flies Aug–Oct. **LARVA** feeds inside stems of Common Reed. **STATUS** Widespread and locally common.

Large Wainscot

Saltern Ear

Saltern Ear

Large Ear

Large Ear

Crinan Ear

Crinan Ear

Ear Moth

Ear Moth

Flounced
Rustic

Flounced Rustic

Flounced Rustic

Large Wainscot

Sandhill Rustic, ssp. *demuthi*

Large Wainscot

Blair's Wainscot *Sedina buettneri* 73.135 (2376) 30–32mm
ADULT forewings have a pointed tip; buff with dark veins and fine black speckling. Flies Sep–Oct. **LARVA** feeds inside stems of Lesser Pond-sedge. **STATUS** Rare and local, resident in a few marshes in Dorset; very rare immigrant elsewhere.

LS

Bulrush Wainscot *Nonagria typhae* 73.136 (2369) 45–50mm
ADULT abdomen projects beyond forewings at rest. Forewings are buff in female, brown in smaller male; both have dark veins and black spots. Flies Jul–Sep. **LARVA** feeds inside stems of Bulrushes. **STATUS** Widespread in marshes; commonest in the S.

LS

Fen Wainscot *Arenostola phragmitidis* 73.137 (2377) 33–36mm
ADULT is pale buff, the forewings mostly unmarked and flushed darker reddish buff on outer third. Flies Jul–Aug. **LARVA** feeds inside stems of Common Reed. **STATUS** Local, associated with reedbeds mainly in S and E England.

LS

Lyme Grass *Longalatedes elymi* 73.138 (2348) 34–36mm
ADULT is grey-buff to warm brown, with subtly darker veins and an outer cross-row of black dots. Flies Jun–Aug. **LARVA** feeds inside stems of Lyme-grass. **STATUS** Scarce and local, restricted to coastal dunes in E England.

LS

Twin-spotted Wainscot *Lenisa geminipuncta* 73.139 (2370) 28–30mm
ADULT abdomen projects beyond forewings at rest. Forewings are brown with faint black and white streaks on margin and 2 spots, either dark or dark-framed white. Flies Aug–Sep. **LARVA** feeds inside stems of Common Reed. **STATUS** Local, confined to reedbeds mainly in S England and S Wales.

LS

White-mantled Wainscot *Archanara neurica* 73.140 (2372) 26–28mm
ADULT has a white 'collar'; abdomen projects beyond forewings at rest. Forewings are buff with a subtle dark streak, partly framing white-framed kidney and oval marks. Undersides of both wings are unmarked (cf. Brown-veined). Flies Jul–Aug. **LARVA** feeds inside stems of Common Reed. **STATUS** Rare, in coastal reedbeds in Suffolk.

LS

Brown-veined Wainscot *Archanara dissoluta* 73.141 (2371) 28–32mm
ADULT abdomen projects beyond forewings at rest. Forewings are brown with subtle dark streaks and white-framed oval and kidney marks. Underwings have a central spot. Flies Jul–Sep. **LARVA** feeds inside stems of Common Reed. **STATUS** Local, in reedbeds in central and S Britain.

LS

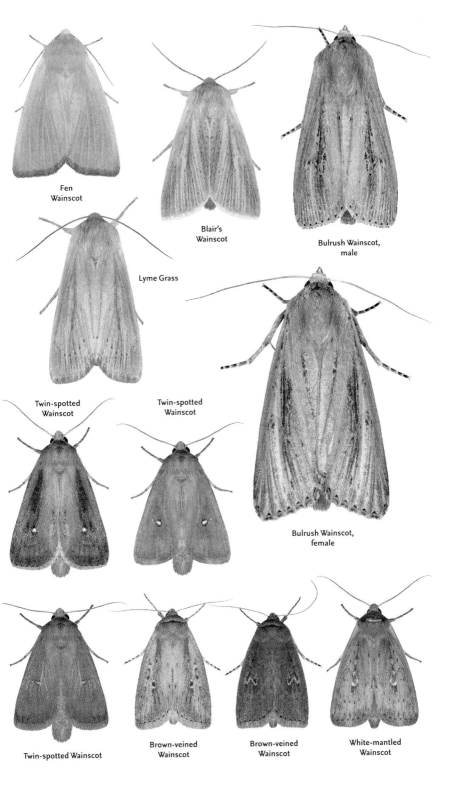

Fen
Wainscot

Blair's
Wainscot

Lyme Grass

Bulrush Wainscot,
male

Twin-spotted
Wainscot

Twin-spotted
Wainscot

Bulrush Wainscot,
female

Twin-spotted Wainscot

Brown-veined
Wainscot

Brown-veined
Wainscot

White-mantled
Wainscot

Small Rufous *Coenobia rufa* 73.142 (2379) 22–24mm
ADULT is buff to reddish brown, the forewings with an outer cross-row of black dots. Flies Jul–Aug. **LARVA** feeds inside stems of rushes. **STATUS** Local in damp habitats in central and S Britain.

Brighton Wainscot *Oria musculosa* 73.143 (2378) 30–32mm
ADULT is buff, the forewings with dark veins and 2 broad lengthways stripes. Flies Jul–Aug. **LARVA** feeds inside stems of cereal grasses. **STATUS** Very local, on arable farmland in central S England.

Small Wainscot

Small Wainscot
Denticucullus pygmina
73.144 (2350) 24–28mm
ADULT ranges from buff to brown, the forewings with indistinct dark veins and an outer cross-row of black dots. Flies Aug–Sep. **LARVA** feeds inside stems of sedges. **STATUS** Widespread and locally common.

Mere Wainscot
Photedes fluxa
73.145 (2349) 28–30mm
ADULT ranges from buff to brown, the forewings with a faint cross-row of black dots and a pale kidney mark. Flies Jul–Aug. **LARVA** feeds inside Wood Small-reed. **STATUS** Very local, in fens and marshes in central and S England.

Least Minor
Photedes captiuncula
73.146 (2344) 16–18mm
ADULT male flies by day as

well as at night. Forewings are broad; brown to buff in ssp. *expolita* with central white cross-lines framing a dark central band; ssp. *tincta* is overall redder brown. Flies Jun–Aug. **LARVA** feeds inside stems of Glaucous Sedge. **STATUS** Rare and very local on limestone; ssp. *expolita* occurs in N England, ssp. *tincta* in W Ireland.

Small Dotted Buff *Photedes minima* 73.147 (2345) 20–22mm
ADULT is buff, the forewings with central cross-rows of black dots; female is smaller than male, with a darker margin and banding. Flies Jun–Aug. **LARVA** feeds inside stems of Tufted Hair-grass. **STATUS** Widespread and locally common.

Morris's Wainscot *Photedes morrisii* 73.148 (2346) 28–32mm
ADULT is very pale buff (almost white), the forewings with faint dark speckling and a cross-row of very subtle black dots. Flies Jun–Jul. **LARVA** feeds inside stems of Tall Fescue. **STATUS** Very rare, restricted to short stretch of undercliff in Dorset and Devon; formerly in Kent.

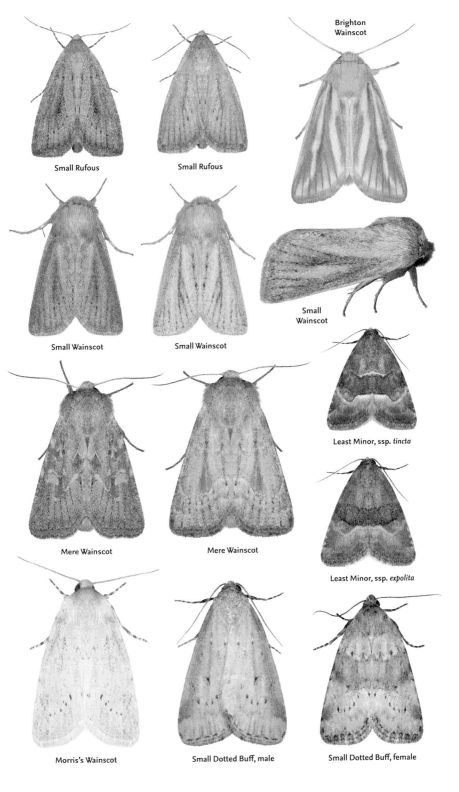

Small Rufous

Small Rufous

Brighton Wainscot

Small Wainscot

Small Wainscot

Small Wainscot

Mere Wainscot

Mere Wainscot

Least Minor, ssp. *tincta*

Least Minor, ssp. *expolita*

Morris's Wainscot

Small Dotted Buff, male

Small Dotted Buff, female

Concolorous *Photedes extrema* 73.149 (2347) 26–28mm
ADULT is pale buff, the forewings with an outer cross-row of black dots, and some individuals also with inner dots. Flies Jun–Jul. **LARVA** feeds inside stems of small-reed grasses. **STATUS** Rare resident of fens in Huntingdonshire; very rare immigrant elsewhere.

L

Fenn's Wainscot *Protarchanara brevilinea* 73.150 (2351) 32–36mm
ADULT is buffish brown, the forewings with dense, dark speckling, pale outer veins with dark streaks between, and subtle dark central and basal stripes. Flies Jul–Aug. **LARVA** feeds on Common Reed. **STATUS** Rare, in a few coastal East Anglian fens.

L

Webb's Wainscot
Globia sparganii
73.151 (2373) 34–38mm
ADULT abdomen projects beyond forewings at rest. Forewings are buff to sandy brown, with an outer cross-row and marginal row of black dots, and a dark central streak, sometimes reduced to 2 black dots. Flies Aug–Sep. **LARVA** feeds inside stems of Yellow Iris. **STATUS** Local in wetlands in E and SE England and S Wales.

L

Rush Wainscot *Globia algae* 73.152 (2374) 34–40mm
ADULT male is reddish brown, while larger female is buff. In both, forewings have an outer cross-row of black dots and a subtle dark central streak and spot. Flies Jul–Aug. **LARVA** feeds inside stems of Bulrush, Common Club-rush and other wetland plants. **STATUS** Very local, in a few wetland sites in E and SE England.

LS

Dusky Brocade *Apamea remissa* 73.154 (2330) 38–40mm
ADULT has a curved leading edge to forewings. In typical form *obscura*, forewings are brown with a subtly darker central band defined by pale cross-lines; pale submarginal cross-line contains letter 'W'. Form *submissa* is similar, but paler overall and with a contrastingly darker central band. Flies Jun–Jul. **LARVA** feeds on a range of grasses. **STATUS** Widespread and common.

LS

Clouded Brindle *Apamea epomidion* 73.155 (2327) 42–44mm
ADULT forewings are variably marbled brown and buff; white submarginal line defines black border with 2 dark wedges; has 2 dark streaks at base. Flies Jun–Jul. **LARVA** feeds on various grasses. **STATUS** Widespread and common except in Scotland.

LS

Clouded-bordered Brindle *Apamea crenata* 73.156 (2326) 38–42mm
ADULT typically has a reddish-brown thorax, and forewings marbled buff overall, the reddish-brown margin with 2 projecting wedges. Much darker brown overall in form *combusta*, which has pale-framed kidney and elongated oval marks. Flies Jun–Jul. **LARVA** feeds on various grasses. **STATUS** Widespread and common.

LS

Concolorous

Fenn's Wainscot

Rush Wainscot, male

Webb's Wainscot

Webb's Wainscot

Rush Wainscot, female

Dusky Brocade

Dusky Brocade

Clouded Brindle

Clouded-bordered Brindle

Clouded-bordered Brindle

Clouded Brindle

Large Nutmeg *Apamea anceps* 73.157 (2333) 36–40mm
ADULT ranges from grey-brown to buff, the forewings with fine dark speckling, pale-framed oval and kidney marks, and no dark basal streak; has 2 pale central cross-lines, the outer one gently scalloped. **LARVA** feeds on Cock's-foot and Annual Meadow-grass. **STATUS** Locally common only in SE England.

Rustic Shoulder-knot *Apamea sordens* 73.158 (2334) 36–40mm
ADULT is grey-buff, the forewings with rather indistinct markings, including pale-framed oval and kidney marks, and a dark basal streak, slightly forked at end. Flies May–Jun. **LARVA** feeds on Cock's-foot and other grasses. **STATUS** Widespread and locally common.

Small Clouded Brindle *Apamea unanimis* 73.159 (2331) 32–36mm
ADULT forewings are marbled brown, with a pale-framed kidney mark and 2 dark basal streaks. Flies Jun–Jul. **LARVA** feeds on Reed Canary-grass and other wetland grasses. **STATUS** Widespread but local, in damp habitats; commonest in the S.

Slender Brindle *Apamea scolopacina* 73.160 (2335) 34–36mm
ADULT is marbled buff with a dark central ridge on thorax; forewings have a dark margin, 2 faint scalloped central cross-lines, and a white-framed kidney mark and adjacent dark patch on leading edge. Flies Jul–Aug. **LARVA** feeds on various grasses, including Wood Millet. **STATUS** Widespread, locally common except in the N.

Slender Brindle

ABOVE: **Slender Brindle**
BELOW: **Dark Arches**

Crescent Striped *Apamea oblonga* 73.161 (2325) 44–48mm
ADULT is grey-brown. Forewings have rather indistinct markings, including a pale outer cross-line containing a 'W', a kidney mark that is pale-framed on outer half, and a smooth, kinked pale outer central cross-line; sometimes shows a dark central bar. Flies Jun–Aug. **LARVA** feeds on saltmarsh-grasses. **STATUS** Very local on coasts of England and Wales; commonest in East Anglia.

Dark Arches *Apamea monoglypha* 73.162 (2321) 48–54mm
ADULT is variable, ranging from grey-buff to dark brown; dark forms predominate in the N. Forewings have large oval and kidney marks, pale-framed except in dark forms; outer pale cross-line contains a 'W'. Flies Jul–Aug. **LARVA** feeds on various grasses. Sides of thorax are marked with dark lines that form a 'V'. **STATUS** Widespread and common in S Britain.

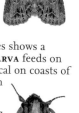

Light Arches *Apamea lithoxylaea* 73.163 (2322) 44–48mm
ADULT is pale buff with a reddish-brown centre to thorax; forewings have dark veins and a reddish-brown mark on leading edge, and a reddish-brown flush to margin and trailing corner. **LARVA** feeds on various grasses. **STATUS** Widespread and common.

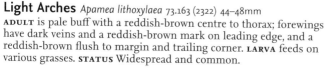

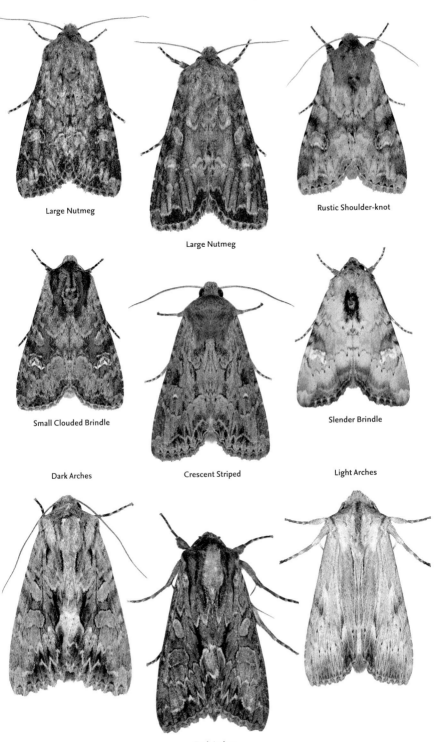

Large Nutmeg

Large Nutmeg

Rustic Shoulder-knot

Small Clouded Brindle

Slender Brindle

Dark Arches

Crescent Striped

Light Arches

Dark Arches

Reddish Light Arches *Apamea sublustris* 73.164 (2323) 44–46mm
ADULT is similar to Light Arches (p. 262) and Clouded-bordered
Brindle (p. 260) but more reddish buff overall. Forewings have darker
reddish-brown marks on border and trailing corner, and a partial
central cross-band; thorax is a similar colour. Flies Jun–Jul. **LARVA**
feeds on grass roots and stems. **STATUS** Local, mainly in central
S England.

LS

Confused *Apamea furva* 73.165 (2329) 36–40mm
ADULT is confusingly similar to a number of other *Apamea* species,
notably Dusky Brocade (p. 260), but grey-brown forewings have a
straight leading edge, smaller oval and kidney marks, and a wavy
white submarginal line that lacks a 'W'. Flies Jul–Aug. **LARVA** feeds
on grass roots and stems. **STATUS** Very local and scattered, mainly
in the W and N.

LS

Northern Arches/Exile *Apamea exulis* 73.167 (2324) 44–48mm
ADULT Northern Arches (ssp. *assimilis*) has rich brown forewings
with greenish tints, and reddish-buff cross-lines and frame to kidney
mark. Exile (ssp. *marmorata*) is similar but 'colder' grey-brown overall,
with more striking markings. Flies Jul–Aug. **LARVA** feeds on moorland
grasses. **STATUS** Local; Northern Arches occurs on Scottish moors,
Exile on Shetland Isles.

LS

Double Lobed *Lateroligia ophiogramma* 73.168 (2336) 33–35mm
ADULT is grey-buff, the forewings with a rich, dark brown 'lobe'
on leading edge that contains a pale kidney mark. Flies Jun–Aug.
LARVA feeds on Reed Sweet-grass and Reed Canary-grass. **STATUS**
Local in wetland habitats; widespread except in the N.

LS

Common Rustic *Mesapamea secalis* 73.169 (2343) 28–30mm;
Lesser Common Rustic *M. didyma* 73.170 (2343a) 24–28mm;
Remm's Rustic *M. remmi* (2343b) 26–30mm (not illustrated)
Until recently, these three moths were considered to be a single
species. They cannot be separated in the field reliably, requiring
dissection of genitalia (dead specimens) to confirm identity. That is
beyond the scope of this book, so here they are treated as a species
complex. **ADULT** is very variable. At one extreme are moths with
rather uniform dark brown wings, except for the white kidney mark.
At the other are buff moths with a dark brown thorax and broad,
dark brown patch on leading edge of forewings containing a pale
kidney mark. Many intermediate forms are known and are common.
LARVA feeds inside the stems of grasses, including Cock's-foot.
STATUS Widespread in a range of habitats; locally common except
in the N.

Common Rustic
LS

Lesser
Common
Rustic
LS

Reddish Light Arches

Exile

Confused

Exile

Northern Arches

Double Lobed

Common Rustic

Common Rustic

Common Rustic

Lesser Common Rustic

Common Rustic

Lesser Common Rustic

Rosy Minor *Litoligia literosa* 73.171 (2342) 26–30mm

LS

ADULT forewings are typically pinkish and grey, with dark central cross-lines defining a subtly darker band containing a black-framed white oval mark. Unusual darker, almost melanic, forms also occur. Flies Jul–Aug. **LARVA** feeds inside the stems of grasses. **STATUS** Widespread and locally common.

Cloaked Minor *Mesoligia furuncula* 73.172 (2341) 24–26mm

LS

ADULT is very variable. One typical form has a brown basal half to forewings (of varying shades) and a pale (almost whitish) outer half. Other forms can show a more obvious darker central bar, like Rosy Minor. Flies Aug–Sep. **LARVA** feeds inside stems of grasses. **STATUS** Widespread, except in the N, and generally commonest in coastal districts.

Marbled Minor *Oligia strigilis* 73.173 (2337) 23–25mm;

Marbled Minor

LS

Tawny Marbled Minor *O. latruncula* 73.174 (2339) 24–26mm;

Rufous Minor *O. versicolor* 73.175 (2338) 24–26mm

Tawny Marbled Minor

LS

These 3 variable species are hard to separate in the field and are treated here as a species complex. However, there are distinctive features which, if present, are helpful in separation and identification although an examination of the genitalia is often required for certain identification. **ADULT** well-marked individuals have a pale outer third to the forewings and a subtle dark central band defined on the inner margin by a white cross-line. Other forms are much darker and more uniform brown, showing just a hint of a pale outerwing and darker central area. Well-marked Marbled Minors usually show a tiny pair of dark-framed white spots aligned centrally on the outer margin of the white outer forewing band; darker forms of Rufous Minor usually have a rufous tint; Tawny Marbled Minors usually have indistinct markings and show the least contrast on the wings of the 3 species. Very dark melanic forms of all 3 species also occur. Flies May–Jul. **LARVA** feeds on a range of grasses. **STATUS** Widespread and locally common, least so in the N.

Rufous Minor

LS

Middle-barred Minor *Oligia fasciuncula* 73.176 (2340) 23–25mm

LS

ADULT ground colour is variable, ranging from grey-buff to brown; forewings have a dark central cross-band defined on trailing half by partial white cross-lines. Flies Jun–Jul. **LARVA** feeds on various grasses. **STATUS** Widespread and locally common, favouring damp grassland.

Beautiful Gothic *Leucochlaena oditis* 73.178 (2226) 30–35mm

LS

ADULT is buff, the forewings with darker brown patches defined by bold white lines. Oval and kidney marks are buff and white-framed. Flies Sep–Oct. **LARVA** feeds on various coastal grasses. **STATUS** Rare and local, restricted to a few coastal habitats from Hampshire to Cornwall.

Rosy Minor

Cloaked Minor

Cloaked Minor

Cloaked Minor

Marbled Minor

Marbled Minor

Marbled Minor

Tawny Marbled Minor

Middle-barred Minor

Rufous Minor

Rufous Minor

Tawny Marbled Minor

Middle-barred Minor

Beautiful Gothic

Middle-barred Minor

Orange Sallow *Tiliacea citrago* 73.179 (2271) 30–32mm
ADULT is orange-buff; pointed forewings are marked with a network of darker, reddish-brown cross-lines and veins. Flies Aug–Sep. LARVA feeds on limes. STATUS Widespread and locally common, especially in urban areas in the S where the larval foodplants occur.

LS

Barred Sallow *Tiliacea aurago* 73.180 (2272) 28–30mm
ADULT is reddish brown; pointed forewings have a broad, paler central cross-band that is either yellow or orange and contains a dark oval. Flies Sep–Oct. LARVA feeds on Field Maple and Beech. STATUS Locally common only in central and S Britain.

LS

Pink-barred Sallow *Xanthia togata* 73.181 (2273) 28–30mm
ADULT is yellow with a pinkish-brown head and front of thorax, and similar colour as a cross-band and markings on pointed forewings. Flies Sep–Oct. LARVA feeds on sallow catkins at first, then on low-growing plants. STATUS Widespread and locally common.

LS

Pink-Barred Sallow

FAR LEFT:
Pink-Barred Sallow
LEFT: **Sallow**

Sallow *Cirrhia icteritia* 73.182 (2274) 28–34mm
ADULT is yellow, the pointed forewings usually marked with a reddish-brown partial basal cross-band and broader submarginal band; in another form, forewings are pure yellow except for dark spot. Flies Sep–Oct. LARVA feeds on sallow catkins at first, then on low-growing plants. STATUS Widespread and locally common, favouring heaths and marshy habitats.

LS

Dusky-lemon Sallow *Cirrhia gilvago* 73.183 (2275) 34–36mm
ADULT is dull yellow, the rounded tip to forewings heavily speckled grey-brown, and with subtly darker cross-bands but pale-framed oval and kidney marks. Flies Aug–Oct. LARVA feeds on elms. STATUS Widespread but local, mainly in England and Wales.

LS

Pale-lemon Sallow *Cirrhia ocellaris* 73.184 (2276) 33–35mm
ADULT is dull buffish yellow; forewings are pointed, with subtle pale cross-lines and veins, and pale-framed oval and pale-framed dark kidney marks. Flies Sep–Oct. LARVA feeds on poplar catkins at first, then on low-growing plants. STATUS Scarce and local, mainly in East Anglia and the S coast of England.

LS

Centre-barred Sallow *Atethmia centrago* 73.219 (2269) 33–35mm
ADULT is typically yellow with a reddish-brown head and thorax, and similar colour on forewings as a margin and central cross-band, the inner edge of which is straight. Unusual dark forms also occur. Flies Aug–Sep. LARVA feeds on Ash. STATUS Widespread and locally common, least so in the N.

LS

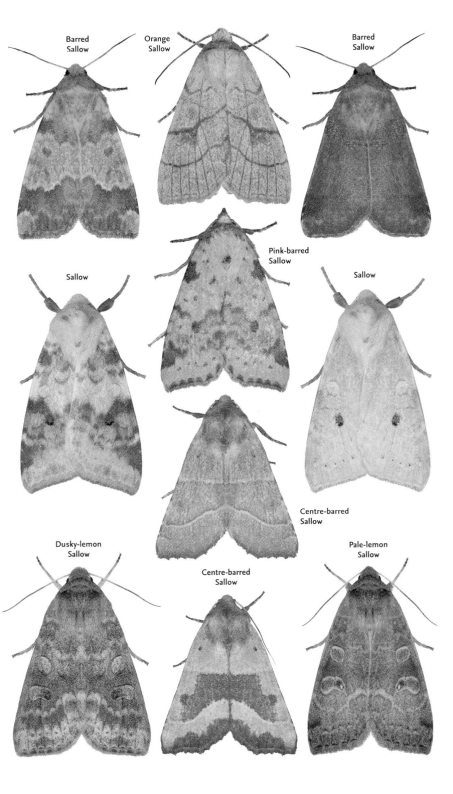

Barred
Sallow

Orange
Sallow

Barred
Sallow

Pink-barred
Sallow

Sallow

Sallow

Centre-barred
Sallow

Dusky-lemon
Sallow

Centre-barred
Sallow

Pale-lemon
Sallow

Beaded Chestnut *Agrochola lychnidis* 73.186 (2267) 32–34mm

ADULT ranges from grey-buff to rich brown, the forewings with narrow dark oval and kidney marks, and black dots on leading edge; darker forms have subtle pale veins and cross-lines. Flies Sep–Oct. **LARVA** feeds on a wide range of plants. **STATUS** Widespread and locally common in central and S Britain.

Brown-spot Pinion *Agrochola litura* 73.187 (2266) 30–34mm

ADULT is rich brown, the forewings with dark dashes on leading edge (the one near tip is boldest), a pale-framed oval mark and a narrow, pale-framed dark kidney mark. Flies Sep–Oct. **LARVA** feeds on low-growing plants at first, then on shrubs and trees. **STATUS** Widespread and locally common, especially in the E.

Flounced Chestnut *Agrochola helvola* 73.188 (2265) 32–34mm

ADULT is reddish brown; forewings are hook-tipped with a dark band near base and a dark submarginal cross-band that is marked on inner edge by pale scallops. Flies Sep–Oct. **LARVA** feeds on shrubs. **STATUS** Locally common; on moors in the N but in woodland further S.

FAR LEFT:
Red-line Quaker
LEFT:
Yellow-line Quaker

Red-line Quaker *Agrochola lota* 73.189 (2263) 34–38mm

ADULT is purplish grey, the forewings with a red submarginal cross-line, and red-framed oval and kidney marks (dark on trailing quarter). Flies Sep–Oct. **LARVA** feeds on willows, eating catkins at first. **STATUS** Widespread and locally common.

Yellow-line Quaker *Agrochola macilenta* 73.190 (2264) 33–35mm

ADULT is buffish brown, the forewings with a dark-edged yellow submarginal cross-line, and pale-framed oval and kidney marks (dark on trailing quarter). Flies Oct–Nov. **LARVA** feeds on deciduous trees and Heather. **STATUS** Widespread and locally common, on moors in the N but in woodland further S.

Southern Chestnut *Agrochola haematidea* 73.191 (2264a) 34–36mm

ADULT is rich brown, the pointed forewings with a subtly paler, broad margin with an inner dark band that extends along trailing edge. Flies Oct–Nov. **LARVA** feeds on Cross-leaved Heath and Bell Heather. **STATUS** Scarce, mainly in Dorset and New Forest heaths.

Brick *Agrochola circellaris* 73.192 (2262) 34–36mm

ADULT ranges from grey-buff to orange-buff. Forewings have a network of subtly darker veins and wavy cross-lines, the outer one often reddish; pale oval and kidney marks are often red-framed, with trailing half of kidney dark. Flies Aug–Oct. **LARVA** feeds on poplars and Wych Elm. **STATUS** Widespread and locally common.

Beaded Chestnut

Beaded Chestnut

Beaded Chestnut

Brown-spot Pinion

Brown-spot Pinion

Flounced Chestnut

Red-line Quaker

Yellow-line Quaker

Southern Chestnut

Brick

Brick

Brick

Lunar Underwing

Lunar Underwing
Omphaloscelis lunosa
73.193 (2270) 34–36mm

LS
ADULT varies from grey-buff to brown. Forewings have narrow dark oval and kidney marks, a dark 'wedge' near tip, and a network of pale veins and cross-lines. Flies Aug–Oct. **LARVA** feeds on grasses. **STATUS** Widespread and locally common in central and S Britain.

Chestnut *Conistra vaccinii*
73.194 (2258) 30–34mm

LS
ADULT is reddish brown. Forewings are rather short, with a curved leading edge; surface is dusted with blue-grey scales, including along jagged cross-lines; kidney mark contains a dark dot. Flies Sep–Apr; hibernates in cold weather. **LARVA** feeds on deciduous trees. **STATUS** Widespread and locally common.

Dark Chestnut *Conistra ligula* 73.195 (2259) 32–36mm

LS
ADULT is usually a rich chestnut brown; rarely paler. Forewings are slightly hook-tipped, with a curved leading edge; markings are indistinct. Flies Oct–Nov. **LARVA** feeds on sallow catkins at first, then on low-growing plants. **STATUS** Widespread and fairly common in central and S Britain.

Dotted Chestnut *Conistra rubiginea* 73.197 (2260) 33–35mm

LS
ADULT is usually orange-yellow, rarely buffish brown. Forewings are marked with numerous black dots, some aligning into rows, particularly along margin. Flies Oct–Nov, and Mar–Apr after hibernation. **LARVA** feeds on deciduous trees. **STATUS** Local and rather scarce, favouring woodland in central S England.

Orange Upperwing *Jodia croceago* 73.199 (2257) 32–34mm

LS
ADULT is orange-brown; forewings have a pointed tip, subtly darker veins and a dark cross-line that embraces a pale kidney mark. Flies Oct–Nov, and Mar–Apr after hibernation. **LARVA** feeds on oaks. **STATUS** Rare in S England woodland; possibly extinct.

Tawny Pinion *Lithophane semibrunnea* 73.200 (2235) 40–42mm
LS
ADULT is grey-brown. Thorax has dark-ridged 'shoulders' and a dark-ridged central crest; colour continues, in resting moth, down aligned trailing margins of narrow forewings. Flies Oct–Nov, and Apr–May after hibernation. **LARVA** feeds mainly on Ash. **STATUS** Local, mainly in central and S Britain.

Pale Pinion *Lithophane socia* 73.201 (2236) 40–42mm
LS
ADULT is pale buff, the thorax with dark-ridged 'shoulders' and a buff central crest. Narrow forewings have a dark smudge towards centre of trailing edge and dark marks on margin. Flies Oct–Nov, and Apr–May after hibernation. **LARVA** feeds on sallows at first, then on low-growing plants later. **STATUS** Local, mainly in central and S Britain.

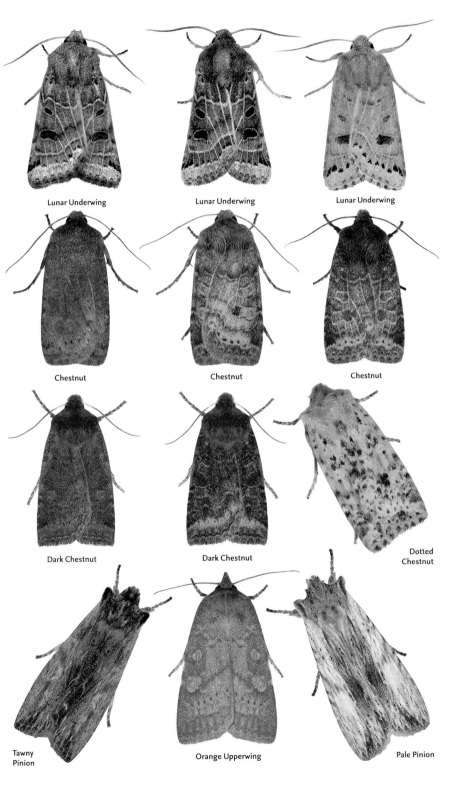

Lunar Underwing

Lunar Underwing

Lunar Underwing

Chestnut

Chestnut

Chestnut

Dark Chestnut

Dark Chestnut

Dotted
Chestnut

Tawny
Pinion

Orange Upperwing

Pale Pinion

Grey Shoulder-knot

Blair's Shoulder-knot

Golden-rod Brindle

Grey Shoulder-knot

Lithophane ornitopus 73.202 (2237) 34–36mm
ADULT is light grey. Narrow forewings have fine black speckling; pale kidney mark is orange-buff towards trailing edge. In resting moth, pale 'shoulders' are framed by a black line with radiating outer streaks. Flies Sep–Oct, and Mar–Apr after hibernation. **LARVA** feeds on oaks. **STATUS** Local, in central and S Britain.

Blair's Shoulder-knot

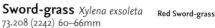

LS

Blair's Shoulder-knot

Lithophane leautieri 73.206 (2240) 40–43mm
ADULT is light grey. Narrow forewings have black veins and streaks, including a long basal streak; kidney mark is orange-buff. **LARVA** feeds on Leyland Cypress and Lawson's Cypress. **STATUS** Recent colonist, now local in central and S Britain.

LS

Golden-rod Brindle

Golden-rod Brindle

Sword-grass

Xylena solidaginis 73.207 (2233) 45–50mm
ADULT is grey-buff. Narrow forewings have a bold, dark-framed white kidney mark and a smaller pale oval; leading edge is orange-brown. Flies Aug–Sep. **LARVA** feeds mainly on Heather and Bilberry. **STATUS** Locally common on moorland habitats in N Britain.

LS

Sword-grass *Xylena exsoleta*
73.208 (2242) 60–66mm

Red Sword-grass

ADULT rests with wings rolled around body. Head and front of thorax are pale buff, thorax is dark above, and narrow forewings are grey-buff with faint dark veins and subtle dark marbling. Flies Sep–Oct, then Mar–Apr after hibernation. **LARVA** feeds on low-growing plants. **STATUS** Local, commonest in central and N Britain on moors and in woodland.

LS

Red Sword-grass *Xylena vetusta* 73.209 (2241) 52–55mm
ADULT is similar to Sword-grass but overall a warmer buffish brown. Narrow forewings are mainly buff with a dark reddish-brown trailing edge; colour continues onto thorax. Head and front of thorax are pale buff. Flies Sep–Oct, then Mar–Apr after hibernation. **LARVA** feeds on a range of plants. **STATUS** Local, mainly on moors and damp habitats in W and N Britain.

LS

Satellite *Eupsilia transversa* 73.210 (2256) 34–40mm
ADULT is orange-brown, the forewings with a white or orange kidney mark and 2 adjacent concolourous 'satellite' dots. Flies Sep–Oct, then Mar–Apr after hibernation. **LARVA** feeds on deciduous trees. **STATUS** Widespread and locally common.

LS

Angle-striped Sallow *Enargia paleacea* 73.211 (2313) 45–55mm
ADULT ranges from yellow to orange-buff. Forewings have a pointed tip, 2 narrow, angled cross-lines, and dark-framed oval and kidney marks, the latter with a dark spot in trailing half. Flies Jul–Aug. **LARVA** feeds on birches. **STATUS** Local, in E England and in Scotland.

LS

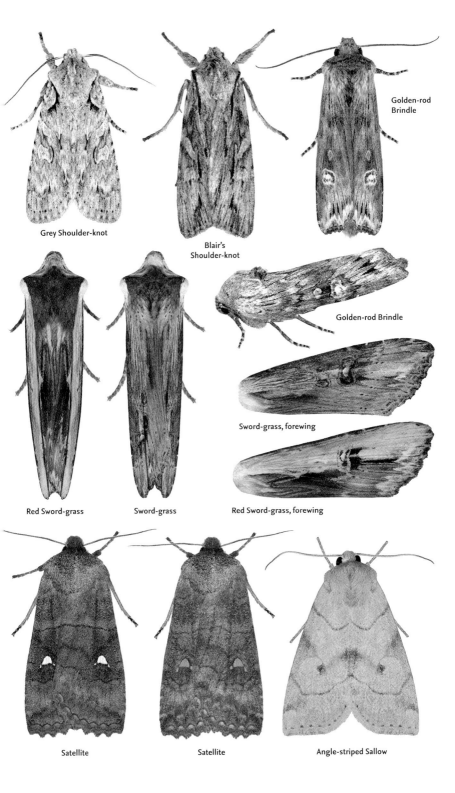

Grey Shoulder-knot

Blair's
Shoulder-knot

Golden-rod
Brindle

Red Sword-grass

Sword-grass

Golden-rod Brindle

Sword-grass, forewing

Red Sword-grass, forewing

Satellite

Satellite

Angle-striped Sallow

Double Kidney *Ipimorpha retusa* 73.212 (2311) 28–30mm
ADULT is grey-buff. Forewings are hook-tipped, with 2 oblique and parallel, dark-edged pale cross-lines, and pale-framed oval and kidney marks. Flies Jul–Sep. **LARVA** feeds on sallows. **STATUS** Locally common only in S Britain.

Olive *Ipimorpha subtusa*
73.213 (2312) 28–30mm
ADULT is grey-buff and similar to Double Kidney. Forewings are hook-tipped, with 2 curved, slightly diverging cross-lines and pale-framed kidney and kidney-like oval marks. Flies Jul–Aug. **LARVA** feeds on poplars, including Aspen. **STATUS** Widespread and locally common in central and S Britain.

Olive

White-spotted Pinion
Cosmia diffinis 73.214 (2317) 30–35mm
ADULT is reddish brown, the forewings with blue-grey marbling and white cross-lines that expand at leading edge into broad patches. Flies Jul–Sep. **LARVA** feeds on English and Wych elms. **STATUS** Rare and local, mainly in central S England.

Lesser-spotted Pinion *Cosmia affinis* 73.215 (2316) 30–35mm
ADULT is reddish brown to buff; forewings have faint pale cross-lines, the outer one kinked and broadening into a white mark towards leading edge. Flies Jul–Aug. **LARVA** feeds on English and Wych elms. **STATUS** Scarce, in central and S Britain.

Dun-bar *Cosmia trapezina*
73.216 (2318) 34–36mm
ADULT forewings range from buff to brown, with 2 dark-edged pale cross-lines, the inner one oblique, the outer one sharply angled midway; dark central band contains a dark spot. Flies Jul–Sep. **LARVA** feeds on deciduous trees. **STATUS** Widespread and locally common.

Dun-bar

Dun-bar

Lunar-spotted Pinion
Cosmia pyralina 73.217 (2319) 34–36mm
ADULT has maroon-buff forewings with 2 cross-lines; outer one kinks at leading edge and abuts a pale blue-grey patch. Flies Jul–Aug. **LARVA** feeds on elms. **STATUS** Local, mainly in S Britain.

Lunar-spotted
Pinion

Heart Moth *Dicycla oo* 73.218 (2315) 34–38mm
ADULT forewings are yellow-buff with dark veins and cross-lines; oval and heart-shaped kidney marks are dark-framed. Flies Jun–Jul. **LARVA** feeds on Pedunculate Oak. **STATUS** Rare and local in the S.

Minor Shoulder-knot *Brachylomia viminalis* 73.220 (2225) 28–32mm
ADULT forewings range from grey to brown; central dark cross-band contains a pale oval mark, while pale kidney mark lies outside. Dark basal streak defines pale 'shoulder'. Flies Jul–Aug. **LARVA** feeds on willows. **STATUS** Widespread and locally common.

Double Kidney

Olive

White-spotted Pinion

Lesser-spotted Pinion

Dun-bar

Dun-bar

Dun-bar

Lunar-spotted Pinion

Heart Moth

Minor Shoulder-knot

Lunar-spotted Pinion

Minor Shoulder-knot

Suspected *Parastichtis suspecta* 73.221 (2268) 30–32mm
ADULT ranges from buff to reddish brown. Forewings have pale cross-lines and pale-framed oval and kidney marks; some forms have yellow marbling, particularly as a marginal band. Flies Jul–Aug. LARVA feeds on birches and sallows. STATUS Widespread but local.

Dingy Shears *Apterogenum ypsillon* 73.222 (2314) 34–40mm
ADULT is grey-brown; forewings have partly dark-framed oval and kidney marks, a forked dark central mark and tooth-like dark projections from outermost cross-line. Flies Jun–Jul. LARVA feeds on sallows. STATUS Widespread in central and S Britain.

Oak Rustic *Dryobota labecula* 73.223 (2246a) 28–30mm
ADULT is dark reddish brown with subtle blue marbling. Forewings have subtle cross-lines, a dark-framed paler oval and a pale kidney mark (white or tinged buff). Flies Oct–Dec. LARVA feeds on Evergreen Oak. STATUS Rare recent colonist in S England.

FAR LEFT:
Merveille du Jour
LEFT: **Brindled Green**

Merveille du Jour

Merveille du Jour *Griposia aprilina* 73.224 (2247) 44–50mm
ADULT is pale blue-green, beautifully patterned with black and white marks and lines, the overall effect resembling tree lichen. Flies Sep–Oct. LARVA feeds on oaks. STATUS Widespread and locally common.

Brindled Green *Dryobotodes eremita* 73.225 (2248) 34–38mm
ADULT is greenish, the forewings marbled with black and white; pale oval, inner cross-line and outer cross-band are usually particularly striking. Flies Aug–Sep. LARVA feeds on oaks. STATUS Widespread, commonest in central and S Britain.

Grey Chi *Antitype chi* 73.228 (2254) 34–36mm
ADULT is very pale grey to grey-buff. Forewings have paler wavy cross-lines and a black central mark, like a laterally compressed 'X'. Flies Aug–Sep. LARVA feeds on low-growing plants. STATUS Widespread on moors in upland and N Britain.

Feathered Brindle *Aporophyla australis* 73.230 (2230) 38–40mm
ADULT forewings are grey with fine black cross-lines, a black basal streak and black marginal streaks. Flies Aug–Oct. LARVA feeds on Sea Campion and other coastal plants. STATUS Scarce and local; on coastal dunes and shingle in the S and SE.

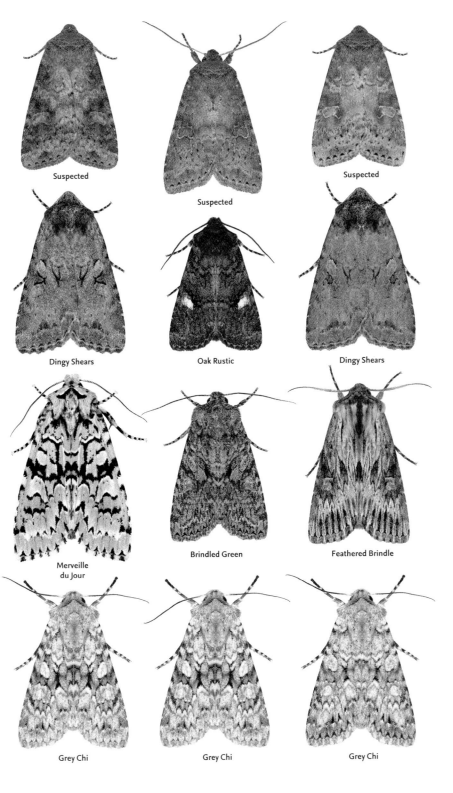

Suspected

Suspected

Suspected

Dingy Shears

Oak Rustic

Dingy Shears

Merveille
du Jour

Brindled Green

Feathered Brindle

Grey Chi

Grey Chi

Grey Chi

Deep-brown Dart *Aporophyla lutulenta* 73.231 (2231) 38–42mm
ADULT is dark grey-brown with subtle jagged cross-lines, the central two defining a darker band. Hindwings are white and usually unmarked. Flies Aug–Oct. **LARVA** feeds on Heather and shrubs. **STATUS** Locally common, mainly in central and S England.

Northern Deep-brown Dart
Aporophyla lueneburgensis 73.232 (2231a) 38–40mm
ADULT is similar to Deep-brown Dart but with more obvious pale cross-lines and more contrast between dark central band and paler rest of wing. White hindwings have a central row of black spots. Flies Aug–Sep. **LARVA** feeds on Heather and other moorland plants. **STATUS** Local, on moors in N Britain.

FAR LEFT:
Black Rustic, flying
LEFT:
Black Rustic, resting

Black Rustic

Black Rustic *Aporophyla nigra* 73.233 (2232) 42–45mm
ADULT is black, the forewings with a subtle bronze sheen in some lights; has a central white mark (outer edge of otherwise black kidney mark). Flies Sep–Oct. **LARVA** feeds on low-growing plants. **STATUS** Widespread and locally common, favouring moors, heaths and grassland.

Brindled Ochre *Dasypolia templi* 73.234 (2229) 40–50mm
ADULT is orange-buff to grey-buff, the forewings with paler oval and kidney marks and marginal cross-bands. Flies Sep–Oct. **LARVA** feeds on roots of Hogweed. **STATUS** Local and scattered; mainly coastal in SW, W and N Britain.

Brindled Ochre

Feathered Ranunculus *Polymixis lichenea* 73.235 (2255) 35–40mm
ADULT is well marked and variable, the forewings typically a shade of grey-green, with fine dark speckling, yellowish marbling and a darker central band containing pale kidney and dark-centred pale oval marks. Male has feathered antennae. Flies Aug–Oct. **LARVA** feeds on Thrift, Sea Plantain and other coastal plants. **STATUS** Mainly coastal, as far N as Yorkshire and Lancashire.

Black-banded *Polymixis xanthomista* 73.236 (2253) 40–42mm
ADULT is yellowish grey with dense dark speckling. Forewings have a dark central cross-band. Flies Aug–Sep. **LARVA** feeds on Thrift and other coastal plants. **STATUS** Scarce, local and entirely coastal, in SW England and SW Wales only.

Large Ranunculus
Polymixis flavicincta 73.237 (2252) 42–48mm
ADULT is light grey to dark grey, with dense dark speckling, orange-yellow markings (particularly along margin) and a subtle dark cross-band. Flies Sep–Oct. **LARVA** feeds on a range of herbaceous plants. **STATUS** Locally common only in S England and S Wales.

Deep-brown Dart

Deep-brown Dart

Northern Deep-brown Dart

Black Rustic

Northern Deep-brown Dart

Northern Deep-brown Dart

Feathered Ranunculus

Feathered Ranunculus

Brindled Ochre

Large Ranunculus

Large Ranunculus

Black-banded

Dark Brocade *Mniotype adusta* 73.238 (2250) 44–46mm

ADULT is brown, the forewings with orange-brown and dark brown marbling, and jagged pale central cross-lines framing a dark central band with pale-framed oval and kidney marks; jagged pale submarginal cross-line includes an indented 'W'. Flies May–Jul. **LARVA** feeds on a range of plants. **STATUS** Widespread and fairly common, favouring heaths and downs in the S, and moors in the N.

LS

Pine Beauty *Panolis flammea* 73.241 (2179) 30–32mm

ADULT is orange-brown with white streaks and veins, and white oval and kidney marks. Flies Mar–Apr. **LARVA** feeds on pines, including Scots Pine. **STATUS** Widespread and locally common.

LS

Pine Beauty

Clouded Drab *Orthosia incerta* 73.242 (2188) 36–38mm

ADULT is very variable, ranging from grey-buff to brown, with fine dark speckling. Forewings are marbled grey and rich brown, with subtle dark patches in centre, particularly around oval and kidney marks; usually show a pale outer cross-line. Flies Mar–May. **LARVA** feeds on oak and other deciduous trees. **STATUS** Widespread and locally common.

L

Clouded Drab

Blossom Underwing

Orthosia miniosa 73.243 (2183) 32–34mm
ADULT is buff, the forewings with an orange-brown central cross-band containing darker brown oval and kidney marks. Hindwings are pinkish. Flies May–Apr. **LARVA** feeds on trees and shrubs, but mainly oaks. **STATUS** Locally common only in S Britain.

LS

Common Quaker *Orthosia cerasi* 73.244 (2187) 36–38mm

ADULT ranges from grey-brown to orange-buff. Forewings have a diffuse dark central band, pale-framed oval and kidney marks, and a pale outer cross-line and outer veins. Flies Mar–Apr. **LARVA** feeds on oaks, sallows and other trees. **STATUS** Widespread and locally common.

LS

Small Quaker *Orthosia cruda* 73.245 (2182) 26–28mm

ADULT is grey-buff, the forewings with a few scattered dark spots, pale-framed oval and pale-framed dark kidney marks, and a pale outer cross-line. Flies Mar–Apr. **LARVA** feeds on oaks, sallows and other trees. **STATUS** Widespread and locally common.

LS

Lead-coloured Drab *Orthosia populeti* 73.246 (2185) 36–38mm

ADULT is blue-grey to grey-brown, the forewings with a diffuse dark (subtly reddish) central band, pale-framed dark oval and kidney marks, and a pale outer cross-line with dark inner spots. Flies Apr. **LARVA** feeds mainly on Aspen. **STATUS** Widespread but local, mainly in central and S Britain, but also central Scotland.

LS

Dark Brocade

Pine Beauty

Pine Beauty

Pine Beauty

Clouded Drab

Clouded Drab

Clouded Drab

Clouded Drab

Blossom Underwing

Blossom Underwing

Common Quaker

Common Quaker

Small Quaker

Small Quaker

Lead-coloured Drab

Lead-coloured Drab

Powdered Quaker
Orthosia gracilis 73.247 (2186) 36–38mm
ADULT ranges from buffish white to orange-brown. Forewings have dark speckling and a powdered texture. Many forms have an outer cross-line and inner row of black dots; oval and kidney marks are usually pale-framed, the latter dark towards trailing half. Some forms have a diffuse dark central cross-band. Flies Apr–May. **LARVA** feeds mainly on sallows. **STATUS** Widespread and common.

Powdered Quaker

Northern Drab
Orthosia opima 73.248 (2184) 36–38mm
ADULT is grey-brown to reddish brown with a hairy thorax. Forewings usually have a pale outer cross-line and diffuse dark central cross-band containing pale-framed oval and kidney marks. Flies Apr–May. **LARVA** feeds on a wide range of plants. **STATUS** Local, found mainly in central and S Britain.

Hebrew Character
Orthosia gothica 73.249 (2190) 32–34mm
ADULT is variably marbled grey-brown to reddish brown, with a striking saddle-shaped mark that is usually black but in some forms is concolourous with wing. Flies Mar–Apr. **LARVA** feeds on trees and shrubs. **STATUS** Widespread and common.

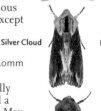

Hebrew Character

Twin-spotted Quaker
Anorthoa munda 73.250 (2189) 40–42mm
ADULT ranges from grey-buff to orange-brown, the forewings with paired streak-like black spots. Flies Mar–Apr. **LARVA** feeds on deciduous trees. **STATUS** Locally common except in the N.

Silver Cloud

Silver Cloud
Egira conspicillaris 73.251 (2181) 38–40mm
ADULT rests with wings creased lengthways. Forewings are typically dark with a pale streak at tip and a

Twin-spotted Quaker

pale trailing edge. Dorsal surface of thorax is also pale. Flies Apr–May. **LARVA** feeds on trees and shrubs. **STATUS** Scarce and local, mainly in woodland in the Severn Valley and on Exmoor.

Hedge Rustic

Hedge Rustic *Tholera cespitis* 73.252 (2177) 36–38mm
ADULT is sooty brown, the broad forewings with red- and yellow-tinged cross-lines and pale-framed oval and kidney marks. Flies Aug–Sep. **LARVA** feeds on various grasses. **STATUS** Locally common.

Feathered Gothic *Tholera decimalis* 73.253 (2178) 34–44mm
ADULT forewings are grey-brown with white veins and white-framed oval and kidney marks. Male has feathered antennae. Flies Aug–Sep. **LARVA** feeds on grasses. **STATUS** Locally common in central and S Britain.

Powdered Quaker

Powdered Quaker

Northern Drab

Hebrew Character

Hebrew Character

Northern Drab

Silver Cloud

Twin-spotted Quaker

Twin-spotted Quaker

Hedge Rustic

Feathered Gothic, male

Feathered Gothic, female

Antler Moth *Cerapteryx graminis* 73.254 (2176) 30–38mm
ADULT is buff to orange-brown, the forewings with a branched (antler-like) white mark and dark marginal 'wedges'. Flies Jun–Sep. LARVA feeds on grasses. STATUS Widespread and common.

Nutmeg *Anarta trifolii* 73.255 (2145) 32–34mm
ADULT is grey-buff with fine black and pale grey speckling, and subtle orange marbling. Oval and kidney marks are usually pale-framed and dark-centred, and pale outermost cross-line includes a 'W'. Flies May–Sep. LARVA feeds on goosefoots and oraches. STATUS Locally common; has an E bias to its range.

Broad-bordered White Underwing *Anarta melanopa* 73.256 (2144) 24–26mm
ADULT is day-flying. Forewings are grey with dark bands and dark oval and kidney marks. Hindwings are black with a white central patch and margin. Flies May–Jun. LARVA feeds on upland moorland plants, including Crowberry. STATUS Very local, on Scottish uplands above 500m.

Broad-bordered
White Underwing

Beautiful Yellow Underwing

Beautiful Yellow Underwing
Anarta myrtilli 73.257 (2142) 21–23mm
ADULT is day-flying. Forewings are orange-brown with white cross-bands and lines. Hindwings are black with a yellow centre and white margin. Flies May–Aug. LARVA feeds on Heather. STATUS Widespread but local, on heaths in the S and moors elsewhere.

Beautiful
Yellow Underwing

Small Dark Yellow Underwing
Coranarta cordigera 73.258 (2143) 25–27mm
ADULT is day-flying. Forewings are black with grey banding, and a white basal cross-line and kidney mark. Hindwings are yellow with a black border and white margin. Flies Apr–May. LARVA feeds on Bearberry. STATUS Scarce, on upland moors in central Scotland.

Small Dark Yellow
Underwing

Silvery Arches *Polia trimaculosa* 73.260 (2149) 44–50mm
ADULT forewings are grey, marbled with grey-brown and hints of orange; outermost cross-line is edged with an interrupted black line that forms dashes centrally and on trailing margin. Thorax has tufts of reddish hairs. Flies Jun–Jul. LARVA feeds on birches and Bog-myrtle. STATUS Very local, mainly on heaths in S England and moors in central Scotland.

Grey Arches *Polia nebulosa* 73.261 (2150) 46–52mm
ADULT is typically grey with dark-framed pale oval and kidney marks, and jagged, black-edged white cross-lines; on outermost of these, dark edging is most obvious centrally and there is no dash on trailing margin (cf. Silvery Arches). Much darker forms also occur, showing a silvery dusting on thorax, oval and kidney marks, and a pale margin. Flies Jun–Jul. LARVA feeds on low-growing plants at first, then on willows. STATUS Locally common.

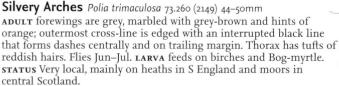

Broad-bordered
White Underwing

Broad-bordered
White Underwing

Nutmeg

Antler Moth

Beautiful Yellow
Underwing

Beautiful Yellow
Underwing

Antler Moth

Small Dark Yellow
Underwing

Small Dark
Yellow Underwing

Silvery Arches

Grey Arches, dark form

Grey Arches, typical form

Pale Shining Brown *Polia bombycina* 73.259 (2148) 45–50mm
ADULT is grey-buff. Forewings are slightly shiny, with an orange-buff central band; kidney mark has a pale outer margin, and outermost cross-line is wavy. Flies Jun–Jul. **LARVA** feeds on low-growing plants. **STATUS** Rare and declining, now mainly on calcareous soils in SE England.

L

Light Brocade *Lacanobia w-latinum* 73.263 (2157) 38–40mm
ADULT is lilac-grey, the forewings with a broad brown central cross-band (which fails to reach trailing margin) containing pale oval and kidney marks. Flies May–Jun. **LARVA** feeds on Broom and related plants. **STATUS** Local, mainly in S England and Wales.

L

Light Brocade

Pale-shouldered Brocade
Lacanobia thalassina 73.264 (2158) 36–38mm
ADULT forewings are brown with a pale basal 'shoulder'; jagged pale central cross-lines frame pale oval and kidney marks; has a dark bar parallel to trailing edge and outer pale cross-line contains a striking 'W' (cf. Dog's Tooth). Flies Jun–Jul. **LARVA** feeds on a range of plants. **STATUS** Widespread and locally common.

L

Beautiful Brocade *Lacanobia contigua* 73.265 (2156) 38–40mm
ADULT is grey-brown, the forewings with marbling and markings that can be greenish or orange-brown; pale diagonal band is striking, and outermost black-edged white cross-line contains a 'W'. Flies Jun–Jul. **LARVA** feeds on a wide range of plants. **STATUS** Local; range is disjunct, with populations in S England and Wales, and central Scotland.

L

Dog's Tooth *Lacanobia suasa* 73.266 (2159) 34–36mm
ADULT ranges from grey-buff to brown, the forewings with a tooth-like black central mark; outermost jagged, dark-edged white cross-line includes a distinct 'W' (fancifully fang-like in some forms). Flies May–Jun. **LARVA** feeds on low-growing plants. **STATUS** Local, mainly in central and S Britain.

L

Bright-line Brown-eye
Lacanobia oleracea
73.267 (2160) 34–36mm
ADULT forewings are brown with pale-framed oval and orange kidney marks; outer cross-line contains a 'W'. Flies May–Jul. **LARVA** feeds on goosefoots and oraches. **STATUS** Widespread and common.

L

Dot Moth *Melanchra persicariae* 73.270 (2155) 38–40mm
ADULT is sooty black, the forewings with a buff-centred white kidney mark; has an orange tuft at rear end of thorax. Flies Jul–Aug. **LARVA** feeds on low-growing plants. **STATUS** Common in central and S Britain.

L

Dot Moth

Pale Shining Brown

Light Brocade

Pale-shouldered Brocade

Beautiful Brocade

Dog's Tooth

Dog's Tooth

Bright-line Brown-eye

Dot Moth

larva

Broom Moth
Ceramica pisi 73.271 (2163) 34–36mm
ADULT ranges from buff to rich brown, but in all forms forewings have a jagged yellow outermost cross-line that is enlarged at trailing edge to form a patch; in many individuals, a subtle dark central cross-band is also present. Flies May–Jul.
LARVA is stippled grey-green, with lengthways yellow stripes; feeds on Broom and Bracken. **STATUS** Widespread and common.

Glaucous Shears *Papestra biren* 73.272 (2162) 34–38mm
ADULT forewings are grey with dark speckling and dark cross-lines; outermost cross-line is edged very pale yellow, and oval and kidney marks are pale. Flies May–Jun. **LARVA** feeds on Heather and other moorland plants. **STATUS** Local on moorland in W and N Britain.

Shears *Hada plebeja* 73.273 (2147) 32–34mm
ADULT ranges from pale grey to grey-brown. Forewings have a straight leading edge; dark partial central band contains a forked white mark, a bit like a pair of shears; oval and kidney marks are pale. Flies May–Jul. **LARVA** feeds on low-growing plants. **STATUS** Widespread and locally common.

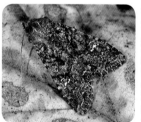

Cabbage Moth *Mamestra brassicae*
73.274 (2154) 38–44mm
ADULT forewings are marbled rich brown and grey, with dark speckling and a white-edged outermost cross-line that includes a 'W'; kidney mark is white-edged, conspicuously so on outer margin. Flies May–Aug. **LARVA** feeds on Cabbage and related plants. **STATUS** Widespread, commonest in S half of Britain.

White Colon *Sideridis turbida* 73.275 (2152) 40–42mm
ADULT forewings are grey-buff with paired white marks; depending on how you view them, they look like a colon punctuation mark or inverted commas; outermost white cross-line is jagged and incomplete, and lacks a 'W'. Flies May–Jul. **LARVA** feeds on low-growing plants. **STATUS** Sandy coasts of England and Wales.

Campion *Sideridis rivularis* 73.276 (2166) 28–30mm
ADULT forewings are marbled brown and pinkish purple; elongated oval and kidney marks are white-framed, the frames typically joined and creating a broad 'V'; outermost cross-line is jagged and pale. Double-brooded in the S: flies May–Jun, and Aug–Sep. **LARVA** feeds inside seed capsules of campions. **STATUS** Widespread and locally common.

Lychnis *Hadena bicruris* 73.281 (2173) 32–38mm
ADULT is very similar to Campion but forewings are typically marbled grey and brown, lacking any hint of purple; elongated oval and kidney marks are white-framed and separate, not linked as in Campion. Flies Jun–Jul. **LARVA** feeds inside seed capsules of campions. **STATUS** Widespread and locally common.

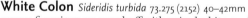

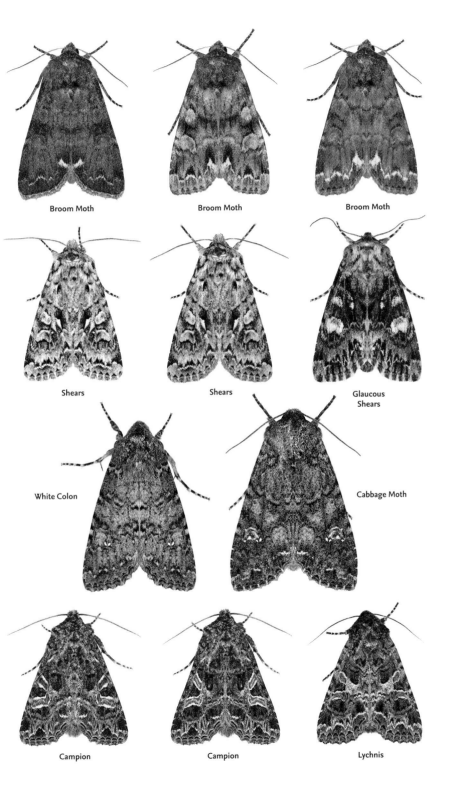

Broom Moth

Broom Moth

Broom Moth

Shears

Shears

Glaucous
Shears

White Colon

Cabbage Moth

Campion

Campion

Lychnis

Bordered Gothic *Sideridis reticulata* 73.277 (2153) 34–36mm
ADULT forewings are grey-brown with a network of white cross-lines
and veins. Similar Gothic (p. 314) has broader wings and more widely
separated veins; similar Feathered Gothic (p. 284) lacks white cross-lines.
Flies Jun–Jul. LARVA feeds on low-growing plants. STATUS Rare, mainly
on coastal grassland in SE England and S Ireland (subtly darker ssp.
hibernica).

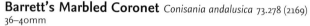

Barrett's Marbled Coronet *Conisania andalusica* 73.278 (2169)
36–40mm
ADULT is grey-buff, the forewings with yellow and dark speckling, a
subtly darker central cross-band containing pale oval and kidney marks,
and an indistinct pale outermost cross-line. Flies Jun–Jul. LARVA feeds
on roots of Sea Campion and other coastal plants. STATUS Very local;
on coasts of SW England and Wales.

Broad-barred White
Hecatera bicolorata
73.279 (2164) 30–34mm
ADULT is greyish white,
the forewings with a broad
dark central cross-band; this
contains pale oval and kidney
marks. Flies Jun–Aug. LARVA feeds on flowers
of low-growing plants. STATUS Widespread,
but commonest in S Britain.

Small Ranunculus
Hecatera dysodea
73.280 (2165) 32–34mm
ADULT is grey with dark
speckling and orange tints.
Forewings have a darker
central cross-band with pale oval and kidney
marks, the latter tinged orange. Flies Jun–Jul.
LARVA feeds on flowers and seeds of lettuces.
STATUS Local in SE England.

Varied Coronet
Hadena compta
73.282 (2170) 26–28mm
ADULT is marbled grey and
white, with a complete broad white central cross-band that embraces
white oval and kidney marks. Flies Jun–Jul. LARVA feeds on seeds of
members of the pink family, including Sweet-William. STATUS Locally
common only in the SE but its range is expanding.

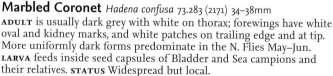

Broad-barred White

Marbled Coronet *Hadena confusa* 73.283 (2171) 34–38mm
ADULT is usually dark grey with white on thorax; forewings have white
oval and kidney marks, and white patches on trailing edge and at tip.
More uniformly dark forms predominate in the N. Flies May–Jun.
LARVA feeds inside seed capsules of Bladder and Sea campions and
their relatives. STATUS Widespread but local.

White Spot *Hadena albimacula* 73.284 (2172) 32–36mm
ADULT is rich brown with white markings; forewings have black-edged
white cross-lines and black-framed white oval and kidney marks. Flies
Jun–Jul. LARVA feeds on Nottingham Catchfly seeds. STATUS Scarce;
on coastal shingle and cliffs in SE England.

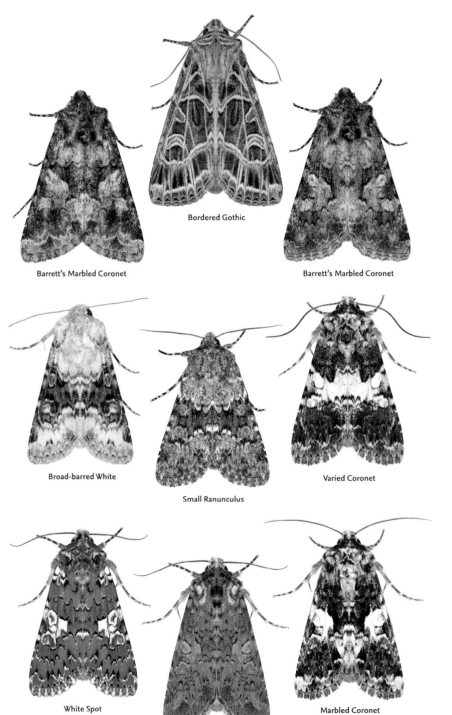

Bordered Gothic

Barrett's Marbled Coronet

Barrett's Marbled Coronet

Broad-barred White

Small Ranunculus

Varied Coronet

White Spot

Marbled Coronet

Marbled Coronet

Grey *Hadena caesia* 73.285 (2174) 38–40mm
ADULT from Ireland is blue-grey; individuals elsewhere are grey-brown with orange marbling. Forewings usually have a diffuse dark basal band, a mark on middle of leading edge and a marginal band. Flies May–Aug. **LARVA** feeds on Sea Campion. **STATUS** Rare and coastal; Western Isles, Isle of Man and SW Ireland.

Tawny Shears *Hadena perplexa* 73.286 (2167) 28–34mm
ADULT ground colour ranges from almost white, through yellow-buff to brown. Forewings have jagged cross-lines, a dark central tooth-like mark and a pale oval; pale kidney mark abuts a dark outer patch. So-called **Pod Lover** (ssp. *capsophila*) is grey-brown. **LARVA** feeds on the seeds of campions. **STATUS** Widespread, commonest in central and S Britain.

Double Line *Mythimna turca* 73.288 (2191) 38–44mm
ADULT forewings are brown with 2 dark central cross-lines, the inner one angled sharply near leading edge and the outer one oblique. Flies Jun–Jul. **LARVA** feeds on Cock's-foot and other grasses. **STATUS** Scarce and local, mainly in SW England and SW Wales.

Brown-line Bright-eye *Mythimna conigera* 73.290 (2192) 32–34mm
ADULT forewings are orange-brown with 2 dark brown cross-lines (the inner sharply angled, the outer oblique) and a white central spot (trailing half of kidney mark). Flies Jun–Jul. **LARVA** feeds on Cock's-foot and other grasses. **STATUS** Widespread and fairly common.

Delicate *Mythimna vitellina*
73.295 (2195) 38–42mm
ADULT forewings range from pale yellow to orange-buff; marked with jagged brown cross-lines, and kidney mark has a dark spot in trailing half. Flies Aug–Oct. **LARVA** feeds on grasses. **STATUS** Regular immigrant, sometimes arriving in good numbers in the SW.

Delicate

White-speck
Mythimna unipuncta
73.296 (2203) 42–46mm
ADULT forewings have curved, pointed tip. Some individuals are buff, tinged orange, with a dark central streak containing a white spot, and a streak at tip; others are much more dark-speckled, the dark streaks bordered with orange. Flies Aug–Oct. **LARVA** feeds on grasses. **STATUS** Regular immigrant, sometimes in good numbers.

White-point *Mythimna albipuncta* 73.297 (2194) 32–34mm
ADULT forewings are orange-brown with scalloped, diffuse pale cross-lines and a white central spot. Flies Aug–Sep. **LARVA** feeds on grasses. **STATUS** Regular immigrant and occasional short-term resident in the SW.

Clay *Mythimna ferrago* 73.298 (2193) 36–38mm
ADULT forewings are buff to grey-buff with a pear-shaped white central spot and curved outer cross-row of black dots. Flies Jul–Aug. **LARVA** feeds on grasses and low-growing plants. **STATUS** Widespread and locally common.

Tawny Shears

Tawny Shears

Grey

Grey

Pod Lover

Double Line

Brown-line Bright-eye

White-speck

White-point

Delicate

White-speck

Clay

Delicate

Silurian *Eriopygodes imbecilla* 73.306 (2175) 25–30mm
ADULT male has a furry orange-red thorax; forewings range from orange to yellow-buff, marked with dark cross-lines and a narrow pale kidney mark. Female is smaller and more uniformly brown, although cross-lines and kidney mark can still be discerned. Flies Jun–Jul. **LARVA** feeds on Heath Bedstraw. **STATUS** Rare; restricted to a few moorland sites in S Wales.

Striped Wainscot *Mythimna pudorina* 73.289 (2196) 36–38mm
ADULT forewings have a curved leading edge; pinkish buff with dark speckling and white veins, some bordered with dark stripes. Flies Jun–Jul. **LARVA** feeds on grasses and rushes. **STATUS** Local; favours marshes and bogs, mainly in S England and S Wales.

Common Wainscot

Common Wainscot
Mythimna pallens
73.291 (2199) 32–34mm
ADULT ranges from buff to orange-buff; forewings have dark-edged white veins and a hint of a dark central streak. Hindwings are typically unmarked white. Overlapping double broods in the S: flies May–Sep. **LARVA** feeds on grasses. **STATUS** Widespread and locally common.

Mathew's Wainscot
Mythimna favicolor
73.292 (2200) 36–38mm
ADULT forewings are buff, tinged orange, and mostly unmarked except for very subtle pale veins and an outer cross-row of black dots. Flies Jun–Jul. **LARVA** feeds on Common Saltmarsh-grass. **STATUS** Scarce and local; restricted to saltmarshes in S and SE England.

Smoky Wainscot *Mythimna impura* 73.293 (2198) 32–36mm
ADULT is similar to Common Wainscot but white veins on grey-buff forewings are more strikingly black-edged, and also shows a bold black central streak. Hindwings are smoky grey. Flies Jun–Aug. **LARVA** feeds on grasses. **STATUS** Widespread and locally common.

Southern Wainscot *Mythimna straminea* 73.294 (2197) 34–38mm
ADULT forewings are pale grey-buff with very finely marked veins, a scattering of black spots (some of which form an outer cross-line) and a marginal row of black dots. Flies Jul. **LARVA** feeds on Common Reed and canary-grasses. **STATUS** Local, restricted to wetlands in S England and S Wales.

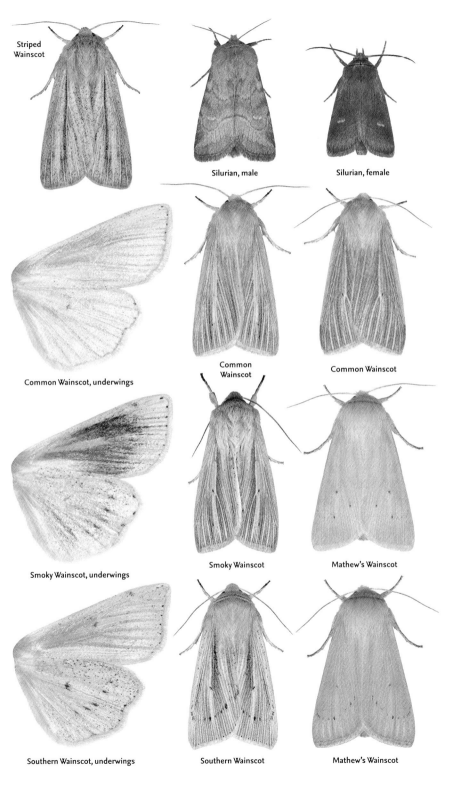

Striped Wainscot

Silurian, male

Silurian, female

Common Wainscot, underwings

Common Wainscot

Common Wainscot

Smoky Wainscot, underwings

Smoky Wainscot

Mathew's Wainscot

Southern Wainscot, underwings

Southern Wainscot

Mathew's Wainscot

Shore Wainscot *Mythimna litoralis* 73.299 (2201) 38–40mm
ADULT forewings are yellow-buff with finely marked veins and a
branched, dark-edged white central streak. Hindwings are white. Flies
Jun–Aug. LARVA feeds on Marram. STATUS Local, restricted to suitable
sandy coasts of England and Wales.

LS

L-album Wainscot *Mythimna l-album* 73.300 (2202) 32–34mm
ADULT is grey-buff. Forewings have a striking L-shaped white streak,
plus fine dark streaks, white veins and a pale oblique stripe from
wingtip. Hindwings are grey-buff. Double-brooded: flies Jul, and Sep–
Oct. LARVA feeds on coastal grasses. STATUS Widespread but local on
coasts of S England and S Wales.

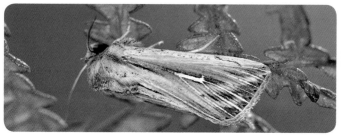

L-album
Wainscot

Shoulder-striped
Wainscot

Shoulder-striped Wainscot *Leucania comma* 73.301 (2205) 34–36mm
ADULT forewings are buff with a black basal streak and white veins (central
one is boldest) that are emphasised towards margin by interspersed
black streaks. Hindwings are grey-brown. Flies Jun–Jul. LARVA feeds on
Cock's-foot and other grasses. STATUS Widespread and locally common,
except in the N.

LS

Obscure Wainscot *Leucania obsoleta* 73.302 (2204) 38–40mm
ADULT forewings are grey-buff with black-edged veins and an outer
cross-row of black dots. Hindwings are whitish with grey streaks. Flies
May–Jul. LARVA feeds on Common Reed. STATUS Local, found in
wetlands in central and S England and S Wales.

LS

Devonshire Wainscot *Leucania putrescens* 73.303 (2206) 33–35mm
ADULT forewings are grey-buff with dark central and marginal streaks,
well-marked veins and an orange suffusion on trailing edge. Hindwings
are white. Flies Jul–Aug. LARVA feeds on coastal plants. STATUS Scarce
and local, on coasts of SW Britain only.

LS

Cosmopolitan *Leucania loreyi* 73.304 (2208) 36–40mm
ADULT forewings are buff to grey-buff with a dark central streak
containing a central white spot; central streak often links to a dark
oblique stripe running from wingtip. Hindwings are white. White-speck
(p. 294) is similar. Flies Aug–Oct. LARVA feeds on grasses. STATUS
Immigrant, often in good numbers in the SW.

LS

Flame Wainscot *Senta flammea* 73.305 (2209) 34–38mm
ADULT forewings have a strongly curved margin and edges, tapering to
a pointed tip; grey-buff with a dark central streak and outer cross-row of
black dots. Flies May–Jul. LARVA feeds on Common Reed. STATUS Scarce
and local in SE England; East Anglian wetlands are its stronghold.

LS

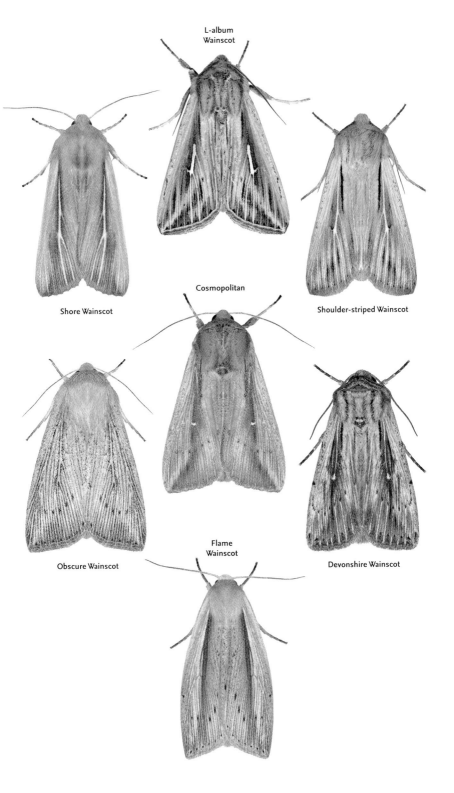

L-album
Wainscot

Shore Wainscot

Cosmopolitan

Shoulder-striped Wainscot

Obscure Wainscot

Devonshire Wainscot

Flame
Wainscot

Pearly Underwing *Peridroma saucia* 73.307 (2119)
46–54mm
ADULT forewings are long and narrow; brown with variable black marbling and speckling, dark-edged pale cross-lines, and pale oval and pale-framed kidney marks. Hindwings have a pearly sheen. Thorax has a pale dorsal stripe. Flies Aug–Oct. **LARVA** feeds on low-growing plants. **STATUS** Immigrant, often in good numbers.

LS

Portland Moth *Actebia praecox* 73.308 (2099) 36–38mm
ADULT forewings are pale green with jagged, black-edged white cross-lines, pale oval and kidney marks (former red-centred), and a brick-red submarginal band. Flies Aug–Sep. **LARVA** feeds on Creeping Willow. **STATUS** Scarce and local; on coastal dunes of Britain and Ireland.

LS

Coast Dart *Euxoa cursoria* 73.311 (2083) 34–38mm
ADULT ranges from grey-buff to brown. Compared to White-line Dart (below) and Sand Dart (p. 302), forewings are narrower; kidney mark is relatively large (roughly same depth as distance between kidney edge and wing's trailing margin). Flies Jul–Sep. **LARVA** feeds on Sea Sandwort and other dune plants. **STATUS** Restricted to coastal dunes; particularly local and scarce in the S.

LS

Square-spot Dart *Euxoa obelisca* 73.312 (2080)
36–38mm
ADULT forewings are grey-brown with a pale stripe on leading edge (particularly broad on 'shoulder'), and pale oval and kidney marks set within a broad black streak. Compared to White-line Dart, outermost cross-line lacks inner dark streaks. Flies Aug–Oct. **LARVA** feeds on low-growing plants. **STATUS** Widespread but scarce, local and mainly coastal.

LS

White-line Dart *Euxoa tritici* 73.313 (2081) 30–38mm
ADULT forewings are brown with dark arrowhead marks inside outermost cross-line; pale oval and kidney marks are set within a broad black streak, and often shows a pale line just inside and parallel to leading edge. Flies Jul–Aug. **LARVA** feeds on low-growing plants. **STATUS** Widespread but local.

LS

Garden Dart *Euxoa nigricans* 73.314 (2082) 30–34mm
ADULT forewings are brown and relatively unmarked except for pale oval and kidney marks, and usually indistinct pale cross-lines. Flies Aug–Sep. **LARVA** feeds on low-growing plants. **STATUS** Widespread and locally common, favouring disturbed ground.

LS

Light Feathered Rustic *Agrotis cinerea* 73.316
(2084) 34–38mm
ADULT ranges from pale grey-buff to dark brown. Forewings have jagged dark cross-lines and a dark kidney mark; lacks dark central dart seen in similar species. Flies May–Jun. **LARVA** feeds on low-growing plants. **STATUS** Local in S England and Wales.

LS

Pearly
Underwing

Pearly Underwing

Portland Moth

Coast Dart

White-line Dart

White-line Dart

White-line Dart

Coast Dart

Square-spot Dart

Garden Dart

Garden Dart

Coast Dart

Light Feathered Rustic

Light Feathered Rustic

Light Feathered Rustic

Heart and Dart *Agrotis exclamationis* 73.317 (2089) 32–38mm
ADULT has a black band on front of thorax, unique among its congeners. Forewings are grey-brown with a dart-shaped black central mark, and dark oval and kidney marks. Flies May–Jul. **LARVA** feeds on low-growing plants. **STATUS** Widespread and common.

LS

Turnip Moth *Agrotis segetum* 73.319 (2087) 30–38mm
ADULT ranges from grey-buff to brown, all individuals with a pale marginal fringe to relatively long, narrow forewings; dart, oval and kidney marks are usually pale but dark-framed. Double-brooded: flies May–Jun, and Aug–Sep. **LARVA** feeds on roots of low-growing plants. **STATUS** Widespread and common in central and S Britain.

LS

Heart and Club *Agrotis clavis* 73.320 (2088) 36–38mm
ADULT is grey-buff, the forewings flecked and speckled with black, and with dark-framed oval, kidney and broad central dart marks. Flies Jun–Jul. **LARVA** feeds on low-growing plants. **STATUS** Locally common in S England; scattered and local elsewhere.

Heart and
Club

LS

Archer's Dart *Agrotis vestigialis* 73.322 (2085) 32–34mm
ADULT is pale grey-buff. Forewings have a broad fang-like dart and black-framed, dark-centred oval and kidney marks, and a submarginal row of dagger-like darts. Flies Jul–Sep. **LARVA** feeds on low-growing plants. **STATUS** Widespread but local; mainly on coasts but also on sandy soils inland (heathland and Breckland).

Archer's Dart

Sand Dart *Agrotis ripae* 73.323 (2093) 34–40mm
ADULT is pale grey-buff, the forewings with relatively small (compared to, e.g. Coast Dart, p. 300) dark-framed oval, kidney and central dart marks. Flies Jun–Jul. **LARVA** feeds on low-growing sand-dune plants. **STATUS** Scarce and local, restricted to coastal sand dunes, mainly in England and Wales.

LS

Sand Dart

Crescent Dart *Agrotis trux* 73.324 (2090) 36–40mm
ADULT male's grey-buff forewings have a broad dark dart, black-framed white oval and black-framed kidney mark. Female has similar markings but blackish-brown forewings, hence only white oval is distinct. Flies Jul–Aug. **LARVA** feeds on coastal plants. **STATUS** Local and coastal, mainly in SW England and NW Wales.

LS

Shuttle-shaped Dart *Agrotis puta* 73.325 (2092) 30–32mm
ADULT pale grey thorax contrasts with forewing colour, which ranges from buff to blackish brown; pale oval is compressed and pointed at both ends, and kidney mark is dark-framed. Flies May–Oct in successive broods. **LARVA** feeds on low-growing plants. **STATUS** Locally common in central and S Britain.

Crescent
Dart

LS

LS

Shuttle-shaped
Dart, female

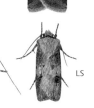

Shuttle-shaped Dart, male

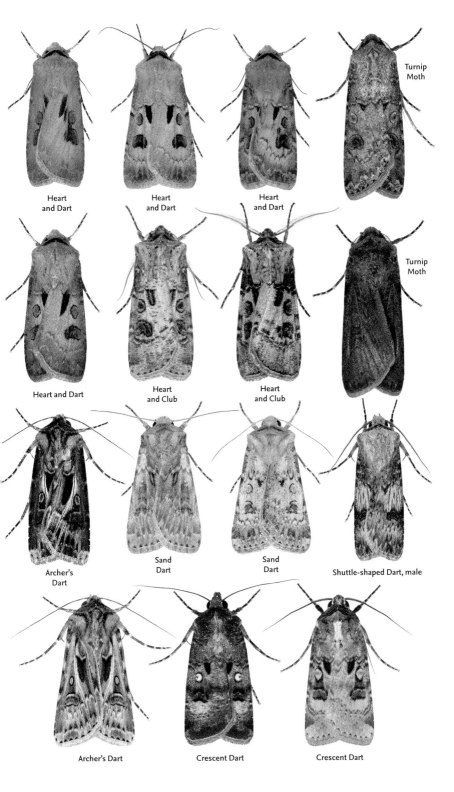

Heart
and Dart

Heart
and Dart

Heart
and Dart

Turnip
Moth

Heart and Dart

Heart
and Club

Heart
and Club

Turnip
Moth

Archer's
Dart

Sand
Dart

Sand
Dart

Shuttle-shaped Dart, male

Archer's Dart

Crescent Dart

Crescent Dart

Dark Sword-grass *Agrotis ipsilon* 73.327 (2091) 40–45mm
ADULT forewings are narrow and overlap at rest; grey-brown to dark brown, with a pale submarginal band containing dark dagger-like marks; scalloped basal cross-line and dark-framed oval and kidney marks are variably distinct. Flies May–Oct. **LARVA** feeds on low-growing plants. **STATUS** Immigrant, sometimes numerous.

LS

Flame *Axylia putris* 73.328 (2098) 28–30mm
ADULT rests with forewings overlapping and rolled around body. Front of thorax is yellow-buff; top of thorax is dark, contrasting with pale buff forewings, which have a dark streak on leading edge and a dark kidney mark. Flies Jun–Jul. **LARVA** feeds on low-growing plants. **STATUS** Widespread and common, except in the N.

LS

Flame Shoulder
Ochropleura plecta 73.329 (2102) 26–28mm
ADULT is reddish brown, the forewings with a pale leading edge and an adjacent black streak containing white-framed oval and kidney marks. Double-brooded: flies May–Jun, and Aug–Sep. **LARVA** feeds on low-growing plants. **STATUS** Common.

LS

Radford's Flame Shoulder
Ochropleura leucogaster 73.330 (2102a) 34–36mm
ADULT is similar to Flame Shoulder but longer forewings lack any reddish hue; white-framed oval and kidney marks are relatively smaller. Flies Aug–Oct. **LARVA** feeds on low-growing plants. **STATUS** Rare immigrant, mainly in SW England.

LS

Barred Chestnut *Diarsia dahlii* 73.331 (2121) 34–40mm
ADULT male is reddish brown and female is yellowish brown. In both sexes, forewings are broad with a strongly curved leading edge, 3 diffuse dark cross-bands, and indistinct pale-framed oval and kidney marks. Flies Aug–Sep. **LARVA** feeds on Bilberry and birches. **STATUS** Widespread but local on moors in N and W Britain; very local on heaths in SE England.

LS

Purple Clay *Diarsia brunnea* 73.332 (2122) 36–38mm
ADULT forewings are rich brown, subtly tinged purple; pale-framed oval and white kidney marks are linked by a dark patch, and there is a dark patch on leading edge. Flies Jun–Aug. **LARVA** feeds on low-growing plants. **STATUS** Locally common in woodland.

LS

Ingrailed Clay *Diarsia mendica* 73.333 (2120) 30–34mm
ADULT ground colour ranges from pale buff to rich brown. Forewings have a marginal row of small dark arrowhead markings; in some pale forms, oval and kidney marks are defined by dark patches; in other forms, especially dark ones, markings are less obvious. Flies Jun–Jul. **LARVA** feeds on a range of plants. **STATUS** Widespread and common.

LS

Flame
Shoulder

Radford's Flame
Shoulder

Flame

Dark Sword-grass

Flame

Purple Clay

Barred Chestnut

Ingrailed Clay

Ingrailed Clay

Ingrailed Clay

Ingrailed Clay

Small Square-spot *Diarsia rubi* 73.334 (2123) 30–32mm
ADULT is similar to Ingrailed Clay (p. 304) and Fen Square-spot; compared to former, marginal black spots on forewings are barely noticeable. Forewings are brown to grey-brown with a square black spot sited between pale oval and kidney marks. Double-brooded in the S: flies May–Jun, and Aug–Sep. LARVA feeds on low-growing plants. STATUS Widespread and common.

Fen Square-spot *Diarsia florida* 73.335 (2124) 33–35mm
ADULT is very similar to Small Square-spot but on average larger and paler. Flight time differs too: Jun–Jul. LARVA feeds on low-growing plants. STATUS Scarce and very local in fens and marshes; scattered populations in East Anglia, central Wales, N England, S Scotland and Orkney.

Red Chestnut *Cerastis rubricosa* 73.336 (2139) 34–36mm
ADULT is reddish brown, the forewings dusted with blue-grey, and with dark spots along the straight leading edge. Flies Mar–Apr. LARVA feeds on low-growing plants. STATUS Widespread and locally common.

White-marked *Cerastis leucographa* 73.337 (2140) 32–32mm
ADULT is similar to Red Chestnut but slightly smaller and with paler, more prominent dark-centred oval and kidney marks. Outermost cross-line is pale, and inside this is a cross-row of pale dashes. Flies Mar–Apr. LARVA feeds on low-growing plants. STATUS Local in woodland; S, SW and NE England, and S Wales.

White-marked

True Lover's Knot
Lycophotia porphyrea
73.338 (2118) 26–28mm
ADULT forewings are rich brown with bold markings, including white cross-lines, white oval and kidney marks, and black central and marginal streaks. Flies Jun–Aug. LARVA feeds on Heather and heaths. STATUS Widespread; locally common on heaths and moors.

True Lover's Knot

True Lover's Knot

Dotted Rustic
Rhyacia simulans
73.339 (2105) 50–60mm
ADULT is yellow-buff and diffuse grey, the forewings with scalloped dark cross-lines (the inner one double) and a cross-row of black dots outside kidney mark. Flies Jun–Jul, then Sep–Oct after aestivation. LARVA feeds on low-growing plants. STATUS Widespread but local; has a strong E bias to range.

Dotted Rustic

Northern Rustic *Standfussiana lucernea* 73.341 (2104) 38–44mm
ADULT is grey-buff to sooty grey, the forewings with dense dark speckling and 2 scalloped, diffuse, dark-edged pale cross-lines. Flies Jul–Aug. LARVA feeds on low-growing plants. STATUS Widespread but very local, on uplands and coastal cliffs in W Britain, from Cornwall to Shetland.

Small Square-spot

Small Square-spot

Fen Square-spot

Red Chestnut

Red Chestnut

Red Chestnut

True Lover's Knot

Northern Rustic

White-marked

Dotted Rustic

True Lover's Knot

Northern Rustic

Large Yellow Underwing *Noctua pronuba*

73.342 (2107) 48–54mm

ADULT forewings range from marbled grey and brown, to dark brown or buff; all forms show a dark wedge or spot on leading edge near tip. Hindwings are yellow with a black submarginal band. Flies Jul–Sep. **LARVA** feeds on low-growing plants. **STATUS** Widespread and very common.

Broad-bordered Yellow Underwing

Noctua fimbriata 73.343 (2110) 48–54mm

ADULT forewings range from buff (typical female) to marbled grey-buff and olive-brown (typical male). Hindwings are yellow with a broad black submarginal band. Flies Jul–Sep. **LARVA** feeds on low-growing plants. **STATUS** Widespread and common.

Lunar Yellow Underwing *Noctua orbona*

73.344 (2108) 40–44mm

ADULT forewings are brown with pale-framed oval and kidney marks, and a black wedge on leading edge near tip. Hindwings are yellow with a black submarginal band and black central crescent. Flies Jul–Sep. **LARVA** feeds on low-growing plants. **STATUS** Local and scarce; on sandy soils, mainly in S England and East Anglia.

Lesser Yellow Underwing *Noctua comes*

73.345 (2109) 38–44mm

ADULT forewings are brown, typically with dark kidney and oval marks, and a scalloped dark inner cross-line; diffuse dark outer cross-line broadens towards leading edge. Individuals from Scilly and Lundy are boldly marked. Hindwings are yellow with a black submarginal band and central crescent. Flies Jul–Sep. **LARVA** feeds on low-growing plants. **STATUS** Widespread and common.

Least Yellow Underwing *Noctua interjecta*

73.346 (2112) 32–34mm

ADULT forewings are reddish brown with dark cross-lines and a diffuse dark cross-band. Hindwings are yellow with a broad black submarginal band that extends up trailing edge, and a dark central spot on leading edge. Flies Jul–Aug. **LARVA** feeds on low-growing plants. **STATUS** Common in central and S Britain.

Lesser Broad-bordered Yellow Underwing

Noctua janthe 73.348 (2111) 32–38mm

ADULT forewings are marbled grey-buff and brown, often with red on outer leading edge. Hindwings are yellow with a broad black submarginal band that extends up trailing edge. Thorax shows a pale 'collar'. Flies Jul–Sep. **LARVA** feeds on low-growing plants. **STATUS** Widespread, commonest in the S. **SIMILAR SPECIES** Langmaid's Yellow Underwing *N. janthina*, 73.347 (2110a), 32–38mm, differs in having mostly black hindwings with a yellow central patch and narrow margin. Scarce immigrant.

Lesser Broad-bordered Yellow Underwing

Langmaid's Yellow Underwing

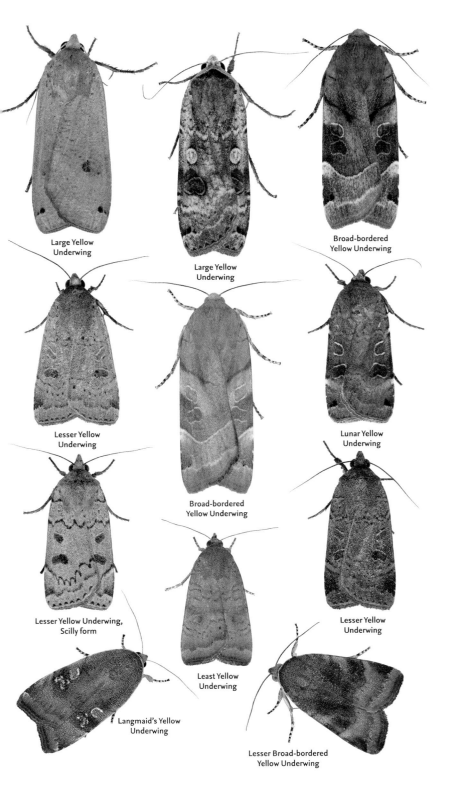

Large Yellow
Underwing

Large Yellow
Underwing

Broad-bordered
Yellow Underwing

Lesser Yellow
Underwing

Broad-bordered
Yellow Underwing

Lunar Yellow
Underwing

Lesser Yellow Underwing,
Scilly form

Least Yellow
Underwing

Lesser Yellow
Underwing

Langmaid's Yellow
Underwing

Lesser Broad-bordered
Yellow Underwing

Stout Dart *Spaelotis ravida* 73.349 (2113) 44–46mm
ADULT is grey-brown, the forewings with a broad red tinge along
leading edge and a dark basal line. Flies Jun–Sep. **LARVA** feeds on
low-growing plants. **STATUS** Local and generally scarce, mainly in
S central and E England.

Great Brocade *Eurois occulta* 73.350 (2137) 55–60mm
ADULT resident form is blackish brown with scalloped pale
cross-lines, pale oval and pale-framed kidney marks, and a black
basal streak. Immigrants are much paler grey, with similar markings.
Flies Jul–Sep. **LARVA** feeds mainly on Bog-myrtle, but also on other
shrubs. **STATUS** Local resident in the Scottish Highlands;
immigrant elsewhere, with an E bias to records.

Double Dart *Graphiphora augur* 73.351 (2114) 36–40mm
ADULT forewings are grey-brown with scalloped pale-
edged cross-lines, partly dark-framed oval and kidney
marks, and 2 dark streaks. Flies Jun–Jul. **LARVA** feeds
on shrubs such as Blackthorn and Hawthorn. **STATUS**
Widespread but generally scarce and local.

Double
Dart

Green Arches
Anaplectoides prasina
73.352 (2138) 42–48mm
ADULT is marbled green
(fading yellow with age),
with a red dorsal ridge
on thorax; forewings have
scalloped, dark-edged
pale cross-lines and
dark-framed oval and
kidney marks. Flies
Jun–Jul. **LARVA** feeds on
a wide range of plants.
STATUS Widespread but
local, favouring deciduous
woodland.

Green
Arches

Dotted
Clay

Dotted Clay *Xestia baja* 73.353 (2130) 36–38mm
ADULT ranges from grey-brown to reddish brown. Forewings have
subtle marbling, faint oval and kidney marks, and paired black marks
on leading edge near tip. Flies Jul–Aug. **LARVA** feeds on Bramble, Bog-
myrtle and other shrubs. **STATUS** Widespread and locally common.

Square-spotted Clay *Xestia stigmatica* 73.354 (2131) 38–42mm
ADULT is dark grey-brown, the forewings with diffuse dark cross-
bands and 2 squarish black spots either side of oval and abutting kidney
mark. Flies Aug. **LARVA** feeds on low shrubs. **STATUS** Scattered and local,
with centres of population in E and NE England, and central Wales.

Neglected Rustic *Xestia castanea* 73.355 (2132) 38–40mm
ADULT forewings range from pale grey-buff to orange-brown; rather
plain except for finely dark-framed oval and kidney marks (the latter
variably black in its trailing half) and a faint cross-row of dark dots.
Flies Aug–Sep. **LARVA** feeds on Heather and heaths. **STATUS** Widespread
but local, on heaths and moors.

Stout Dart

Great Brocade

Double Dart

Green Arches,
fresh individual

Dotted Clay

Green Arches,
faded individual

Square-spotted Clay

Neglected Rustic

Neglected Rustic

Heath Rustic *Xestia agathina* 73.356 (2135) 30–35mm
ADULT is grey-buff to reddish brown. Subtly paler leading edge on forewings abuts a dark band-like streak that frames the elongated white oval, and abuts edge of white-framed kidney mark. Flies Sep. **LARVA** feeds on Heather. **STATUS** Widespread but local, on heaths and moors.

Square-spot Rustic *Xestia xanthographa* 73.357 (2134) 32–34mm
ADULT is grey-buff to reddish brown. Forewings are broad, with a dark patch between pale oval and squarish kidney marks; also has variable scalloped dark cross-lines. Flies Aug–Sep. **LARVA** feeds on low-growing plants. **STATUS** Widespread and common.

FAR LEFT: **Six-striped Rustic**
LEFT: **Setaceous Hebrew Character**

Six-striped Rustic *Xestia sexstrigata* 73.358 (2133) 36–38mm
Six-striped Rustic
ADULT is grey-buff, the forewings with a network of dark veins and cross-lines. Flies Jul–Aug. **LARVA** feeds on low-growing plants. **STATUS** Widespread and locally common.

Setaceous Hebrew Character *Xestia c-nigrum* 73.359 (2126) 36–40mm
ADULT is grey-brown; forewings have a pale buff triangle on leading edge, framed by a saddle-shaped black mark, and a pale basal cross-line. Thorax has a pale 'collar'. Flies Aug–Sep. **LARVA** feeds on low-growing plants. **STATUS** Widespread and locally common.

Triple-spotted Clay *Xestia ditrapezium* 73.360 (2127) 36–42mm
ADULT is reddish brown. Forewings have 2 dark spots, partly framing pale oval and abutting kidney mark, an additional spot on leading edge near tip, and a pale basal cross-line. **LARVA** feeds on shrubs and trees. **STATUS** Widespread but local; mainly in central and S Britain, but also NW Scotland.

Double Square-spot
Xestia triangulum 73.361 (2128) 38–44mm
ADULT is grey-buff, the forewings with 2 squarish black spots either side of oval and abutting kidney mark; also has black basal marks and a black wedge on leading edge near tip. Flies Jun–Jul. **LARVA** feeds on shrubs and trees. **STATUS** Widespread and locally common.

Double Square-spot

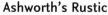

Ashworth's Rustic
Xestia ashworthii 73.362 (2129) 36–40mm
ADULT is grey-buff, the forewings with scalloped, pale-edged dark cross-lines, diffuse dark cross-bands, and pale oval and kidney marks separated by a dark patch. Flies Jun–Aug. **LARVA** feeds on upland plants. **STATUS** Scarce; restricted to N Wales mountains.

Heath Rustic

Square-spot Rustic

Square-spot Rustic

Six-striped Rustic

Setaceous
Hebrew Character

Setaceous
Hebrew Character

Triple-spotted Clay

Ashworth's Rustic

Double Square-spot

Northern Dart *Xestia alpicola* 73.363 (2125) 36–40mm
ADULT forewings are grey or brown, with variable dark streaking, mainly central and on margins; large pale oval and kidney marks are often suffused orange. Flies Jun–Aug. **LARVA** feeds on Crowberry. **STATUS** Local; upland moors in the Scottish Highlands.

Rosy Marsh Moth *Coenophila subrosea* 73.364 (2115) 36–40mm
ADULT male is rosy buff, while female is grey-buff. Both have broad forewings with a dark streak framing oval and abutting kidney mark. Flies Jul–Aug. **LARVA** feeds on Bog-myrtle. **STATUS** Rare and very local; moorland bogs in W Wales and Cumbria.

Rosy Marsh Moth

Autumnal Rustic

Autumnal Rustic
Eugnorisma glareosa
73.365 (2117) 34–36mm
ADULT is typically pale grey-buff. Forewings have black patches either side of oval and abutting kidney mark, and paired black dots at base. Dark forms occur on N Scottish islands. Flies Aug–Sep. **LARVA** feeds on a range of plants. **STATUS** Widespread and locally common.

Plain Clay *Eugnorisma depuncta* 73.366 (2103) 38–42mm
ADULT has broad buff forewings with black basal dots and a broken cross-row of black spots. Flies Jul–Sep. **LARVA** feeds on low-growing plants. **STATUS** Local in deciduous woodland in central Scotland, N England, Wales, Dartmoor and Exmoor.

Plain Clay

Cousin German *Protolampra sobrina* 73.367 (2116) 36–38mm
ADULT forewings are reddish brown, flushed with grey scales, especially at base; has a diffuse, subtly darker cross-band and kidney is darker in trailing half. Flies Jul–Aug. **LARVA** feeds on Bilberry, heaths and birches. **STATUS** Local, restricted to birch woodland in central Scottish Highlands.

Gothic
Naenia typica
73.368 (2136) 34–38mm
ADULT forewings are broad with white veins and cross-lines, and a dark patch between white-framed oval and kidney marks. Similar to Feathered Gothic (p. 284), which lacks white cross-lines and flies later; and rare Bordered Gothic (p. 292), whose inner cross-line curves in opposite direction. Flies Jul–Aug. **LARVA** feeds on low-growing plants. **STATUS** Widespread and common.

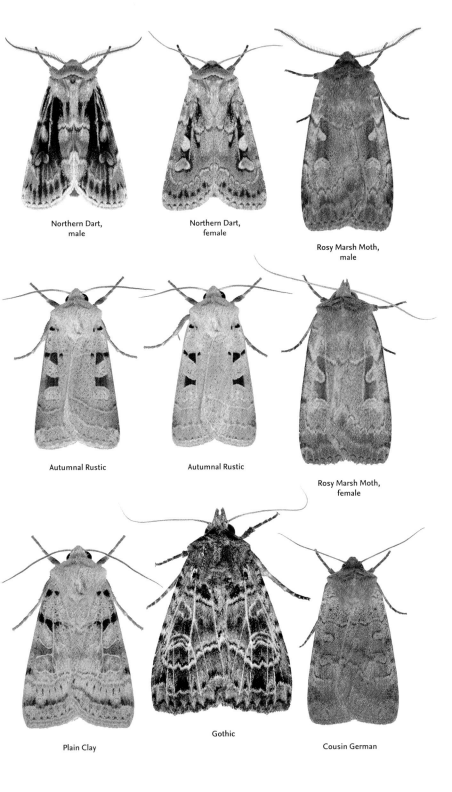

Northern Dart,
male

Northern Dart,
female

Rosy Marsh Moth,
male

Autumnal Rustic

Autumnal Rustic

Rosy Marsh Moth,
female

Plain Clay

Gothic

Cousin German

Oak Nycteoline *Nycteola revayana* 74.009 (2423) 20–24mm

ADULT resembles a *Tortrix* micromoth at rest. Forewings can be grey, buff or brown. Has a dark central spot but other markings are variable and include: a black central streak and dark leading edge; or an array of black spots and an inner-central cross-line. Flies Jul–Sep, then Apr–Jun after hibernation. **LARVA** feeds on oaks. **STATUS** Widespread and locally common.

Small Black Arches *Meganola strigula* 74.001 (2075) 20–24mm
ADULT recalls a micromoth. Forewings are broad with a strongly curved leading edge; grey-buff with fine dark speckling, ragged dark cross-lines and a marginal row of faint black streaks. Flies Jun–Jul. **LARVA** feeds on oaks. **STATUS** Scarce and local, in deciduous woodland in central S England.

Kent Black Arches *Meganola albula* 74.002 (2076) 20–24mm

ADULT forewings are broad and very pale grey, with diffuse buff cross-bands, the central one containing a subtly darker cross-line. Flies Jun–Aug. **LARVA** feeds on Dewberry. **STATUS** Scarce; restricted to coastal districts in S and SE England.

Kent Black Arches

Short-cloaked Moth *Nola cucullatella* 74.003 (2077) 16–18mm

ADULT forewings are broad and rather angular, with a curved dark inner cross-line defining the dark brown basal area. Flies Jun–Jul. **LARVA** feeds on Hawthorn, Blackthorn and other shrubs. **STATUS** Widespread and locally common in central and S Britain.

Least Black Arches *Nola confusalis* 74.004 (2078) 16–18mm

ADULT forewings are angular and pointed, with inner half markedly paler than outer half, and with 2 dark cross-lines, the inner one usually sharply angled towards leading edge and the outer shaped like a question mark. **LARVA** feeds on trees, including limes and Evergreen Oak. **STATUS** Widespread but local.

Scarce Silver-lines *Bena bicolorana* 74.007 (2421) 40–44mm

ADULT forewings are broad and bright green with white edges and 2 white cross-lines. Flies Jun–Aug. **LARVA** feeds on oaks. **STATUS** Widespread and locally common in central and S Britain.

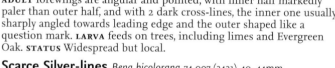

Green Silver-lines
Pseudoips prasinana
74.008 (2422) 30–34mm

ADULT forewings are green with 3 oblique, diffuse pale cross-lines and a reddish-pink margin; legs and antennae are also reddish pink. Flies Jun–Jul. **LARVA** feeds mainly on oaks and birches. **STATUS** Widespread and locally common.

Cream-bordered Green Pea *Earias clorana* 74.011 (2418) 18–20mm

ADULT rests with wings angled, not flat like the similar micromoth Green Oak Tortrix *Tortrix viridana* (p. 335). Forewings are green, with a curved white-bordered leading edge. Flies May–Jun. **LARVA** feeds on willows. **STATUS** Local, in wetlands in S and SE England.

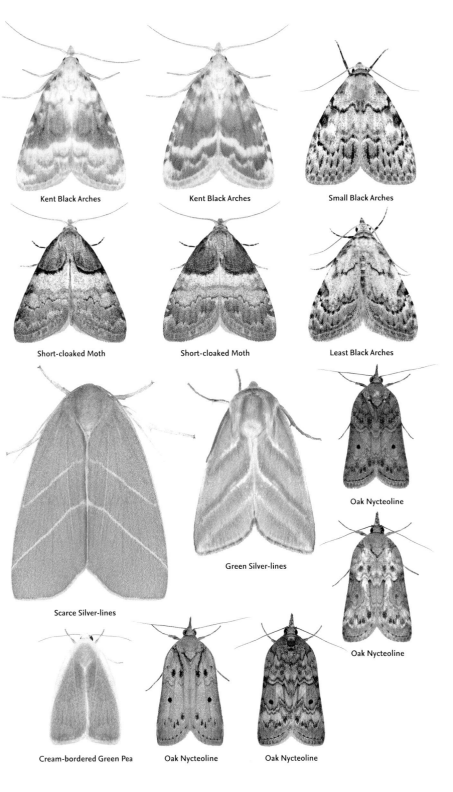

Kent Black Arches

Kent Black Arches

Small Black Arches

Short-cloaked Moth

Short-cloaked Moth

Least Black Arches

Scarce Silver-lines

Green Silver-lines

Oak Nycteoline

Oak Nycteoline

Cream-bordered Green Pea

Oak Nycteoline

Oak Nycteoline

RAREST OF THE RARE

Goosefoot Pug *Eupithecia sinuosaria* 70.167 (1842a)
20–24mm Well-marked pug with a dark-framed
chestnut central cross-band on forewings.
Flies Jun–Aug. Very rare immigrant, with
just a few records.

Rusty Wave *Idaea inquinata* 70.0042
(1703) 18–20mm Rather similar to Weaver's Wave
(p. 108) but colour and markings are more intense.
Flies Jun–Jul. Very rare; probably imported with
dried flowers.

Goosefoot
Pug

Lydd Beauty *Peribatodes ilicaria* 70.261
(1937b) 28–32mm Similar to Willow Beauty
(p. 180) but with more intense markings and
denser dark speckling. Flies Jul–Sep. Rare
immigrant from mainland Europe.

Rusty Wave

Olive-tree Beauty *Peribatodes umbraria* 70.259
(1937c) 36–38mm Similar to Great Oak Beauty (p. 182) but with much bolder dark
markings. Flies May–Jun, and Aug–Sep. Very rare immigrant from S Europe.

Speckled Beauty *Fagivorina arenaria* 70.269 (1946) 26–28mm Recalls a well-
marked Brussels Lace (p. 186). Flies Jun–Jul. Extinct former resident.

Common Forest Looper *Pseudocoremia*
suavis 70.290 (1965a) 26–32mm Recalls a
barred yellowish form of July Highflier
(p. 126) but noticeably narrower-winged.
Flies May–Sep. Very rare accidental
introduction from New Zealand.

Essex Emerald *Thetidia smaragdaria*
maritima 70.301 (1668) 34–36mm Bright green
forewings have a golden-yellow leading
edge and white central spot and cross-line.
Flies Jun–Jul. Extinct former resident of
saltmarshes in SE England.

Essex Emerald

Large Dark Prominent *Notodonta torva* 71.014
(2001) 44–46mm Similar to Great Prominent (p. 196),
but smaller, less colourful and less heavily marked.
Flies May–Jun. Extremely rare immigrant from
mainland Europe.

Large Dark
Prominent

Three-humped Prominent *Notodonta*
tritophus 71.015 (2002) 45–50mm Well-marked moth
with similarities to both Pebble and Iron
prominents (p. 196). Flies May–Jun. Very rare
immigrant from mainland Europe.

Reed Tussock *Laelia coenosa* 72.014
(2024) 48–50mm Pale buff moth, like a large plain
silky wainscot (*Mythimna* spp.; p. 296); male has very
large feathery antennae. Flies Jul–Aug. Extinct former resident.

Three-humped
Prominent

Nine-spotted *Amata phegea* 72.0343
(2070) 38–40mm Well-marked and unmistakable.
Flies Jun–Jul. Extremely rare and doubtful
immigrant.

Plumed Fan-foot
Pechipogo plumigeralis 72.057
(2488a) 24–46mm Recalls a
small Snout (p. 202), but male
has feathery antennae. Flies
May–Sep. Very rare immigrant
from S Europe.

Nine-spotted

Jubilee Fan-foot *Zanclognatha lunalis* 72.058
(2490) 34–36mm Similar to Fan-foot (p. 218) but with subtle
differences in markings: in particular, kidney mark is more
curved. Flies Jun–Aug. Very rare immigrant from mainland
Europe.

Lesser Belle

Dusky Fan-foot *Zanclognatha zelleralis* 72.059 (2491a) 32–
34mm Similar to Fan-foot (p. 218) but greyer buff, with more
intense markings. Flies Jun–Jul. Very rare immigrant from
mainland Europe.

Levant Blackneck *Tathorhynchus exsiccata* 72.065
(2296) 30–32mm Recalls a Silky Wainscot (p. 246), but buff
forewings have black basal and central streaks. Flies May–
Jun, and Sep–Oct. Rare immigrant from S Europe.

Lesser Belle *Colobochyla salicalis* 72.068 (2472) 28–30mm Recalls a small version of
unrelated July Belle (p. 116), but lacks central forewing spot. Flies Jun–Jul. Extinct
former resident and very rare immigrant from mainland Europe.

Alchymist *Catephia alchymista* 72.085 (2464) 44–46mm Dark forewings have a pale buff
margin; hindwings are black and white. Flies May–
Jul. Rare immigrant from mainland Europe.

Accent
Gem

Accent Gem *Ctenoplusia accentifera* 73.006
(2431) 28–34mm Recalls a small pale Silver Y (p. 228);
white forewing mark is more like a tick than a 'Y'.
Flies Jun–Sep. Very rare immigrant.

Tunbridge Wells Gem *Chrysodeixis acuta* 73.009
(2429) 36–42mm Recalls a Golden Twin-spot (p. 226), but greyer overall,
with a contrasting orange hue to trailing half of central cross-band.
Flies Sep–Oct. Rare immigrant from S Europe.

Spotted Sulphur *Acontia trabealis* 73.029
(2414) 19–20mm Unmistakable black and yellow moth. Flies Aug–Oct.
Extinct former resident and
potential immigrant.

Sorcerer *Aedia
leucomelas* 73.030 (2464a) 34–
36mm Forewings are marbled
brown; hindwings are dark
brown with a white centre.
Flies Aug–Oct. Very rare
immigrant.

Spotted Sulphur

Sorceror

Marsh Dagger *Acronicta strigosa* 73.041 (2285) 32–34mm Recalls a small Knot Grass (p. 236) but with 3 slightly misaligned black streaks along trailing half of forewings. Flies Jun–Jul. Extinct former resident; very rare immigrant.

Scarce Dagger *Acronicta auricoma* 73.043 (2287) 38–40mm Similar to Light Knot Grass (p. 236) but dagger-like streak near trailing corner is more striking; black-framed pale oval has a dark central spot. Flies May–Aug. Extinct former resident; very rare immigrant.

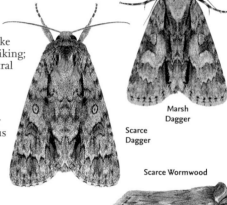

Marsh Dagger

Scarce Dagger

Scarce Wormwood

Scarce Wormwood *Cucullia artemisiae* 73.051 (2213) 34–38mm Similar to Shark (p. 238), but with more obvious dark cross-lines and dark-framed oval and kidney marks; margin has a row of black dots, not streaks. Flies Jun–Aug. Rare immigrant.

Cudweed *Cucullia gnaphalii* 73.054 (2218) 40–44mm Similar to Wormwood (p. 238); diffuse dark central cross-band on forewings emphasises pale oval and kidney marks. Flies May–Jul. Extinct former resident.

Cudweed

Water Betony

Water Betony *Cucullia scrophulariae* 73.056 (2220) 46–48mm Very similar to Mullein (p. 238) and not distinguishable with certainty without dissection of genitalia. Flies May–Jul. Very rare immigrant.

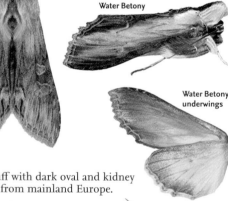

Water Betony underwings

Spotted Clover *Protoschinia scutosa* 73.071 (2405) 32–34mm Distinctive moth; forewings are grey-buff with dark oval and kidney marks. Flies Jul–Sep. Scarce immigrant from mainland Europe.

Eastern Bordered Straw *Heliothis nubigera* 73.075 (2404) 38–40mm Similar to Bordered Straw (p. 242) but smaller and with finer markings; grey-buff forewings have dark patches on leading edge. Flies Jul–Sep. Rare and irregular immigrant.

Latreille's Latin *Callopistria latreillei* 73.081 (2309) 24–26mm Beautifully patterned moth with a dart-shaped pinkish patch near leading corner. Flies Jun–Oct. Extremely rare immigrant.

Shining Marbled *Pseudeustrotia candidula* 73.086 (2413a) 20–24mm Forewings are creamy white, marbled buff and brown, and with a dark patch on leading edge. Flies Jun–Sep. Very rare immigrant.

Latreille's latin

Shining Marbled

Clancy's Rustic *Caradrina kadenii* 73.093 (2387a) 28–30mm Recalls Pale Mottled Willow (p. 246), but pale grey-buff forewings have limited markings, of which the red kidney mark is most obvious. Flies Sep–Oct. Very rare immigrant.

Clancy's Rustic

Lorimer's Rustic *Caradrina flavirena* 73.094 (2388) 30–32mm Recalls a Pale Mottled Willow (p. 246), but forewings are more uniformly brown, with an orange spot in outer portion of kidney mark. Flies Sep–Oct. Very rare immigrant.

Lorimer's Rustic

Powdered Rustic *Hoplodrina superstes* 73.098 (2383) 34–36mm Similar to Vine's Rustic (p. 246) but with more extensive dark speckling and an outer cross-row of black spots. Flies Jun–Sep. Very rare immigrant; possibly overlooked.

Powdered Rustic

Porter's Rustic *Athetis hospes* 73.104 (2392a) 28–30mm Recalls a small Pale Mottled Willow (p. 246) but forewings are plain grey-brown except for indistinct central streak. Flies Jun–Sep. Very rare immigrant.

Guernsey Underwing *Polyphaenis sericata* 73.108 (2302) 38–42mm Forewings are marbled green and black; hindwings are orange. Flies Jun–Aug. Resident on Channel Islands; potential rare immigrant to S England.

Cameo *Crypsedra gemmea* 73.117 (2252a) 42–44mm Recalls a White Spot (p. 292) but orange-brown forewings are even more beautifully patterned with white. Flies Jul–Sep. Very rare immigrant.

Dumeril's Rustic

Dumeril's Rustic *Luperina dumerilii* 73.130 (2355) 32–34mm Recalls a pale Sandhill Rustic (p. 254), but central cross-band is usually more obvious and highlights the elongated pale kidney mark. Flies Aug–Oct. Rare immigrant.

Union Rustic *Pabulatrix pabulatricula* 73.153 (2332) 34–46mm Recalls a Double Lobed (p. 264), but ground colour of forewings is paler grey, and central band is complete. Flies Jul–Aug. Extinct former resident.

Scarce Brindle

Scarce Brindle *Apamea lateritia* 73.166 (2328) 44–48mm Similar to dark form of Clouded-bordered Brindle (p. 260), but forewings are more uniform brown except for wavy white outer edge to kidney mark. Flies Jul–Aug. Rare immigrant from mainland Europe.

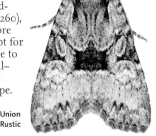

Union Rustic

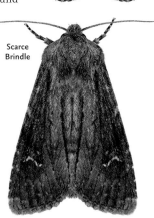

Red-headed Chestnut *Conistra erythrocephala* 73.198 (2261) 36–40mm Reddish-brown forewings are variably marbled with grey; pale kidney mark contains 3 black spots. Flies Oct–Nov. Very rare immigrant.

Conformist *Lithophane furcifera* 73.203 (2238) 45–50mm Extinct native ssp. *suffusa* had narrow, dark brown forewings with an orange-buff basal patch and kidney mark. Flies Apr–May. Very rare immigrant ssp. *furcifera* has a paler grey ground colour.

Beautiful Arches *Mniotype satura* 73.24 (2249) 42–48mm Similar to Dark Brocade (p. 282) but with richer brown coloration on forewings. Flies Jul–Oct. Occurrence in Britain is doubtful.

Sombre Brocade *Dichonioxa tenebrosa* 73.227 (2248b) 36–38mm Similar to Dark Brocade (p. 282), but smaller and kidney mark lacks white edging. Flies Oct–Dec. Very rare immigrant.

Flame Brocade *Trigonophora flammea* 73.229 (2251) 46–50mm Distinctive moth; pinkish-buff forewings have a broad pale trailing edge and large pale kidney mark with a projection. Flies Oct–Nov. Extinct former resident (except perhaps on the Channel Islands); now a very rare immigrant.

Beautiful Arches

Flame Brocade

Feathered Ear *Pachetra sagittigera* 73.262 (2151) 40–48mm Forewings are grey-buff, with pale oval and kidney marks, a pale patch on trailing edge and dark marginal streaks; male has feathered antennae. Flies Jun–Jul. Extinct former resident.

Splendid Brocade *Lacanobia splendens* 73.268 (2160a) 34–36mm Forewings are yellow-buff to pinkish buff with pale oval and kidney marks, the latter dark grey in trailing half. Flies Jun–Jul. Rare immigrant from mainland Europe.

Viper's Bugloss *Hadena irregularis* 73.287 (2168) 33–35mm Similar to well-marked yellow-buff form of Tawny Shears (p. 294), but forewings lack a tooth-like dark central mark. Flies Jun–Jul. Extinct former resident of East Anglian Breckland.

Splendid Brocade

Viper's Bugloss

Feathered Ear

Black Collar *Dichagyris flammatra* 73.310
(2101) 45–50mm Thorax has a distinct black 'collar'. Grey-buff forewings have a broken black streak framing the pale oval, with a rufous patch between oval and kidney mark. Flies Jul–Sep. Very rare immigrant.

Great Dart *Agrotis bigramma* 73.315 (2094) 42–46mm Brown forewings are well marked with pale-edged, black-framed jagged cross-lines and oval and kidney marks; also has a tooth-like central mark, and dark arrowhead streaks inside outermost cross-line. Flies Aug–Sep. Very rare immigrant from S Europe.

Woods's Dart *Agrotis graslini* 73.318 (2083a) 36–38mm Similar to Archer's Dart (p.302); forewings have a long dark central streak containing a small, dark-centred white oval and a white-edged kidney mark. Fies Jun–Jul. Potential rare immigrant from mainland Europe; resident on Jersey.

Black Collar

Great Dart

Spiny Bollworm *Earias biplaga* 74.0121
(2419) 20–24mm Yellow-green overall, the forewings with variable dark markings but invariably a brown marginal fringe. Flies Aug–Oct. Very rare immigrant and probable accidental import.

Egyptian Bollworm *Earias insulana* 74.012
(2420) 24–26mm Rather uniform green or brown, the forewings with concentric, faint dark cross-lines. Flies Aug–Oct. Very rare immigrant and probable accidental import.

Egyptian Bollworm

Scarce Black Arches *Nola aerugula* 74.005
(2079) 16–20mm Similar to Least Black Arches (p. 316); forewings are white with dark and buff speckling, and variably intense dark cross-lines and diffuse buff cross-bands. Flies Jun–Aug. Rare immigrant.

Eastern Nycteoline *Nycteola asiatica* 74.010 (2423a) 25–27mm Similar to Oak Nycteoline (p. 316) and requires expert inspection for certain identification. Flies Sep–Oct. Very rare immigrant.

INTRODUCTION TO MICRO-MOTHS

The bulk of the British Lepidoptera fauna comprises so-called 'micro-moths', most families of which are tiny and hard to identity without the experience of an expert eye. Within this diverse group are representatives that are so small they are hard to recognise as being moths at all. But at the other extreme are species that are larger than many so-called 'macro-moths'. All very confusing!

Where all members of a given micro-moth family are of a comparable size to their macro-moth cousins (such as burnets and clearwings), they have been included in the main section of this book. The remaining micro-moth families are covered in the following introduction to the group, detailing their characteristics and depicting species that are typical representatives of the group, or are large and showy enough to allow identification with a reasonable degree of certainty. Not every micro-moth family is illustrated here, and readers who are interested in the subject are advised to use the excellent *Field Guide to the Micro Moths of Great Britain and Ireland* (2012) by Sterling, Parsons and Lewington (see 'Further Reading', p. 346).

Very few micro-moths have common English names. In addition to its scientific name, each species mentioned is assigned a unique checklist number: this comprises the *Checklist of the Lepidoptera of the British Isles* (Agassiz *et al.* 2013) number, followed by the *A Recorder's Log Book or Label List of British Butterflies and Moths* (Bradley and Fletcher 1979) number in brackets. And the 2013 *Checklist* has been used as a guide to the current number of species contained within each family.

Family Micropterigidae (not illustrated)
Group comprises 5 species of tiny moths, in the range 4–5mm long. Wings are rather broad and rounded, with a metallic sheen; held in a tent-like manner at rest. Antennae are relatively short. Generally day-flying, adults feeding on pollen. Little is known about larval habits.

Family Eriocraniidae
Group comprises 8 species of tiny day-flying moths, in the range 4–6mm long, with rather broad, rounded wings, held in a tent-like manner at rest. Antennae are relatively short. Larvae form blotch mines in leaves of deciduous trees.

Dyseriocrania subpurpurella 2.001 (0006) Length 6mm Common in oak woodland in S Britain. Flies Apr–May. Larva feeds on oaks.

×3

Family Nepticulidae
Group comprises 100 or so species of tiny nocturnal moths, in the range 3–5mm long. Rounded forewings have a fringed edge; held in a shallow tent-like manner at rest. Larvae form either blotch or gallery mines in leaves.

Stigmella aurella 4.045 (0050) Length 5mm Widespread and common in woodland and scrub. Flies May–Jun. Larva forms squiggly galleries in Bramble leaves.

Stigmella aurella

Ectoedemia intimella 4.082 (0025) Length 3mm Local, in damp woodland. Flies Jun. Larva mines sallow leaves.

×3

×3

Ectoedemia intimella

Family Opostegidae
Group comprises 4 species, in the range 4–7mm long, whose relatively broad whitish forewings have a fringed outer edge. Antennae are relatively long, base with scaly 'eye-caps'. Little is known about the life cycles.

Opostega salaciella 5.001 (0119) Length 7mm Widespread and locally common in open grassland. Flies Jun–Jul. Larva is presumed to feed on Sheep's Sorrel.

Opostega salaciella

×3

Family Heliozelidae (not illustrated)

Group comprises 5 species of tiny day-flying moths, in the range 4–5mm long. Wings are relatively broad and rounded. Larvae mine leaves and shoots.

Family Adelidae

Group comprises 15 species of distinctive moths, in the range 5–10mm long. Most are day-flying, with long antennae (known as 'longhorns'). Wings are broad, with a metallic sheen in most species. Larvae are case-builders living in leaf litter.

Adela reaumurella

Adela reaumurella 7.006 (0150) Length 8–9mm Widespread and locally common in woodland. Flies May–Jun. Has metallic green wings and extremely long antennae. Males swarm around oaks on sunny days. Larva feeds on leaf litter.

×3

Adela cuprella 7.007 (0149) Length 7–8mm Widespread but local on heaths and moors. Flies Apr–May. Has metallic coppery-green wings, males with extremely long antennae. Males swarm around willow bushes. Larva feeds on leaf litter.

Adela cuprella

×3

Nematopogon metaxella 7.014 (0143) Length 7–8mm Widespread but local in damp woods and marshes. Flies Jun–Jul. Larva feeds on leaf litter.

×3

Nematopogon metaxella

Family Incurvariidae

Group comprises five species of tiny day-flying moths, in the range 5–7mm long. Forewings are broad and held in a tent-like manner. Antennae are short and pectinate in males of some species. Larvae are leaf miners.

Incurvaria masculella 8.002 (0130) Length 6–7mm Widespread and common in woodland scrub and gardens. Flies Apr–May. Larval foodplant is Hawthorn.

×3

Family Prodoxidae

Group comprises 7 species, in the range 5–8mm long. Antennae are short and thread-like. Forewing is rounded and held in a tent-like manner. Larvae feed internally in plant tissue, including fruits.

Raspberry Moth *Lampronia corticella* 9.003 (0136) Length 5mm Local in gardens and hedgerows. Flies Jun. Larva feeds inside Raspberry fruits.

×3

Family Tischeriidae

Group comprises 6 species, in the range 4–5mm long. Antennae are short and thread-like. Forewing is rounded and held in a tent-like manner. Larvae are leaf miners.

Tischeria ekebladella 10.001 (0123) Length 5mm Widespread and common in deciduous woodland. Flies May–Jun. Larva mines leaves of oaks and Sweet Chestnut.

×3

Family Psychidae

Group comprises 18 species, females wingless and males in the range 5–12mm long. Males have broad, rounded wings and feathery antennae; most fly on sunny afternoons. Larvae live in cases (like those of caddis-fly larvae) and feed on decaying matter, and are sometimes called bagworms.

Psyche casta 11.012 (0186) Length 6mm (male) Widespread and common in gardens, scrub and woods. Flies May–Jul. Larva feeds on organic detritus.

Family Tineidae

Group comprises 60 or so species, in the range 6–9mm long. Wings are elongate, with a curved outer edge. Antennae are thread-like and held pressed against wings at rest. Larvae feed on organic matter, from woven natural fibres, to dead animal skin, birds' nests and fungi.

Cork Moth *Nemapogon cloacella* 12.016 (0216) Length 7–8mm Widespread and common in gardens, woods and farms. Flies Jun–Jul. Larva feeds on stored dried food goods (including grain and cereal) and bracket fungi.

×3

Case-bearing Clothes Moth *Tinea pellionella* 12.027 (0240) Length 6–7mm Widespread and common in houses, barns and storage areas. Flies May–Oct. Larva constructs a case and feeds on dry organic matter, including wood, fur and stored goods.

×3

Skin Moth *Monopis laevigella* 12.036 (0227) Length 8–9mm Widespread and common around outbuildings and farms. Flies May–Sep. Larva feeds on dead animal remains, droppings and birds' nest detritus.

×3

Family Roeslerstammiidae

Group includes just 1 regularly encountered species (plus 1 rarity).

Roeslerstammia erxlebella 13.002 (0447) Length 6–7mm Local in woodland, commonest in the S. Elongated wings are held in a tent-like manner at rest; antennae are thread-like. Flies Jun–Aug. Larva feeds on birches in particular, mining leaves at first, then creating a rolled-leaf case.

×3

Family Bucculatricidae

Group comprises 12 species of small micro-moths, most 3–5mm long. Wings are held in a tent-like manner or rolled around body depending on species. Antennae are thread-like. Larvae are leaf miners at first, external feeders when older.

Bucculatrix cidarella 14.008 (0272) Length 4mm Flies May–Jun. Local on moors and in wetlands. Larva feeds on alders and Bog-myrtle.

×3

Family Gracillariidae

Group comprises 93 species, in the range 4–8mm long. Wings are narrow and held in a tent-like manner at rest. Antennae are thread-like. Many species rest with head end elevated. Larvae are leaf miners at first, external feeders when older.

Caloptilia robustella 15.009 (0287) Length 7mm Widespread and common in oak woodland. Flies Jun–Sep. Larva mines oak leaves.

×3

Phyllonorycter harrisella 15.034 (0315) Length 4–5mm Widespread and common in oak woodland. Flies Apr–Jun, and Aug–Sep. Larva mines oak leaves.

Horse Chestnut Leaf Miner *Cameraria ohridella* 15.089 (0366a) Length 4–5mm Widespread and common in parks and towns. Flies May–Sep. Larva mines leaves of Horse Chestnut.

Family Yponomeutidae

Group comprises 24 species, in the range 7–13mm long. At rest, wings are held in a tent-like manner. Antennae are thread-like and almost as long as forewings. Larvae are leaf miners at first, external feeders when older; some are colonial, living in extensive silk webs.

Bird-cherry Ermine *Yponomeuta evonymella* 16.001 (0424) Length 12–14mm Widespread and common in scrub and woods. Flies Jul–Aug. Larva feeds on Bird Cherry.

Yponomeuta sedella 16.008 (0431) Length 9mm Local in ancient woodland, rocky areas and gardens. Flies Apr–May, and Aug. Larva feeds on Orpine and cultivated Iceplant.

Family Yposolophidae

Group comprises 16 species, in the range 8–15mm long. At rest, wings are rolled around body or held in a tent-like manner depending on species. Larvae of most species live inside a silken tent on underside of leaf.

Ypsolopha nemorella 17.002 (0452) Length 15mm Locally throughout Britain. Flies Jun–Aug. Larva feeds on Honeysuckle.

Honeysuckle Moth *Ypsolopha dentella* 17.003 (0453) Length 11–12mm Widespread and common in gardens, hedges and woods. Flies Jul–Aug. Larva feeds on Honeysuckle.

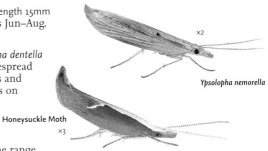

Ypsolopha nemorella

Honeysuckle Moth

Family Plutellidae

Group comprises 7 species, in the range 8–10mm long. At rest, wings are held in a tent-like manner; thread-like antennae point forwards at rest. Larvae are web-builders and feed on members of the cabbage family.

Diamond-back Moth *Plutella xylostella* 18.001 (0464) Length 8mm Common immigrant from mainland Europe. Flies Jun–Sep. Larva feeds on members of the cabbage family.

Family Glyphipterigidae

Group comprises 14 species, in the range 5–14mm long. At rest, wings are held in a range of positions depending on species, but mostly in a tent-like manner. Some species are day-flying. Larvae feed inside seedpods or stems.

Glyphipterix thrasonella 19.002 (0397) Length 10mm Widespread and common in damp habitats. Flies May–Aug. Larva probably feeds inside stems of rushes.

Family Argyresthiidae

Group comprises 24 species, in the range 4–7mm long. At rest, wings are pressed close to body with head end pointing downwards. Many species fly in daytime. Larvae feed inside shoots, leaves and catkins.

Argyresthia goedartella 20.012 (0411) Length 6–7mm Widespread and common in woods, hedges and scrub. Flies Jun–Sep. Larva feeds inside shoots and catkins of birches and Alder.

Argyresthia albistria 20.023 (0422) Length 5mm Widespread and common in hedgerows and scrub. Flies Jul–Aug. Larva feeds inside shoots of Blackthorn.

×3

Family Lyonetiidae

Group comprises 8 species, in the range 3–5mm long. At rest, wings are held a tent-like manner. Larvae are leaf miners.

Apple Leaf Miner *Lyonetia clerkella* 21.001 (0263) Length 5–6mm Widespread and common in gardens, hedges and orchards. Flies Jul–Sep. Larva is a leaf miner on shrubs, notably apples, Wild Cherry, Hawthorn and Rowan.

×3

Family Praydidae

Group comprises 5 species, in the range 5–9mm long. At rest, wings are held in a tent-like manner with antennae aligned with body. Larvae feed inside buds or mine leaves.

Ash Bud Moth *Prays fraxinella* 22.002 (0449) Length 8–9mm Widespread and locally common wherever Ash occurs. Flies Jun–Aug. Larva mines leaves, buds and twigs of Ash.

×3

Family Bedelliidae

Group comprises 1 species. At rest, narrow wings are rolled around body; sits with head end up.

Bedellia somnulentella 24.001 (0264) Length 5–6mm Local in S Britain. Flies Aug–Oct, then hibernates. Larva mines leaves of bindweeds.

×3

Family Scythropiidae

Group comprises 1 species. At rest, narrow wings are held in a shallow tent-like manner. Larvae are gregarious, living in a silk web on their foodplant.

Hawthorn Moth *Scythropia crataegella* 25.001 (0450) Length 6–7mm Common in scrub in S Britain. Flies Jun–Jul. Larva feeds on Blackthorn and Hawthorn.

×3

Family Douglasiidae (not illustrated)

Group comprises 2 species, in the range 4–5mm long. At rest, narrow wings are held in a shallow tent-like manner. Larvae feed inside stems of their foodplant.

Tinagma ocnerostomella 26.001 (0398) Length 4–5mm Local in dry grassland in S England. Flies Jun–Jul. Larva feeds on Viper's-bugloss.

Family Autostichidae

Group comprises 4 species, in the range 8–9mm long. At rest, narrow wings are held flattish, with thread-like antennae carried alongside. Larvae feed on leaf litter and decaying matter.

Oegoconia quadripuncta 27.001 (0870) Length 6–8mm Locally common in S Britain. Flies Jul–Aug. Larva feeds on decaying leaf litter.

×3

Family Oecophoridae

Group comprises 26 species, in the range 4–12mm long. At rest, wings are mostly held in a tent-like manner. Larvae feed on organic detritus, fungi, etc.

White-shouldered House-moth *Endrosis sarcitrella* 28.009
(0648) Length 8–9mm Widespread and common in houses and sheds. Flies mainly May–Oct. Larva feeds on detritus and stored dry foodstuff.

×3

Brown House-moth *Hofmannophila pseudospretella* 28.010
(0647) Length 9–10mm Widespread and common in houses, sheds and outdoors generally. Flies Jun–Aug. Larva feeds on a range of detritus and decaying matter.

Brown
House-moth

×3

Family Chimabachidae

Group comprises 3 species, in the range 9–15mm long. All show sexual dimorphism, with females being flightless. Wings are held in a shallow tent-like manner. Larvae live in webs on leaves of their foodplant.

Diurnea fagella 29.001 (0663) Length 15mm (male), 10mm (female) Widespread and common in woodland and scrub. Flies Mar–Apr. Larval foodplants include a range of deciduous trees and shrubs.

Diurnea fagella

Family Lypusidae

Group comprises 4 species, in the range 5–11mm long. At rest, wings are held in a shallow tent-like manner. Larvae are case-builders, feeding on leaves and flowers.

×2

Pseudatemelia josephinae 30.003 (0660) Length 10–12mm Local in woodland in S Britain. Flies Jun–Jul. Larva feeds on Bilberry.

Pseudatemelia josephinae

×3

Family Peleopodidae

Group comprises 1 species. At rest, wings are held flat.

Carcina quercana 31.001 (0658) Length 8–9mm Widespread and common in woodland, hedgerows and gardens. Flies Jun–Sep. Larva feeds on oaks and Beech, spinning 2 leaves together.

×3

Carcina quercana

Family Depressariidae

Group comprises 51 species, in the range 9–15mm long. At rest, wings are held flat and slightly overlapping. Larvae feed on shoots and construct a silk web.

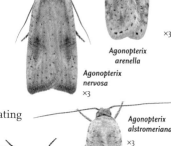

Agonopterix arenella 32.017 (0697) Length 9–11mm Widespread and common in rough grassland and disturbed ground. Flies Mar–Oct, hibernating in winter. Larva feeds on thistles, knapweeds and burdocks.

Agonopterix nervosa 32.030 (0706) Length 11–12mm Widespread and common in rough grassland and heaths. Flies Aug–Sep. Larva feeds on Broom, gorses and their relatives.

Agonopterix arenella

Agonopterix nervosa
×3

Agonopterix alstromeriana 32.031 (0695) Length 9–11mm Locally common in S Britain. Flies Oct–Mar, hibernating in winter. Larva feeds on Hemlock.

Agonopterix alstromeriana
×3

Parsnip Moth *Depressaria radiella* 32.036 (0672) Length 14–15mm

Widespread and common in rough grassland and on waste ground. Flies Sep–Oct, then Apr after hibernation. Larva feeds on flowers and fruits, and in stems, of Wild Parsnip and Hogweed.

×2

Parsnip Moth

Family Ethmiidae

Group comprises 6 species in the range 6–10mm long. At rest, wings are held close to body in a tent-like manner. Larvae live within a silken web constructed on their foodplant.

Ethmia dodecea 33.001 (0718) Length 9–11mm Local in S England, on dry ground. Flies Jun–Jul. Larva feeds on Common Gromwell.

Ethmia bipunctella 33.006 (0720) Length 10–14mm Local, on shingle beaches in S England. Flies May–Jun. Larva feeds on Viper's-bugloss.

Ethmia dodecea ×3   **Ethmia bipunctella** ×3

Family Cosmopterigidae

Group comprises 16 species, in the range 5–12mm long. At rest, wings are held in a steep tent-like manner, often slightly rolled around body. Larval lifestyles vary: some are leaf miners, while others live in stems and roots.

Cosmopterix orichalcea 34.007 (0896) Length 5–6mm Scarce in marshes and damp grassland. Flies Jun–Aug. Larva mines leaves of various wetland grass species.

×3

Cosmopterix pulchrimella 34.009 (0896b) Length 4–5mm Scarce, in vicinity of old walls and mainly on S coast. Flies Sep–Oct. Larva mines leaves of Pellitory-of-the-wall.
×3

Family Gelechiidae

Group comprises 160 species, in the range 4–12mm long. At rest, wings are held in a range of postures, but often flattish and slightly rolled. Larval lifestyles vary: some are leaf-miners while others live in stems and roots.

Syncopacma larseniella 35.003 (0844) Length 6–8mm Local in S England in rough, damp grassland. Flies Jun–Jul. Larva feeds on Greater Bird's-foot Trefoil, binding leaves together with silk.

Anacampsis populella 35.011 (0853) Length 8–10mm Common in England and Wales. Flies Jul–Aug. Larva feeds on poplars, Aspen and willows, binding leaves together with silk.

Nothris congressariella 35.016 (0839) Length 10–11mm Rare, restricted to coastal SW England. Flies Aug–Sep. Larva feeds on Balm-leaved Figwort.

Bryotropha terrella 35.040 (0787) Length 7–9mm Widespread and common in grassland. Flies Jun–Jul. Larva feeds on grasses.

Athrips mouffetella 35.085 (0762) Length 8–9mm Common in England and Wales, in woods and gardens. Flies Jul–Aug. Larva feeds on Honeysuckle and Snowberry.

Pseudotelphusa scalella 35.152 (0764) Length 6–7mm Scarce in oak woodland in S Britain. Flies May–Jun. Larva feeds on mosses growing on oaks.

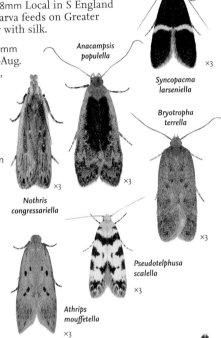

Anacampsis populella ×3

Syncopacma larseniella ×3

Bryotropha terrella ×3

Nothris congressariella ×3

Pseudotelphusa scalella ×3

Athrips mouffetella ×3

Family Batrachedridae

Group comprises 3 species, in the range 5–9mm long. At rest, narrow wings are held slightly rolled around body, with head end elevated and antennae aligned with body. Larvae feed inside flowers and fruits of trees.

Batrachedra praeangusta 36.001 (0878) Length 7–8mm Widespread and locally common. Flies Jul–Aug. Larva feeds on catkins of Aspen, poplars and willows.

×3

Family Coleophoridae

Group comprises 109 species, in the range 4–12 mm long. At rest, narrow wings are held pressed close to body, with antennae outstretched. Larvae are generally case-bearers, grazing leaves of their foodplants. Most species are impossible to identify to species level without dissection and the aid of an expert eye. The family is illustrated by images of coleophorids that have not been identified to species, plus 2 common species whose identity was confirmed.

×3   ×3   ×3

Coleophora serratella 37.015 (0493) Length 6–7mm Widespread and common in woods and hedgerows. Flies May–Jul. Larva feeds on birches, elms, Hazel and alders.

×3

Coleophora alcyonipennella 37.035 (0517) Length 6–7mm Local in rough grassland. Flies Jul–Sep. Larva feeds in seedheads of White Clover.

Family Elachistidae

Group comprises 49 species, in the range 4–18mm long. At rest, wings are held either flat and slightly overlapping, or in a tent-like manner, depending on species. Larvae are leaf miners of grasses and sedges.

Elachista maculicerusella 38.039 (0609) Length 6–7mm Widespread and common in wetland habitats. Flies May–Jul. Larva feeds on Common Reed and Reed Canary-grass.

Family Parametriotidae

Group comprises 6 species, in the range 5–7mm long. At rest, narrow wings are held slightly rolled around body in a shallow tent-like manner. Larvae mine twigs and bark of trees.

Blastodacna hellerella 39.001 (0905) Length 6–7mm Widespread and common in scrub and hedgerows. Flies Jun–Jul. Larva feeds inside Hawthorn berries.

Family Momphidae

Group comprises 15 species, in the range 4–9mm long. At rest, wings are held in a tent-like manner and antennae are aligned with body and wings. Forewings have tufts. In some species larvae are leaf miners, while others feed internally in shoots.

Mompha subbistrigella 40.008 (0892) Length 4–6mm Locally common in England and Wales, in gardens and on disturbed ground. Flies Aug–Apr, hibernating in winter. Larva feeds on willowherbs.

Family Blastobasidae

Group comprises 6 species, in the range 7–12mm long. At rest, wings are held slightly rolled around body, with antennae aligned with body and wings. Larvae live a debris-coated silk tube on, or in, foodplant.

Blastobasis lacticolella 41.003 (0874) Length 7–11mm Widespread and common in woods, hedgerows and gardens. Flies May–Sep. Larva feeds on a range of organic matter, from detritus to plant seedpods.

Staphmopoda pedella

Family Stathmopodidae

Group comprises 1 native species (with 2 aliens occurring accidentally). Rests with wings rolled around body and with hind legs at right angles to body.

Blastobasis lacticolella

Staphmopoda pedella 42.002 (0877) Length 6–8mm Scarce in damp woodland. Flies Jun–Jul. Larva feeds on catkins and buds of alders.

Scythris grandipennis

Family Scythrididae

Group comprises 12 species, in the range 4–9mm long. At rest, wings are held tightly pressed to the body. Larvae live in a silk tube coated with debris.

Scythris grandipennis 43.002 (0911) Length 7–10mm Scarce on heaths and downs in S England. Flies Jun. Larva feeds on gorses.

×3

amily Alucitidae

roup comprises 1 species that rests with wings spread flat,
ch wing divided into 6 'plumes'.

Many-plumed Moth *Alucita hexadactyla* 44.001
288) Wingspan 14–16mm Widespread and common in
rdens, hedgerows and woods. Flies throughout the year,
xcept the dead of winter. Larva feeds on Honeysuckle leaves
nd buds.

x2

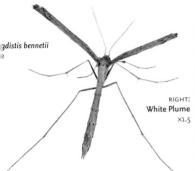

gdistis bennetii
2

RIGHT:
White Plume
×1.5

amily Pterophotoridae

roup comprise 42 species of familiar 'plume moths', with a wingspan range of 20–35mm.
ests with narrow wings at right angles to body, closely aligned or with forewing
verlapping hindwing depending on species. Larvae feed externally on foodplant.

gdistis bennetii 45.001 (1488) Wingspan 20–22mm Rests with wings angled forwards. Local
n saltmarshes in S England. Flies Jun–Jul. Larva feeds on Common Sea-lavender.

White Plume *Pterophorus pentadactyla* 45.030 (1513) Wingspan 30–35mm Widespread and
common on rough ground and in gardens. Flies Jun–Aug. Larva feeds on bindweeds.

Common Plume *Emmelina monodactyla* 45.044 (1524)
Wingspan 20–25mm Widespread and common in
gardens, hedgerows and on rough ground. Flies
Sep–Apr, hibernating in winter. Larva feeds on a
range of plants, particularly bindweeds.

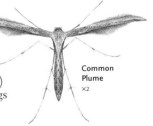

**Common
Plume**
x2

Family Schreckensteiniidae (not illustrated)

Group comprises 1 species that rests with its narrow wings
held flat and legs splayed.

Schreckensteinia festaliella 46.001 (0485) Length 5–6mm
Widespread and common in scrub, open woodland and gardens. Flies
Apr–Sep. Larva feeds on Bramble and Hazel, spinning a web under leaf.

Family Epermeniidae (not illustrated)

Group comprises 8 species, in the range 4–8mm long. Rests with wings in a steep tent-
like manner, pressed close to body. Larvae feed externally, spinning a web on foodplant.

Epermenia chaerophyllella 47.005 (0483) Length 6–7mm Widespread and common in rough
grassland. Flies Mar–Sep. Larva feeds on Hogweed, Cow Parsley and related plants.

Family Choreutidae

Group comprises 6 species, in the range 5–7mm long. At rest, wings are held flattish or in a shallow tent-like manner. Larvae feed externally, spinning a web on foodplant.

Nettle-tap *Anthophila fabriciana* 48.001 (0385) Length 6–7mm Widespread and common on rough ground, and in hedges and gardens. Flies May–Sep. Larva feeds on Common Nettle.

Family Tortricidae

A diverse and varied family that includes 386 species. Resting positions vary and include species that hold their wings flat, in a tent-like manner or rolled around the body. Overall, the Tortricidae are relatively large micro-moths and, confusingly, some species are similar in size and appearance to the smallest species of macro-moths. Larval lifestyles vary according to species: some spin webs of leaves of their foodplants, while others feed internally.

Large Fruit-tree Tortrix *Archips podana* 49.013 (0977) Length 10–12mm Widespread and common in woods, hedgerows and gardens. Flies mainly Jun–Jul. Larva feeds on deciduous trees and shrubs.

Variegated Golden Tortrix
Archips xylosteana 49.015 (0980) Length 8–10mm Widespread and common in woods. Flies Jul–Aug. Larva feeds on deciduous trees.

Choristoneura hebenstreitella 49.018 (0983) Length 11–12mm Local in woods, commonest in the S. Flies Jun–Jul. Larva feeds on deciduous trees and shrubs.

Chequered Fruit-tree Tortrix *Pandemis corylana* 49.024 (0969) Length 11–12mm Common in gardens, hedgerows and woods. Flies Aug. Larva feeds on deciduous trees and shrubs.

Barred Fruit-tree Tortrix
Pandemis cerasana 49.025 (0970) Length 10mm Common in gardens, hedgerows and woods. Flies Jun–Aug. Larva feeds on deciduous trees and shrubs.

Dark Fruit-tree Tortrix
Pandemis heparana 49.026 (0972) Length 10mm Common in gardens, hedgerows and woods. Flies Jun–Aug. Larva feeds on deciduous trees and shrubs, particularly fruit-bearing species.

Lozotaenia forsterana 49.029 (1002) Length 13–14mm Common in gardens, hedgerows and woods. Flies Jun–Jul. Larva feeds on trees and shrubs.

Large Fruit-tree Tortrix ×3

Variegated Golden Tortrix ×3

Choristoneura hebenstreitella ×3

Chequered Fruit-tree Tortrix ×3

Barred Fruit-tree Tortrix ×3

Dark Fruit-tree Tortrix ×3

Lozotaenia forsterana ×3

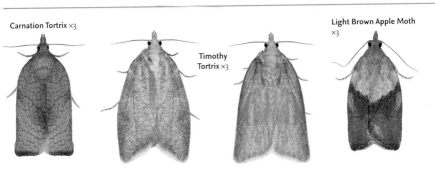

Carnation Tortrix ×3

Timothy Tortrix ×3

Light Brown Apple Moth ×3

Carnation Tortrix *Cacoecimorpha pronubana* 49.030 (0985) Length 10mm Common in gardens, hedgerows and woods. Flies May–Jun, and Aug–Sep. Larva feeds on deciduous trees and shrubs.

Timothy Tortrix *Aphelia paleana* 49.031 (0989) Length 11–12mm Locally common in grassland. Flies Jun–Aug. Larva feeds on grasses and low-growing herbaceous plants.

Light Brown Apple Moth *Epiphyas postvittana* 49.039 (0998) Length 10–12mm Australian resident, now established here and widespread and locally common in gardens. Flies Apr–Oct. Larva feeds on a range of shrubs.

Lozotaeniodes formosana 49.040 (1001) Length 14–15mm Locally common in pine woodland. Flies Jun–Aug. Larva feeds on Scots Pine.

Light Grey Tortrix *Cnephasia incertana* 49.049 (1024) Length 10–12mm Common in a wide range of open habitats. Flies Jun–Jul. Larva feeds on low-growing plants, notably plantains and sorrels.

Grey Tortrix *Cnephasia stephensiana* (1020) Length 10–12mm Common in a wide range of open habitats. Flies Jul. Larva feeds on low-growing herbaceous plants.

Cnephasia communana 49.055 (1018) Length 10–12mm Local in dry grassland. Flies May. Feeds on low-growing herbaceous plants. This species is similar to, and virtually indistinguishable from, *C. incertana* and *C. stephensiana*; genitalia dissection is needed to confirm identification.

Green Oak Tortrix *Tortrix viridana* 49.059 (1033) Length 10mm Widespread and locally common in oak woodland. Flies May–Jun. Larva feeds on oaks and occasionally other deciduous trees.

Aleimma loeflingiana 49.060 (1032) Length 9mm Widespread and locally common on oak woodland. Flies Jul–Aug. Larva feeds on oaks.

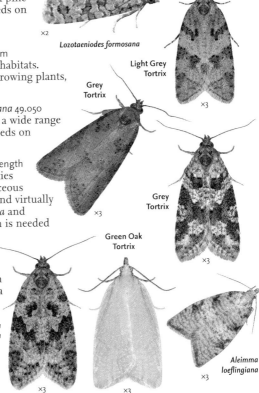

×2

Lozotaeniodes formosana

Light Grey Tortrix

Grey Tortrix

×3

×3

Grey Tortrix

×3

Green Oak Tortrix

Cnephasia communana

×3

×3

Aleimma loeflingiana

×3

Acleris forsskaleana 49.062 (1036) Length 8mm Common in gardens and woods. Flies Jul–Aug. Larva feeds on Sycamore and Field Maple.

Acleris laterana 49.066 (1038) Length 10mm Widespread and common in woods and scrub. Flies Aug. Larva feeds on shrubs, including Blackthorn and willows.

Acleris emargana 49.071 (1062) Length 10–11mm Widespread and common in gardens, hedgerows and woods. Flies Aug–Sep. Larva feeds on birches, poplars and sallows.

Garden Rose Tortrix

Acleris variegana 49.077 (1048) Length 8mm Widespread and common in woods and gardens. Flies Aug–Sep. Larva feeds on roses, both cultivated forms and wild species.

Acleris literana 49.087 (1061) Length 10–12mm Locally common in oak woodland. Flies Aug–Sep, and Apr after hibernation. Larva feeds on oaks.

Eulia ministrana 49.090 (1015) Length 10mm Widespread and common in woods and on heaths. Flies May–Jun. Larva feeds on a range of deciduous trees and shrubs.

Pseudargyrotoza conwagana 49.091 (1011) Length 7–8mm Common in gardens, hedgerows and scrub. Flies Jun–Jul. Larva feeds on Ash and privets.

Acleris forsskaleana ×3

Acleris emargana ×3

Acleris laterana ×3

Garden Rose Tortrix ×3

Eulia ministrana

Acleris literana ×3

Pseudargyrotoza conwagana ×3

Agapeta hamana ×3

Aethes cnicana ×3

Agapeta zoegana ×3

Cochylis atricapitana ×3

Agapeta hamana 49.109 (0937) Length 11–12mm Widespread and common in rough grassland. Flies Jul–Aug. Larva feeds on roots of thistles.

Agapeta zoegana 49.110 (0938) Length 11–12mm Locally common in dry grassland. Flies Jun–Aug. Larva feeds on roots of Small Scabious and Common Knapweed.

Aethes cnicana 49.127 (0945) Length 8–9mm Locally common in rough grassland. Flies Jun–Jul. Larva feeds on seeds of various thistles.

Cochylis atricapitana 49.139 (0966) Length 7–8mm Locally common in rough grassland and on chalk downs. Flies May–Jun, and Aug. Larva feeds on roots of Ragwort.

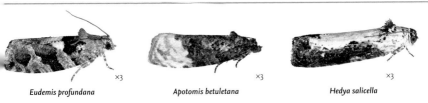

Eudemis profundana

Apotomis betuletana

Hedya salicella

Eudemis profundana 49.144 (1113) Length 10–11mm Common in oak woodland in the S half of Britain. Flies Jul–Aug. Larva feeds on oaks.

Apotomis betuletana 49.150 (1093) Length 10–11mm Common on heaths and in open birch woodland. Flies Jul–Aug. Larva feeds on birches.

Hedya salicella 49.155 (1086) Length 11–12mm Common in gardens, hedgerows and woods in the S half of Britain. Flies Jul–Aug. Larva feeds mainly on willows and Aspen.

Ancylis badiana

Epinotia brunnichana

Eucosma campoliliana

Ancylis badiana 49.214 (1126) Length 7mm Common in a wide range of habitats. Flies Apr–May, and Jul–Aug. Larva feeds on various vetches and clovers.

Epinotia brunnichana 49.231 (1155) Length 9–11mm Common in open woodland and on heaths. Flies Jul–Aug. Larva feeds on birches, sallows and Hazel.

Eucosma campoliliana 49.269 (1197) Length 8–9mm Common in rough grassland. Flies Jun–Jul. Larva feeds on Ragwort.

Gypsonoma sociana 49.281 (1168) Length 7–8mm Common in gardens, hedgerows and woods. Flies Jul–Aug. Larva feeds on catkins of sallows and Aspen.

Notocelia cynosbatella 49.292 (1174) Length 11–12mm Widespread and common in hedgerows, scrub and gardens. Flies May–Jul. Larva feeds on wild and cultivated roses.

Bramble Shoot Moth *Notocelia uddmanniana* 49.294 (1175) Length 9–10mm Common in gardens, hedgerows and woods. Flies Jun–Jul. Larva feeds on shoots of Bramble and related plants.

Codling Moth *Cydia pomonella* 49.338 (1261) Length 9–10mm Widespread and common in gardens, orchards and hedgerows. Flies Jul–Aug. Larva feeds inside apples and other fruits.

Cydia splendana 49.341 (1260) Length 10–11mm Locally common in deciduous woodland; commonest in S Britain. Flies Jul–Aug. Larva feeds inside acorns and Sweet Chestnut fruits.

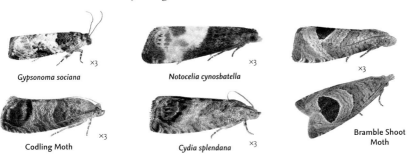

Gypsonoma sociana

Notocelia cynosbatella

Codling Moth

Cydia splendana

Bramble Shoot Moth

Family Pyralidae

Group comprises 87 species, in the range 9–17mm long. Very varied in appearance, resting with wings held flat like certain macro-moths, or with wings rolled around the body or in a tent-like manner. Pyralids are relatively large by micro-moth standards, and a few are comparable in size, or larger than, many small macro-moths.

Bee Moth
×2

Bee Moth *Aphomia sociella* 62.001 (1428)
Length 16–17mm Locally common in a range of habitats, its presence dependent upon that of bee and wasp nests. Flies Jun–Aug. Larva feeds on nest detritus and life-cycle stages of bees and wasps.

Wax Moth *Galleria mellonella* 62.006 (1425)
Length 16–17mm Locally common in the vicinity of beehives. Flies Jun–Sep. Larva feeds inside beehive honeycomb.

Wax Moth

Phycita roborella

Dioryctria abietella

Dioryctria abietella 62.028 (1454) Length 15mm Locally common in pine woodland in S England. Flies Jul–Aug. Larva feeds on Scots Pine, European Larch and Norway Spruce.

×2

×2

Phycita roborella 62.029 (1452)
Length 15mm Common in S Britain in oak woodlands, hedgerows and rural gardens. Flies Jul–Aug. Larva feeds mainly on oaks.

Phycita roborella

Hypochalcia ahenella 62.030 (1457) Length 13–14mm Locally common, mainly in the S, in dry grassy habitats. Flies Jun–Aug. Larval foodplants are unknown.

Hypochalcia ahenella

×3

Thistle Ermine

Thistle Ermine *Myelois circumvoluta* 62.042 (1458) Length 15–16mm Common in S Britain, in rough grassland. Flies Jun–Jul. Larva feeds on flowers and in stems of thistles and Greater Burdock.

×2

Euzophera pinguis 62.048 (1470)
Length 10–11mm Locally common in S Britain, in hedgerows and woods. Flies Jul–Aug. Larva feeds on Ash.

Euzophera pinguis

×3

Large Tabby *Aglossa pinguinalis* 62.074 (1421) Length 14–15mm Local in S Britain, in rural outbuildings, stables and barns. Flies Jun–Aug. Larva feeds on debris associated with stored grain and animal feed.

×2

Large Tabby

Gold
Triangle
×3

Gold Triangle
Hypsopygia costalis
62.075 (1413) Length 11–12mm
Common in England and
Wales, in a range of habitats.
Flies Jul–Aug. Larva feeds on
stored hay and other vegetable
matter, and on thatch.

*Hypsopygia
glaucinalis*

*Endotricha
flammealis*

×2   ×2

Hypsopygia glaucinalis
62.076 (1415) Length 14–15mm
Common in S Britain, in
gardens, hedgerows and woods. Flies Jun–Aug. Larva
feeds on stored hay, decaying plant material and thatch.

Endotricha flammealis 62.077 (1424) Wingspan 16–19mm Local in S Britain, in gardens
and deciduous woodland. Flies Jul–Aug. Larva feeds mainly on fallen and
decaying leaves of deciduous trees.

Family Crambidae
Group comprises 37 species of
relatively large micro-moths, in the
range 10–23mm long. Includes the
distinctive 'grass moth' group, whose
members rest with their relatively
narrow wings held in a tent-like
manner, creating a distinctive
narrow, attenuated outline. Some
other Crambidae members have broad triangular wings
and rest with them held flat like many macro-moths;
these include the 'china-marks', and large and familiar
species like Small Magpie and Mother of Pearl.

*Pyrausta
aurata*

*Pyrausta
purpuralis*

×3

×3

Pyrausta aurata 63.006 (1361) Length 9–10mm Local, mainly
on chalk downs and grassland. Flies May–Jun, and Jul–Aug.
Larva feeds on mints, thymes and Marjoram.

Pyrausta purpuralis 63.007 (1362) Length 11–12mm Local on chalk
downs and in close-cropped grassland. Flies May–Jun, and
Jul–Aug. Larva feeds on thymes and Corn Mint.

Small Magpie *Anania hortulata* 63.025 (1376)
Length 20–23mm Widespread and common in
gardens, hedgerows and on rough ground.
Flies Jun–Jul. Larva feeds on Common Nettle and
Small Nettle.

×2

Small Magpie

European Corn-borer *Ostrinia nubilalis*
63.028 (1375) Length 14–15mm A fairly recent
arrival, now local but increasing in England.
Flies Jun–Jul. Larva feeds on Mugwort.

European
Corn-borer

×3

Rusty Dot Pearl *Udea ferrugalis*
63.031 (1395) Length 10–11mm Regular immigrant
from mainland Europe, commonest on S
coasts. Flies mainly Aug–Oct. Larva feeds
on low-growing herbaceous plants.

Udea olivalis 63.037 (1392) Length 14–15mm
Widespread and common in gardens and
woods and on rough ground. Flies Jun–Jul.
Larva feeds on a range of herbaceous
plants, notably Common Nettle and
Common Sorrel.

European
Corn-borer
×3

Udea olivalis
×2

×1

×3
Rusty Dot Pearl

Mother of Pearl

Mother of Pearl *Pleuroptya ruralis* 63.038 (1405)
Length 16–17mm Widespread and common in gardens
and on rough ground. Flies Jul–Aug. Larva feeds
mainly on Common Nettle.

Palpita vitrealis 63.048 (1408)
Wingspan 28–30mm
Regular immigrant
from mainland Europe,
commonest on S coasts.
Flies Sep–Oct. Larva
feeds on privets and
related plants, but
probably does not
breed here.

*Palpita
vitrealis*

×1.5

Rush
Veneer

×3

Rush Veneer *Nomophila*
noctuella 63.052 (1398) Length
14–15mm Common immigrant from mainland Europe.
Flies Jun–Oct. Larva feeds on members of the pea family.

×3

Garden Pebble *Evergestis forficalis* 63.057 (1356)
Length 13–14mm Widespread and common
in gardens and on open rough ground.
Flies May–Jun, and Jul–Aug. Larva
feeds on various members of the
cabbage family.

Garden
Pebble

×3

Evergestis pallidata 63.060 (1358) Length 12–13mm Widespread but local in damp grassy woods and marshes. Flies Jun–Aug. Larva feeds on various members of the cabbage family.

Evergestis pallidata

Scoparia ambigualis 63.064 (1334) Length 10–11mm Widespread and common in woods and on moors. Flies May–Jul. Larva feeds on various mosses.

×3

Scoparia ambigualis

×3

Eudonia truncicolella 63.073 (1340) Length 15–16mm Widespread and common in a range of habitats, from gardens to woods. Flies Jul–Aug. Larva feeds on various mosses.

Eudonia mercurella 63.074 (1344) Length 10–11mm Widespread and common in a range of wooded habitats. Flies Jul–Sep. Larva feeds on mosses.

×2

Eudonia truncicolella

×3

Eudonia mercurella

Chrysoteuchia culmella 63.080 (1293) Length 13–14mm Widespread and common in rough grassy areas. Flies Jun–Jul. Larva feeds on roots of various grasses.

Crambus perlella

×3

Chrysoteuchia culmella

×2

Crambus perlella

Crambus lathoniellus 63.086 (1301) Length 10–11mm Widespread and common in rough grassland. Flies May–Jul. Larva feeds inside lower stems and roots of grasses.

×3

Crambus lathoniellus

×2

Crambus perlella

Crambus perlella 63.088 (1302) Length 15–16mm Widespread and common in rough grassy areas. Flies Jul–Aug. Larva feeds on stems of various grasses.

Agriphila tristella

Agriphila tristella 63.089 (1305) Length 16–17mm Widespread and common in rough grassy areas. Flies Jun–Aug. Larva feeds inside stems of various grasses.

×2

Catoptria pinella 63.099 (1313) Length 12–13mm Widespread and common in damp habitats, including marshes and wet heaths. Flies Jul–Aug. Larva feeds inside roots of various grasses of damp habitats.

Catoptria pinella

×3

Catoptria falsella 63.102 (1316) Length 11–12mm Widespread, commonest in S Britain, particularly in villages with thatched houses and old walls. Flies Jul–Aug. Larva feeds on a range of mosses.

Catoptria falsella

×3

Platytes alpinella 63.112 (1325) Length 12–13mm Very local and scarce on coastal dunes and shingle beaches, from Devon to Yorkshire. Flies Jul–Aug. Larva feeds on coastal mosses.

Platytes alpinella   ×3

Brown China-mark *Elophila nymphaeata*

63.114 (1345) Length 12–13mm Widespread and locally common, associated with vegetated still and slow-flowing waters (e.g. ponds, lakes and canals). Flies Jul–Aug. Larva lives submerged, feeding on aquatic plants such as water-lilies and *Potamogeton* pondweeds.

Water Veneer

Acentria ephemerella
63.115 (1331) Length 12–13mm Widespread and locally common, associated with vegetated ponds, lakes and slow-flowing rivers. Flies Jun–Aug. Larva lives submerged, feeding on aquatic plants such as Canadian Waterweed and *Potamogeton* pondweeds.

Brown China-mark
×3

Water Veneer
×3

Ringed China-mark

Parapoynx stratiotata
63.117 (1348) Length 11–13mm Local in S Britain, associated with ponds, lakes and canals. Flies Jun–Aug. Larva lives submerged, feeding on aquatic plants such as Canadian Waterweed and *Potamogeton* pondweeds.

Ringed China-mark
×3

Beautiful China-mark

Nymphula nitidulata
63.118 (1350) Length 10–11mm Widespread but local, associated with vegetated still and slow-flowing waters. Flies Jul–Aug. Larva lives submerged, feeding on aquatic plants such as Yellow Water-lily and bur-reeds.

Beautiful China-mark
×3

Schoenobius gigantella 63.120 (1328) Length 23–28mm Local in S and SE England, in reedbeds. Flies Jun–Jul. Larva feeds in stems of Common Reed and Reed Sweet-grass.

Donacaula forficella 63.121 (1329) Length 23–28mm Local in reedbeds and marshes in S Britain. Flies May–Jul. Larva feeds on shoots of Common Reed, Reed Sweet-grass and sedges.

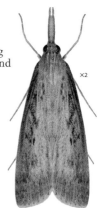

×2

×2

Schoenobius gigantella

Donacaula forficella

PLANT LIST

The following plant species are mentioned in the text of the book, reference being made there to just the English common name. Here they are shown with their scientific names, too, allowing the reader to refer to botanical texts. The plants are listed in alphabetical order by common name, and the names are those used in the most up-to-date British flora: *New Flora of the British Isles* by Clive Stace (third edition, 2010), published by Cambridge University Press.

Alder	*Alnus glutinosa*
alders	*Alnus* spp.
Angelica, Wild	*Angelica sylvestris*
apples	*Malus* spp.
Ash	*Fraxinus excelsior*
Aspen	*Populus tremula*
Aster, Sea	*Aster tripolium*
Balsam, Orange	*Impatiens capensis*
Balsam, Touch-me-not	*Impatiens noli-tangere*
Barberry	*Berberis vulgaris*
Bartsia, Red	*Odontites verna*
Bearberry	*Arctostaphylos uva-ursi*
beard lichens	*Usnea* spp.
Bedstraw, Heath	*Galium saxatile*
Bedstraw, Lady's	*Galium verum*
bedstraws	*Galium* spp.
Beech	*Fagus sylvatica*
Beet, Sea	*Beta vulgaris maritima*
Bellflower, Nettle-leaved	*Campanula trachelium*
bellflowers	*Campanula* spp.
Bent, Bristle	*Agrostis curtisii*
bent grasses	*Agrostis* spp.
Bilberry	*Vaccinium myrtillus*
Bindweed, Field	*Convolvulus arvensis*
bindweeds	*Convolvulus* spp.
Birch, Downy	*Betula pubescens*
Birch, Silver	*Betula pendula*
birches	*Betula* spp.
Bird's-foot Trefoil, Common	*Lotus corniculatus*
Bird's-foot Trefoil, Greater	*Lotus pedunculatus*
bird's-foot trefoils	*Lotus* spp.
Bitter-vetch	*Lathyrus linifolius*
Blackthorn	*Prunus spinosa*
Bluebell	*Endymion non-scripta*
Bog-myrtle	*Myrica gale*
Bracken	*Pteridium aquilinum*
Bramble	*Rubus fruticosa agg.*
Brome, False	*Brachypodium sylvaticum*
Broom	*Cytisus scoparius*
Buckthorn	*Rhamnus cathartica*
Buckthorn, Alder	*Frangula alnus*
Bugle	*Ajuga reptans*
Bulrush	*Typha latifolia*
Bulrush, Lesser	*Typha angustifolia*
bulrushes	*Typha* spp.
Burdock, Greater	*Arctium lappa*
burdocks	*Arctium* spp.
Burnet-rose	*Rosa pimpinellifolia*
Burnet-saxifrage	*Pimpinella saxifraga*
bur-reeds	*Sparangium* spp.
Buttercup, Meadow	*Ranunculus acris*
Butterbur	*Petasites hybridus*
Cabbage	*Brassica oleracea*
Campion, Bladder	*Silene vulgaris*
Campion, Red	*Silene dioica*
Campion, Sea	*Silene uniflora*
campions	*Silene* spp.
Canary-grass, Reed	*Phalaris arundinacea*
canary-grasses	*Phalaris* spp.
Carrot, Sea	*Daucus carota maritima*
Catchfly, Nottingham	*Silene nutans*
Chamomile	*Chamaemelum nobile*
Cherry, Bird	*Prunus padus*
Cherry, Wild	*Prunus avium*
Chestnut, Horse	*Aesculus hippocastanum*
Chestnut, Sweet	*Castanea sativa*
Cinquefoil, Creeping	*Potentilla reptans*
Cinquefoil, Marsh	*Comara palustre*
Clover, White	*Trifolium repens*
clovers	*Trifolium* spp.
Club-rush, Common	*Scirpus lacustris*
Cock's-foot	*Dactylis glomerata*
comfreys	*Symphytum* spp.
Cottongrass, Hare's-tail	*Eriophorum vaginatum*
cottongrasses	*Eriophorum* spp.
Couch, Common	*Elytrigia repens*
Couch, Sand	*Elytrigia juncea*
Cow-parsley	*Anthriscus sylvestris*
Cowslip	*Primula veris*
Cow-wheat, Common	*Melampyrum pratense*
Crane's-bill, Dove's-foot	*Geranium molle*
Crowberry	*Empetrum nigrum*
crucifers	Brassicaceae
Cuckoo-flower	*Cardamine pratensis*
currants	*Ribes* spp.
Cypress, Lawson's	*Chamaecyparis lawsoniana*
Cypress, Leyland	*Cupressocyparis leylandii*
Cypress, Monterey	*Cupressus macrocarpa*
cypresses	*Cupressus* spp.
delphiniums	*Delphinium* spp.
Dewberry	*Rubus caesius*
Dock, Water	*Rumex hydrolapathum*

docks	*Rumex* spp.	knotgrasses	*Polygonum* spp.
Dog-rose	*Rosa canina*	lady's-mantles	*Achemilla* spp.
Dog-violet, Common	*Viola riviniana*	Larch, European	*Larix decidua*
Douglas-fir	*Pseudotsuga menziesii*	larches	*Larix* spp.
		lettuces	*Lactuca* spp.
Elder	*Sambucus nigra*	lilacs	*Syringa* spp.
Elm, English	*Ulmus procera*	Lime, Large-leaved	*Tilia platyphyllos*
Elm, Wych	*Ulmus glabra*	Lime, Small-leaved	*Tilia cordata*
elms	*Ulmus* spp.	limes	*Tilia* spp.
eyebrights	*Euphrasia* spp.	Loosestrife, Yellow	*Lysimachia vulgaris*
		Lucerne	*Medicago sativa*
Fescue, Red	*Festuca rubra*	Lyme-grass	*Elymus arenarius*
Fescue, Tall	*Festuca arundinacea*		
fescues	*Festuca* spp.	Mallow, Common	*Malva sylvestris*
Figwort, Balm-leaved	*Scrophularia scorodonia*	mallows	*Malva* spp.
firs	*Abies* spp.	Maple, Field	*Acer campestre*
Fleabane, Common	*Pulicaria dysenterica*	marigolds, cultivated	*Tagetes* sp.
Flixweed	*Descurania sophia*	Marjoram	*Origanum vulgare*
Foxglove	*Digitalis purpurea*	Marram	*Ammophila arenaria*
		Marsh-bedstraw,	*Galium palustre*
Garlic Mustard	*Alliaria petiolata*	Common	
geraniums	*Geranium* spp.	Marsh-mallow	*Althaea officinalis*
ginger-lilies	*Hedychium* spp.	Mat-grass	*Nardus stricta*
Goldenrod	*Solidago virgaurea*	Meadow-grass, Annual	*Poa annua*
Gooseberry	*Ribes uva-crispa*	Meadow-grass, Smooth	*Poa pratensis*
goosefoots	*Chenopodium* spp.	Meadow-rue, Common	*Thalictrum flavum*
gorse	*Ulex* spp.	Meadowsweet	*Filipendula ulmaria*
Groundsel, Sticky	*Senecio viscosus*	Milk-parsley	*Peucedanum palustre*
Guelder-rose	*Viburnum opulus*	milkworts	*Polygala* spp.
		Mint, Corn	*Mentha arvensis*
Hair-grass, Early	*Aira praecox*	Mint, Water	*Mentha aquatica*
Hair-grass, Tufted	*Deschampsia cespitosa*	mints	*Mentha* spp.
Hair-grass, Wavy	*Deschampsia flexuosa*	Moor-grass, Blue	*Sesleria caerulea*
Hawthorn	*Crataegus monogyna*	Moor-grass, Purple	*Molinia caerulea*
Hazel	*Corylus avellana*	Mouse-ear, Common	*Cerastium holosteoides*
Heath, Cross-leaved	*Erica tetralix*	Mouse-ear, Field	*Cerastium arvense*
Heather (Ling)	*Calluna vulgaris*	Mugwort	*Artemisia vulgaris*
Heather, Bell	*Erica cinerea*	Mullein, Dark	*Verbascum nigrum*
Hedge Mustard	*Sisymbrium officinale*	Mullein, Great	*Verbascum thapsus*
Hemlock	*Conium maculatum*		
Hemp-agrimony	*Eupatorium cannabinum*	Nasturtium	*Tropaeolum majus*
Hemp-nettle, Common	*Galeopsis tetrahit*	Nettle, Common	*Urtica dioica*
Hog's-Fennel	*Peucedanum officinale*	Nettle, Small	*Urtica urens*
Hogweed	*Heracleum sphondylium*		
Holly	*Ilex aquifolium*	Oak, Evergreen	*Quercus ilex*
Honeysuckle	*Lonicera periclymenum*	Oak, Pedunculate	*Quercus robur*
Hop	*Humulus lupulus*	Oak, Sessile	*Quercus petraea*
		oaks	*Quercus* spp.
Iceplant	*Hylotelephium spectabile*	Oleander	*Nerium oleander*
Iris, Yellow	*Iris pseudocorus*	oraches	*Atriplex* spp.
Ivy	*Hedera helix*	Orpine	*Sedum telephium*
		Osier	*Salix viminalis*
Juniper	*Juniperus communis*		
junipers	*Juniperus* spp.	Parsley, Cow	*Anthriscus sylvestris*
		Parsnip, Wild	*Pastinaca sativa*
Knapweed, Common	*Centaurea nigra*	pelargoniums	*Pelargonium* spp.
Knapweed, Great	*Centaurea scabiosa*	Pellitory-of-the-wall	*Parietaria judaica*
knapweeds	*Centaurea* spp.	perwinkles	*Vinca* spp.

Petty Whin	*Genista anglica*	Spurge, Wood	*Euphorbia amygdaloides*
Pignut	*Conopodium majus*	spurges	*Euphorbia* spp.
Pine, Scots	*Pinus sylvestris*	stonecrops	*Sedum* spp.
pines	*Pinus* spp.	Stork's-bill, Common	*Erodium cicutarium*
Plantain, Buck's-horn	*Plantago coronopus*	Strawberry, Wild	*Fragaria vesca*
Plantain, Ribwort	*Plantago lanceolata*	Sweet-grass, Reed	*Glyceria maxima*
Plantain, Sea	*Plantago maritima*	Sweet-William	*Dianthus barbatus*
Ploughman's-spikenard	*Inula conyzae*	Sycamore	*Acer pseudoplatanus*
Pond-sedge, Lesser	*Carex acutiformis*		
Poplar, Black	*Populus nigra*	Tamarisk	*Tamarix gallica*
poplars	*Populus* spp.	Thistle, Carline	*Carlina vulgaris*
Potato	*Solanum tuberosum*	Thistle, Stemless	*Cirsium acaule*
Primrose	*Primula vulgaris*	thistles	*Cirsium* spp. and
Privet, Wild	*Ligustrum vulgare*		*Carduus* spp.
privets	*Ligustrum* spp.	Thrift	*Armeria maritima*
		Thyme, Wild	*Thymus polytrichus*
Ragged Robin	*Lychnis flos-cuculi*	thymes	*Thymus* spp.
Ragwort	*Senecio vulgaris*	Toadflax, Common	*Linaria vulgaris*
Raspberry	*Rubus idaeus*	toadflaxes	*Linaria* spp.
Reed, Common	*Phragmites communis*	tobacco-plants	*Nicotiana* spp.
Restharrow	*Ononis repens*	Tor-grass	*Brachypodium pinnatum*
restharrows	*Ononis* spp.	Traveller's-joy	*Clematis vitalba*
Rocket, Sea	*Cakile maritima*	Treacle Mustard	*Erysimum cheiranthoides*
Rock-rose, Common	*Cistus nummularium*		
roses	*Rosa* spp.	Valerian, Common	*Valeriana officinalis*
Rowan	*Sorbus aucuparia*	Vetch, Horseshoe	*Hippocrepis comosa*
rushes	*Juncus* spp.	Vetch, Kidney	*Anthyllis vulneraria*
		Vetch, Tufted	*Vicia cracca*
Saltmarsh-grass, Common	*Puccinellia maritima*	Vetch, Wood	*Vicia sylvatica*
saltmarsh-grasses	*Puccinellia* spp.	vetches	*Vicia* spp.
Scabious, Devil's-bit	*Succisa pratensis*	Vetchling, Meadow	*Lathyrus pratensis*
Scabious, Field	*Knautia arvensis*	Violet, Hairy	*Viola hirta*
Scabious, Small	*Scabiosa columbaria*	violets	*Viola* spp.
St John's-worts	*Hypericum* spp.	Viper's-bugloss	*Echium vulgare*
sallows	*Salix* spp.		
Sandwort, Sea	*Honkenya peploides*	water-lilies	*Nymphaea* and
Saw-wort	*Serratula tinctoria*		*Nuphar* spp.
saxifrages	*Saxifraga* spp.	Water-lily, Yellow	*Nuphar lutea*
Sea-buckthorn	*Hippophae rhamnoides*	Waterweed, Canadian	*Elodea canadensis*
Sea-lavender, Common	*Limonium vulgare*	Wayfaring-tree	*Viburnum lantana*
sea-lavenders	*Limonium* spp.	Willow, Creeping	*Salix repens*
Sea-spurrey, Rock	*Spergularia rupicola*	Willow, Eared	*Salix aurita*
Sedge, Glaucous	*Carex flacca*	Willow, Goat	*Salix caprea*
sedges	*Carex* spp.	Willow, Grey	*Salix cinerea*
Sheep's-fescue	*Festuca ovina*	Willowherb, Rosebay	*Chamerion*
Sheep's-bit	*Jasione montana*		*angustifolium*
Small-reed, Wood	*Calamagrostis epigejos*	willowherbs	*Epilobium* spp.
small-reeds (grasses)	*Calamagrostis* spp.	willows	*Salix* spp.
Sneezewort	*Achillea ptarmica*	Wood Millet	*Milium effusum*
Snowberry	*Symphiocarpos albus*	Wood-sage	*Teucrium scorodonia*
Sorrel, Common	*Rumex acetosa*	Wormwood	*Artemisia absinthium*
Sorrel, Sheep's	*Rumex acetosella*	Wormwood, Sea	*Artemisia maritima*
sow-thistles	*Sonchus* spp.		
Spindle	*Euonymus europaeus*	Yarrow	*Achillea millefolium*
Spruce, Norway	*Picea abies*	Yellow-rattle	*Rhinanthus minor*
spruces	*Picea* spp.	Yew	*Taxus baccata*
		Yorkshire-fog	*Holcus lanatus*

FURTHER READING AND USEFUL WEBSITES

FURTHER READING

Agassiz, J.L., Beavan, S.D. and Heckford, R.J. (2013). *Checklist of the Lepidoptera of the British Isles*. Field Studies Council.

Bradley, J.D. and Fletcher, D.S. (1979). *A Recorder's Log Book or Label List of British Butterflies and Moths*. Curwen Books.

Bradley, J. (2000). *Checklist of Lepidoptera Recorded from the British Isles*, 2nd edition. D. Bradley.

Goater, B. (1986). *British Pyralid Moths*. Harley Books.

Manley, C. (2008). *British Moths and Butterflies – A Photographic Guide*. A&C Black.

Porter, J. (1997). *The Colour Identification Guide to the Caterpillars of the British Isles*. Viking.

Skinner, B. and Wilson, D. (1984). *Colour Identification Guide to the Moths of the British Isles*. Viking.

Sterling, P., Parsons, M. and Lewington, R. (2012). *Field Guide to the Micro Moths of Great Britain and Ireland*. British Wildlife Publishing.

Sterry, P. (2006). *Collins Complete British Wild Flowers*. HarperCollins.

Townsend, M., Waring, P. and Lewington, R. (2009). *Field Guide to the Moths of Great Britain and Ireland*, 2nd edition. British Wildlife Publishing.

USEFUL WEBSITES

British Butterflies – britishbutterflies.co.uk

British Entomological and Natural History Society – benhs.org.uk

Buglife – buglife.org.uk

Butterfly Conservation – butterfly-conservation.org

Hants Moths – hantsmoths.org.uk

The Wildlife Trusts – wildlifetrusts.org

UK Butterflies – ukbutterflies.co.uk

UK Moths – ukmoths.org.uk